Batch 668706LV00024B

668706LVX01234B PERFECT	9783752210903 5.83X8.27	BABADADA black-and-white, Tradition 94 GLOSS	(1)
668706LVX01235B PERFECT	9783752210125 5.83X8.27	BABADADA black-and-white, Tradition 94 GLOSS	(1)
668706LVX01236B PERFECT	9783752210842 5.83X8.27	BABADADA black-and-white, Traditiona 94 GLOSS	(1)
668706LVX01237B PERFECT	9783752211085 5.83X8.27	BABADADA black-and-white, Tradition 94 GLOSS	(1)
668706LVX01238B PERFECT	9783752210439 5.83X8.27	BABADADA black-and-white, Traditiona 94 GLOSS	(1)
668706LVX01239B PERFECT	9783752211016 5.83X8.27	BABADADA black-and-white, Tradition 94 GLOSS	(1)
668706LVX01240B PERFECT	9783752210453 5.83X8.27	BABADADA black-and-white, Traditiona 94 GLOSS	(1)
668706LVX01241B PERFECT	9783752211061 5.83X8.27	BABADADA black-and-white, Tradition 94 GLOSS	(1)
668706LVX01242B PERFECT	9783752210682 5.83X8.27	BABADADA black-and-white, Traditiona 94 GLOSS	(1)
668706LVX01243B PERFECT	9783752210897 5.83X8.27	BABADADA black-and-white, Traditiona 94 GLOSS	(1)
668706LVX01244B PERFECT	9783752210613 5.83X8.27	BABADADA black-and-white, Tradition 94 GLOSS	(1)
668706LVX01245B PERFECT	9783752210569 5.83X8.27	BABADADA black-and-white, Tradition 94 GLOSS	(1)
668706LVX01246B PERFECT	9783752210668 5.83X8.27	BABADADA black-and-white, Tradition 94 GLOSS	(1)
668706LVX01247B PERFECT	9783752210354 5.83X8.27	BABADADA black-and-white, Traditiona 94 GLOSS	(1)
668706LVX01248B PERFECT	9783752210330 5.83X8.27	BABADADA black-and-white, Traditiona 94 GLOSS	(1)
668706LVX01249B PERFECT	9783752210996 5.83X8.27	BABADADA black-and-white, Traditiona 94 GLOSS	(1)
668706LVX01250B PERFECT	9783752210224 5.83X8.27	BABADADA black-and-white, Tradition 94 GLOSS	(1)

Computer Programming

This Book Includes:

SQL, Linux, Java, Python, C#, Arduino, C# For Intermediates, Arduino For Intermediates

Learn Any Computer Language In One Day Step by Step (#2020 Version)

Steve Tudor

Text Copyright

All rights reserved. No part of this guide may be reproduced in any form without permission in writing from the publisher except in the case of brief quotations embodied in critical articles or reviews.

Legal & Disclaimer

The information contained in this book and its contents is not designed to replace or take the place of any form of medical or professional advice; and is not meant to replace the need for independent medical, financial, legal or other professional advice or services, as may be required. The content and information in this book has been provided for educational and entertainment purposes only.

The content and information contained in this book has been compiled from sources deemed reliable, and it is accurate to the best of the Author's knowledge, information and belief. However, the Author cannot guarantee its accuracy and validity and cannot be held liable for any errors and/or omissions. Further, changes are periodically made to this book as and when needed. Where appropriate and/or necessary, you must consult a professional (including but not limited to your doctor, attorney, financial advisor or such other professional advisor) before using any of the suggested remedies, techniques, or information in this book.

Upon using the contents and information contained in this book, you agree to hold harmless the Author from and against any damages, costs, and expenses, including any legal fees potentially resulting from the application of any of the information provided by this book. This disclaimer applies to any loss, damages or injury caused by the use and application, whether directly or indirectly, of any advice or information presented, whether for breach of contract, tort, negligence,

personal injury, criminal intent, or under any other cause of action.

You agree to accept all risks of using the information presented inside this book.

You agree that by continuing to read this book, where appropriate and/or necessary, you shall consult a professional (including but not limited to your doctor, attorney, or financial advisor or such other advisor as needed) before using any of the suggested remedies, techniques, or information in this book.

TABLE OF CONTENTS

CHAPTER 1. INTRODUCTION *SQL* 22
    A. INTRODUCTION TO SQL 23
    B. HOW TO START CODING 29
        Data Definition Language..29
        Data Query Language..30
        Data Control Language...30
        Data Administration Commands..30
        Transactional Control Commands..31
    C. HOW TO INSTALL MySQL APPLICATIONS 32
    D. HOW TO LAUNCH MySQL WORKBENCH 33
    E. WRITING THE FIRST MySQL CODE. 35

CHAPTER 2. DATABASE 37
    A. HOW TO CREATE A SQL DATABASE 37
    B. HOW TO USE A DATABASE 44
    C. HOW TO DELETE A DATABASE 44
    D. HOW TO ADMINISTRATE THE DATABASE 45

CHAPTER 3. TABLES 46
    CREATE TABLES 46
    DELETING TABLES 50
    INSERTING DATA INTO A TABLE 52
    DROPPING A TABLE..55
    USING THE ALTER TABLE QUERY 56

CHAPTER 4. DATA..62
    CONSTRAINTS IN MySQL 63
    UPDATING DATA..64
    PIVOTING DATA 69
    DELETING DATA 71

CHAPTER 5. SELECTING DATA 72
    SELECTING ROWS AND COLUMNS 72
    FILTERING ROWS AND COLUMNS 74
    UPDATING DATA 78
    CREATING INDEXES 82
    FUNCTIONS...83

MySQL Functions 83
Joins 86
Union 88
ALIASES 88

CHAPTER 6. VIEWS 90

CHAPTER 7. WHAT IS A VIEW, HOW TO CREATE A VIEW, HOW TO ALTER A VIEW, DELETING A VIEW 93

CHAPTER 8. TRIGGERS 99

CHAPTER 9. VARIABLES AND STORED ROUTINES 101

Variables 101
Stored routines 106
Stored procedures 111
Stored functions 120
Deleting stored routines 125

CHAPTER 10. CONTROL FLOW TOOLS 134

IF statement 134
CASE statement 135
WHILE statement 136
LOOP statement 136

CHAPTER 11. CURSORS 138

CHAPTER 12. COMMON BEGINNER MISTAKES AND HOW TO FIX THEM 140

CHAPTER 13. TIPS AND TRICKS OF SQL 143

Four Tips That Make Using SQL Easier! 146

CHAPTER 14. WORKBOOK 148

What is the schema? 148
How to create a new table 150
How to create a table with one that already exists 150
How to drop tables 151
How to Do Your Own Search Results Through SQL 152
How to create a new query *153*
How to work with the SELECT command *154*
How does case sensitivity work? *156*

CHAPTER 15. SQL QUIZ 159
CONCLUSION 161

INTRODUCTION *LINUX* 167
CHAPTER 1: WHAT IS LINUX? 170
    A.   THE STORY OF LINUX 170
    B.   THE DIFFERENT RANGE OF USES 171
    C. CERTIFICATIONS 171
    D. FROM UNIX TO LINUX 172
CHAPTER 2: LINUX EVERYDAY 175
    A.   LINUX DISTRIBUTIONS 175
    B.   LINUX DISTRIBUTIONS LIST 176
CHAPTER 3 : SETTING UP 185
    A.   DIFFERENT TYPES OF INSTALLATIONS 185
    B. HOW TO INSTALL LINUX STEP BY STEP 186
    C. HOW TO CONFIGURE LINUX 189
    D. HOW TO ADD A GRAPHICAL USER INTERFACE 190
    E. HOW TO ADD ADDITIONAL SOFTWARE 192
CHAPTER 4 : NAVIGATE LINUX 195
    A.   HOW TO NAVIGATE WITH LINUX 195
    B.   COMMANDS FOR DIRECTORIES 195
    C.   TERMINAL-BASED FILE MANAGER 196
    D.   GRAPHICAL FILE MANAGER 198
    E.   LINUX TERMINAL TERMINAL 198
CHAPTER 5: ESSENTIAL COMMANDS 200
    A. INTRO TO FILE AND DIRECTORIES 200
        1. SHELL FEATURES 200
        2. BASIC FILE OPERATIONS 200
        3. DIRECTORY OPERATIONS 203
        4. FILE VIEWING 204
        5. FILE CREATION AND EDITING 205
        6. FILE PROPERTIES 206

  7. FILE LOCATION 207
  8. FILE COMPRESSION AND PACKAGING 209

B. OUTPUT AND TEXT PROCESSING 212

C. USERS AND GROUPS 214

D. PROCESS MANAGEMENT 221

  1. BACKUPS AND REMOTE STORAGE 221
  2. VIEWING PROCESS 222
  3. LOGINS, LOGOUTS, SHUTDOWNS 222
  4. HOST INFORMATION 225
  5. HOST LOCATION 227
  6. NETWORK CONNECTIONS 228

E. NETWORK AND SYSTEM INFORMATION 231

  1. NETWORK CONNECTIONS 231
  2. WEB BROWSING 231
  3. EMAILS 232
  4. COPY AND PASTE 233
  5. MATH AND CALCULATIONS 233
  6. GRAPHICS 233
  7. AUDIO AND VIDEO 234

CHAPTER 6: WORKBOOK 236

CHAPTER 9: QNA FOR BEGINNERS QUESTIONS 241

  QUIZ 241
  ANSWERS 242

CHAPTER 10: TIPS AND TRICKS 247

CONCLUSION 251

INTRODUCTION *JAVA* 257

CHAPTER 1 : GETTING READY 259

  INTRODUCTION TO JDK AND NETBEANS 260
  INSTALL JDK AND NETBEANS 262
  BASIC STRUCTURE OF A JAVA PROGRAM 267

THE STRUCTURE OF JAVA CODE AND HOW TO RUN PROGRAMS 267
HOW TO DOWNLOAD AND INSTALL JAVA ON LINUX, WINDOWS AND MAC. 269

CHAPTER 2: JAVA BASICS 271

JAVA TOKENS 271
KEYWORDS 271
IDENTIFIERS 272
OPERATORS 272
SEPARATORS 273
LITERALS 273
COMMENTS 274

CHAPTER 3 : VARIABLES 275

WHAT ARE VARIABLES 275
TYPES OF VARIABLES IN JAVA 275
NAMING A VARIABLE 277
JAVA PRIMITIVE TYPES 278
HOW TO INITIALIZE A VARIABLE 280

CHAPTER 4 : JAVA OPERATORS 285

ARITHMETIC OPERATORS 285
ARITHMETIC OPERATORS 285
ASSIGNMENT OPERATORS 286
LOGICAL OPERATORS 287
ASSIGNMENT OPERATORS 288
BITWISE OPERATORS 289

CHAPTER 5 : ARRAYS AND STRING 290

WHAT ARE STRINGS 290
STRING METHODS 290
ARRAYS 290
ARRAY METHODS 291
PRIMITIVE TYPES 292
REFERENCE TYPES 293

CHAPTER 6 : INTERACTIVE 295

HOW TO DISPLAYING OUTPUT 295
CONVERTERS 296
FORMATTING OUTPUTS 296

ESCAPE SEQUENCES 297

CHAPTER 7: CONTROL FLOW STATEMENTS 299

IF STATEMENTS 299
NESTED IFS 300
IF … ELSE 300
IF … ELSE IF 301
NESTED IF STATEMENTS 302
BOOLEAN VALUES 302
SWITCH STATEMENTS 302

CHAPTER 8 : LOOPS IN JAVA 304

CHAPTER 9: CLASSES AND OBJECTS IN JAVA 309

THE FUNDAMENTALS OF CLASS 309
THE BASIC STYLE OF A CLASS 309
DEFINITION OF A CLASS 311
REFERENCE VARIABLES AND ASSIGNMENT 313
WE GIVE A METHOD THE JAVA VEHICLE CLASS 315
RETURNING TO A METHOD 317
RETURNING A VALUE 318

CHAPTER 10 : ENCAPSULATIONS IN JAVA 320

JAVA ENCAPSULATION 320
ABSTRACTION 321

CHAPTER 11: POLYMORPHISM IN JAVA 322

STATIC POLYMORPHISM 322
DYNAMIC POLYMORPHISM 322
INHERITANCE AND COMPOSITION 322

CHAPTER 12: EXAMPLES WITH JAVA 324

HOW TO BUILD A SMALL GAME WITH JAVA 324

CHAPTER 13: MOST SEARCHED BEGINNER'S QUESTIONS . 326

INSTALLING JAVA 326
INSTALLING JAVA ON WINDOWS 326
INSTALLING JAVA ON LINUX 327
INSTALLING JAVA ON MAC 328

CHAPTER 14: TIPS AND TRICKS 330

CHAPTER 15: WORKBOOK 334
    ANSWERS 334
CONCLUSION 335

CHAPTER 1. *WHAT IS PYTHON* 341

    A. WHY TO LEARN PYTHON 341
    B. DIFFERENT VERSIONS OF PYTHON...342
    C. HOW TO DOWNLOAD AND INSTALL PYTHON 350
    D. WRITING THE FIRST PYTHON PROGRAM 356

CHAPTER 2. BASIC OF PYTHON 365

CHAPTER 3. FULL INSTRUCTIONS ON HOW TO CODE 368

CHAPTER 4. HOW TO MAKE PREDICTIONS WITH ALGORITHM 373

    WHAT IS PREDICTIVE ANALYTICS?...373
    WORKFLOW IN PREDICTIVE ANALYTICS: 377
    WHAT IS DIFFERENCE BETWEEN PREDICTIVE ANALYTICS & PRESCRIPTIVE ANALYTICS?...379

CHAPTER 5. INTRODUCTION TO BASIC DATA TYPES...........380

    IMPLEMENTATION OF PYTHON 381
    STANDARD DATA 381

CHAPTER 6. INTERMEDIATE AND ADVANCED DATA TYPES 383

    PYTHON NUMBERS: 383
    PYTHON LIST: 383
    PYTHON TUPLE: 384
    PYTHON SET...384
    PYTHON DICTIONARY 384
    CONVERSION BETWEEN DATA TYPES: 385

CHAPTER 7. FUNCTIONS AND MODULES IN PYTHON 386

CHAPTER 8. PYTHON FILE MANAGEMENT 389

CHAPTER 9. INTRODUCTION TO OBJECT ORIENTED PROGRAMMING **397**

CHAPTER 10. REAL WORLD EXAMPLES OF PYTHON **403**

    THINGS WE CAN DO IN PYTHON *406*
        READING AND WRITING.. *406*
        TRIPLE QUOTES.. *408*
        ESCAPE SEQUENCES *408*
        OPERATOR PRECEDENCE *408*
        THE SCOPE OF A VARIABLE *409*
        MODIFYING VALUES... *410*
        THE ASSIGNMENT OPERATOR *410*

CHAPTER 11. EXAMPLES OF CODING.. **412**

    LOOPS 412
    WORKING AND STRINGS 412

CHAPTER 12. QUIZ AND WORKBOOK **414**

    QUIZ 416
    ANSWERS.. 416

CHAPTER 13. BONUS: WORKBOOK... **418**

    HOW TO MAKE NEW CONCEPTS STICK 431

CONCLUSION **436**

INTRODUCTION *C#* **442**

    GETTING STARTED WITH THE C# LANGUAGE 445
    WRITING OUT A PROGRAM WITH C# 445
    ANALYZING THE PROGRAM... 446
    COMMENTS IN C# 448

CHAPTER 1 DATA TYPES.. **450**

CHAPTER 2 DATA TYPE CONVERSION **452**

CHAPTER 3 ARRAYS AND LOOPS **456**

CHAPTER 4 OPERATORS... **467**

    OPERATORS... 467

VALUES 476
CHAPTER 5 CLASSES **477**
   ENCAPSULATION AND MEMBER FUNCTIONS 480
   STATIC MEMBERS 487
CHAPTER 6 THE C LANGUAGE VARIABLES **491**
CHAPTER 7 LOOPS IN C **500**
   THE WHILE LOOP: 500
   THE DO...WHILE LOOP 501
   THE FOR LOOP 502
   THE BREAK KEYWORD 504
   THE INFINITE LOOP 504
CHAPTER 8 APPLICATION OF GRAPHICAL USER INTERFACE
.... **506**
   THE GRAPHICAL HARDWARE AND SOFTWARE 506
   THE GRAPHIC HARDWARE 506
CHAPTER 9 DECISION MAKING IN C **514**
CHAPTER 10 CONSTANTS AND LITERALS **522**
   INTEGER LITERALS 522
   FLOATING POINT LITERALS 522
   CHARACTER LITERALS 523
   STRING LITERALS 525
CHAPTER 11 COMMAND LINE ARGUMENTS **526**
   TYPECASTING 530
CHAPTER 12 EXTENSION METHODS **536**
CHAPTER 13 NULLABLE TYPES **543**
   CONCLUSION 553

INTRODUCTION *C# FOR INTERMEDIATES* 558
CHAPTER 1 DATA TYPES **560**
   INTEGER TYPES 560

FLOATING POINT DATA TYPES 562
THE VOID TYPE 564

CHAPTER 2 DATA STRUCTURES, HANDLING AND FUNCTIONS 566

LINKED LISTS 573
Stack *574*
Queue *574*
HASH TABLE (DICTIONARY IMPLEMENTATION) 575
HASH TABLE (SET IMPLEMENTATION) 575
BALANCE TREE (DICTIONARY IMPLEMENTATION) 576
BALANCE TREE (SET IMPLEMENTATION) 576
PRACTICAL EXAMPLE OF CHOICE OF A DATA STRUCTURE 576

CHAPTER 3 HOW TO DEFINE YOUR CLASSES IN C# 586

HOW TO WORK WITH THESE CLASSES 586
ORGANIZING THE CLASSES 588
HOW TO ACCESS OUR CLASSES 589

CHAPTER 4 CREATING LOOPS IN C# 592

CHAPTER 5 VALUE TYPES AND REFERENCE TYPES 603

VALUE TYPES 603
REFERENCE TYPES 603
COPYING VALUE & REFERENCE TYPES 603
NULL VALUES 604
NULLABLE TYPES 605
THE SYSTEM.OBJECT CLASS 606
BOXING 606
UNBOXING 607
CASTING DATA SAFELY 608
THE IS OPERATOR 609
THE AS OPERATOR 610

CHAPTER 6 ENUMERATIONS 611

STRUCTURES 612
DIFFERENCES BETWEEN STRUCTURES AND CLASSES 613

CHAPTER 7 DECISION-MAKING 616

IF STATEMENT 616

If Else Statement 617
Nested If Statements 618
Switch Statement 619
Nested Switch Statements 620
Conditional Operator 620

CHAPTER 8 ARRAYS 621

Declaring Arrays 621
Initializing Arrays 621
Assigning Values 622
Accessing Elements 623
Foreach Loop 624
Arrays in C# 625

CHAPTER 9 CREATING OBJECTS AND MAKING THEM WORK 626

Classes and objects 626
What is OOP? 626
Classes 628
How to use these classes in your code 629
How to create your own objects 632
Creating the object 632
System classes 633
How to assign a parameter to the object 634
Releasing your objects 635
The constructors 635
The basics of working with classes 638
Components of classes 638
Custom classes 639
How to organize your classes 640
Accessing the classes 641
A final word about classes 642

CONCLUSION 645

INTRODUCTION *ARDUINO* 650

CHAPTER 1 CHOOSING AND SETTING UP THE ARDUINO 666

15

CHAPTER 2 INPUTS AND OUTPUTS 671
   VERTICAL INTEGRATION PROJECTS 676
CHAPTER 3 MODULATING THE ON-BOARD LED AND PERSISTENCE OF VISION 692
   WHAT YOU NEED TO KNOW AND WHAT YOU WILL LEARN IN THIS EXPERIMENT 692
   THE BASIC PULSE TRAIN PATTERN 694
   WHAT IS THE FLICKER RATE? 695
   CHANGING THE APPARENT BRIGHTNESS 698
   NEW FEATURES: INTRODUCING VARIABLES AND VARIABLE TYPES 699
   NEW FEATURES: VARIABLE NAMES 708
   ON-TIME, OFF-TIME, PERIOD AND DUTY CYCLE 712
   MY SKETCH TO MODULATE THE LED WITH A PERIOD AND DUTY CYCLE 714
   SUMMARY OF THE COMMANDS INTRODUCED SO FAR 714
CHAPTER 4 CODING FOR THE ARDUINO 718
CHAPTER 5 ULTRASONIC SENSOR 730
CONCLUSION 733

INTRODUCTION *ARDUINO FOR INTERMEDIATES* 737
CHAPTER 1 KEY TERMS IN UNDERSTANDING ARDUINO 743
CHAPTER 2 WORKING WITH USER-DEFINED FUNCTIONS . 747
CHAPTER 3 THE SERIAL 752
CHAPTER 4 CONNECTING SWITCH 756
CHAPTER 5 TEMPERATURE SENSOR 759
   WATER DETECTOR AND SENSOR 761
   PIR SENSOR 763
CHAPTER 6 USING THE STREAM CLASS 768

THE SERIAL 770

CHAPTER 7 CALCULATED DIGITAL REPRESENTATIONS ... 774

CHAPTER 8 UNDERSTANDING THE ARDUINO FRAMEWORK 778

    CONSTANTS 780
    FUNCTIONS 781

CHAPTER 9 LEARN THE IMPLEMENTATION OF ALGORITHMS 783

CHAPTER 10 TROUBLESHOOTING 792

CHAPTER 11 PROJECTS 797

CHAPTER 12 SPEND TIME THINKING OUTSIDE THE BOX (AND THE ARDUINO) 806

CHAPTER 13 TROUBLESHOOTING 810

    CONCLUSION 814

SQL

The Practical Beginner's Guide to Learn SQL Programming in One Day Step-by-Step (#2020 Updated Version | Effective Computer Programming)

Steve Tudor

Text Copyright

All rights reserved. No part of this guide may be reproduced in any form without permission in writing from the publisher except in the case of brief quotations embodied in critical articles or reviews.

Legal & Disclaimer

The information contained in this book and its contents is not designed to replace or take the place of any form of medical or professional advice; and is not meant to replace the need for independent medical, financial, legal or other professional advice or services, as may be required. The content and information in this book has been provided for educational and entertainment purposes only.

The content and information contained in this book has been compiled from sources deemed reliable, and it is accurate to the best of the Author's knowledge, information and belief. However, the Author cannot guarantee its accuracy and validity and cannot be held liable for any errors and/or omissions. Further, changes are periodically made to this book as and when needed. Where appropriate and/or necessary, you must consult a professional (including but not limited to your doctor, attorney, financial advisor or such other professional advisor) before using any of the suggested remedies, techniques, or information in this book.

Upon using the contents and information contained in this book, you agree to hold harmless the Author from and against any damages, costs, and expenses, including any legal fees potentially resulting from the application of any of the information provided by this book. This disclaimer applies to any loss, damages or injury caused by the use and application, whether directly or indirectly, of any advice or information presented, whether for breach of contract, tort, negligence, personal injury, criminal intent, or under any other cause of action.

You agree to accept all risks of using the information presented inside this book.

You agree that by continuing to read this book, where appropriate and/or necessary, you shall consult a professional (including but not limited to your doctor, attorney, or financial advisor or such other advisor as needed) before using any of the suggested remedies, techniques, or information in this book.

Chapter 1. INTRODUCTION

If you are interested in learning a new coding language, there are a lot of different options that you can choose from, and it really depends on what you are looking for and what you want to do with them. Some of these languages are good for helping you to create a good website. Some are good for creating a smartphone application or for working on your own game to share with others. And then you can also choose a coding language that is like SQL, which are meant to help businesses stay organized and keep track of their information without all the challenges that can come with this.

Traditionally, many companies would choose to work with the 'Database Management System,' or the DBMS to help them to keep organized and to keep track of their customers and their products. This was the first option that was on the market for this kind of organization, and it does work well. Some newer methods that have changed the way that companies can sort and hold their information. Even when it comes to the most basic management system for data that you can choose, you will see that there is a ton more power and security than you would have found in the past.

Big companies will be responsible for holding onto a lot of data, and some of this data will include personal information about their customers like address, names, and credit card information. Because of the more complex sort of information that these businesses need to store, a new 'Relational Database Management System' has been created to help keep this information safe in a way that the DBMS has not been able to.

Now, as a business owner, there are some different options that you can pick from when you want to get a good database management system. Most business owners like to go with SQL because it is one of the best options out there. The SQL language is easy to use, was designed to work well with businesses, and it will give you all the tools that you need to make sure that your information is safe. Let's take some more time to look at this SQL and learn how to make it work for your business.

a. Introduction to SQL

It is best to start at the beginning. SQL is a programming language that stands for 'Structured Query Language,' and it is a simple language to learn considering it will allow interaction to occur between the different databases that are in the same system. This database system first came out in the 70s, but when IBM came out with its own prototype of this programming language, then it really started to see a growth in popularity and the business world started to take notice.

The version of SQL that was originally used by IBM, known back then as ORACLE, was so successful that the team behind it eventually left IBM and became its own company. ORACLE, thanks to how it can work with SQL, is still one of the leaders in programming languages and it is always changing so that it can keep up with everything that is needed in the programming and database management world.

The SQL is a set of instructions that you can use to interact with your relational database. While there are a lot of languages that you can use to do this, SQL is the only language that most databases can understand. Whenever you are ready to interact with one of these databases, the software can go in and translate the commands that you are given, whether you are giving them in form entries or mouse clicks. These will be translated into SQL statements that the database will already be able to interpret.

If you have ever worked with a software program that is database driven, then it is likely that you have used some form of SQL in the past. It is likely that you didn't even know that you were doing this though. For example, there are a lot of dynamic web pages that are database driven. These will take some user input from the forms and clicks that you are making and then will use this information to compose a SQL query.

This query will then go through and retrieve the information from the database to perform the action, such as switch over to a new page.

To illustrate how this works, think about a simple online catalog that allows you to search. The search page will often contain a form that will just have a text box. You can enter the name of the item that you would like to search using the form and then you would simply need to click on the search button. As soon as you click on the search button, the web server will go through and search through the database to find anything related to that search term. It will bring those back to create a new web page that will go along with your specific request.

For those who have not spent that much time at all learning a programming language and who would not consider themselves programmers, the commands that you would use in SQL are not too hard to learn. Commands in SQL are all designed with a syntax that fits in with the English language.

At first, this will seem really complicated, and you may be worried about how much work it will be to get it set up. But when you start to work on a few codes, you will find that it is not actually that hard to work with. Often, just reading out the SQL statement will help you to figure out what the command will do. Take a look at the code below:

How this works with your database

If you decide that SQL is the language that you will work on for managing your database, you can take a look at the database. You will notice that when you look at this, you are basically just looking at groups of information. Some people will consider these to be organizational mechanisms that will be used to store information that you, as the user, can look at later on, and it can do this as effectively as possible. There are a ton of things that SQL can help you with when it comes to managing your database, and you will see some great results.

There are times when you are working on a project with your company, and you may be working with some kind of database that is very similar to SQL, and you may not even realize that you are doing this. For example, one database that you commonly use is the phone book. This will contain a ton of information about people in your area including their name, what business they are in, their address, and their phone numbers. And all this information is found in one place so you won't have to search all over to find it.

This is kind of how the SQL database works as well. It will do this by looking through the information that you have available through your company database. It will sort through that information so that you are better able to find what you need the most without making a mess or wasting time.

Client and server technology

In the past, if you were working with a computer for your business, you were most likely using a mainframe computer. What this means is that the machines were able to hold onto a large system, and this system would be good at storing all the information that you need and for processing options. The user would be able to get onto these computers and interact with the mainframe, which in this case would be a 'dumb' terminal or one that is not able to interact all on its own. To get the information to show up the correct function, the dumb terminal would need to rely on all the information that is inside the computer, such as the memory, processor, and storage.

Now, these systems were able to work, and they got the job done for a very long time. If your company uses these and this is what you are most comfortable with using, it does get the work done. But there are some options on the market that will do a better job. These options can be found in the client-server system.

These systems will use some different processes to help you to get the results that are needed. With this one, the main computer that you are using, which would be called the 'server,' will be accessible to any user who is on the network. Now, these users must have the right credentials to do this, which helps to keep the system safe and secure. But if the user has the right information and is on your network, they can reach the information without a lot of trouble and barely any effort. The user can get the server from other servers or from their desktop computer, and the user will then be known as the 'client' so that the client and server are easily able to interact through this database.

How to work with databases that are online

There are a lot of business owners who will find that the client and server technology is the one that works for them. This system is great for many companies, but there are some things that you will need to add or take away at times because of how technology has been changing lately. There are some companies that like the idea that their database will do better with the internet so that they can work on this database anywhere they are located, whether they are at home or at the office. There are even times when a customer will have an account with the company, and they will need to be able to access the database online as well. For example, if you have an account with Amazon, you are a part of their database, and you can gain access to certain parts through this.

As the trend continues for companies to move online, it is more common to see that databases are moving online as well and that you must have a website and a good web browser so that the customer can come in and check them out. You can always add in usernames and passwords to make it more secure and to ensure that only the right user can gain access to their information. This is a great idea to help protect personal and payment information of your customers. Most companies will require that their users pick out security credentials to get on the account, but they will offer the account for free.

Of course, this is a system that is pretty easy to work with, but there will be a number of things going on behind the scenes to make sure that the program will work properly. The customer can simply go onto the system and check the information with ease, but there will be a lot of work for the server to do to make sure that the information is showing up on the screen in the right way, and to ensure that the user will have a good experience and actually see their own account information on the screen.

For example, you may be able to see that the web browser that you are using uses SQL or a program that is similar to it, to figure out the user that your data is hoping to see. The SQL system will be used to reach your database, as soon as the customer can put in what they are looking for. The SQL system, will see this query. And then bring back information on the website that will show up on the web browser, and if the system is working properly, the right information will show up on the page.

Why is SQL so great?

The various types of database management systems that you can work with, it is time to discuss why you would want to choose SQL over some of the other options that are out there. You not only have the option of working with other databases but also with other coding languages, and there are benefits to choosing each one. So, why would you want to work with SQL in particular? Some of the great benefits that you can get from using SQL as your database management system includes:

Incredibly fast

If you would like to pick out a management system that can sort through the information quickly and will get the results back in no time, then SQL is one of the best programs to use for this. You will be surprised at how much information you can get back, and how quickly it will come back to you. In fact, out of all the options, this is the most efficient one that you can go with.

Well defined standards

The database that comes with SQL is one that has been working well for a long time. In addition, it has been able to develop some good standards that ensure the database is strong and works the way that you want. Some of the other databases that you may want to work with will miss out on these standards, and this can be frustrating when you use them.

You do not need a lot of coding

If you are looking into the SQL database, you do not need to be an expert in coding to get the work done. We will take a look at a few codes that can help, but even a beginner will get these down and do well when working in SQL.

Keeps your stuff organized

When it comes to running your business, it is important that you can keep your information safe and secure as well as organized. And while there are a ton of great databases that you can go with, none will work as well as the SQL language at getting this all done.

Object-**oriented** DBMS

The database of SQL relies on the DBMS system that we talked about earlier because this will make it easier to find the information that you are searching for, to store the right items, and do so much more within the database.

The benefits that you can get when you choose to work with the SQL program. While some people do struggle with this interface in the beginning, but overall there are a ton of good features to work on with SQL, and you will really enjoy how fast and easy it is to work with this language and its database.

b. how to start coding

SQL is easy to learn, and you won't have a lot of different commands in order to bring up the information that you want. In this chapter, we are going to spend some time learning some of these commands as well as separating the commands into the six different categories that are the best for them. These six categories include:

Data Definition Language

This one is also known as the DDL, and it is one of the aspects that is inside of your SQL program that is in charge of allowing you to generate objects into the database before arranging them the way that you enjoy the best. For example, this is the aspect of the system that you will use when you would like to make changes, such as adding or deleting objects, out of the table. The commands that you would be able to use for this including:

- Drop index
- Drop view
- Create index
- Alter index
- Alter table
- Drop table
- Create table

Data Query Language

When you are working in DQL, you are working with what many consider a really powerful aspect of what they are able to do with SQL, especially when you are working on a database system that is considered more modern. There is just one command that is needed in order to work with the DQL part, and this command is the "Select" command. You are able to use this command in various ways including using it to run queries when you are inside of a relational database. If you were interested in getting results that are more detailed, you would need to use the Select command through DQL to make this happen.

Data Control Language

The DCL is another component of SQL that you should learn to use, and it is the commands that the user works with any time that they want to control who is allowed to get on the database. If you are dealing with personal information like credit card information, it is a good idea to have some limitations on who can get onto the system and get the information. This DCL command is used to help generate the objects that are related to who can access the information in the database, including who will be able to distribute the information. There are a few commands that are helpful when you are working on DCL including:

- Create synonym
- Grand
- Alter password
- Revoke

Data Administration Commands

When it comes to some of the commands that you can use inside SQL, you can also use them in order to audit or analyze the operation that is inside of the database. To access the performance of the database overall with the help of some of these commands. If you would like to fix something that is causing issues on the system or you would like to get rid of some of the bugs on the system, these are the commands that you are going to need to work with. While there are some options that you can choose from with these commands, the two most popular options include:

- Stop audit
- Start audit

One of the things that you need to remember when working with SQL is that data administration and database administration are going to be two different ideas inside the system. For example, database administration is going to be the part that will manage all your database, including the different commands that you are setting up in SQL and they will also be more specific to the implementation that is done in SQL.

Transactional Control Commands

If you are trying to manage and keep track of some of the transactions that are going on with your database with you and the customer, the transactional control commands are the right ones to use. If you are a company that uses their website in order to sell products online, the transactional control commands are going to help make sure that you can keep all of this in line. There are several things that you will be able to use these transactional control commands for, including:

Commit
This is the command that you will need to use in order to save information that relates to the different transactions that are inside your database.

Savepoint
This is the command that you will be able to use in order to generate different points inside the group of transactions. This

is also the one that you can use at the same time as the Rollback Command.

Rollback

This command is the one that you will use whenever you are looking through the database, and you would like to undo at least one of the transactions inside.

Set transaction

This command is the one that you can use any time that you are trying to take the transactions in your database and give them names. You will often use this one whenever you are trying to label things for a bit more organization.

All six of these types are going to be important based on the results that you would like to get out of your search. Each of these will be explored a bit more as we go through this guidebook so that you understand better how to use them, when to use them, and how to divide up the information in the proper way to avoid issues and to keep your database nice and organized with the help of the SQL language.

c. how to install MySQL applications

MySQL is a tool (database server) that uses SQL syntax to manage databases. It is an RDBMS (Relational Database Management System) that you can use to facilitate the manipulation of your databases.

If you are managing a website using MySQL, ascertain that the host of your website supports MySQL too.

Here's how you can install MySQL in your Microsoft Windows. We will be using Windows because it is the most common application used in computers.

How to install MySQL on Microsoft Windows in your

Installing MySQL

- Download MySQL from the internet.
- Run the install file. You will be asked some questions, following which you should run the setup of the program.
- Troubleshoot MySQL.
- If the downloaded MySQL fails to work on your server, you will just have to buy a server running Mac OS X. Such servers will come with a pre-installed software and most of their configuration issues are already sorted out.

d. how to launch MySQL Workbench

MySQL is a server program for querying databases, an open source relational database management system. It can be referred to as a client-server system. It is able to support a number of administrative tools, libraries, and programs, as well as, application programming interfaces.

This is a branded version of SQL. It allows its users to get data that they need from their databases, managing the database as well as receiving any reports pertaining to that database.

You can get it easily and for free from MySQL website, or you can choose to pay for a commercial release which comes with additional functionality.

MySQL runs on different platforms which include Windows, Mac OS X, and Linux. If it is possible, find and download it on your computer if you have a supporting platform. Some web hosting services provide it as their implementation as part of their package though, and each comes with a different interface to connect you to the database.

If you are using it as part of a website or application, those people that will visit the site will not have to download any additional software in order to use the features of MySQL.

Its performance

MySQL is written in C and C++, and it uses the kernel thread. This allows for multi-threading so as to take advantage of the many CPUs if they are available. It uses thread-based memory allocation which is joined by optimized nested-loop so as to improve its speed.

It uses hash tables as temporary tables whenever you are executing your queries. It uses SQL functions in an optimized class library in order to improve speed and reduce the need for accessing memory whenever you are querying tables in a database.

MySQL databases

With MySQL, you can add, access, modify and also delete any data that is stored within the database of a MySQL server.

The only limitation will be on the number of tables you can create, and all this depends on the file system.

If you have large MySQL databases, you can partition them so as to improve performance and management.

When you are querying, you are free to include tables from different databases on the same query.

MySQL Tables

There is a large amount of data that you can create with MySQL. You can create about 4,096 columns and store as many records as you want with no limitation at all whenever you are designing MySQL tables.

Each field can contain an assorted range of data. You can always fix the length of a certain field set primary and index keys, require that they have values and even increment numbers automatically.

SQL syntax is utilized to query tables. Use functions such as select, insert, update, show, join, and delete, among other syntaxes that are allowed by SQL languages.

Connecting to MySQL server

To add or modify any data that is located on MySQL server, you will have to connect to MySQL server. To succeed in this connection, you are required to have its hostname, port, username, and password.

Creating MySQL database

This is typically a simple and interesting thing to do once you master the basics of MySQL. Choose between phpMyAdmin interface or Secure Shell Command Line.

e. Writing the first MySQL code.

When using phpMyAdmin:

- Get onto the internet and log in to phpMyAdmin interface. Use the username and the password that is assigned to your web hosting provider.

- On the main frame of the page, click on 'Create New Database.'

- Choose and enter the name of the database that you want to create in the blank space that has been provided

- Click 'Create' and you will have created your database already. You will get a confirmation message stating your database is successfully created.

When using SSH Command Line:

- Go to the internet and log in using an appropriate SSH client. You will need a username and password that has been provided by your web hosting provider.

- Into the command line, enter mysql -uUSERNAME –pPASSWORD using your own username and password in capital letters.

- Choose a database name and enter into the prompt that will be provided.

- Create the database and wait for the confirmation that the database has been created.

Chapter 2. DATABASE

a. How to create a SQL database

Before you can be able to do anything on your data, create a database. My assumption is that you have installed either **MySQL** or **SQL Server** in your computer.

To create a database in SQL, we use the CREATE DATABASE statement. This statement takes the syntax given below:

CREATE DATABASE database_name;

First, login to MySQL by running the following command:

mysql -u root –p

Now you have logged into the MySQL database, it is time for you to create a new database. In the command given below, we are creating a database named *school* :

CREATE DATABASE school;

```
mysql> CREATE DATABASE school;
Query OK, 1 row affected (0.00 sec)

mysql>
```

The output shows that the database was created successfully. However, it will be good for you to confirm whether or not the database was created. To do this, use the **SHOW command** as shown below:

SHOW databases;

The above output shows that the school database was created successfully. The above command returns the list of databases you have in your system.

```
mysql> SHOW databases;
+--------------------+
| Database           |
+--------------------+
| information_schema |
| company1           |
| easydrive          |
| library_system     |
| movies             |
| mysql              |
| performance_schema |
| school             |
| sys                |
| wordpress          |
+--------------------+
10 rows in set (0.00 sec)

mysql>
```

An attempt to create a database that already exists generates an error. To confirm this, try to recreate the school database by running the following command:

CREATE DATABASE school;

```
mysql> CREATE DATABASE school;
ERROR 1007 (HY000): Can't create database 'school'; database exists
mysql>
```

The above output shows an error because the database already exists. To avoid this error, we can use the optional clause **IF NOT EXISTS**. This is showed below:

```
mysql> CREATE DATABASE IF NOT EXISTS school;
Query OK, 1 row affected, 1 warning (0.00 sec)
mysql>
```

The statement executed without returning an error.

Once you have created a database, it doesn't mean that you have selected it for use. You must select the target database using the **USE statement**. To select the school database, for example, run the following command:

USE school;

After running the above command, the school database will receive all the commands you execute.

RENAME Database

Sometimes, you may need changing the name of a database. This is after you realize that the name you have given to the database is not much relevant to it. You may also need giving the database a database name. This can be done using the SQL **RENAME DATABASE command.**

The command takes the syntax given below:

RENAME DATABASE old_database_name TO new_database_name;

For example, in my case, I have the following list of databases:

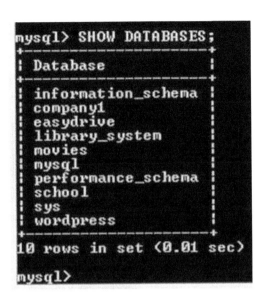

Let us rename the database named *movies* by giving it the name *movies_db*. This means we run the following command:

RENAME DATABASE movies TO movies_db;

The database should be renamed successfully.

Database Backup

It is always important to back up your database. This is because an unexpected and unforeseen event may happen to the database. Examples of such unforeseen events include Cyber-criminality and natural disasters. In case of such an occurrence, it will be impossible for you to recover your database if you had not backed it up. However, if your database had been backed up, it will be easy to recover the database and resume normal operations. You also need to back up your database to prevent the loss of your data. SQL provides you with an easy way of creating a backup of your database.

To create a database backup, you use the **BACKUP DATABASE command**. This command takes the syntax given below:

BACKUP DATABASE database_name

TO DISK = 'file_path';

The *database_name* parameter denotes the name of the database you need to back up. The *file_path* parameter denotes the file leading to the directory where you need to back up your database. The above command should be done when you need to back up the database from the beginning.

However, you can use the *differential command* if you need to create a **differential backu**p. When you do this, the backup will only be created from the time you did your last full backup of the database. To do this, you must change the command to:

BACKUP DATABASE database_name

TO DISK = 'file_path'

WITH DIFFERENTIAL;

We have changed the command by adding the **WITH DIFFERENTIAL** statement. This means that the command will perform a differential backup on the database.

Suppose we need to create a full backup of the database named *school*. We will store the backup file in the local disk **D**.

The following command will help us accomplish this:

BACKUP DATABASE school

TO DISK = 'D:\schoolDB.bak';

If you need to create a differential backup of the database, just run the following command:

BACKUP DATABASE school

TO DISK = 'D:\schoolDB.bak'

WITH DIFFERENTIAL;

We have just added the **WITH DIFFERENTIAL** statement to the command.

Note that with a differential backup, the backup will be created within a short time. This is because you are only backing up changes that have occurred within a short period. However, a full backup will take a longer time to complete.

b. how to use a database

This database is the one that you will want to use when you want to work with databases that are aggregated into logical units or other types of tables, and then these tables have the ability to be interconnected inside of your database in a way that will make sense depending on what you are looking for at the time. These databases can also be good to use if you want to take in some complex information, and then get the program to break it down into some smaller pieces so that you can manage it a little bit better.

The relational databases are good ones to work with because they allow you to grab on to all the information that you have stored for your business, and then manipulate it in a way that makes it easier to use. You can take that complex information and then break it up into a way that you and others are more likely to understand. While you might be confused by all the information and how to break it all up, the system would be able to go through this and sort it the way that you need in no time. You are also able to get some more security so that if you place personal information about the customer into that database, you can keep it away from others, in other words, it will be kept completely safe from people who would want to steal it.

c. how to delete a database

So now, let's see how you can drop a database using the SQL Server's graphical user interface.

Right click on the name of any database that you want to delete (make sure you have created a test database for this exercise).

After you right click on the name of a database, you will see the delete option; click on it. A new window will open up; make sure you check the box that says close existing connections available at the bottom of the window.

Closing existing connections allows you to safely delete your databases. With queries, this happens automatically, but when you delete your database using the GUI, you need to select this option so that if some project is using this database, the connection to that project will be closed before the drop option goes on. That's all you need to know about databases at this point of your learning curve. Let's move to the next chapter where I will talk about tables and operations related to tables.

d. how to administrate the database

Let's see how to rename MySql and SQL Server databases.

Rename MySQL database

To rename the mysql database, you need to follow the following syntax:

RENAME DATABASE old_db_name TO new_db_name;

Rename SQL server database using T-SQL

This command is useful for SQL server 2005, 2008, 2008R2 and 2012.

ALTER DATABASE old_name MODIFY NAME = new_name

SQL SELECT Database

USE DATABASE database_name;

In oracle, you don't need to select database.

Chapter 3. TABLES

Your tables are used to store the data or information in your database. They are composed of rows and columns as discussed in chapter 1. Specific names are assigned to the tables to identify them properly and to facilitate their manipulation. The rows of the tables contain the information for the columns.

Create tables

The following are the simple steps:

Step #1– Enter the keywords CREATE TABLE

These keywords will express your intention and direct what action you have in mind.

    Example: CREATE TABLE

Step #2–Enter the table name

Right after your CREATE TABLE keywords, add the table name. The table name should be specific and unique to allow easy and quick access later on.

    Example: CREATE TABLE "table_name"

The name of your table must not be easy to guess by anyone. You can do this by including your initials and your birthdate. If your name is Henry Sheldon, and your birthdate is October 20, 1964, you can add that information to the name of your table.

Let's say you want your table to be about the traffic sources in your website, you can name the table"traffic_hs2064"

Take note that all SQL statements must end with a semicolon (;). All the data variables must be enclosed with quotation marks (" "), as well.

    Example: CREATE TABLE traffic_hs2064

Step #3– Add an open parenthesis in the next line

The parenthesis will indicate the introduction of the columns you want to create.

    Example: CREATE TABLE "table_name"
             (

Let's apply this step to our specific example.

    Example: CREATE TABLE traffic_hs2064
             (

In some instances, the parentheses are not used.

Step #4– Add the first column name

What do you want to name your first column? This should be related to the data or information you want to collect for your table. Always separate your column definitions with a comma.

    Example: CREATE TABLE "table_name"
             ("column_name" "data type",

In our example, the focus of the table is on the traffic sources of your website. Hence, you can name the first column "country".

Example: CREATE TABLE traffic_hs2064

(country

Step #4 – Add more columns based on your data

You can add more columns if you need more data about your table. It's up to you. So, if you want to add four more columns, this is how your SQL statement would appear.

Example: CREATE TABLE "table_name"

("column_name1" "data type",

"column_name2" "data type",

"column_name3" "data type",

"column_name4" "data type");

Let's say you have decided to add for column 2 the keyword used in searching for your website, for column 3, the number of minutes that the visitor had spent on your website, and for column 4, the particular post that the person visited. This is how your SQL statement would appear.

Take note:

- The name of the table or column must start with a letter, then it can be followed by a number, an underscore, or another letter. It's preferable that the number of the characters does not exceed 30.

- You can also use a VARCHAR (variable-length character) data type to help create the column.

- **Common data types are:**
    - **date** – date specified or value
    - **number (size)** – you should specify the maximum number of column digits inside the open and close parentheses
    - **char (size)** – you should specify the size of the fixed length inside the open and close parentheses.
    - **varchar (size)** – you should specify the maximum size inside the open and close parentheses. This is for variable lengths of the entries.
    - **Number (size, d)** – This is similar to number (size), except that 'd' represents the maximum number of digits (from the decimal point) to the right of the number.

        Hence if you want your column to show 10.21, your date type would be:

        number (2,2)

Example: CREATE TABLE traffic_hs2064

(country varchar (40),

keywords varchar (30),

time number (3),

post varchar (40));

Step #5 – Add CONSTRAINTS, if any

CONSTRAINTS are rules that are applied for a particular column. You can add CONSTRAINTS, if you wish. The most common CONSTRAINTS are:

- o **"NOT NULL"** – this indicates that the columns should not contain blanks
- o **"UNIQUE"** – this indicates that all entries added must be unique and not similar to any item on that particular column.

In summary, creating a table using a SQL statement will start with the CREATE TABLE, then the "table name", then an open parenthesis, then the "column names", the "data type", (add a comma after every column), then add any "CONSTRAINTS".

Deleting Tables

Deleting tables, rows or columns from your database is easy by using appropriate SQL statements. This is one of the commands that you must know to be able to optimize your introductory lessons to SQL.

Here are steps in deleting tables:

Step #1– Select the DELETE command

On your monitor, choose the DELETE command and press the key. Downloading Window's MySQL Database, MySQL Connectors and MySQL Workbench can facilitate your process.

Expert SQL users may laugh and say that these steps should not be included in this book. But for beginners, it is crucial to state specifically what steps should be done. Imagine yourself learning a totally new language; Russian for example, and you'll know what I mean.

Step #2– Indicate from what table

You can do this by adding the word "FROM" and the name of the table

    DELETE FROM 'table_name"

Make sure you have selected the proper table_name. Using our first sample example from the previous chapter, this is how your SQL statement would appear:

    Example: DELETE from traffic_hs2064

Step #3–Indicate the specific column or row by adding "where"

If you don't indicate the "where" all your files would be deleted, so ensure that your statement is complete.

    Example: DELETE FROM 'table_name"
        WHERE "column_name"

Hence, if you want to delete the entire table, simply choose:

    DELETE FROM "table_name";

Using our previous example from chapter 1, this is how your SQL statement would appear:

>Example: DELETE FROM traffic_hs2064

>>where time = (10)

>>DELETE from traffic_hs2064

>>where time = (5);

Step #4–Complete your DELETE statement by adding the necessary variables

>Example: DELETE FROM "table_name"

>>WHERE "column_name"

>>OPERATOR "value"

>>[AND/OR "column"

>>OPERATOR "value"];

Deleting the wrong tables from your database can cause problems, so, ascertain that you have entered the correct SQL statements.

Inserting Data into a Table

You can insert a new data into an existing table through the following steps.

Step #1–Enter the key words INSERT INTO

Select the key words INSERT INTO. The most common program, which is compatible with SQL is windows MySQL. You can use this to insert data into your table.

Step #2 - Add the table name

Next, you can now add the table name. Be sure it is the correct table

> Example: INSERT INTO"table_name"

Using our own table:

> Example: INSERT INTO traffic_hs2064

Step #3–Add Open parenthesis

You can now add your open parenthesis after the table name and before the column_names. Remember to add commas after each column.

> Example: INSERT INTO"table_name"
>
> (

Using our own table:

> Example: INSERT INTO traffic_hs2064
>
> (

Step #4–Indicate the column

Indicate the column where you intend to insert your data.

Example: INSERT INTO"table_name"

("column_name",. . . ."column_name"

Step #5– Close the columns with a close parenthesis

Don't forget to add your closing parenthesis. This will indicate that you have identified the columns accordingly.

Example: INSERT INTO"table_name"

("first_columnname", . . ."last_columnname")

Step #6–Add the key word values

The key word values will help your selection be more specific. This is followed by the list of values. These values must be enclosed in parentheses too.

Example: INSERT INTO"table_name"

("first_columnname", . . ."last_columnname")

values (first_value, . . . last_value

Step #7– Add the closing parenthesis

Remember to add the close parenthesis to your SQL statement. This will indicate that the column does not go no further.

Example: INSERT INTO"table_name"

("first_columnname", ..."last_columnname")

values (first_value, . . . last_value)

Step #8–Add your semicolon

All SQL statements end up with a semicolon, with the exception of a few.

Example: INSERT INTO"table_name"

("first_columnname", ..."last_columnname")

values (first_value, . . . last_value);

Take note that strings must be enclosed in single quotation marks, while numbers are not.

Using our sample table, you can come up with this SQL statement:

Example: INSERT INTO"traffic_hs2064"

(country, keyword. time)

values ('America','marketing', 10);

You can insert more data safely without affecting the other tables. Just make sure you're using the correct SQL commands or statements.

Dropping a Table

You can drop or delete a table with a few strokes on your keyboard. But before you decide to drop or delete a table, think about the extra time you may spend restoring it back, if you happen to need it later on. So, be careful with this command.

Dropping a table

Dropping a table is different from deleting the records/data in the table. When you drop a table, you are deleting the table definition plus the records/data in the table.

>Example: DROP TABLE "table_name"

Using our table, the SQL statement would read like this.

>Example: DROP TABLE traffic_hs2064;

Deleting data in a table

As discussed in the earlier chapters, this action will delete all the records/data in your table but will not delete the table itself. Hence, if your table structure is not deleted, you can insert data later on.

The complete steps in deleting data or record in a table are discussed in another chapter.

DROPPING your table is easy as long as you are able to create the proper SQL.

Using the ALTER TABLE Query

There will be several times you need to use the ALTER TABLE command. This is when you need to edit, delete or modify tables and constraints.

The basic SQL statement for this query is:

Example: ALTER TABLE "table_name"

    ADD "column_name" data type;

You can use this base table as your demo table:

Traffic_hs2064

Country	Searchword	Time	Post
America	perfect	5	Matchmaker
Italy	partner	2	NatureTripping
Sweden	mate	10	Fiction
Spain	couple	3	News
Malaysia	team	6	Health
Philippines	island	5	Entertainment
Africa	lover	4	Opinion

If your base table is the table above, and you want to add another column labeled City, you can create your SQL query this way:

Examples: ALTER TABLE Traffic_hs2064

    ADD City char(30);

The output table would appear this way:

    Traffic_hs2064

Country	Searchword	Time	Post	City
America	perfect	5	Matchmaker	NULL
Italy	partner	2	NatureTripping	NULL
Sweden	mate	10	Fiction	NULL
Spain	couple	3	News	NULL
Malaysia	team	6	Health	NULL
Philippines	island	5	Entertainment	NULL
Africa	lover	4	Opinion	NULL

You can also ALTER a table to ADD a constraint such as, NOT NULL.

Example: ALTER TABLE Traffic_hs2064

MODIFY City datatype NOT NULL;

This will modify all entries that are NOT NULL.

You can also ALTER TABLE to DROP COLUMNS such as, the example below:

Example: ALTER TABLE Traffic_hs2064 DROP COLUMN Time;

Using the second table with this SQL query, the resulting table will be this:

Traffic_hs2064

Country	Searchword	**Post**	City
America	perfect	**Matchmaker**	NULL
Italy	partner	**NatureTripping**	NULL
Sweden	mate	**Fiction**	NULL
Spain	couple	**News**	NULL
Malaysia	team	**Health**	NULL
Philippines	island	**Entertainment**	NULL
Africa	lover	**Opinion**	NULL

You can ALTER TABLE by adding a UNIQUE CONSTRAINT. **You can construct your SQL query this way:**

Example: ALTER TABLE Traffic_hs2064

ADD CONSTRAINT uc_Country UNIQUE (Country, SearchWord);

In addition to these uses, the ALTER TABLE can also be used with the DROP CONSTRAINT **like the example below.**

Example: ALTER TABLE Traffic_hs2064
DROP CONSTRAINT uc_City;

Here are examples of CONSTRAINTS.

- **NOT NULL**

This constraint indicates that the NOT NULL values should not be present in the columns of a stored table.

- **CHECK**

This will ensure that all parameters have values that have met the criteria.

- **UNIQUE**

This ascertains that all values in the columns are distinct or unique.

- **PRIMARY KEY**

This indicates that the values in two or more columns are NOT NULL and simultaneously UNIQUE.

- **FOREIGN KEY**

This will ascertain that the values of columns from different tables match.

- **DEFAULT**

There is a specified DEFAULT value for columns. This may appear as blanks or appear as NULL.

Make sure you use these constraints properly to make the most out of your SQL queries.

Chapter 4. DATA

The purpose of database systems is to store the data in tables. This data is supplied by application programs running on top of the database. SQL has the INSERT command that helps us enter data into a table for storage. The command creates a new row in the table.

The command the following syntax:

INSERT INTO tableName(column_1,column_2,...)

VALUES (value1, value2, ...);

Note that we have specified the name of the table to insert data into, followed by the names of columns in which we need to insert the data, then the data values that are to be inserted. If you need to insert data into all the columns of the table, there is no need for you to specify the column names. However, if you need to insert into some columns while skipping the others, specify the columns into which you need to insert data.

The following command shows how to insert data into all the columns of the table:

INSERT INTO EMPLOYEES VALUES (1, 'jOHN', 'John12', 26, 3000.00);

```
mysql> INSERT INTO EMPLOYEES VALUES (1, 'jOHN', 'John12', 26, 3000.00 );
Query OK, 1 row affected (0.00 sec)

mysql>
```

The command ran successfully as shown above. This means that a row has been created in the table.

However, you may need to insert data into some columns only. This is the time you must specify the names of columns into which you need to insert the data.

Suppose we don't know the salary of the employee. We can insert data into the other columns as shown below:

INSERT INTO EMPLOYEES (ID, NAME, ADDRESS, AGE) VALUES (2, 'Mercy', 'Mercy32', 25);

```
mysql> INSERT INTO EMPLOYEES (ID, NAME, ADDRESS, AGE) VALUES (2, 'Mercy', 'Mercy
32', 25);
Query OK, 1 row affected (0.02 sec)

mysql>
```

The salary column has not been affected by the above command.

Constraints in MySQL

Constraints are required to restrict the values that are stored in a particular field. You can limit the type of data entered into a table with the help of constraints. Constraints can be applied at column level and at table level. Constraints are defined when the table is created. The following are the constraints available to you with MySQL:

- **PRIMARY KEY: you have already used the Primary Key constraint while creating the family_data table. The primary key is required to accept unique data for one or more columns, for faster access of values stored in the database.**

- **NOT NULL: this constraint specifies that a particular cannot accept blank entry.**

- **UNIQUE: this constraint does not allow duplicate entry in a column.**

- **FOREIGN KEY: in relational database management systems, the link between two tables is created with the help of a FOREIGN KEY. The primary key of one table when used in another table for retrieving related records is called the FOREIGN KEY.**
- **CHECK: as the name suggests, this constraint is used to check whether a valid value has been entered as per the logical statement.**

- **DEFAULT: default is a value that must be fed into a column if no value is defined while inserting data.**

Updating Data

Updating or changing data is one task you must learn and engage in as a beginner SQL learner.

The key word for this SQL query is UPDATE. You can follow the steps below.

Step #1–Create your UPDATE syntax

Prepare your update SQL query or syntax by using the key word UPDATE.

Example: UPDATE"table_name"
SET"column_name1"= value1,"column_name2"= value2;

Step #2–Add the WHERE clause

Be sure to include the WHERE clause to identify the columns to be updated, otherwise, all of your data will be updated.

Example: UPDATE"table_name"
SET"column_name1"= value1,"column_name2"= value2
WHERE some _"column_name"= some_value;

Step #3–Double check your SQL syntax

You must double check your statement before clicking the enter button. One error can cause problems in your database.

Let's practice making UPDATE SQL statements from the table below. The table below is on"Online Students".

Students

StudentNo	LastName	FirstName	Age	Address	City
1	Potter	Michael	17	130 Reed Ave.	Cheyenne
2	Walker	Jean	18	110 Westlake	Cody
3	Anderson	Ted	18	22 Staten Sq.	Laramie
4	Dixon	Allan	18	12 Glenn Rd.	Casper
5	Cruise	Timothy	19	20 Reed Ave.	Cheyenne
6	Depp	Adam	17	276 Grand Ave.	Laramie
7	Lambert	David	19	32 8th St.	Cody
8	Cowell	Janine	18	140 Center St.	Casper
9	Kennedy	Daniel	17	11 21st St.	Laramie
10	Budzinak	Leila	20	24 Wing St.	Cheyenne

EXERCISE #1

Let's say you want to update or change the student "Walker, Jean" with a new address and city. How would you state your SQL query?

ANSWER:

Your SQL statement should appear this way:

    Example: UPDATE students

               SET Address ='34 Staten Sq', City ='Laramie'

               WHERE LastName ='Walker';

REMINDER: AGAIN, Always indicate the WHERE clause to prevent updating all the data in your table.

If you have submitted the correct SQL query, your resulting table will appear like this:

Students

StudentNo	LastName	FirstName	Age	Address	City
1	Potter	Michael	17	130 Reed Ave.	Cheyenne
2	Walker	Jean	18	34 Staten Sq.	Laramie
3	Anderson	Ted	18	22 Staten Sq.	Laramie

4	Dixon	Allan	18	12 Glenn Rd.	Casper
5	Cruise	Timothy	19	20 Reed Ave.	Cheyenne
6	Depp	Adam	17	276 Grand Ave.	Laramie
7	Lambert	David	19	32 8th St.	Cody
8	Cowell	Janine	18	140 Center St.	Casper
9	Kennedy	Daniel	17	11 21st St.	Laramie
10	Budzinak	Leila	20	24 Wing St.	Cheyenne

EXERCISE #2

You want to update the address of Cowell, Janine to 20 18th St. Laramie City. What would your SQL syntax be?

Try creating your SQL statement without looking at the answer.

ANSWER:

UPDATE students

SET Address ='2018ᵗʰSt.', City ='Laramie'

WHERE LastName ='Budzinak';

If your SQL query is correct, your table will be updated according to your recent input.

Pivoting Data

Pivoting data is converting your data, which are presented in rows, into column presentations.

Through the use of PIVOT queries, you can manipulate the rows and columns to present variations of the table that will help you in analyzing your table. PIVOT can present a column into multiple columns. You have also the option to use UNPIVOT query. UNPIVOT does the opposite of what PIVOT does.

It is extremely useful in multidimensional reporting. You may need it in generating your numerous reports.

How can you compose your PIVOT query?

Step #1–Ascertain that your SQL can allow PIVOT queries

Is the version of your SQL server appropriate for PIVOT queries. If not, then you cannot accomplish these specific queries.

Step #2 - Determine what you want displayed in your results

Identify the column or data you want to appear in your results or output page.

Step #3–Prepare your PIVOT query, using SQL

Use your knowledge of SQL to compose or create your PIVOT query.

To understand more about PIVOT, let's use the table below as a base table.

ProductSales

ProductName	Year	Earnings
RazorBlades1	2015	12000.00
BarHandles1	2016	15000.00
RazorBlades2	2015	10000.00
BarHandles2	2016	11000.00

Let's say you want an output that will show the ProductName as the column headings. This would be your PIVOT query:

Example #1:

```
SELECT * FROM ProductSales

PIVOT (SUM(Earnings)

    FOR ProductNames IN ([RazorBlades1],
    [BarHandles1],            [RazorBlades2],
    [BarHandles2]) AS PVT
```

With the PIVOT query above, your ProductSales table will now appear like this:

#ProductNamesPIVOTResults

ProductName	RazorBlades1	BarHandles1	RazorBlades2	BarHandles2
Year	2015	2016	2015	2016
Earnings	12000.00	15000.00	10000.00	11000.00

You can also manipulate the table based on your preferences.

Deleting data

This action will delete all the records/data in your table but will not delete the table itself. Hence, if your table structure is not removed, you can insert data later on.

The complete steps in deleting data or record in a table are discussed in another chapter.

DROPPING your table is easy as long as you can create the proper SQL.

Chapter 5. SELECTING DATA

Selecting rows and columns

Selecting a datum from your database can be done through the SELECT key. You only have to specify the data you want to select.

Step #1–Choose the SELECT statement

Choose SELECT to identify your SQL command.

Step #2– Choose the column

Choose the specific column where you want to retrieve the data.

    Example: SELECT"column_name"

Step #3–Use the asterisk * to select all columns

If you want to select all columns use *, or you can also choose as many columns as you want.

    Example: SELECT"column_name1"

        ["column_name2","column_name3"]

Step #4–Add FROM and the table name, where the data will come from

You can enclose the identified columns and where conditions with open and close square brackets [ ], but this is optional.

Example: SELECT "column_name"

["column_name","column_name"]

FROM 'table_name'

WHERE "colum_name";

You can also write the above example in this way:

Example: select column_name, column_name, column_name

from table_name

where column_name;

Step #5–Specify the "CONDITION"

You can specify the condition through the common operators that are presented in chapter 4.

Example #1: SELECT "column_name"

["column_name","column_name"]

FROM 'table_name'

[where "colum_name" "condition"];

You can also write the above example in this way: (no open and close square brackets)

Example #2: select column_name, column_name, column_name

from table_name

where column_name condition;

Example #3: SELECT "column_name"

[, "column_name", "column_name"]

FROM "table_name"

[WHERE "column_name" LIKE 'Am'];

In the example above, all entries that start or match with 'Am' will be displayed.

Example: SELECT "column_name"

FROM "table_name"

WHERE "column_name"='America';

In the example above, only the rows that exactly matches or equals 'America' will be selected.

Reminder:

You can remove the double quotes when using the actual names of the tables and columns.

Filtering rows and columns

Filtering data is an essential skill that you can learn as a beginner. There are various filtering activities that have been previously discussed in the past chapters by the use of the SQL keyword WHERE.

Filtering the data is similar to selecting the data you want to be displayed on your monitors.

WHERE indicates the content/file that can be found in your table.

Without the WHERE key word, your SQL query would be 'lost in space' not knowing what data to filter and select.

You can use the following steps to filter your data.

Steps #1–Decide what data to filter

Know specifically what date in your table you would like to filter. Once you have decided, go to the next step.

Steps #2–Select the data

Write your SQL query with the key word SELECT to indicate your selected data.

Make sure you have chosen properly. Inaccuracies in your query can produce wrong results.

You can write the SQL query like this:

Student No	LastName	FirstName	Age	Address	City
1	Potter	Michael	17	130 Reed Ave.	Cheyenne

2	Walker	Jean	18	110 Westlake	Cody
3	Anderson	Ted	18	22 Staten Sq.	Laramie
4	Dixon	Allan	18	12 Glenn Rd.	Casper
5	Cruise	Timothy	19	20 Reed Ave.	Cheyenne
6	Depp	Adam	17	276 Grand Ave.	Laramie
7	Lambert	David	19	32 8th St.	Cody
8	Cowell	Janine	18	140 Center St.	Casper
9	Kennedy	Daniel	17	11 21st St.	Laramie
10	Budzinak	Leila	20	24 Wing St.	Cheyenne

Example:
SELECT
"column_name1,'column_name2,"column_name3"

Remember to separate the column names with commas.

Using the table displayed below, compose your SQL query based on the stated premise.

Let's say you have chosen to filter all students below age 17, and want to display all students, who are older than 17.

How would you write your SQL statement?

Students

You can write the SQL query like this:

    Example: SELECT LastName, FirstName, Address, City

Step #3–Indicate FROM what table the data came from

After selecting the columns you want displayed, indicate FROM what table they should come from.

    Example: Example: SELECT LastName, FirstName, Address, City FROM Students

Step #4–Add the WHERE clause

This is significant in filtering data, so remember to always use the WHERE clause. What data do you want to filter?

In the above exercise, you want to display all students above the age of 17. Hence, your resulting SQL statement would appear like this.

Example: SELECT LastName, FirstName, Address, City FROM students WHERE Age => 17;

Step #5–Always add the semicolon

SQL queries or statement almost always end with a semicolon. The semicolon is already added to the example above.

Updating Data

Updating or changing data is one task you must learn and engage in as a beginner SQL learner.

The key word for this SQL query is UPDATE. You can follow the steps below.

Step #1 – Create your UPDATE syntax
Prepare your update SQL query or syntax by using the keyword UPDATE.

Double check your SQL syntax
You must double check your statement before clicking the enter button. One error can cause problems in your database.

Let's practice making UPDATE SQL statements from the table below. The table below is on "Online Students".

Students

Student No	LastName	FirstName	Age	Address	City
1	Potter	Michael	17	130 Reed Ave.	Cheyenne
2	Walker	Jean	18	110 Westlake	Cody
3	Anderson	Ted	18	22 Staten Sq.	Laramie
4	Dixon	Allan	18	12 Glenn Rd.	Casper
5	Cruise	Timothy	19	20 Reed Ave.	Cheyenne
6	Depp	Adam	17	276 Grand Ave.	Laramie
7	Lambert	David	19	32 8th St.	Cody
8	Cowell	Janine	18	140 Center St.	Casper
9	Kennedy	Daniel	17	11 21st St.	Laramie

| | 10 | Budzinak | Leila | 20 | 24 Wing St. | Cheyenne |

EXERCISE #1

Let's say you want to update or change the student "Walker, Jean" with a new address and city. How would you state your SQL query?

ANSWER:

Your SQL statement should appear this way:

Example: UPDATE students

    SET Address = '34 Staten Sq', City = 'Laramie'

    WHERE LastName = 'Walker';

REMINDER: AGAIN, Always indicate the WHERE clause to prevent updating all the data in your table.

If you have submitted the correct SQL query, your resulting table will appear like this:

Students

Student No	LastName	FirstName	**Age**	Address	City
1	Potter	Michael	**17**	130 Reed Ave.	Cheyenne

2	Walker	Jean	18	34 Staten Sq.	Laramie
3	Anderson	Ted	18	22 Staten Sq.	Laramie
4	Dixon	Allan	18	12 Glenn Rd.	Casper
5	Cruise	Timothy	19	20 Reed Ave.	Cheyenne
6	Depp	Adam	17	276 Grand Ave.	Laramie
7	Lambert	David	19	32 8th St.	Cody
8	Cowell	Janine	18	140 Center St.	Casper
9	Kennedy	Daniel	17	11 21st St.	Laramie
10	Budzinak	Leila	20	24 Wing St.	Cheyenne

EXERCISE #2

You want to update the address of Cowell, Janine to 20 18th St. Laramie City. What would your SQL syntax be?

Try creating your SQL statement without looking at the answer.

ANSWER:

UPDATE students

SET Address = '2018ᵗʰ St.', City = 'Laramie'

WHERE LastName = 'Budzinak';

If your SQL query is correct, your table will be updated according to your recent input.

Creating Indexes

Creating indexes is also essential knowledge that you should learn as a SQL beginner.

These indexes are essential when searching for data or tables because they provide an immediate and efficient result to queries.

To save time and effort, create indexes only for tables that you often use.

The basic CREATE INDEX SQL query is:

Example: CREATE INDEX "Index_name"

ON "table_name"; (you can include the "colum_name", if you need that data)

Example: CREATE INDEX Studex

ON Students (Name, Age, City);

The SQL above will display all files - even duplicate files. If you want your result table to show only unique data, you can use the keywords CREATE UNIQUE INDEX, instead.

The basic SQL statement is similar with that of CREATE INDEX.

Here it is:

Example: CREATE UNIQUE INDEX "Index_name"

ON "table_name"; (you can include the "colum_name", if you need that data)

Retrieve your tables quickly by using CREATE INDEX.

Functions

User-defined functions often come to play when creating your Python codes. These functions can be used when you want a task or code done repeatedly. Functions can also help in maintaining your codes.

Keep in mind that you have also your built-in functions, which you can easily 'call', whenever you need them.

SQL has numerous functions that can be used to work with date and time values. Let us discuss them.

MySQL Functions

MySQL databases

With MySQL, you can add, access, modify and also delete any data that is stored within the database of a MySQL server.

There is no limitation as to the number of databases that you can create on a MySQL server. The only limitation will be on the number of tables you can create, and all this depends on the file system.

If you have large MySQL databases, you can partition them so as to improve performance and management.

When you are querying, you are free to include tables from different databases on the same query.

MySQL Tables

There is a large amount of data that you can create with MySQL. You can create about 4,096 columns and store as many records as you want with no limitation at all whenever you are designing MySQL tables.

Each field can contain an assorted range of data. You can always fix the length of a certain field set primary and index keys, require that they have values and even increment numbers automatically.

SQL syntax is utilized to query tables. Use functions such as select, insert, update, show, join, and delete, among other syntaxes that are allowed by SQL languages.

Connecting to MySQL server

To add or modify any data that is located on MySQL server, you will have to connect to MySQL server. To succeed in this connection, you are required to have its hostname, port, username, and password.

Creating MySQL database

This is typically a simple and interesting thing to do once you master the basics of MySQL. Choose between phpMyAdmin interface or Secure Shell Command Line.

When using phpMyAdmin:

- Get onto the internet and log in to phpMyAdmin interface. Use the username and the password that is assigned to your web hosting provider.
- On the main frame of the page, click on 'Create New Database.'
- Choose and enter the name of the database that you want to create in the blank space that has been provided
- Click 'Create' and you will have created your database already. You will get a confirmation message stating your database is successfully created.

When using SSH Command Line:

- Go to the internet and log in using an appropriate SSH client. You will need a username and password that has been provided by your web hosting provider.

- Into the command line, enter mysql -uUSERNAME –pPASSWORD using your own username and password in capital letters.

- Choose a database name and enter into the prompt that will be provided.

- Create the database and wait for the confirmation that the database has been created.

Joins

The databases used in industries have very complex structures. The data selection is often done from more than one table. Sometimes, tens of tables combine together to return a meaningful result set. To combine the records of multiple tables and select them, we use joins. Joins allow you to query data from multiple tables. There are six types of joins available in SQL:

- Inner Join
- Left join
- Right Join
- Full Join
- Self Join

Cartesian product

Before we move on towards discussing the details about all the types of joins, let's first create another SQL table inside the Employee database. The name of the table will be Customers. In our scenario, I am assuming that the database Employee contains the details of all employees in a retail store. This database also keeps the details about the customers who are served by its employees. Let's start with creating a customer table.

CREATE TABLE CUSTOMERS(

CustID   INT   Identity(1,1)   NOT NULL,

CustNAME VARCHAR (20)   NOT NULL,

CustAGE INT   NOT NULL,

CustADDRESS CHAR (25) ,

CustSALARY   DECIMAL (18, 2),

EmpFKID INT NOT NULL,

PRIMARY KEY (CustID),

   FOREIGN KEY (EmpFKID) References Employee (EmpID)

);

Output:
Command(s) completed successfully.

The customer id in the customers table is an identity column. An identity column is a column whose value gets incremented automatically whenever a record is inserted into the table. This means that while writing an insert query for this table, you will not need to pass a customer id for each record. Another interesting thing about the customer table is the presence of a foreign key. A foreign key defines a relationship between two tables. In our case, we can use this foreign key to figure out which employee served which customer. Due to the presence of foreign key, the referential integrity constraint is in place.

Union

The union keyword combines unique results of two select statements. Union keyword only works when the select statements involved bring result sets with the same structure (equal number of column and rows), the same order of column selection, and the same datatypes. The query below is combining the results of a left joined query and a right joined query using the UNION keyword.

Select EmpID as Employee_ID,EmpNAME as Employee_Name, EmpAGE as Employee_Age,

EmpADDRESS as Employee_Address, CustNAME as Customer_Name from

Employee LEFT JOIN CUSTOMERS On Employee.EmpID = CUSTOMERS.CustID

ALIASES

Sometimes you need to rename a table to facilitate your SQL query. This renamed table are termed ALIASES.

They are only temporary and do not change the name of your base table in your databases.

ALIASES are useful when your SQL query uses more than one table; when you want to combine columns; when your column_names are long or vague and you want to change them for something simpler and clearer.

You can also use ALIASES when you want to define the functions in your SQL statement.

Here is an example of a SQL query using ALIASES:

For tables:

Example:
SELECT"column_name1,"column_name2"

    FROM"table_name"AS"alias_name"

    WHERE [condition];

For columns:

Example: SELECT"column_name"AS"alias_name"

    FROM"table_name"

    WHERE [condition];

Chapter 6. VIEWS

VIEWS are virtual tables or stored SQL queries in the databases that have predefined queries and unique names. They are actually the resulting tables from your SQL queries.

As a beginner, you may want to learn about how you can use VIEWS. Among their numerous uses is their flexibility can combine rows and columns from VIEWS.

Here are important pointers and advantages in using VIEWS:

1. You can summarize data from different tables, or a subset of columns from various tables.

2. You can control what users of your databases can see, and restrict what you don't want them to view.

3. You can organize your database for your users'easy manipulation, while simultaneously protecting your non-public files.

4. You can modify, or edit, or UPDATE your data. Sometimes there are limitations, though, such as, being able to access only one column when using VIEW.

5. You can create columns from various tables for your reports.

6. The VIEWS can display only the information that you want displayed. You can protect specific information from other users.

7. You can provide easy and efficient accessibility or access paths to your data to users.

8. You can allow users of your databases to derive various tables from your data without dealing with the complexity of your databases.

9. You can rename columns through views. If you are a website owner, VIEWS can also provide domain support.

10. The WHERE clause in the SQL VIEWS query may not contain subqueries.

11. For the INSERT keyword to function, you must include all NOT NULL columns from the original table.

12. Do not use the WITH ENCRIPTION (unless utterly necessary) clause for your VIEWS because you may not be able to retrieve the SQL.

13. Avoid creating VIEWS for each base table (original table). This can add more workload in managing your databases. As long as you create your base SQL query properly, there is no need to create VIEWS for each base table.

14. VIEWS that use the DISTINCT and ORDER BY clauses or keywords may not produce the expected results.

15. VIEWS can be updated under the condition that the SELECT clause may not contain the summary functions; and/or the set operators, and the set functions.

16. When UPDATING, there should be a synchronization of your base table with your VIEWS table. Therefore, you must analyze the VIEW table, so that the data presented are still correct, each time you UPDATE the base table.

17. Avoid creating VIEWS that are unnecessary because this will clutter your catalogue.

18. Specify "column_names" clearly.
19. The FROM clause of the SQL VIEWS query may not contain many tables, unless specified.
20. The SQL VIEWS query may not contain HAVING or GROUP BY.
21. The SELECT keyword can join your VIEW table with your base table.

Chapter 7. What is a view, how to create a view, how to alter a view, deleting a view

How to create VIEWS

You can create VIEWS through the following easy steps:

Step #1 - Check if your system is appropriate to implement VIEW queries.

Step #2 - Make use of the CREATE VIEW SQL statement.

Step #3–Use key words for your SQL syntax just like with any other SQL main queries.

Step #4–Your basic CREATE VIEW statement or syntax will appear like this:

Example: Create view view_"table_name AS

    SELECT"column_name1"

    FROM"table_name"

    WHERE [condition];

Let's have a specific example based on our original table.

    EmployeesSalary

Names	Age	Salary	City
Williams, Michael	22	30000.00	Casper
Colton, Jean	24	37000.00	San Diego
Anderson, Ted	30	45000.00	Laramie
Dixon, Allan	27	43000.00	Chicago
Clarkson, Tim	25	35000.00	New York
Alaina, Ann	32	41000.00	Ottawa
Rogers, David	29	50000.00	San Francisco
Lambert, Jancy	38	47000.00	Los Angeles

| Kennedy, Tom | 27 | 34000.00 | Denver |
| Schultz, Diana | 40 | 46000.00 | New York |

Based on the table above, you may want to create a view of the customers' name and the City only. This is how you should write your statement.

Example: CREATE VIEW EmployeesSalary_VIEW AS

SELECT Names, City

FROM EmployeesSalary;

From the resulting VIEW table, you can now create a query such as the statement below.

SELECT * FROM EmployeesSalary_VIEW;

This SQL query will display a table that will appear this way:

EmployeesSalary

Names	City
Williams, Michael	Casper
Colton, Jean	San Diego
Anderson, Ted	Laramie
Dixon, Allan	Chicago
Clarkson, Tim	New York
Alaina, Ann	Ottawa
Rogers, David	San Francisco

Lambert, Jancy	Los Angeles
Kennedy, Tom	Denver
Schultz, Diana	New York

Using the keyword WITH CHECK OPTION

These keywords ascertain that there will be no return errors with the INSERT and UPDATE returns, and that all conditions are fulfilled properly.

Example: CREATE VIEW"table_Name"_VIEW AS

SELECT"column_name1","column_name2"

FROM"table_name"

WHERE [condition]

WITH CHECK OPTION;

Applying this SQL statement to the same conditions (display name and city), we can come up now with our WITH CHECK OPTION statement.

Example: CREATE VIEW EmployeesSalary_VIEW AS

SELECT Names, City

FROM EmployeesSalary

WHERE City IS NOT NULL

WITH CHECK OPTION;

The SQL query above will ensure that there will be no NULL returns in your resulting table.

DROPPING VIEWS

You can drop your VIEWS whenever you don't need them anymore. The SQL syntax is the same as the main SQL statements.

Example: DROP VIEW EmployeesSalary_VIEW;

UPDATING VIEWS

You can easily UPDATE VIEWS by following the SQL query for main queries.

Example: CREATE OR REPLACE VIEW"tablename"_VIEWS(could also be VIEWS_'tablename") AS

SELECT"column_name"

FROM"table_name"

WHERE condition;

DELETING VIEWS

The SQL syntax for DELETING VIEWS is much the same way as DELETING DATA using the main SQL query. The difference only is in the name of the table.

If you use the VIEW table example above, and want to delete the City column, you can come up with this SQL statement.

Example: DELETE FROM EmployeesSalary_VIEW

WHERE City ='New York';

The SQL statement above would have this output:

EmployeesSalary

Names	Age	Salary	City
Williams, Michael	22	30000.00	Casper
Colton, Jean	24	37000.00	San Diego
Anderson, Ted	30	45000.00	Laramie
Dixon, Allan	27	43000.00	Chicago
Alaina, Ann	32	41000.00	Ottawa
Rogers, David	29	50000.00	San Francisco
Lambert, Jancy	38	47000.00	Los Angeles
Kennedy, Tom	27	34000.00	Denver

INSERTING ROWS

Creating an SQL in INSERTING ROWS is similar to the UPDATING VIEWS syntax. Make sure you have included the NOT NULL columns.

Example: INSERT INTO"table_name"_VIEWS "column_name1"

WHERE value1;

VIEWS can be utterly useful, if you utilize them appropriately.

Chapter 8. TRIGGERS

Sometimes there are cases when certain SQL operations or transactions need to occur after performing some specific actions. This is a scenario that describes an SQL statement triggering another one to take place. A trigger is simply an SQL procedure compiled in the database that executes certain transactions based on previously occurring transactions. Such triggers can be performed before or after executing a DML statement (INSERT, DELETE and UPDATE). Moreover, triggers can validate the integrity of data, maintain consistency of information, undo certain transactions, log operations, read and modify data values in different databases.

Creating a Trigger - Once a trigger has been created, it cannot be altered or modified anymore (you can just either re-create or replace it). How a trigger works depends on what conditions are specified – whether it will be executed all at once when a DML statement is performed or it will be run multiple times for each table row that is affected by the given DML statement. A threshold value or a Boolean condition can also be included, which will trigger a course of action when the specified condition is met.

The standard syntax for creating a trigger is:

CREATE TRIGGER **TRIGGER_NAME**

TRIGGER_ACTION_TIMETRIGGER_EVENT

ON **TABLE_NAME**

[REFERENCING **OLD_OR_NEW_VALUE_ALIAS_LIST**]

TRIGGERED_ACTION

TRIGGER_NAME - the trigger's unique identifying name

TRIGGER_ACTION_TIMETRIGGER_EVENT - the specified time or duration that the set of triggered actions will occur (either before or after the triggering event).

TABLE_NAME – the database table for which the DML statements have been specified

TRIGGERED_ACTION – indicates the actions to be performed once an event is triggered

Dropping a Trigger

The basic syntax for dropping or destroying a trigger is the same as dropping a table:

DROP TRIGGER **TRIGGER_NAME**;

Chapter 9. VARIABLES AND STORED ROUTINES

Variables

Python makes use of variables. As previously discussed, variables can contain a string of words, an integer (number) or other items. Hence, they act as containers.

Step #1–Specify the value of your variable.

In the example below, the value of your variable is 50.

Example:

Let's say you want your variable to be 50, you can enter this in your Python.

    myVariable = 50

This is for the Python version 3. The first letter is in the lower case and the first letter of the next words are in the upper case. This is termed the 'camel case declaration'.

You must remember that Python is case sensitive, so use the upper case and lower case letters whenever necessary.

    myVariableTitle = 50

Step #2–Press 'enter'.

After entering or assigning the value, you can press 'enter', and the value 50 will appear. This is your value.

You can make use of it in math operations to compute whatever you want to compute.

If your syntax is wrong, a syntax error appears in red ink, informing you of the mistake.

You can assign values to your variables by using the equal (=) sign. You have to name your variable before the equal sign and assign its values after the equal sign.

Examples:

>**name ="Billy"**
>**surname ="Trump"**
>**age = 45**
>**height = 5**

Your variables are: name, surname, age and height and the values assigned are:"Billy","Trump", 45, and 5.

If you want to print your variables, you can create your statement or code this way:

>**name ="Billy"**
>**surname ="Trump"**
>**age = 45**
>**height = 5**
>
>**print name**

print surname

print age

print height

See image below:

The original shell was used; thus, the variables are printed one by one by pressing your 'enter' tab/key.

Unlike if you open a 'New File', the results will be displayed all at once in a new shell:

```
>>>
>>> name="Billy"
>>> surname="Trump"
>>> age=45
>>> height=5
>>>
>>> print name
Billy
>>> print surname
Trump
>>> print age
45
>>> print height
5
```

If you decide to open a 'New File', the syntax/statement will appear this way:

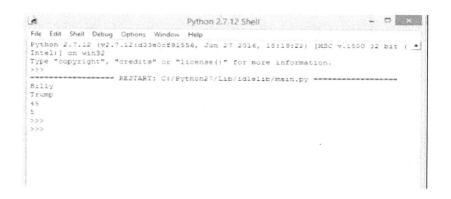

When you click 'Run', and then 'Run Module', the results will appear in a new shell:

It's smart to name your variables according to their objects/content, so you won't get confused accessing them later on.

As discussed, variables can contain names or integers, or different types of data. Just be sure to separate them with commas.

For variables that you want printed literally in a string, don't include them inside braces [ ]. These will appear in the final output.

Multiple assignments for variables

You can also assign, simultaneously, a single value to multiple variables. Here's an example:

Variables a, b, c, and d are all assigned to "1" memory location.

a=b=c=d=1

Another example is where variables are assigned individual values:

a, b, c, d, = 1, 2, "Potter", 3

The value of a=1

The value of b=2

The value of c = "Potter"

And the value of d = 1

Take note again, that numbers or integers are not enclosed in quotes (quotation marks– ''), while word-strings are enclosed in single, double quotes, or triple quotes. (' ', or " ", or """" """").

Stored routines

Python contains built-in modules and functions that come with the program when you download it into your computer. Downloading the Python versions 2 and 3 in the same computer may not work, because some of their contents/functions are incompatible with each other, although they are both from Python.

The following are quick steps in accessing and learning these built-in modules and functions:

Step #1– On your shell, type help('modules) and press'enter'.

This command or function will provide all the modules of Python available in your downloaded Python.

When you press'enter', it will take a few seconds for the list of modules to appear.

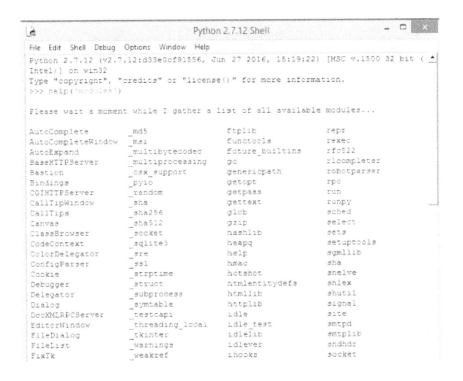

Step #3– Narrow down your search.

You can narrow down the search by being more specific. You can specify the type of module you want to find. Let's say, you want to accessmodules about'profile', you can enter or type on your Python shell the following:

help("modulesprofile")

And then press'enter'. The matching modules related to your designated search word will appear in your shell. See image below.

```
>>> help('modules profile')

Here is a list of matching modules. Enter any module name to get more help.

_lsprof - Fast profiler
cProfile - Python interface for the 'lsprof' profiler.
hotshot - High-perfomance logging profiler, mostly written in C.
profile - Class for profiling Python code.
pstats - Class for printing reports on profiled python code.
test.profilee - Input for test_profile.py and test_cprofile.py.
test.test_cprofile - Test suite for the cProfile module.
test.test_profile - Test suite for the profile module.
test.test_sys_setprofile

>>>
```

The above image is only an example to demonstrate how to be more specific in your search for modules.

Step #4 – Find the built-in functions and modules.

You can access the Python built-in functions through your shell by typing the following:

dir(['__builtin__'])

See image below:

```
>>>
>>> dir(['__builtin__'])
['__add__', '__class__', '__contains__', '__delattr__', '__delitem__', '__delsli
ce__', '__doc__', '__eq__', '__format__', '__ge__', '__getattribute__', '__getit
em__', '__getslice__', '__gt__', '__hash__', '__iadd__', '__imul__', '__init__',
 '__iter__', '__le__', '__len__', '__lt__', '__mul__', '__ne__', '__new__', '__r
educe__', '__reduce_ex__', '__repr__', '__reversed__', '__rmul__', '__setattr__'
, '__setitem__', '__setslice__', '__sizeof__', '__str__', '__subclasshook__', 'a
ppend', 'count', 'extend', 'index', 'insert', 'pop', 'remove', 'reverse', 'sort'
]
>>>
```

The different functions will appear on your Python shell. You can choose any of the functions you want to use.

You can also access the built-in functions or modules by importing them. This is done by opening your idle shell, and then typing:

> import urllib

and then, type

> dir(urllib)

When you press 'enter', all the Python modules will be displayed on your shell.

See image below:

```
Python 2.7.12 Shell
File Edit Shell Debug Options Window Help
Python 2.7.12 (v2.7.12:d33e00f91556, Jun 27 2016, 15:19:22) [MSC v.1500 32 bit (
Intel)] on win32
Type "copyright", "credits" or "license()" for more information.
>>> import urllib
>>> dir(urllib)
['ContentTooShortError', 'FancyURLopener', 'MAXFTPCACHE', 'URLopener', '__all__'
, '__builtins__', '__doc__', '__file__', '__name__', '__package__', '__version_
_', '_asciire', '_ftperrors', '_have_ssl', '_hexdig', '_hextochr', '_hostprog',
 '_is_unicode', '_localhost', '_noheaders', '_nportprog', '_passwdprog', '_portpro
g', '_queryprog', '_safe_map', '_safe_quoters', '_tagprog', '_thishost', '_typep
rog', '_urlopener', '_userprog', '_valueprog', 'addbase', 'addclosehook', 'addin
fo', 'addinfourl', 'always_safe', 'basen64', 'basejoin', 'c', 'ftpcache', 'ftperr
ors', 'ftpwrapper', 'getproxies', 'getproxies_environment', 'getproxies_registry
', 'i', 'localhost', 'noheaders', 'os', 'pathname2url', 'proxy_bypass', 'proxy_b
ypass_environment', 'proxy_bypass_registry', 'quote', 'quote_plus', 're', 'repor
thook', 'socket', 'splitattr', 'splithost', 'splitnport', 'splitpasswd', 'splitp
ort', 'splitquery', 'splittag', 'splittype', 'splituser', 'splitvalue', 'ssl', '
string', 'sys', 'test1', 'thishost', 'time', 'toBytes', 'unquote', 'unquote_plus
', 'unwrap', 'url2pathname', 'urlcleanup', 'urlencode', 'urlopen', 'urlretrieve'
]
>>>
```

Step #5 – Find the uses of function words.

You can now explore the uses/functions of the function words displayed on your shell. That is, if you don't know the function of the word.

Let's say you want to learn more about the uses of the function word 'max', you can use the help function by entering the following command:

> help(max)

Press enter or execute. The use or functions of the word 'max' will be displayed on your shell, just like in the image below:

```
Python 2.7.12 Shell
File Edit Shell Debug Options Window Help
Python 2.7.12 (v2.7.12:d33e0cf91556, Jun 27 2016, 15:19:22) [MSC v.1500 32 bit (
Intel)] on win32
Type "copyright", "credits" or "license()" for more information.
>>> help(max)
Help on built-in function max in module __builtin__:

max(...)
    max(iterable[, key=func]) -> value
    max(a, b, c, ...[, key=func]) -> value
    
    With a single iterable argument, return its largest item.
    With two or more arguments, return the largest argument.

>>>
```

Based on the results in the image shown above, apparently, the function of 'max' is to show or display the largest item or largest (maximum) argument.

Therefore, if you want to know the largest item in a certain string, type max and then the values, and press enter.

The item with the highest value will be selected, just like the example below:

See image below:

[Screenshot of Python 2.7.12 Shell showing max() function help and examples: max(7,8,9,10) returning 10 and max(3,6,9,11) returning 11]

As shown above, the highest value of the first set is 10, and the second is 11.

Step #5 - Access the Python modules and built-in functions from your downloaded file.

Another alternative is to access the different Python functions from the files that you have saved.

Remember, if your Python syntax or statement is wrong, the words will be colored red. So, it's easy to detect errors in your commands or statements.

Stored procedures

You can create and save your Python files, so you can easily access and run them, whenever you need them. There are standard data types used in Python that you have to learn; these are: strings, lists, numbers, tuples and the dictionary.

But how do you create, save and run your own files?

Here's how:

Step #1 – Open your Python shell.

As instructed in the earlier chapter, after you have downloaded and saved the Python program in your computer/device, you can open your Python shell by clicking your saved Python and click IDLE (for Python version 3) or follow the instructions for version 2 as discussed in chapter 7.

Step #2 – Click on the 'File' menu of your shell.

At the left, uppermost portion of your Python shell, click the 'File' menu. The scroll down options will appear. Click on 'New File'. See image below:

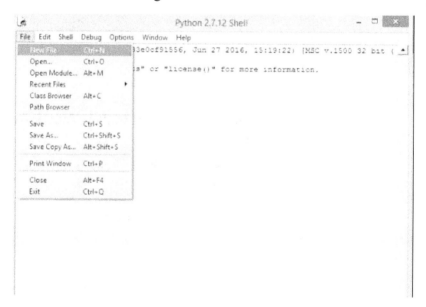

Step #3 – Create your 'New File'.

When you click on the 'New File' option, a blank box will appear. See image below:

The new box is where you can create your file for saving. If you have noticed, the file is still untitled because you will be assigning the title before you can save it. You may save the file first before proceeding, or proceed to write your Python statement/code before saving.

Write your file.

For example, you want to create a file to provide the maximum or largest value of your variables (a, b, c, d), you can enter in your new file in the following manner:

      a=int(input("Please enter 1stnumber"))

      b=int(input("Please enter 2ndnumber"))

      c=int(input("Please enter 3rdnumber"))

      d=int(input("Please enter 4thnumber"))

      print (max(a,b,c,d))

See image below:

```
a=int(input("Please enter 1st number"))
b=int(input("Please enter 2nd number"))
c=int(input("Please enter 3rd number"))
d=int(input("Please enter 4th number"))

print (max(a,b,c,d))
```

Make sure you enter the correct items and had used the necessary quotes and parentheses.

Any error in the signs, indentations, and quotes in your statement will yield errors.

Python won't be able to execute your command, and says so in red ink.

Step #4 – Save your New File.

You can save your 'New File' before writing it. Just access the 'File' menu, and choose 'Save As'.

See image below:

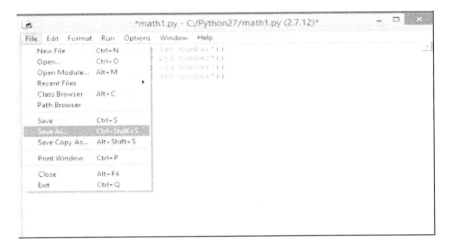

When you click on the 'Save As' option, a box will appear allowing you to select the name of your file, and where you want to save your file. Ascertain that your file is with the suffix .py.

Let's say you want to name your file math1. Type the name on the provided box, and press 'Save'.

See image below:

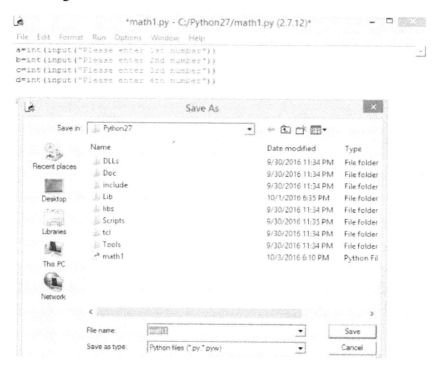

Step #5 – Run your 'New File' (math 1) or module.

You can now run your 'New File' by clicking on the 'Run' option, or key in F5 on your computer's keypads.

See image below:

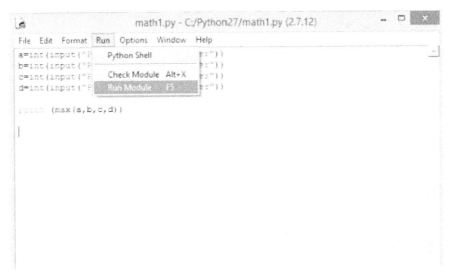

When you click on the 'Run Module' option, a new shell will appear. You can now enter your variables or values.

See image below:

```
Python 2.7.12 (v2.7.12:d33e0cf91556, Jun 27 2016, 15:19:22) [MSC v.1500 32
bit (Intel)] on win32
Type "copyright", "credits" or "license()" for more information.
>>>
==================== RESTART: C:/Python27/math1.py ====================
>>>
Please enter 1st number:
```

Test your file if it's working by providing the values required. Let's say the values of your items - a, b, c, and d - are 1356, 1827, 1359 and 1836. When you press 'enter', the value 1836 will appear, because it is the largest or highest value.

See image below.

```
Python 2.7.12 Shell
File Edit Shell Debug Options Window Help
Python 2.7.12 (v2.7.12:d33e0cf91556, Jun 27 2016, 15:19:22) [MSC v.1500 32 bit (
Intel)] on win32
Type "copyright", "credits" or "license()" for more information.
>>> 
================================ RESTART: C:/Python27/math1.py ================================
Please enter 1st number1356
Please enter 2nd number1827
Please enter 3rd number1359
Please enter 4th number1836
1836
>>>
>>>
```

Of course, you can add more statements/codes, if you wish. This is just an example on how to create and save your Python file.

You can add another item/command, ("Please press enter to exit"), to provide easier access. Save your file again.

See image below.

```
math1.py - C:/Python27/math1.py (2.7.12)
File Edit Format Run Options Window Help
a=int(input("Please enter 1st number"))
b=int(input("Please enter 2nd number"))
c=int(input("Please enter 3rd number"))
d=int(input("Please enter 4th number"))

print (max(a,b,c,d))

input("Please press enter to exit")
```

Remember to ALWAYS save any changes you made in your Python statement, and double check that your saved file is a .py file.

Take note that Python doesn't compile your programs, you have to run them directly.

Deleting files

To delete files, use the key 'del'.

>Example:
>
>**myname="Lincoln"**
>
>**myage=20**
>
>**del myname**

This will delete your variable 'myname', and whatever is specified in your command or code.

You can delete as many variables as you want. Don't worry, you can always create new files, if you want to.

Stored functions

You can create and utilize your own user-defined functions.

Step #1 – Use a keyword to define function.

The function should be defined first making use of the word 'def', and then the name of its function.

When you want to define a function, you can use the general code below:

>def functionname (arg1, arg2, arg3)
>
>statement1
>
>statement2
>
>statement3

Press 'enter' twice to access results.

Take note: arg stands for argument.

Example:

You are an employer, and you want to print the numbers (num) of your employees, thus, you defined 'employee' as the name of your file.

    def employee(num)

    print ("num")

See image below:

```
                    Python 2.7.12 Shell
File Edit Shell Debug Options Window Help
Python 2.7.12 (v2.7.12:d33e0cf91556, Jun 27 2016, 15:19:22) [MSC v.1500 32 bit (
Intel)] on win32
Type "copyright", "credits" or "license()" for more information.
>>>
>>> def employee(num):
        print ('employee', num)
```

When you press enter, and input a number, the function will keep going until you decide to stop. So, the function can work repetitively. See image below:

```
Python 2.7.12 Shell
File Edit Shell Debug Options Window Help
Python 2.7.12 (v2.7.12:d33e0cf91556, Jun 27 2016, 15:19:22) [MSC v.1500 3.
Intel)] on win32
Type "copyright", "credits" or "license()" for more information.
>>>
>>> def employee(num) :
        print ('employee', num)

>>> employee (101)
('employee', 101)
>>>
>>> employee (301)
('employee', 301)
```

You can also create the Python syntax this way:

    def employee(num)

        print 'employee', num

Press 'enter' twice and then you can begin entering the numbers. The program will print it ad infinitum.

See image below:

```
Python 2.7.12 Shell
File Edit Shell Debug Options Window Help
Python 2.7.12 (v2.7.12:d33e0cf91556, Jun 27 2016, 15:19:22) [MSC v.1500 32 bit (
Intel)] on win32
Type "copyright", "credits" or "license()" for more information.
>>>
>>> def employee(num) :
        print 'employee', num

>>> employee (101)
employee 101
>>> employee (301)
employee 301
>>> employee (34)
employee 34
>>> employee (1)
employee 1
>>> |
```

Functions can have no arguments, or have a couple of arguments. The arguments can be numbers, or strings.

You can also make use of the keyword 'return' to 'return' results (the 'return' key indicates that answers to the computation specified will be 'returned' – (displayed in the results).

Example:

If you want to obtain the average of the grades of students in 4 subjects, you can create the code this way: You can use this code for as long as you don't exit the shell. If you want to save it, you can create a New File so you could save it.

>   def grades(a,b,c,d) :

>   return ((a+b+c+d)/4)

See image below:

```
Python 2.7.12 Shell
File  Edit  Shell  Debug  Options  Window  Help
Python 2.7.12 (v2.7.12:d33e0cf91556, Jun 27 2016, 15:19:22) [MSC v.1500 32 bit ( 
Intel)] on win32
Type "copyright", "credits" or "license()" for more information.
>>>
>>> def grades(a,b,c,d) :
        return ((a+b+c+d)/4)

>>>
```

When you, or the student enters his grades following the syntax/statement, the 'return' results would be the computed value already. See image below:

```
Python 2.7.12 Shell
File Edit Shell Debug Options Window Help
Python 2.7.12 (v2.7.12:d33e0cf91556, Jun 27 2016, 15:19:22) [MSC v.15
Intel)] on win32
Type "copyright", "credits" or "license()" for more information.
>>>
>>> def grades(a,b,c,d) :
        return ((a+b+c+d)/4)

>>>
>>> grades(80,79,81,84)
81
>>> grades(77,95,87,77)
81
>>> grades(90,88,86,85)
87
>>> grades(88,80,79,85)
83
>>> |
```

The student has to type in the shell, after the arrows (>>>), following the given format:

grades(80,90,85,75)

Through this method, you can compute the grades of your students- ad infinitum.

Take note that 'return' results are different from 'return' statements. Refer to the chapter involved.

Keep in mind that you have first to define (def) the function, before your code can work, and print the results.

Remember to add the colon (:) after your def statement. You must also separate the arguments by commas.

In default parameters, the originally assigned value is printed, when the user doesn't enter any value.

In multiple parameters, an asterisk (*) can be used to indicate this.

Be adventurous and discover the joy of knowing how to make your codes work with Python.

Deleting stored routines

Classes, as defined earlier, are data that contain objects that are related to each other. The functions that are applied to these classes are also related to each other.

The keyword 'self' is a sparring partner for class data because it's used in creating your class statements.

For classes to be used correctly, it's important to create correct Python statements and syntax.

How do use your classes? Here's how.

For example, you're the 'big boss' of a company, and you want to compile the personal information of your employees, you can create a Python class code to do this.

Step #1 – Use the 'class' keyword.

Open a New File and save it. Use the 'class' keyword in introducing your class code.

Step #2 – Add the name of your 'class'.

Add the name of your class (file name). Since the data is the personal information of your employees, you may want to name it - PersonnelInfo .

Step #3 – Add the colon at the end of the first statement.

Hence, it will appear this way: class PersonnelInfo :

Step #4 – Define your variables

You have to define or assign variables to your data. You need to use the word 'self' to indicate that the code is referring to the class.

In general, a class statement appears this way:

      class ClassName :

<statement-1>

.

.

.

<statement – last>

Step #5 – Run your module.

See image below:

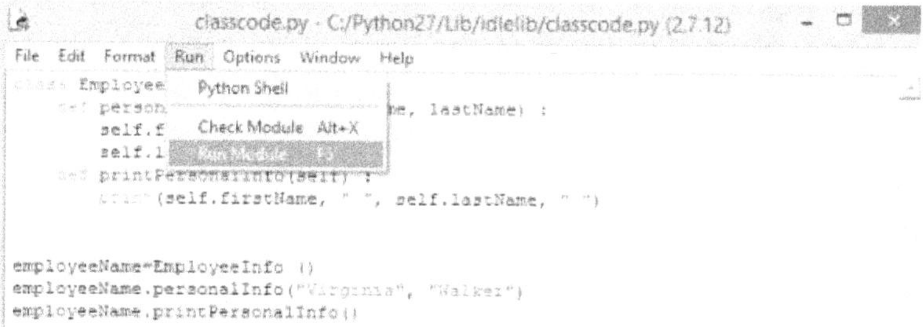

e

Two types of class object operations

1. **Class instantiation** – this type utilizes function notations in calling a class object. A special method, (double underscore)__init__(double underscore) ( ) (bracket), can be defined by a class. __init__is called a class constructor and it's used to initialize (init) a value. Python uses this keyword to indicate (initialization).

Example:

def __init__self :

self.data = [ ]

The class instantiation using the __init__ ( ) method, automatically raises __init__( ) for the newly formed class instance.

Save and click 'Run', and then 'Run Module'.

When you click 'Run Module', a new shell will be opened with this image:

```
Python 2.7.12 Shell
File Edit Shell Debug Options Window Help
Python 2.7.12 (v2.7.12:d33e0cf91556, Jun 27 2016, 15:19:22) [MSC v.1500 32 bit (
Intel)] on win32
Type "copyright", "credits" or "license()" for more information.
>>>
================= RESTART: C:/Python27/Lib/idlelib/classcode.py =================
Employee Information Data.
('Virginia', ' ', 'Walker', ' ')
>>> |
```

You can now enter your employees' names. See image below.

```
Python 2.7.12 Shell
File Edit Shell Debug Options Window Help
Python 2.7.12 (v2.7.12:d33e0cf91556, Jun 27 2016, 15:19:22) [MSC v.1500 32 bit (
Intel)] on win32
Type "copyright", "credits" or "license()" for more information.
>>>
================= RESTART: C:/Python27/Lib/idlelib/classcode.py =================
Employee Information Data.
('Virginia', ' ', 'Walker', ' ')
>>> 'Donnie, Tell'
'Donnie, Tell'
>>> 'Venus', 'Potter'
('Venus', 'Potter')
>>> ('Miriam', 'Wells')
('Miriam', 'Wells')
>>> |
```

We have also what we call 'destructors' represented by the Python keyword __del__( ): (double underscore + del + double underscore + brackets + colon.

This function will destroy or delete specified data or acts as a trash can for the data. Just like __init__, it automatically functions even without 'calling' it out.

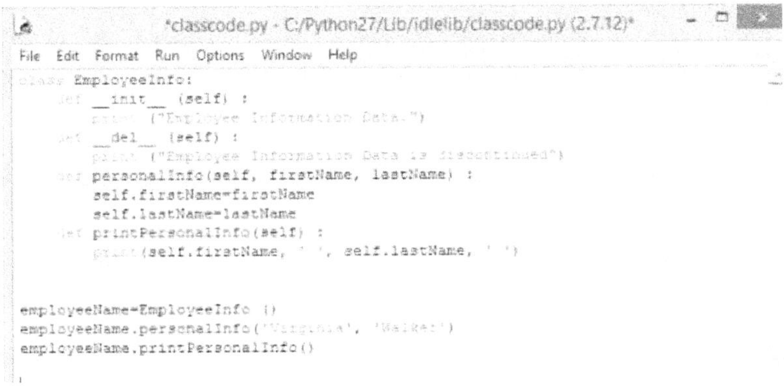
classcode.py - C:/Python27/Lib/idlelib/classcode.py (2.7.12)
File Edit Format Run Options Window Help
class EmployeeInfo:
def __init__ (self) :
__del__ (self) :
personalInfo(self, firstName, lastName) :
self.firstName=firstName
self.lastName=lastName
printPersonalInfo(self) :
(self.firstName, ' ', self.lastName, ' ')
employeeName=EmployeeInfo ()
employeeName.personalInfo('Virginia', 'Walker')
employeeName.printPersonalInfo()

If you use the del keyword in the object or instance, for example:

Adding employeeName.__del__ ( )

The resources or employees' name will be deleted or destroyed.

See image below:

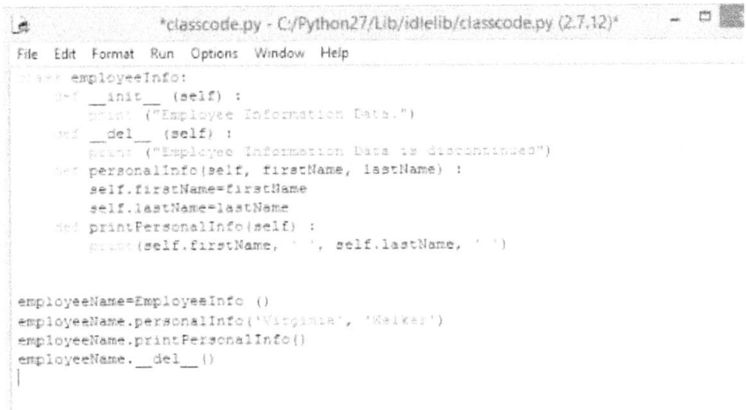
classcode.py - C:/Python27/Lib/idlelib/classcode.py (2.7.12)
File Edit Format Run Options Window Help
class employeeInfo:
__init__ (self) :
__del__ (self) :
personalInfo(self, firstName, lastName) :
self.firstName=firstName
self.lastName=lastName
printPersonalInfo(self) :
(self.firstName, ' ', self.lastName, ' ')
employeeName=EmployeeInfo ()
employeeName.personalInfo('Virginia', 'Walker')
employeeName.printPersonalInfo()
employeeName.__del__()

When you click 'Run', and then 'Run Module', a new shell will open.

See image below:

When you click 'Run', and then 'Run Module', another Python shell will open, printing the results. See image below:

You can edit your code to produce results that are in congruence with your preferences. Isn't it fun?

Reminders:

For each definition, a colon (:) is added at the end of the statement.

'self' is always included in each member function, even if there are no arguments. Example of arguments are those values found inside the parentheses (self, firstName, LastName).

Double quotes or single quotes can be used with the arguments.

The constructor and destructor can contain arguments other than self. You can include any arguments you want. Example of arguments are (self, firstName, lastName). Make sure though that your __init__ arguments are included in the instances or objects' statements that come after the 'def'.

2. **Attribute references** – this type uses the 'object.name' of common Python syntax. Whenever you define a function of a class always pass an argument on 'self'. This is because the 'self' is pointing to the class.

Example:

We will be using the same code above – without the __init__ function. If you want the data about your employees, you can create your code this way:

```
class EmployeeInfo:
    def personalInfo(self, firstName, lastName) :
        self.firstName=firstName
        self.lastName=lastName
    def printPersonalInfo(self) :
        print(self.firstName, " ", self.lastName, " ")

employeeName=EmployeeInfo ()
employeeName.personalInfo("Virginia", "Walker")
employeeName.printPersonalInfo()
```

In the example above, in each definition (def) of a class, 'self' is always added for every function of the class. Notice also the indentations for the 'def' statements.

The following entries are not indented because the statements are not part of the definition of the class, but they are objects, or instances of the class.

employeeName=EmployeeInfo ( )

employeeName.personalInfo("Virginia", "Walker")

employeeName.printPersonalInfo ( )

If you run the class code above, this would appear in your Python shell:

```
Python 2.7.12 Shell
File Edit Shell Debug Options Window Help
Python 2.7.12 (v2.7.12:d33e0cf91556, Jun 27 2016, 15:19:22) [MSC v.1500 32 bit (
Intel)] on win32
Type "copyright", "credits" or "license()" for more information.
>>>
============ RESTART: C:/Python27/Lib/idlelib/classcode.py ============
('Virginia', ' ', 'Walker', ' ')
>>>
```

Tweak the codes and see what happens. Curiosity doesn't always kill the cat.

Chapter 10. CONTROL FLOW TOOLS

IF statement

In Python, you can use various condition statements. However, you have to ascertain that you follow the Python syntax rules and indentation. One of these rules is to provide an indentation after the 'if' and 'else' statements, when you enter their codes. Simply press the tab once to provide the indentation.

Anyway, the program will assist you in determining errors in your Python syntax. If there's an error, it will display the errors, and what's wrong with them. You can also press for help, if you're lost in the sea of Python lingo.

Therefore, relax and enjoy the experience.

Functions

The 'IF ELSE' statements, which execute codes, are generally used to compare values, or determine their correctness. 'if' is expressed, if the condition is 'true', while 'else' is expressed when the condition is 'false'.

General code is:

    if expression:

        Statement/s

   else:

        Statement/s

Example:

Assign a base statement first. Let's say you're teaching chemistry to freshmen college students and you want to encourage them to attend your tutorials. You can compose this Python code:

```
hours = float(input('How many hours can you allot for your chemistry tutorials?'))
if hours < 1:
    print ('You need more time to study.')
else:
    print ('Great! Keep it up!')
print ('Chemistry needs more of your time.')
```

CASE statement

Ruby language is common in organizations for web application development. Ruby on Rails is a framework that allows for rapid development, and business teams focus on other business processes instead of coding functions from scratch. This framework provides a separator known as MVC structure (Model-view-controller). The MVC provides support in separating data, user interface, and business functions.

On the other hand, Python has the most popular MVC frameworks known as Django web framework for web application development. In addition, Python is also famous beyond the domains of web applications. For example, the Pandas library is useful for data preparation. Other libraries such as numpy and stats-model are also supportive in this case. Matplotlib is a powerful Python library for data visualization. Tensorflow is popular for machine learning tasks and projects. Besides, SciPy is another open-source library for Python, which is used for scientific computing and solving math functions that used to make engineering students sweat.

WHILE statement

The **while** statement is the main looping statement and is mostly used whenever simple iterations are required. Its structure is as follows:

Counter = 10

while counter>0:

   print counter

   counter = counter-1

   print 'Backward counting from 10 to 1'

This simple **while** loop will keep on checking the **while** condition again and again until the condition becomes false. Until the condition becomes false, every time the cycle goes through the loop. Then after the condition becomes false the interpreter resumes the former activity and continues with the program statements just after the loop. Following diagram illustrates the flow of while controls.

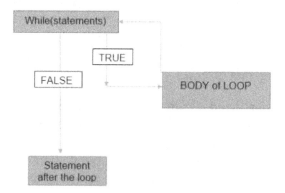

LOOP statement

As defined in the previous chapter, it is a symbol used to represent repeated (iterated) word/s or sentence/s in Python programming. Anything that is being repeatedly used can employ a loop (a piece of code). Hence, it facilitates the task that you would want to accomplish.

Types of loops

1. **The 'while' loop** – this is used to implement a piece of code repeatedly.

Example:

Let's say you have these values: a – for individual numbers; t – for sum of the numbers:

a=1

t=0

And you want the user to 'Enter numbers to add to the total.', you write the code for the 'while; loop this way:

print ('Enter numbers to add to the total.')

print ('Enter x to quit.')

(Now use the 'while' function to allow the action to become repetitive.)

while a ! = 0:

    print ('Current Total: ' , t)

    a = float(input("Number? '))

    a = float (a)

    t+ = a

print ('Grand Total = ' , t)

This is how your code will look like.

Chapter 11. CURSORS

In general, SQL commands manipulate, or work around, database objects using set-based operations, meaning transactions are performed on a block or group of data. A cursor, on the other hand, retrieves and processes a subset of data from the database one row at a time. It is actually like a pointer that refers to a specific table row. When cursor is activated, a user can select, update or delete the row at which it is pointing. It also enables the SQL program to retrieve table rows one at a time and send it to a procedural code for processing. In this way, the entire table is processed row by row.

To use the cursor functionality, its existence is declared first using a compound statement that could also be destroyed upon exit. The following is the standard syntax for declaring a cursor (but may differ for every SQL implementation):

Syntax:

DECLARE CURSOR **CURSOR_NAME**

IS {**SELECT_STATEMENT**}

After the cursor has been declared or defined, the following operations can now be performed:

Opening a Cursor - Once declared, the OPEN operation can be executed to gain access to the cursor, followed by the specified SELECT statement. The results of the database query will be saved in a certain area in the memory. The following is the standard format of the syntax when opening a cursor:

OPEN **CURSOR_NAME**;

Fetching Data from a Cursor - The FETCH statement is executed if the query results are to be retrieved after opening the cursor. The following is the standard syntax for fetching data from a cursor:

FETCH NEXT FROM **CURSOR_NAME** [INTO **FETCH_LIST**]

The statement inside the square brackets is optional, which will let you allocate the data fetched into a particular variable.

Closing a Cursor - There is a corresponding CLOSE statement that can be executed when you have opened a particular cursor. All the names and resources used will be released once the cursor has been closed. Thus, it is no longer available or usable in the program. The following is the standard syntax when a cursor is to be closed:

CLOSE **CURSOR_NAME**

Chapter 12. Common beginner mistakes and how to fix them

Achieving an error-free implementation or design is considered to be one of the ultimate goals in handling any programming language. A database user can commit errors by simply performing inappropriate naming conventions, writing improperly the programming syntax (typographical errors like a missing apostrophe/parenthesis) or even when the data value entered does not correspond to the data type being defined.

To simplify things, SQL has SQL has created a way to return error messages so that users or programmers will be aware of what is happening in the database system. This will further lead to taking corrective measures to improve the situation. Some of the common error-handling error-handling features are the WHENEVER clause and the SQLSTATE status parameter.

SQLSTATE

The host variable or status parameter SQLSTATE is one of the SQL error-handling tools that includes a wide selection of anomalous programming conditions. It is a five-character string that consists of uppercase letters from A to Z and numeral values from 0 to 9. The first two characters refer to the class code, while the next three signify the subclass code. The indicated class code is responsible for identifying the status after an SQL statement has been completed – whether it is successful or not. If the execution of the SQL statement is not successful, then one of the major types of error conditions will be returned. Additional information about the execution of the SQL statement is also indicated in the subclass code.

The SQLSTATE is always updated after every operation. If its value is set to **'00000'**, this means that the execution was successful, and you can proceed to the succeeding operation. If it contains a string other than the five zeroes, then the user has to check his programming codes to correct the error committed. There are multiple ways on how to handle a certain SQL error, which normally depends on the on the class and subclass codes indicated by the SQLSTATE.

WHENEVER Clause

Another error-handling mechanism tool, the WHENEVER clause focuses on execution exceptions. Through this, an error is acknowledged and provides the programmer an option to rectify it. This is a lot better instead of not doing anything if an error occurs. If you cannot correct or reverse the error that was committed, then the application program can just be gracefully terminated.

The WHENEVER clause should be written before the executable part of the SQL code, in the declaration section to be exact. The standard syntax for the said clause is:

WHENEVER CONDITION ACTION;

CONDITION – the value can either be set to **'SQLERROR'** (will return TRUE if the class code value is not equivalent to **00, 01** or **02**) or **'NOT FOUND'** (will return TRUE if the SQLSTATE value is equivalent to 02000)

ACTION – the value can either be set to **'CONTINUE'** (program execution is continued as per normal) or **'GOTO address'** (a designated program address is executed)

Chapter 13. Tips and tricks of SQL

SQL stands for structured query language. This language is a domain specific language that you are going to use if you are programming or trying to manage data inside of a RDBMS (relational database management system).

SQL was started with math, both tuple relational calculus and relational algebra. There is a lot of data definitions and manipulations along with control language that is going to be inside of SQL. SQL involves the use of things such as delete, update, insert, and query.

In essence, you are going to be able to update, delete, insert, and search for the things that you are going to be putting into the program. It is very common for SQL to be described as a declarative language, however, the program also allows for procedural elements.

This is one of the first languages that was able to use the relational model that was created by Edgar F Codd. Although it is not going to work with all of the rules that are set forth for this model, it is one of the most widely used languages for data bases.

In '86, SQL became part of the ANSI. Then, in '87 it became part of the ISO. However, there have been updates since then that have made it to where the language can include larger sets. Just keep in mind that the code for SQL is not going to be one hundred percent portable between data bases unless there are some adjustments to the code so that it fits the requirements for that data base.

Learning SQL can be one of the better decisions that you make about your career because you can push yourself forward with it that way that you can rely on using your own knowledge rather than having to go to someone else for their knowledge. In fact, people are going to be coming to you to learn what it is that you know about the program.

By learning SQL, you are going to be able to do more than you may have been able to before. Here are a few things that are going to give you a good reason as to why you should learn SQL.

Money

Learning SQL makes it to where you have the opportunity to earn some extra money. Developers that work with SQL earn around $92,000 a year! An administrator for an SQL data base is going to make about $97,000 a year. So, just learning SQL makes it to where you are able to earn around twice as much as what the average American household is going to make in a year.

Highly sought after

Employers are wanting people who know SQL! The more knowledge that you have about SQL the more sought after you are going to by employers. Knowing SQL is not only going to benefit you but your employer as well because they are not going to have to pay for you to learn the program. The interviewing process is going to be better than any other process that you have gone through and you may find that they are going to be willing to give you more money just for knowing SQL over the other person. With SQL knowledge, you are going to be opening yourself up for more careers than you might have been able to apply for before.

Get answers

SQL is going to give you the answers that you are looking for to any questions that you may have about business or data that is being stored inside of your data base. Therefore, you are going to be more self-sufficient and not as dependent on others when it comes to business. If you are able to answer questions on your own that you so that you are not stopping someone else from doing their job, then an employer is going to be able to save money by hiring you because you are going to be able to answer questions on hiring someone else to answer those questions. Knowing SQL is going to even help you if you are wanting to start your own business or push your business that you have already started to the next step that has just been out of your reach.

More stable than Excel

When you are using Excel for large amounts of data, you may notice that it is too much for the program and therefore the program tends to crash. A crash leads to lost data and extra time that you are going to have to go in and fix anything that may be wrong or entering data that was not saved. SQL is going to be much more reliable for you to use when you are trying to work with large amounts of data and it is going to save you some time working with it because it is not going to require too much for you to work with the processes that SQL offers.

Making reports

Searching in SQL is relatively easy and you can reuse that search when you have to double check to make sure that the data in the data base is accurate. Excel does not give you the proper processes that you need to get ahold of the data that you are wanting to get ahold of.

SQL coding only has to be written once and saved and then it is going to run each time that you need it to. This is yet another way that SQL makes it to where your life is easier because you are not having to take up as much time trying to get the data that you need.

Do not think that SQL is going to be simple, it is complicated and is going to take a lot of time to learn, but the more effort that you put into it, the more it is going to pay off for you. You are going to not only be saving money by learning SQL, but you are going to be increasing what you will be able to make with SQL.

Four Tips That Make Using SQL Easier!

1. Changing the language on the user interface: close out the program if you have it open and then go to the installation folder. You will right click on the short cut that is on your desk top and open the file location. From there you will open the SQL developer folder and then the first folder that is listed will need to be opened nexted. The next thing that you are going to click on is the SQL developer.conf. You are going to be adding in a new setting inside of the text that is already there to change the language to what it is that you are wanting to see. You can put this new setting anywhere. Putting a comment in the code is going to be a good idea so that you know what you have done if you have to get back into it at a later date. You will AddVMOption before adding in the Duser.lanaguage and you can set it to any language that you are wanting. Now reopen your SQL developer and it will be in the language that you want it in.

2. Constructdata base connections: right click on the connection on the left of the screen and click on new connection. You will need to title the connection whatever it is that you want. You will need to enter the usertitle and password for it. You should change the color if you are going to be working with multiple connections at once. In the role you are going to change the role if you are using a system connection title. You can leave the home host alone if you are using your home computer. However, if you are using a different location, you will need to input the IP address for where the system is going to be running. Leave your part alone and xe should be left alone as well unless you are not working with an express edition

of SQL. You can test the connection and if it is successful, you can close the connection down and you have created your connection. If everything is correct it is going to open with no errors and you are going to be able to put in SQL code.

3. Disabling features: there are a lot of features that SQL offers and if you do not use them, then you should disable them so that they are not slowing down the developer. You will go to the tools menu and go down to the features option. Each feature has different folders, it is up to you to decide which features you want to keep running and which ones you want to disable. You can expand each folder down so that you are able to see what each folder contains. All you are going to do is uncheck the feature and it will turn that feature off and cause the system to start to run faster. Be sure that you are going to apply the changes so that they are not turning themselves back on without you turning them on yourself.

4. Executing commands and scripts: use the tool bar that is at the top of the developer and press the play button. Make sure that you have added in your semi colon. You can also use ctrl and enter so that you are not having to pull your hand off the keyboard. To run a script, you are going to you can use the toolbar again just select run scrpts so you run both commands. Or, press the F5 key if that is easier for you. Should your file be external use the at sign and the path file to import it and run it.

Chapter 14. Workbook

This guidebook has taken a lot of time to look over many different topics when it comes to SQL, such as which data types you should use to work with your database in SQL. We even spent some time looking at the various commands that you would be able to choose when you are in SQL so you can initiate queries and search around inside the database.

Now that you have some of these basics down, it is time to move on to learn about the steps that you should take when you want to manage the objectivity that comes in the database. There are many things that we would be able to touch upon with regards to this in the guidebook, but some of the ones that we will spend our time on include tables, views, clusters, sequences, and synonyms. Let's start looking at these right now to help you understand how all of them will work in your code.

What is the schema?

When you are working with what is known as a 'schema' inside of SQL, you should always think of it as using a set of objects that are already found inside of the database, but which will be linked to just one user on the database, rather than being linked to all of the users. The user who has the access will be the one who is the owner of the schema, and they will be the ones you can set the objects. These objects will then be linked directly back to the username that the owner picked. The user will have the power to generate their objects, and then when this is done, they can generate their own schema. This allows the user to have a ton of control over what is found in their databases and they could have the control to change it as much as they want.

You will find that this can be helpful in several ways. Let's say that your users just want to place an order with you. If they have their own account and schema, they would be able to make an order, and then they would be able to change or delete that order if they so choose.

Another example of this is when the user is trying to set up their own account in your store. This is something that they can sign up for and then they will have an account for your store. This is something that they can choose to do, and then they will go through and pick out the username and the password that they would like to use.

After the user has been able to set up their own account, they will have access to all parts of the database that pertain to them. They can make changes as well, such as updating their address, changing their payment options, and even making changes to the orders that they placed. In addition, any time that the user would like to be able to get into their account, all they need to do is use the username and password that they picked the first time and log in to mess around on the database.

Let's take a better look at how this will work by bringing out an example. Let's say that you are the person who has the credentials that are needed to log in. For this example, we will use the username 'PERSON1.' You can decide what you would like to place inside this database and you can even create a brand new table, for this one we will call it 'EMPLOYEES_TBL.' When you then go into the records, you will notice that for this new table, it will be called PERSON1 EMPLOYEES_TBL. This is how others will see the table name as well so they know who created the table. The schema will be the same for each person who created this table and owns it.

When you or your user would like to access their own schema, one that is prepared already, you will not have to list out the exact name of the schema. Instead, you would simply need to pull up the name that you gave it. So, for the example that we went through before, you would be able to call up EMPLOYEES_TBL. Remember that this is just with schemas that are in your own account. If you would like to be able to pull up schemas that are present somewhere else, you must add the username ahead of it.

How to create a new table

There are many times when you are creating something new in a database, and you will need to bring out a table. These tables are nice because they can store and present the information that you would want to use. You will find that SQL makes it easy to create tables, and you will then be able to add information as needed. Whenever you want to create a new table, you just have to use the simple command of 'CREATE TABLE.' This command will allow you to bring up the table and start using it, but if you would like to fill it in and make the table look a certain way, there will be a few more steps that you will need to accomplish.

It is important to think about what you would like to have in the table, how you would like the table to look, how big it should be, and other information about the table to ensure that it is made properly. Almost all of the versions of SQL will provide you with characters that will make it easy to submit or terminate a statement to the server. With ORACLE, the semicolon will be the option that you would use, but with the Transact-SQL version, it is better to work with the GO command. But for most of these versions, you would be able to use the CREATE TABLE command and then when you are ready, you can start filling them out.

How to create a table with one that already exists

There will be times that when you are working with SQL where you will want to take the information that you have from one table and then use that information to create a new table. This is something that you can do with SQL, you just need to learn the right commands to make sure that it works right. The commands that work the best for making this happen include the 'CREATE TABLE' and the 'SELECT' commands. Once you have been able to use these two commands, you will see that it worked to create a new table that will have the same parameters and definitions as your older table. This would like to create a new table that you can customize, but it would have the information that you need from an older table.

There is a little bit of coding to make all of this work for your needs. If you would like to take one of your older tables and use it as the basis of your new table, you would be able to use the following syntax:

CREATE TABLE NEW_TABLE_NAME AS

SELECT ["|COLUMN1, COLUMN2]

FROM TABLE_NAME

[WHERE];

As you take a look at this syntax, you should be able to see that the new syntax will use the keyword SELECT. This is the right keyword to use here because it is something that you can bring out any time that you would like to work on a query for that particular database. This SELECT keyword will help you to work on your new table, even while you are creating it, with the help of your search results.

How to drop tables

The next thing that we will work on doing with the SQL system is how to drop tables. If you use a new keyword, the keyword 'RESTRICT' and then you reference a particular table by using the view or the constraint that is set up, the command 'DROP' will be used, but it will give you a message alerting you that there is an error in the system. It is also possible to add in the 'CASCADE' command along with the DROP command. This will make sure that the DROP command will work properly and that all the views and the constraints that are inside of your table will be dropped. To ensure that all of this will work out well for you, you can use the following syntax to drop a new table:

DROP TABLE TABLE_NAME [RESTRICT | CASCADE]

Any time that you are interested in dropping your new table inside of the SQL database, you should make sure that you are telling the program who is the owner of this new table that you are working on. This is not always necessary, but it is a good habit to get into. This will ensure that you do not drop the wrong table and it will often help to prevent loss of information inside of the table. If you have access to some of the other accounts inside of your database which is not your own, it is important that you check that you are working inside the account that you want so that you do not change the wrong things and have to fix that mess later on.

Since you will work with a lot of information and databases when you work with SQL, it makes sense that these tables are an important part of working inside the SQL system. These tables will help you to gather information and present it in a way that you are easily able to read. The tables will then be able to take the information, or perhaps the products that you would like to sell, and they can present them to you in a way that is easier for you to look through. Or, you can set up the table so that it is easier for the user to look at it when they are on your website. As you can see, creating these tables is not something that has to be too difficult to work with, but they will certainly help you to keep the information in your database as safe as possible.

How to Do Your Own Search Results Through SQL

As we have gone through this guidebook, we have spent a lot of time talking about search results and how SQL can help out with this. You can use SQL to make it easier for you and for your users to search for terms or items and have the right things show up. This is a great way to sort through all the information that is inside of the database, so you can organize it the right way and ensure that you are getting the right things.

Once you have set up your own database for your business, and you have taken the time to learn how to create some of your own tables, it is now time to learn how to do various search queries on this system. You can make the SQL language work for you to ensure that you can find any result that you would like as long as that information is found in the database. You do need to make sure that you have set up the database in the proper way so that your search will find the right information without encountering any kind of issue.

A good way to think about it is that there are times when people will come to visit your website, and they are there because they are looking for some particular product that you are trying to sell. Are you more interested in working with a database that is slow and brings back the wrong results for your user? No, this will make the user mad, and they will go and use a different store for their needs. It is much better to go with a database that is set up right so that it is fast and will return the results that are needed.

How to create a new query

The first thing that we need to take a look at is how to create a new query. Before you even start this process, just keep in mind you are basically sending out information to the database that you already set up. Make sure that you are using the right command, which in this case will be the SELECT command so that you can send out the query that you are planning to use.

One example that you can look at for this is when you are working with a table that is responsible for holding onto all of the products that are in your database. To do this, you would just use your SELECT command to find out which products are on that table. Your user will then be able to type in the specific products that they are interested in finding, such as your best-selling items, ones that fit a certain price point, size, color, or brand, and so on. You will also be able to use any type of query that you want to make sure that the user can get the product that they want out of your database if it is there.

How to work with the SELECT command

Any time that you are on your website, or you would like to create a new query inside of your database, you will also be able to use the SELECT command to make this happen. This command can take over the tasks of starting and executing the queries that you are trying to send out to the database and in most cases, you will simply need to add something into the statement rather than sending out the SELECT command. You can add anything that you would like such as the brand of the item and more before using the command.

Whenever you are ready to work with the SELECT command while working with SQL, there will be four main keywords that you will need to watch out for. Remember that these are commonly known as the four clauses. These clauses are listed below:

SELECT

This command must be combined with the 'FROM' command to obtain the necessary data in a format that is readable and organized. You will use this to help determine the data that will show up. The SELECT clause will introduce the columns that you would like to see out of the search results, and then you can use the FROM to find the exact point that you need.

FROM

The SELECT and the FROM commands often go together. It is mandatory because it takes your search from everything in the database, down to just the things that you would like. You will need to have at least one FROM clause for this to work. A good example of a syntax that would use both the SELECT and the FROM properly are these:

SELEC [* | ALL | DISTINCT COLUMN1, COLUMN2]

FROM TABLE1 [, TABLE2];

WHERE

This is what you will use when there are multiple conditions within the clause. For example, it is the element in the query that will display the selective data after the user puts in the information that they want to find. If you are using this feature, the right conditions to have along with it are the 'AND' and 'OR' operators. The syntax that you should use for the WHERE command is this:

SELEC [* | ALL | DISTINCT COLUMN1, COLUMN2]

FROM TABLE1 [, TABLE2];

WHERE [CONDITION1 | EXPRESSION 1]

[AND CONDITION2 | EXPRESSION 2]

ORDER BY

You can use this clause to arrange the output of your query. The server can decide the order and the format that the different information comes up for the user after they do their basic query. The default for this query will be organizing the output going from A to Z, but you can make changes that you would like. The syntax that you can use for this will be the same as the one above, but add in the following line at the end:

ORDER BY COLUMN 1 | INTEGER [ASC/DESC]

All of these will need to be in place if you would like to see the SELECT command working properly and pulling out the right information that you are searching for with your query into the database.

How does case sensitivity work?

As you are doing things inside your SQL database, you will not need to worry so much about the case sensitivity that you put in as you would with some of the other coding languages that you may have used in the past. You can work with both the upper case and the lower case letters that you would like, and they will work the same when you do your own searches. You even have the choice to look for the clauses and the statements and see how those will show up in your code.

Now that we have said this, there will be some times when this case sensitivity is really important. For example, let's say you're in a situation where you are working with objects of data. For the most part, that data that you will use will be written in upper case letters. The reason for this is because it will let other users see that something is consistent with the code and they will know why. It makes the code look better and makes much more sense as well.

Without this rule with the upper case, you would end up with one user typing in 'JOHN', and the other user will go with John and still, another user may go with john. A beginner who goes through the SQL language may be wondering if these mean the same things or not, and this can get confusing. It is better to have everything in upper case so that it matches and some issues with writing this code will be avoided.

Those who work with the SQL language agreed that using an upper case format was the best idea for avoiding this confusion because these are easier to read, and it matches up with what you may have done in some other databases that you worked with. If you are not using this upper case format when you are writing things out, you need to at least go with another method that will keep your titles consistent with what you are doing. If you write out all the names with the format of 'Name,' then this is the way that you will do it with all of them.

There are also many times when you will work with transactions in your database as well as the queries that we talked about earlier, and sometimes these will go together. These transactions are really important, although you may feel that this is some unimportant information that the user is not going to care all that much about. But if you don't use case sensitivity the right way, or make sure that the table is set up the way that it should be, you will end up with the wrong results showing up and everyone getting frustrated. No one wants to type words into a query and find out the results that keep coming up have nothing to do with what they want.

When you are creating a new database and working inside of it, you must make sure that the query is set up well. This will make it easier for your user to find the products and other items that they are looking for. No user wants to come onto your page and run into issues with finding the information that they need. When the user types in the keyword, they want to be able to get the right information.

Imagine how well it would go if the user was on your website and typed in the keywords for what they are looking for, and then the wrong product came up? Let's say that they went on and started looking for some new boots. If they typed that in and started getting results for kids' toys, they probably would be really mad at it. Most people would not even try it a second time and would leave the page to try some other site, leaving you without the sale.

Working with the right queries and making sure that they work the right way with your database is so critical so that the above scenario does not happen. You want to make sure that when the user types in a keyword that they want to use, they can get the items that match with what they are searching for. These queries can make sure that you can keep the customer happy, and it will avoid a ton of frustrations that will come from not being able to find what they want on your website.

Even if this is the way that you would like to use the database, there will still be times that you would want to make sure that there is a good search function for your user. If the user wants to be able to look through the database and find specific information, such as their account, information on which payment method they have available, or what kind of services you can provide, you will still want to make sure that you have the transactions set up so that it goes smoothly. Working to make sure that the database is set up well so you and the user can find what they want when they do a query in the search bar will ensure that the user is happy and that your business can run smoothly.

As a beginner, it is important that you learn how to set up the right queries that can be used inside of your database. This is important to help organize your SQL database and make sure the user finds what they're looking for. This is important whether you are trying to sell products on your website, whether you want to keep track of payment, and other personal information for the customer or you want to use the database for another reason. Make sure to use some of the steps that we outlined earlier in this chapter to help you set up the database in a manner that makes a lot of sense based on what your users need and will provide the right information as soon as a customer does a search on your database.

Chapter 15. SQL Quiz

1. Transcribe SQL.
2. What is the keyword in creating tables?
3. What is the SQL syntax in selecting tables?
4. What is the keyword in deleting tables?
5. What is the SQL statement if you want to display only the names and the city of the table above?
6. What is the SQL statement if you want to retrieve only the data of employees who are 25 years old and above?
7. What is the SQL command if you want to arrange the names in an ascending order?
8. What is the SQL query if you want to fetch the data of employees, who have a salary of more than 20000.00?
9. What is the SQL command if you want to select only the employees coming from Denver?
10. What is the SQL if you want to change the Name of Lambert Jancy to Walker Jean?

ANSWERS:

1. STRUCTURED QUERY LANGUAGE
2. CREATE TABLE
3. SELECT "column_name1", "column_name2 FROM "table_name";

(Remember to remove the double quotes when substituting the names of your columns and tables.)

4. DELETE TABLE

5. SELECT Names, City FROM EmployeesSalary;

6. SELECT * FROM EmployeesSalary WHERE Age >= 25;

7. SELECT * FROM EmployeesSalary ORDER BY Names ASC;

8. SELECT * FROM EmployeesSalary WHERE Salary >20000;

9. SELECT * FROM EmployeesSalary WHERE City = 'Denver';

10. UPDATE EmployeesSalary
SET Names = 'Walker Jean'
WHERE Names = 'Lambert Jancy';

CONCLUSION

For a long time now, data analysis has always been done as a part of business. The business intelligence team has always been the part of business that has been mandated with information retrieval as well as pulling down databases and relying information to other parts of business through the local machines. This has changed so much with the advancement of computer technology.

All businesses are now into digital businesses. Everyone is in the data business and so some of the important skills have to be mastered in order to make things easy to run such businesses. Every day, new data is created for a business and by the time you realize it, a business has produced and consumed digital data. This is the point where the querying and analysis of digital quantitative data becomes an important skill that everyone must learn.

SQL is like an emerging new skill that is quite vital to businesses. Just like basic literacy is important for any job out there, mastery of SQL skills is increasingly becoming important for anyone that wants to succeed in the business sector.

You realize that if everyone you work with is data literate, working can be very easy since everyone can create, access and manipulate data in the databases and perform all the required tasks without waiting for the other.

LINUX

The Practical Beginner's Guide to Learn Linux Programming in One Day Step-by-Step (#2020 Updated Version | Effective Computer Programming)

Steve Tudor

Text   Copyright   ©   Steve   Tudor

All rights reserved. No part of this guide may be reproduced in any form without permission in writing from the publisher except in the case of brief quotations embodied in critical articles or reviews.

Legal & Disclaimer

The information contained in this book and its contents is not designed to replace or take the place of any form of medical or professional advice; and is not meant to replace the need for independent medical, financial, legal or other professional advice or services, as may be required. The content and information in this book has been provided for educational and entertainment purposes only.

The content and information contained in this book has been compiled from sources deemed reliable, and it is accurate to the best of the Author's knowledge, information and belief. However, the Author cannot guarantee its accuracy and validity and cannot be held liable for any errors and/or omissions. Further, changes are periodically made to this book as and when needed. Where appropriate and/or necessary, you must consult a professional (including but not limited to your doctor, attorney, financial advisor or such other professional advisor) before using any of the suggested remedies, techniques, or information in this book.

Upon using the contents and information contained in this book, you agree to hold harmless the Author from and against any damages, costs, and expenses, including any legal fees potentially resulting from the application of any of the information provided by this book. This disclaimer applies to any loss, damages or injury caused by the use and application, whether directly or indirectly, of any advice or information presented, whether for breach of contract, tort, negligence, personal injury, criminal intent, or under any other cause of action.

You agree to accept all risks of using the information presented inside this book.

You agree that by continuing to read this book, where appropriate and/or necessary, you shall consult a professional (including but not limited to your doctor, attorney, or financial advisor or such other advisor as needed) before using any of the suggested remedies, techniques, or information in this book.

INTRODUCTION

Linux is basically just an operating system. "Operating system" is probably a word that you use on a pretty regular basis, but most people don't understand what an OS actually is.

All of the software and hardware on your computer is run through the OS. That is why, if you have an Android phone, you have to download Android apps, and if you have an iPhone, you have to download Apple apps. Different operating systems have different requirements for both their hardware and software, and you have to abide by these requirements for the programs on your computer to work. Most computers come with an OS already installed, which enables users to immediately begin to access the information and capabilities of their computers. If you have an Apple computer or phone, a Mac OS will be pre-installed so that Mac software can be run on it. Most other computers come with a Windows OS pre-installed. They allow you to get started with your computer right away.

An OS is basically the interface that allows you to interact with the information on the computer. The earliest operating systems used a command line interface, which meant that users had to type out a code in order to access a program. The most common one was MS-DOS, which was released by Microsoft in the year 1981. Operating systems today use a graphics user interface, or GUI. This means that you can physically see, as images, the different applications and programs that you want to access. You just have to click on the icons, and they open up. Different operating systems use a different GUI, so switching from one OS to another can cause some confusion at first. The look and feel will be different and may take some getting used to.

Operating systems have to be continually updated in order to keep up with the ever-growing software and hardware improvements. You may have experienced this frustration if you have tried to use the newest version of Microsoft Word (or any other program) and found that it is incompatible with your computer. The problem isn't that your computer has malfunctioned but that your operating system isn't advanced enough to handle the latest version of the software. You will need to either update your OS or use an older version of the program that you are trying to access. Updating an OS can take up a lot of memory, so having an up-to-date one may mean getting a computer that has more memory. You may have to choose between getting a new computer and working with an outdated OS.

The three most common operating systems are Windows, Mac, and Linux. Windows was created by Microsoft in the 1980s to replace MS-DOS. It was much more user-friendly because people no longer had to keep track of different codes necessary to access their programs. Instead, they could just click on the icons that appeared on the computer's desktop. Today, approximately 80% of computers operate through a Windows OS. The Windows OS has undergone multiple iterations. Windows 95, Windows 97, Windows 2000, Windows Vista, and Windows 10 are just some of the versions that have come and gone through the years. Each version represents an improvement. Mac, the OS used by Apple products, also has multiple versions. The iOS system is used by iPhones, with a higher number indicating a higher-level OS. Apple computers have used Lion, Mountain Lion, Mavericks, Yosemite, El Capitan, and High Sierra, amongst others. Every time Apple releases a new OS, changes are made that improve the computer's performance. Like Windows, each update represents improvements and enable different software capabilities. Linux, the third most popular OS, was released in 1991 by a man named Linus Torvalds. It has also undergone multiple iterations over the process of improvement in its protocols.

Linux is different from other operating systems in some pretty significant ways. How it is different will be explained in the next section, which will detail the history of Linux and the Linux community.

CHAPTER 1: WHAT IS LINUX?

If you have spent much time in the world of computer technology, you have probably come across the name "Linux" several times. You may have heard that it is open source and available for free download, but that information doesn't explain what Linux actually is. This chapter will give you some solid background understanding for Linux so that you can navigate through all of the information about Linux.

A. THE STORY OF LINUX

Similar to UNIX, the Linux operating system has different roots and is based on the work of quite a few masterminds. Among others, this includes Richard M. Stallman, Andrew S. Tanenbaum and Linus Torvalds.

Richard M. Stallman, a hacker and developer at MIT, is the first president of the Free Software Foundation (FSF), and the father of the GNU project. GNU abbreviates the slogan GNU is Not UNIX. The goal of the project was to develop a free UNIX operating system. Until the beginning of the 1990s a collection of tools were available, but the kernel was still missing. The entire software was published under the GNU Public License (GPL) around 1983.

The next step for Linux came from Andrew S. Tanenbaum. At that time he was a professor at the University of Amsterdam. For his students he developed Minix, an operating system for educational purposes to demonstrate and understand the UNIX principles. As he pointed out, Minix was not intended to be used in practice.

Linus Torvalds, a Finish student at the University of Helsinki, was a user of Minix and quite unhappy with its boundaries. In 1990 he began to develop a new operating system based on the ideas of Minix, the UNIX principles, and the POSIX standard. His motivation was to have his own system that was understandable, and maximized to the boundaries of the hardware. He also wanted to have fun, and had no commercial intent in mind. The entire story behind Linux is described in his autobiographical book titled **Just for Fun.** Today, Linus Torvalds oversees the development of the Linux kernel.

To make Linux attractive to the outside world it needed a nice logo. Based on a competition for mascots, a large number of proposals were handed in. Larry Ewing sent in his idea for a penguin as seen on the cover of this book, and his proposal won. Designed with a cheeky smile and a well-fed body this penguin, named Tux, represents the image of a happy and satisfied user.

B. THE DIFFERENT RANGE OF USES

Originally designed for Intel-based systems, Linux runs on a variety of platforms today. Among others this includes the ARM architectures (named arm and arm64), Motorola/Freescale's 68k architecture (m68k), Intel x86 (i386 and amd64), IBM s390 (s390), PowerPC (powerpc) and SPARC (sparc).

Right from the beginning Linux focused on server systems. It is in constant use as a web server, file server, mail and news server, internet gateway, wireless router and firewall. Used as a computing unit, it helped to render video sequences and entire films such as Titanic, Shrek and Toy Story. Furthermore, Linux is in use in automotive products, astronautics, military, logistics and the engineering environment. Since 2006, Linux servers run all the world's stock exchanges. It also runs almost all internet search engines.

C. CERTIFICATIONS

The widespread use of Linux has increased the demand for engineers and users who know exactly what they are doing. At this point a certification for Linux becomes advantageous. These certifications can be divided into programs that are general (not specific to a distribution) and focused (specific to a Linux distribution). The lists below give an overview of the primary certifications that currently exist.

Non-specific Certifications

- Linux Essentials
- LPIC-1: Linux Server Professional Certification
- LPIC-2: Linux Engineer
- Linux Foundation Certified System Administrator (LFCS)
- Linux Foundation Certified Engineer (LFCE)
- CompTIA A+
- CompTIA Network+

Distribution-specific Certifications

- RedHat Certified Engineer (RHCE)
- RedHat Certified System Architect (RHCSA)
- RedHat Certified Architect (RCA)
- SUSE Certified Administrator (SCA)
- SUSE Certified Engineer (SCE)
- SUSE Enterprise Architect (SEA)

D. FROM UNIX TO LINUX

The history of Linux can be traced back to the 1990s. In order to understand the story behind Linux, we also have to look back briefly at the early days of computing after the 2nd World War.

At that time computing machines filled entire buildings and the transformation from mechanical to electronic components, like microprocessors and the usage of multi-layer circuits, was underway. Moreover, in the 1960s and 1970s hardware and software components were quite expensive and not standardized. Various vendor-specific platforms existed and each of them had their own interface, protocols to transfer and exchange data, as well as operating system. The communication between these single computing devices required specific knowledge and the understanding of its protocols. The development of UNIX was an aim to circumvent these obstacles and to simplify the usage of computing devices on a larger scale.

UNIX

At the beginning of 1965 the development of the Multiplexed Information and Computing Service (Multics) started. Multics was the result of a collaboration between the Massachusetts Institute of Technology (MIT), General Electric (GE) and Bell Labs/AT&T. Led by the developers Ken Thompson and Dennis Ritchie, the main product they developed was Unics. Later on it was renamed to UNIX. The UNIX operating system was mainly in use at the University of California in Berkeley.

UNIX Variants

The concept of UNIX became licensed to several companies that developed and maintained their own variant of UNIX. This included Solaris/SUN OS (SUN Microsystems, nowadays owned by Oracle), AIX (IBM), Scenix (Siemens), SCO UNIX, Xenix (Microsoft), as well as HP-UX (Hewlett-Packard), NeXTSTEP, Mac OS (Apple) and Android (Google).

Open-source implementations comprised of the Berkeley System Distribution (BSD) with its variants: NetBSD, OpenBSD, and FreeBSD. Today, Linux is the most popular free software among open source developers. There is also a strong commercial support for the systems mentioned above.

The UNIX Philosophy

UNIX is designed with a number of strict principles in mind. These principles cover portability, multi-tasking and multi-user orientation in combination with a time-sharing approach. Furthermore, it is based on network connectivity following the TCP/IP scheme.

The original development was done in the C programming language that resulted in independence from a hardware platform. Delivered with a selection of development tools and libraries, it allows you to easily extend it to your specific needs. It is simple, but has a powerful ability to automate tasks that supports complex but maintainable scripts.

Similar to a toolbox, UNIX consists of a variety of tools. Each of them having a specific purpose and being designed exactly for that task. The idea is to use one tool per task. In order to achieve more complex goals, you would combine several tools into a chain. The following example combines the two commands 'ls' and 'wc' by means of a pipe to be able to count the number of Python files in the current directory.

CHAPTER 2: LINUX EVERYDAY

There are a few terms that may confuse Linux beginners. The first thing is its name, Linux vs GNU/Linux. The term Linux refers to the Linux kernel only. In reality many users refer to Linux as the operating system as a whole, the kernel plus libraries and tools. Also the term Linux is used to include all the programs that run on Linux, or that are available for this great operating system.

Furthermore, the description GNU/Linux needs understanding. Linux distributions with this name prefix are fleshed out with GNU implementations of the system tools and programs. One such example is Debian GNU/Linux. The GNU project goes back to the initiative of Richard M. Stallman and his dream to develop a free UNIX system. Based on his experiences at MIT and the collaboration with other colleagues he choose to use free software that was already available to rewrite the tools he needed. This included the TeX typesetting system as well as X11 window system. He published the rewritten tools under the GPL license whenever possible to make his work available freely to everyone who was interested in it.

A. LINUX DISTRIBUTIONS

A Linux distribution is a collection of software packages that fit together. A distribution is maintained by a team of software developers. Each member of the team focuses on a different package of the distribution. Together as a team they ensure that the single software packages are up-to-date and do not conflict with the other packages of the same release of the distribution.

As of 2018 for Debian GNU/Linux 9, the official repositories contain more than 51,000 different packages. A repository is a directory of packages with a certain purpose. Debian GNU/Linux sorts its packages according to the development state. The official repository is named **stable** and reflects the current release of stable packages. The other repositories are named **testing** and unstable, and work in the same way but do not count as official packages.

Typically a Linux distribution comprises of packages for a Linux kernel, a boot loader, GNU tools and libraries, a graphical desktop environment with a windows environment, as well as additional software like a web browser, an email client, databases and documentation. The software is provided in two ways; as the source code and as the compiled binary packages. This allows you to understand how the software is designed, to study it and to adjust it according to your personal needs.

Depending on the focus of the Linux distribution, it also contains packages for a specific purpose like network or forensic tools, scientific software for educational purposes, and multimedia applications.

B. LINUX DISTRIBUTIONS LIST

According to Distrowatch, more than 600 different Linux distributions exist. Major distributions are Debian GNU/Linux, Ubuntu, Linux Mint, Red Hat Enterprise Linux (RHEL), Fedora, CentOS, openSUSE Linux, Arch Linux, Gentoo and Slackware. One of the major questions is: which Linux distribution to use? Based on our experience these are the recommendations:

- For beginners: Ubuntu, Xubuntu, openSUSE, Linux Mint

- For advanced users with experience: Debian GNU/Linux, Red Hat Enterprise Linux (RHEL), Fedora, CentOS

- For developers: Arch Linux, Gentoo, Slackware

For the examples in this book we use Debian GNU/Linux. Even though this distribution is recommended for advanced users it is still very beginner friendly, which we will show later in the guide. But the most important reason for this selection is its stability and the trust in this Linux distribution that was built up during the last 20 years of permanent use as a server and desktop system. Other Linux distributions fluctuate too much for comfort.

You are more than welcome to choose a different Linux distribution. The majority of this book applies to most distributions. But if you are a complete novice, we highly recommend sticking to Debian GNU/Linux at least for the duration of this guide, as we will go step by step through its setup and configuration.

In general, choosing a Linux distribution can depend on several criteria as stated below:

- By its availability: free or commercial use
- By its purpose: desktop, server, Wi-Fi router/network appliance
- By the intended audience: end user, network engineer, system administrator, developer
- By the package format: .deb, .rpm, .tar.gz
- By the time updates are available: every Linux distribution follows its own update cycle
- By the support that is provided: support can be free (community-based) or with costs (based on a support contract)

When selecting a distribution, we recommend one that is stable, that is updated regularly and fits into the purpose you need the computer for. Below you will find a short description for each of the Linux distributions mentioned above.

Debian GNU/Linux

Established in 1993, Debian GNU/Linux (Debian for short) is an entirely free and community-based operating system that follows the GNU principles. More than 1,000 developers continuously work on it based on their own free will. Behind Debian is no company and there are no business interests involved.

One design goal is to have a stable and reliable operating system for computers that are actively delivering services. It is targeted to users who know what they want and have experience. The Debian developers maintain and use their own software. The packages are made available in .deb format, and are divided into categories according to the following licenses:

- Main: free software
- Contrib: free software that depends on non-free software
- Non-free: packages that have a non-free license

Debian works excellent on both servers and desktop systems. A range of architectures are supported like ARM EABI (arm), IA-64 (Itanium), mips, MIPSel, powerpc, s390 (32 and 64 bit), as well as sparc, i386 (32 bit) and amd64 (64 bit). The code name of each release is based on the name of a character from the film Toy Story, such as **Stretch** for Debian GNU/Linux 9.

Ubuntu

Ubuntu is a free Linux distribution that is financed by the company Canonical Ltd. It is based on Debian but focuses on beginners instead. That's why it contains just one tool per task. Also, the Ubuntu team tries to incorporate brand new elements that lack stability. The packages are made available in .deb format, and are divided into categories according to their support from Canonical:

- Main: free software, supported by Canonical
- Restricted: non-free software, supported by Canonical
- Universe: free software, unsupported
- Multiverse: non-free software, unsupported

Ubuntu is available in three official editions: Ubuntu Desktop, Ubuntu Server, and Ubuntu Core (for the Internet of Things). Supported are a range of architectures like i386, IA-32, amd64, ARMhf (ARMv7 VFPv3-D16), ARM64, powerpc (64 bit) and s390x.

Initially published in 2004, there are two releases per year: one in April and another in October. The release is reflected by the version number: 18.04 refers to the April release of the year 2018. The code name of a release is based on an adjective and an animal, such as Utopic Unicorn for Ubuntu 14.10.

Linux Mint

Linux Mint is a non-commercial distribution that is based on Ubuntu and follows its release scheme. The initial publication dates back to the year 2006. As of 2014 there have been two releases per year following the release from Ubuntu by one month. The code name for the release is a female name that ends with an **a**, such as Felicia for version 6. Linux Mint supports the two architectures IA-32 and amd64. The target of the distribution is desktop users that can use it easily.

Red Hat Enterprise Linux (RHEL)

RHEL is a commercial Linux distribution. It is based on the combination of Red Hat Linux (available between 1995 and 2004) plus Fedora 19 and 20. Its original release dates back to the year 2000. Its focus on business customers includes long-term support, training, and a certification program.

The packages are made available in .rpm format (Red Hat Package Manager). RHEL supports the architectures arm (64 bit), i386, amd64, powerpc, as well as s390 and zSeries. The distribution targets both servers and desktops. The code name for the release looks rather random, as it does not follow a similar scheme as used for Debian or Ubuntu.

Fedora

Fedora is a community Linux distribution, aimed mainly at desktop usage. It is based on Red Hat Enterprise Linux (RHEL) and sponsored by Red Hat. It was launched in 2003 at the time the support for Red Hat Linux ended. As of 2018 it is available in the following versions:

- Workstation: for pc
- Server: for servers
- Atomic: for cloud computing

Fedora supports the architectures amd64, ArmHF, powerpc, mips, s390 and RISC-V. The distribution has a rather short lifecycle where a new release follows roughly every 6 months. The code name for a release does not follow a fixed naming scheme but mostly consists of city names.

CentOS

CentOS abbreviates from the name Community Enterprise Operating System. As with Fedora it is based on Red Hat Enterprise Linux, and compatible in terms of the binary packages. This allows the use of software on CentOS that is initially offered and developed with RHEL in mind. In contrast to Fedora it focuses on enterprise use for both desktop and server, with long-term support. The initial release of CentOS goes back to May 2004. The software packages come from three different repositories:

- Base: regular, stable packages
- Updates: security, bug fix or enhancement updates
- Addons: packages required for building the larger packages that make up the main CentOS distribution, but are not provided upstream

CentOS is available for the architectures i386 and amd64. Other architectures are not supported.

openSUSE

The Linux distribution openSUSE has its roots in the distributions SUSE Linux and the commercial SUSE Linux Professional that saw its first release in 1994. The name SUSE is an abbreviation for the original German owner named **Gesellschaft für Software- und Systementwicklung GmbH**.

OpenSUSE is based on the structures of Red Hat Linux and Slackware, and uses .rpm as a software archive format. It is available for the architectures i586, x86-64 and ARM. The openSUSE project aims to release a new version every eight months. As with Fedora, the code name for a release does not follow a fixed naming scheme.

Arch Linux

Arch Linux is a free Linux distribution that saw its first release in 2002. It follows the principle of a rolling release, which results in monthly releases of the distribution. Currently the core team consists of about 25 developers and is supported by a number of other developers, called trusted users. Arch Linux uses Pacman as a package management system. The single packages are held in four software repositories:

- Core: packages for the basic system
- Extra: additional packages like desktop environments and databases

- Community: packages that are maintained by trusted users
- Multilib: packages that can be used on several architectures

Arch Linux supports the architecture amd64. The early releases until 2007 had code names that do not follow a specific scheme.

Gentoo

As with Arch Linux, Gentoo follows the principle of a rolling release. New installation images are available weekly, with the first release available in 2002. Gentoo is special due to being a source code based distribution. Before installing the software, it has to be compiled first. Supported architectures are alpha, amd64, arm, hppa, IA-64, m68k, mips, powerpc, s390, sh and sparc.

Slackware

Slackware is the oldest active Linux distribution. The first release dates back to 1992. Regular releases are available without a fixed interval. It targets the professional user, and gives him/her as much freedom as possible. Slackware uses compressed tar.gz archives as a package format, and supports the four architectures i486, alpha, sparc and arm. The distribution was also ported to architecture s390.

CHAPTER 3 : SETTING UP

A. DIFFERENT TYPES OF INSTALLATIONS

Debian offers a variety of methods for a proper setup. This includes a graphical and a text-based installation; we will use the former. For installation media the Debian developers offer three variants:

- A CD or DVD for 32 bit and 64 bit
- A network image for 32 bit and 64 bit (a so-called Netinst-ISO)
- A tiny CD for 32 bit or 64 bit

We also have test media available. These include live images for 32 bit and 64 bit, and allow you to try Debian before installing it on your computer. During the time of writing this document, version 9.5 is the current stable release of Debian. The setup described here is based on this release and the amd64 architecture.

After downloading the network image from **www.debian.org/distrib** no further static images are required to be referenced in the system. Instead, it depends on the internet connection to retrieve the packages to be installed and keep your operating system up-to-date.

The entire process will take you about an hour and it allows you to have a lean software selection according to your specific needs. Software packages that you do not use will not be available on your system. They can be added whenever you feel the need for them.

The target system of our installation is an XFCE-based desktop system for a single user with a web browser and a music player. For the web browser we use Mozilla Firefox and for the music player, VLC. Both programs are a permanent component of the Linux distribution. The environment we use for demonstration purposes is a virtual machine based on VirtualBox with 4 GB of RAM and 15 GB of disc space.

B. HOW TO INSTALL LINUX STEP BY STEP

This example will give you an idea of what to do when the time to install your chosen Linux distribution will come. Being the most popular Linux distribution, its installation process is not any different from others. The step by step installation process will make things much easy for you.

1. CD/DVD Installation

Booting Ubuntu Linux from a CD or DVD is one of the two ways through which you can install the system on your computer.

- Download the Ubuntu ISO file from Ubuntu software. This form of file is one that will be burned to a CD or DVD before you can use it.

- Burn the ISO file using your burning program of choice. There are free and paid programs available that can burn an ISO file to a CD or DVD without having to download a separate program. You can choose the one you prefer the most.

- Boot from the disk. Once the program is burned into the disk, you can restart your computer and choose to boot from the CD or DVD. You may be required to change your boot preferences. Do this by hitting the Setup key when the computer is restarting.

- Linux gives users an option of trying it out before you can install it in order first to be sure that this is just what you need. You can do this at this level; try Ubuntu first, and if you feel that it is the operating system you want to use, you can install it. You will be able to view the layout of the operating system when it is still running from the disc.

- Install Ubuntu. You will have to be connected to a power source if you are using a laptop because the process could drain your battery. You need to be connected to an internet source as well.

- Decide what to do with your other operating system. You will be given two options; whether to install Ubuntu Linux alongside the other operating system or to replace the old operating system with Ubuntu. If you choose to have the two, you will always be required to choose the operating system to use every time you reboot your computer.

- Set your partition size. This will be necessary if you will choose to have the two operating systems on your computer. You can use the slider to adjust the amount of space you want to set aside for Ubuntu. Remember that you will also need enough space for files and programs, therefore, leave out enough space for your new system.

- Choose your location. This happens automatically if you are connected to the internet.

- Set your keyboard layout. The right thing to do here is to click detect keyboard layout in order for Ubuntu to automatically choose the right one.

- Enter your login information. Set a username and password. You can choose to have Ubuntu log you in automatically, or you can always enter your login information whenever you want to use your computer.

- Wait for the installation process to finish. Restart the computer once the installation is finished and Ubuntu will load.

2. Windows Installer

Important Note:

1) It is always a good idea to run such a program on CD or DVD in order to have a first look at it; then, install it if you like what you see. Test driving will help you in making a decision you will not regret when it comes to installing operating systems.

2) Make sure that you backup all your files, programs, personal data and settings first before installations begin so that you will not lose them.

Installing New Software on Linux

Installing new software on Linux Operating System is as easy as it is when you are installing the operating system itself. Everything has been made very easy for the users. This is, therefore, no reason to worry if you have been having a hard time installing a new system on other operating systems in the past.

Most of the Linux distributions have an app store, or something close to that, which represents a central area where all applications are stored. What you do is to go through them and install the apps that you want to use on your machine. This makes it so easy for you to locate the app that you want to install on your computer. The Ubuntu Software Center is an example of such a centralized place for the Ubuntu Linux. Deepin has the Deepin Software Center. Some distributions rely on GNOME software while others rely on Synaptic.

All these tools mean and do the same thing; they provide a central place from where you can search and install Linux software with ease. The presence of a GUI is important though, for you to go through the installation process of another software. If you do not have a GUI, you will have to rely on command line interface to do the installations.

What users need to know is that it is very easy to install a software on any Linux machine. New computer users will also find this very easy and less time-consuming. The operating system has been designedin order to give computer users an easy time on everything that they do, and this is just one of them. After the installation of the operating system, you can start installing any app that you will need in the use of your machine or device.

C. HOW TO CONFIGURE LINUX

After you have decided what to run at a specific time (schedule), you have to place it in a place that makes it easier for your daemon to discover it for reading. Even though there are a few places to place it, the user crontab is the most common. The crontab is the file that holds a schedule of jobs on cron. Each user has their own file located at **var/spool/cron/crontab**; the file should not be edited directly. To edit, use the crontab command. Here is the command that you require:

crontab –e

The above command calls up the text editor. You can use the text editor to input your job schedule. Each job should be on a new line. If you would like to view your crontab without editing it, use the command below:

crontab -l

Below is the command to erase the crontab

crontab –r

If you are a user with all the privileges of an admin, here is how you edit another user

crontab -u <user> -e

D. HOW TO ADD A GRAPHICAL USER INTERFACE

At its current stage, the Debian system is fully active and can be used in production. For a desktop system suitable for a regular user, it still lacks a nice and easy-to-use graphical user interface. In this step we will change that and install the XFCE desktop manager.

In order to do so, we will install the following packages:

- The aptitude package manager
- The xdm display manager
- The xfce4 desktop environment

Debian uses the package manager **apt** to handle the installation, the update and the removal of software packages and the related package lists. Also, apt resolves all the package dependencies and ensures that the relevant software is available on the system. In our case a total of roughly 450 MB of data/software have to be retrieved from the package mirror and installed. As pointed out earlier, this requires a working internet connection to download the needed software packages.

In order to install the three packages, type in the following commands at the command-line prompt. Just type the command after the # symbol:

```
root@debian95 ~# apt-get install aptitude xdm xfce4
```

apt will display further information regarding the packages to be installed. This includes the list of depending packages and recommended packages. At the end you will see a command-line prompt. Type Y or press Enter to install aptitude, xdm and xfce4 as well as the depending packages.

The retrieval of the software packages to be installed takes a while. When finished, the command-line prompt will appear again. In order to activate the changes regarding the graphical desktop environment, restart the system. Type the command **reboot** at the command-line prompt as follows:

```
root@debian95 ~# reboot
```

A few seconds later a graphical login screen will be visible (see image below). Log in to the system with the regular user named **user** as created earlier. Type in **user**, press Enter and type in the password for the user. Then, press Enter again to confirm and log in.

The desktop comes with a number of default elements: an upper navigation bar, a lower navigation bar and desktop icons.

- Upper navigation bar: this shows buttons to access the different applications, the four virtual desktop screens, the clock and a button for various user actions such as to lock the screen, change the user, change to standby mode and exit the current session

- Lower navigation bar: this bar contains several buttons to hide all the opened windows and show the empty desktop, to open a terminal, the file manager, a web browser, to find an application and to open the file manager directly with your home directory.

E. HOW TO ADD ADDITIONAL SOFTWARE

Up until now the software available to be used on your Linux system has been rather limited. The next thing to do is to add the following four Debian packages to make your life a bit easier:

- firefox-esr: the web browser Mozilla Firefox (Extended Support Release)
- gnome-terminal: a terminal emulation maintained by the GNOME project
- xscreensaver: a basic screensaver for the X11 system
- vlc: the video player Video Lan Client (VLC)

The installation of the three packages will be done using the command-line in a terminal emulator (we will look at terminals in detail later in the guide). Currently, on your system the X11 terminal emulator **xterm** is installed. In order to open xterm, click on the terminal button in the lower navigation bar or select the entry Application > System > Xterm from the context menu.

As step one, open xterm. Next, type in the command **su** next to the command-line prompt as follows and press Enter:

```
        user@debian95: ~$ su
Password:
```

You may remember from the previous steps that only an administrative user can install, update or remove software on a Debian system. The **su** command abbreviates **switch user** and changes your current role. Used without an additional name, the role changes to the administrative root user. At the password prompt type in the password for the administrative user and press Enter.

As an administrative user, install the packages: firefox-esr, gnome-terminal, xscreenserver and vlc as follows:

> root@debian95: ~# apt-get install firefox-esr gnome-terminal xscreensaver vlc

The output is seen below:

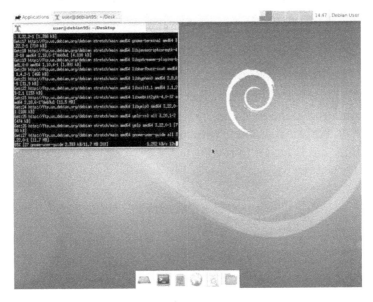

After the installation of the four packages, you can switch back to your role as a regular user. Press Ctrl+D to quit the admin part, and press Ctrl+D again to close xterm.

The installation of Firefox has the following effects:

- The new software **Firefox** is available from the application menu

- The new command **firefox** is available from the command-line
- The earth icon from the lower navigation bar links to the Firefox web browser
- The installation of the GNOME terminal package has the following effects:
- The new software **gnome-terminal** is available from both the command-line and the application menu
- The terminal icon from the lower navigation bar links to the GNOME terminal
- The entry **Open Terminal Here** from the context menu refers to the GNOME terminal

In order to see the changes, select the entry **Open Terminal Here** from the context menu. The image below shows the terminal window. It comes with a white background and a bigger font that is easier to read.

CHAPTER 4 : NAVIGATE LINUX

A. HOW TO NAVIGATE WITH LINUX

In order to move around inside your system, and access various files and software, you will need to learn how to navigate Linux. This sounds more difficult than it actually is. While different versions of Linux vary in how they deal with navigation, the process is pretty easy to pick up. If you click on your system settings, you will be taken to a list of options. Clicking on an option will take you to more options, etc., until you arrive where you want to go. The main menus are like tables of contents, and they will show you the more detailed sections of each part of your computer system.

If you are used to using Windows or Mac OS, it should not take you long to figure out how to navigate through your computer. If you cannot find something, simply perform a search, and type in what you want to find. Ubuntu is especially powerful in this respect, as you can access a system, and online, search by using the Windows key on your keyboard.

B. COMMANDS FOR DIRECTORIES

Command line is based on text, unlike the GUIs (graphical user interfaces) that people generally use these days. However, it can often be must simpler to use command line, especially when you want to get something done quickly. Do you remember the old days when Microsoft DOS was popular? You might recall seeing people working on computers, using nothing but text commands to get things done. That is what Linux command line does. There are different pieces of software for command line, and distributions will have their own versions. You can also install your own choice of command line application.

The very thought of using command line scares a lot of people, and they have no desire to do so. However, since you are reading this section, let's assume that you want to learn about command line, and begin with some basic commands. One great thing about working with command line is that you can work with a range of different Linux distributions, and always be able to do things the same way, with command line. Another reason that people like using command line is the pure power it gives them, although it is a little more complex to learn than graphical user interfaces.

Open up your command line software, which is also knows as your system's shell. This is called Terminal in Ubuntu, and you can find your shell with a quick system search. The keyboard shortcut to access Terminal is Ctrl + Alt + T, and this shortcut is the same for many versions of Linux.

C. TERMINAL-BASED FILE MANAGER

In order to access different parts of your system, you will need to look at directories, and the files they contain. Directories are the folders of your system, containing files, and more folders with files, etc.

Here is a list of commands that will help you to navigate your files and directories:

- "~" indicates your home directory, such as /home or /home/user (with your user name in the place of user).

- "ls" This will display a list of the files in the directory that you are currently looking at.

- "pwd" means "print working directory" and will tell you which directory you are currently in.

- "cd" will let you "change directory", so that you can move around to different parts of your system.

- If you type "cd /" you will be taken to your root, or base-level directory, so that's a good starting point if you become lost.

- "cd" and "cd ~" are two commands that will take you to your home directory.

- "cd .." Will go back up one directory.

- "cd -" will simply go back to the previous directory that you were in.

- You don't have to go through one directory at a time, if you know where you want to navigate. Let's say that you want to go to your "Documents" directory, which is located in a directory called "My Stuff". This might involve the command, "cd /my stuff/documents".

- If you want to copy a file, use "cp" by entering "cp file mine /directory" where "mine" is the name of the file that you wish to copy, and "directory" is where you want to copy the file to. You can copy a directory in the same way, with the command "cp -r directory mine" where "mine" is a directory instead of a file.

- If you want to move a file (as with cut & paste), use the "mv" command instead of "cp".

- To delete a file, use "rm" with the name of the file, where "rm" stands for remove.

- To delete an empty directory, use "rmdir".

- To delete a directory, as well as anything that is inside, including directories and files, use "rm -r"

- Create a new directory with the command "mkdir".

- "man" will show you a manual of commands. If you want a manual of the types of manuals, you can enter "man man".

Those are the basics of navigating files and directories with command line, as well as moving them around. In a graphical interface, these are similar to dragging, dropping, cutting, and pasting files and folders, as well as simply clicking into different folders.

D. GRAPHICAL FILE MANAGER

Now that you have an idea of how to move around in your system, using the command line, it's time to run some files. It's pretty simple, and you can do it with this command:

"./nameoffile.extension"

In this example, "nameoffile" is the name of the file that you want to run, while ".extension" is the extension of the file. If you wanted to run text document called "story", you would type "./story.txt", as ".txt" is the correct extension for text files.

Firstly, you will need to go to the directory that contains the file, as discussed in the previous section. Remember that you can "ls" (list) the files in a directory, to make sure that it contains the one that you want to run.

If this is becoming too complex for you to understand, don't worry. You can always go back to using the graphical interface when you become stuck, and keep practicing with the command line in your own time.

E. LINUX TERMINAL TERMINAL

Working with the Linux operating system requires you to have knowledge about the terminal and the command line. It is essential to know what these things are, to be at least slightly familiar with their usage and the standard commands available.

What is a Terminal?

To be precise, a terminal is simply the outside. Inside a terminal runs a command line interpreter that is called a shell.

Debian Linux supports a long list of terminal software. This includes the Aterm, as well as the GNOME terminal, the Kterm, the Mate Terminal, the Rxvt, the Xterm and the Xvt. These different implementations of terminal software vary in terms of stability, support for character sets, design, colors and fonts, as well as the possibility to apply background images or work with transparency

In this book we will use the GNOME terminal because of its stability, simplicity and adjustability. In order to increase and decrease the size of the content that is displayed inside the terminal window; use the two-key combinations CTRL+ and CTRL-.

CHAPTER 5: ESSENTIAL COMMANDS

A. INTRO TO FILE AND DIRECTORIES

1. SHELL FEATURES

Simply speaking, a shell is a sophisticated command-line interpreter. In a loop the shell reads characters, modifies them under certain conditions, and executes the result.

Under certain conditions, between reading from the command-line and the execution of the actual result, the shell has to interpret special characters that are part of your input.

Available Shells

Your Linux system allows the usage of various shells. Each shell is available as a separate software package through the Debian package manager, Aptitude, we installed earlier.

Unless otherwise stated the examples in this document are based on the Bourne Again Shell (bash). At the time of writing this document this is the default shell on Debian.

2. BASIC FILE OPERATIONS

Am sure that you are eager and keen to get stuck into more commands and begin doing some actual playing around with the system. We need to cover some theories first before we get into that. When you begin to play around with the system you are able to understand why it is behaving in such a way and you can also be able to learn the commands further.

Everything is a file

The first thing that we need to know is that everything is a file. For example a text file is a file, your keyboard is a file, a directory is a file and even a monitor is a file.

Linux is an Extensionless System

A file extension is usually a set of 2 – 4 characters subsequent to the end of a file, which determines the type of file it is.

Common extension includes:

File.exe – an executable program or file,

File.txt – a plain text file.

File [path]

Quotation Marks

First, you can surround an entire item with quotation marks. Single or double quotation marks are both acceptable, though slightly different in ways that will be addressed later. Anything within a set of quotation marks will be interpreted as an individual item.

cd 'My Photos'

pwd

/home/mike/Docs/My Photos

Escape Characters

You can also define an item with a space in it by using an escape character, also known as a backslash (\ ). The backslash nullifies the meaning of the character directly following it.

cd Happyday\ Pictures

pwd

/home/mike/Docs/My Photos

You can see above that the space between 'Happyday' and 'Pictures,' which would normally have a special meaning (separating into unique command line arguments). Thanks to the backslash, the special meaning is ignored in the argument.

If Tab Completion is used before the space in a director name, the terminal will automatically remove the special function of any spaces in the name.

Hidden Files and Directories

The mechanism to specify whether a file or directory is hidden is very elegant in Linux. By beginning a file or directory's name with a '.' (full stop), it will be interpreted as hidden - it doesn't even require any sort of special command or action. There are several reasons for a file or directory to be hidden. For example, a user's configuration files (stored in the home directory) are generally hidden in order to declutter the space for the user's everyday tasks.

In order to make a file or directory hidden, create or rename it with its name beginning with a '.'. In the same fashion, you can rename a hidden file without the '.' in order to make it unhidden. It is possible to modify it with the command line option -a in order to show the hidden files and directories.

ls Docs

MYFILE1.txt Myfile1.txt myfile1.TXT

...

ls -a Docs

... MYFILE1.txt Myfile1.txt myfile1.TXT .hidden .file.txt

...

As you can see, when all items in the current directory are listed, the first two items are '.' and '..' ..

3. DIRECTORY OPERATIONS

In Linux, there is a directory called **The Root Directory**. It serves as the main directory and as programmers and system administrators would refer to it, it is the directory of all directories.

With The Root Directory come the subdirectories. These subdirectories manage files according to their assigned tasks.

Subdirectories and their content:

- /home – home directory
- /boot – the kernel and startup files; files that attempt to eliminate unnecessary bootloaders
- /initrd – data regarding booting information
- /dev – contains references to all CPU hardware peripherals
- /bin – common shared system programs
- /etc – important systems configuration data
- /lib – library files
- /lost+found – retrieved data from failures
- /opt – files from third party sources
- /net – remote file systems' standard mount point
- /misc – miscellaneous data
- /proc – information regarding system resources
- /mnt – external file systems' standard mount point

4. FILE VIEWING

With vi, we can edit files. It's possible to use it to view files, but there are other commands that do so much more conveniently. The first, cat, means concatenate. The main purpose of this command is to join files together, but can be used in a more basic form to simply view files.

cat

If you run cat, an individual command line argument file will display the contents of the file on the screen, as well as a prompt.

Run without a command line argument, cat will do nothing. When a file isn't specified, it will read from STDIN which is the keyboard, by default. By typing something and following it with space, cat will mirror your input onscreen. To cancel, use +c, the universal cancellation signal in Linux.

Generally, anytime you make a mistake and need to get out of it, pressing +c will get you out of it.

cat myfirstfile

here you will see

whatever content you

entered in your file

This command is most useful when you have a small file. Larger files, however, will have their content fill the entire screen and only the last page of it will be accessible. For these files, another command is more well suited:

less

The command less lets you move around within a fill with the arrow keys on the keyboard. Spacebar will move you forward an entire page, and b will move you back. When finished, q will quit the command.

Go ahead and use these command to take a look at the file you just created.

5. FILE CREATION AND EDITING

So far in this book we have looked at the history of Linux , the differences between Linux and Windows, and how to work with command lines. Now that you have that basic knowledge, it is time to know how to create, edit, and remove different files from your computer using the command line interface.

The best reason to learn how to manipulate files in the command line is the command line makes complicated tasks easier to handle. For example, if you wanted to copy just one file to a particular directory, which could easily be done in the graphic file manager. The same applies if you would like to copy a group of files to a new, empty directory. However, if you wanted to copy a group of text files from one directory to another, and the second directory already had some of those text files in it, then this could create a problem.

Whereas it may take you a little bit of time to figure out just exactly how to sort it out in the file manager, with the command line, it is as easy as typing in the following command:

[me@mylinux me]$ cp –u *.txt destination

There are many commands that can be used to create, edit, or delete files, but there are four that are used more frequently than all the others. These are **rm/rmdir, mkdir, cp, mv.**

6. FILE PROPERTIES

Navigating a File in Vi

Now we can return to our created file and add more content to it. Using insert mode, the arrow keys will move the cursor around through the file. Add two more paragraphs of content, then return to edit mode using the esc key.

The following commands will allow you to move around within a file. Go ahead and try them out.

Arrow keys - Move the cursor.

j,k,h,l – These keyshort letters will manipulate the cursor down, up, left, and right (essentially the same function as the arrow keys.)

^ (caret) - Places the cursor at the start of the current line.

$ - Places the cursor at the end of the current line.

nG - Places your cursor on the nth line (for example, 5G will move you to the 5th line.)

G - Places your cursor on the last line.

w - Places your cursor at the beginning of the next word.

nw - Places your cursor n words forward (for example, 2w will move the cursor two words forward).

b - Places your cursor at the beginning of the previous word.

nb - Places your cursor back n words.

{ - Moves your cursor back one paragraph.

} - Moves your cursor forward one paragraph.

Turning on line numbers can help make navigating a file much easier. To do so, type ':set nu' while in edit mode.

Deleting Content

Clearly, there are plenty of ways to move around within a file in vi. Most of them allow for preceding with a number in order to move a specific distance. Deletion works in much the same way as movement - indeed, many delete commands allow for movement commands to be incorporated as a too to indicate what should be deleted.

Next we will look at several of the ways we can delete content within vi.

x - Deletes one character.

nx - Deletes n characters.

dd - Deletes the current line.

dn - d, with a movement command afterwards. Will delete up to where the movement command would have taken.

Undoing

Undoing a change is very simple. It is done with the character u.

u - Undoes the last action you took (can be repeated).

U (capital) - Undoes all changes to the current line.

7. FILE LOCATION

Also, directories are definitely a special type of file. It can be correct to say that a path is a way to find a particular location in the system and the location is a file.

Case Sensitivity

Many people who are new to learning Linux struggle with one specific problem - while many other systems, such as Windows, don't pay attention to the case of a character in file reference, Linux does. Thanks to this feature, it's possible to have multiple files or directors than have the same name, but letters in different cases.

ls Docs

MYFILE1.txt Myfile1.txt myfile1.TXT

...

file Docs/myfile1.txt

Docs/myfile1.txt: ERROR: cannot open 'fil1.txt' (No such file or directory)

In Linux, all of these are interpreted as completely separate files.

It's important to be aware of case sensitivity while working with command line options. For example, in the command line the two options 's' and 'S' perform completely different actions - it's common to read an option in upper case, enter it in lower case, and then wonder why your input doesn't return the expected output.

Name Spaces

While it is possible to incorporate spaces in perfectly valid file and directory names, it's important to be careful with them. Spaces in a command line signify separate items - that's how we can know what a program name is and identify each argument in the command line. For example, if the goal were to move into a director called 'My Photos,' the following command would not work properly:

ls Docs

MYFILE1.txt Myfile1.txt myfile1.TXT My Photos

...

cd My Photos

bash: cd: Happyday: No such file or directory

In this example, 'My Photos' is interpreted as two separate arguments in the command line. The first argument specifies the directory into which cd moves. In order to make this work properly, you can use one of two valid options.

8. FILE COMPRESSION AND PACKAGING

Compiling source code from a third-party source. If you wish to compile source code that someone else designed, such as from an already-existing program, you will need to download a tar file, also referred to as a tar ball. Tar files are common file extensions used in Linux and other Unix-based programming because they allow large amounts of information to be compressed, for the purposes of being archived, sent over the internet, or downloaded. You know that a certain file is a tar file if its name ends with .tar.

On your first time working with a tar file, you may experience some frustration with opening it. However, the process is actually quite easy. You need to understand that a tar file is very similar to a zip file; it is basically just a container that holds a lot of information in a very small space. You can easily extract the information contained in the file using a conversion tool. You can upload the file to an online converter, like online-covert.com or Zamzar, or you can download a dedicated converter.

You need to extract the tar file into a directory, because in the next step, you will need to open up the directory. Go to the terminal on your desktop (this is the same as the shell program) and type cd, a space, and then the name of the directory in which you stored the file.

Next, you need to execute a command to automatically configure the source code. You do this by typing "./configure" into the terminal after the name of the directory. Next, execute the "make" command. At this point, the source code will begin to compile into the program. Depending on the size of the file and the speed of your computer, this process can take from a few seconds to a few hours. If it takes a long time, don't worry.

Now, you need to install the program. You do this by executing the command "make install." This will take you to an install wizard that will guide you through the process of installing the program to run on your computer.

Compiling your own source code. If you are keen on writing your own code to use with Linux, great! The steps involved in compiling your own source code are remarkably similar to compiling third-party source code.

First, you need to use your text editor to write out the actual code. This book won't get into any kind of detail about how to write code for Linux, but later books in this series will. After you type out the code for your program, you need to use a compiler to compile it. The compiler that you use will depend on the programming language that you use (more on that in later books in this series). You should be able to find a free compiler as a Linux-based application that you can either download or use online.

Once you compile your code, you want to use a sandbox to execute it. This step will prevent long-term damage to your entire system should there be a flaw in your code. As with a compiler, you should be able to find a Linux-compatible sandbox that is available for free. If there are any problems with your program, like if it doesn't execute as you had hoped it would or some of the code is defective, go back and re-write the code until the program runs in a satisfactory way. Each time you change the code, you will need to re-compile it. This process makes sure that the human-readable language that you use to write the code is able to be interpreted by the machine that executes it.

Once you are finished writing and compiling the code, you need to save the file to a directory. After that, you follow the exact same steps as when you compiled the source code from a third party.

B. OUTPUT AND TEXT PROCESSING

The result of the above redirected input will show up on the screen, which is also labeled the **standard output.** However, just as with the standard input, the standard output can be redirected and it is usually redirected to a particular file. This is accomplished using the ">" symbol as follows:

[me@mylinux me]$ ls > name_list.txt

The **ls** command in this example will be successfully executed as usual, however, the output of this command will not appear on the display as is expected, and instead it will be redirected to the file **name_list.txt**.

It is important to note that every time the above command is carried out, it will overwrite the original **name_list.txt**file and create a whole new file. However, if you would like to keep adding to the file rather than overwriting it from the beginning every time, the symbol ">>" should be used as in the example below:

[me@mylinux me]$ ls >> name_list.txt

When this command is run, it will add the new results to the end of the file, making it larger and longer every time it is carried out. If you do attempt to carry out this command and the target file has not been created, Linux will do that for you.

There are situations where the standard input and the standard output need to be redirected. Unlike many other command line programs though, the order in which you write down these commands in Linux does not matter, as long as the characters used to redirect (the "<" and ">") the input and output are in the command line AFTER the options or arguments that they are redirecting then the action will be carried out.

If we were to revert to the standard input command **[me@mylinux me]$ sort < file_list.txt** and change it so that it also has a redirected standard output, the result may resemble something like this:

[me@mylinux me]$ sort < file_list.txt> sorted_file_list.txt

In this case, the sort command will be executed, and the result shall be saved to the **sorted_file_list.txt** text file.

C. USERS AND GROUPS

These commands deal with a variety of actions in order to manage the users and groups of your Linux system. Unless explicitly stated, these commands can be run as a regular user.

whoami

This command returns your current user ID as follows:

```
$ whoami
user
$
```

users, who and w

The **users**, **who** and the **w** commands show the users that are currently logged into your Linux system. **w** extends the output of **who** by the uptime information and another column that contains the last command that was executed. In contrast, **users** simply outputs the name of the users as a space-separated list in a single line (see image below).

The single columns for **who** start with the login name of the user. The output is followed by the name of the terminal, where "console" represents a login terminal, and "pts/1" abbreviates the first pseudo terminal session. The last two columns contain the login time and the host the user comes from, in brackets (see image below).

```
user@debian95: ~
File  Edit  View  Search  Terminal  Help
         :~$ who
user      console      2018-08-20 09:36 (:0)
user      pts/2        2018-08-20 09:47 (:0)
user      pts/3        2018-08-20 09:47 (:0)
         :~$
```

The single columns for **w** contain the login name of the user (titled LOGIN), the name of the terminal (titled TTY), the name of the host the user comes from (titled FROM), the login time (titled LOGIN@), the activity (idle time and CPU usage titled IDLE, JCPU, and PCPU) as well as the last command the user executed (titled WHAT) (see image below).

```
user@debian95: ~
File  Edit  View  Search  Terminal  Help
         :~$ w
09:49:23 up 9 min,  3 users,  load average: 0.15, 0.03, 0.01
USER     TTY       FROM         LOGIN@   IDLE    JCPU    PCPU WHAT
user     console   :0           09:36    13:14   0.00s   0.04s -:0
user     pts/2     :0           09:47    2:03    0.02s   0.02s xterm
user     pts/3     :0           09:47    2:03    0.01s   0.01s bash
         :~$
```

id and groups

The **id** command outputs the user and group information of the current user (see image below). From left to right the columns show the user ID (uid=1000(user)), the group id (gid=1000(group)) and the name of the groups the user is a member of.

In order to list the names of all the groups the user belongs to, you can also invoke the **groups** command (see image below). The output is a space-separated list of the group names.

215

passwd

As shown below, type in the current password first, press Enter, type in the new password, press Enter to confirm, retype the new password and press Enter to confirm, again.

The password is stored as a hashed value in the configuration file "/etc/shadow". The content of this file is only visible to the administrative user. The example below shows how to extract the information for the user "user" with the help of the **grep** command.

chfn

This command is also from the Debian "passwd" package and changes the user information that is stored on your system in the file /etc/passwd. During the installation of your Debian system the basic setup was already done. In order to modify this information you can run **chfn** without further parameters in interactive mode, or with one or more of the following options to adapt only a specific value:

- -f or --full-name: change the full name of the user
- -h or --home-phone: change the home phone of the user
- -r or --room: change the room number of the user
- -w or --work-phone: change the work phone of the user

The following example changes the entry for the home phone number to 135:

```
         $ chfn -h 135
Password:
$
```

chsh

This command (also from the Debian "passwd" package) changes the entry for the shell that you use to log into your Linux system. Again, this information is stored in the file /etc/passwd. Which shells are allowed to be used are limited by the entries in the configuration file /etc/shells.

chsh works similar to the **chfn** command. Invoked without further options an interactive method is used (see image below).

```
:~$ chsh
Password:
Changing the login shell for user
Enter the new value, or press ENTER for the default
        Login Shell [/bin/sh]: /bin/bash
:~$
```

chsh accepts the option **-s** (short for --shell) in order to set the shell in non-interactive mode. The following example shows the according command line call:

```
$ chsh -s /bin/bash
$
```

In order to modify the shell for a different user other than yourself, invoke the **chsh** command with the username as a parameter. Note that only the administrative user can do this for a different user. The next example shows how to do that for the user "felix".

```
# chsh felix
Changing the login shell for felix
Enter the new value, or press ENTER for the new value
        Login shell [/bin/bash]:
#
```

su and sudo

In order to change your role from one user to another, you utilize the **su** command. **su** abbreviates "switch user". Invoked without further options you change to the root user as follows:

```
$ su
```

218

```
Password:
#
```

Working as the administrative root user comes with great responsibility and presumes that you know exactly what you are doing. To work as a different user than root, invoke the **su** command with the desired username as follows:

```
        $ su felix
Password:
$
```

The **su** command changes the current role permanently. In order to run only a single command as an administrative user, use the **sudo** command. This requires the Debian "sudo" package to be installed and the additional user to be added to the configuration file /etc/sudoers using the **visudo** command. This step will be explained in further detail later on.

adduser

The command **adduser** creates new user accounts. The image below shows the information that is required. This includes a new entry in the file /etc/passwd as well as the creation of a new group, plus home directory. Furthermore, prepared data from the directory /etc/skel is copied into the previously created home directory. Afterward, the account information is modified using the **chsh** command.

```
user@debian95: ~
File  Edit  View  Search  Terminal  Help
root@debian95:~# adduser caro
Adding user `caro' ...
Adding new group `caro' (1002) ...
Adding new user `caro' (1002) with group `caro' ...
Creating home directory `/home/caro' ...
Copying files from `/etc/skel' ...
Enter new UNIX password:
Retype new UNIX password:
passwd: password updated successfully
Changing the user information for caro
Enter the new value, or press ENTER for the default
        Full Name []: Caro
        Room Number []:
        Work Phone []:
        Home Phone []:
        Other []:
Is the information correct? [Y/n] y
root@debian95:~#
```

Having set up the new user, the entry in the file /etc/passwd looks as follows:

Deleting user accounts and modifying user accounts is done with the help of the two commands **deluser** and **usermod**. The usage of these commands will be explained in further detail later on.

D. PROCESS MANAGEMENT

1. BACKUPS AND REMOTE STORAGE

These days the very best thing to trust when selecting a server is a Linux Storage Server. Linux is the most effective operating system for all computers including servers.

These Servers are the best because they offer top security because it's very hard to infiltrate them, even for seasoned cyber criminals.

Whenever you work on the web, you want safety and the greatest method to have a safe business on the web is with Linux.

An additional great thing about Linux is its speed. Systems similar to Ubuntu Storage Server have shown to be the quickest within the industry. As you can see, selecting such servers will provide you with the newest speeds and security.

You increase your quality whenever you tackle speed and security which will mean much more customers for your company.

The Protection used by Linux Storage Server is unable to be cracked; it's even malware proof simply because the device is so well designed that files fail to access other parts of the PC or servers without permission from the system manager.

In the event, you work on the web you would like to have your files safely kept from any damage. You can only achieve that with a Linux Server.

You can have your server at home, or you can rent a server from another company. When choosing a company to provide hosting you should make sure that it has Linux Network Storage Server because only that way you can rest assure to have all your files safe from harm. The Linux modern systems are always being updated so that you don't need to worry about anything.

When you work with the internet, you want to be always able to deliver; that isn't easy when you have tacky systems running your files. Every time you rent a server on the internet make sure it has Linux Storage Server or you can be under great risks.

2. VIEWING PROCESS

The primary purposes for this demand is the name that has been achieved by the Linux operating system. Now, let us find how this operating system has become the top most among dedicated systems:

Better control: The best thing about this alternative is that it provides better control to the users as compared to other alternatives available in the market.

The server is offered with many applications that can be used free of cost to access the source code. Also, installation of additional applications is also possible. Manual installation of applications is needed as it provides the facility of automatic application installation.

Better security: Users are saying that Linux provides better security as compared to Windows dedicated server. The reason is that as it uses open source technology, where others can view the code written by the programmer, he will be highly careful about making mistakes. Furthermore, attacks on systems are not done through the source code and so it can provide better security to the users.

3. LOGINS, LOGOUTS, SHUTDOWNS

When you start up your computer, you might be logged in automatically. Otherwise, you will be faced with the login screen. This screen will be different for various versions of

Linux, and you will be able to change how you want them to act.

You will be asked for your user name, which you selected during the installation process. After this, you will need to enter your password, to prove that you are in fact the owner of this user name. The login screens will usually have some other items, like the system's name, a clock, and options to restart or shut down your computer.

It is extremely common nowadays that a person includes an internet site. It may be a small business enterprise website, a hobby blog or perhaps a forum. Though, diverse web sites get the different thing; each internet site has one common will need, an internet hosting provider.

Web hosting could be the podium on which the internet site is positioned so that it could be visible to the total globe through World Wide Web.

In making positive that your website resides with suitable website hosting service, you will find several points which can be had to be looked at. The initial point you'll need to pick is the hosting server kind. Website hosting server would be the computers and they also need working a good operating system to take care of applications and services.

Probably the most extensively employed operating system is Linux. Linux system is extremely well-known simply because it's tested to become a secure, applications as well as the efficient operating system. Any time is picking the Linux system web hosting package you'll need to take into account many points.

One of all crucial points you need to think is info back-up. Files recovery and information backup are really crucial to the web site. Who knows, anything at all might happen at any time, so you need a backup of your web sites time to time.

Thus make sure that the web Hosting provider gives you backup at least one time in a week.

You might have to consider concerning limitless bandwidth and space given by your internet hosting business. Even though an individual does not require a lot of data transfer or web space, getting limitless data transfer along with web space may assure that you've adequate room in order to include any kind of technologies.

You are able also to host data transfer programs and don't concern yourself with extreme uninformed caps. An excellent Linux hosting will give you unlimited web space and consequently you will be capable of location anything you desire on your web server.

It is very crucial to recognize your essentials and to get a Linux web hosting by having a helpful choice of characteristics. Just about any great Linux hosting giver gives numerous useful features.

Most typical software formation utilized for Linux hosting is usually referred to as LAMP structure, which positions for Linux, Apache, MySQL, PHP, and also Linux respectively.

This is the most generally used combination of application to sustain the expansion of powerful web sites.

The majority of Linux web hosting businesses give one click installation software totally free for content management systems like Drupal, Joomla, WordPress, vBulleting, phpBB, etc.

Registering with any Linux web hosting organization consumes software for profitable management of the web site.

And last and not the least, make confident the service provider give just about all basic features just like firewall, virus protection, servers load balance, safety and so on anytime pick Linux hosting providers.

You will also find some extra features offered like extra FTP creation, MYSQL database, add-on domains, Sub domains solutions and several other services.

4. HOST INFORMATION

Two main reseller hosting organizations that rule the industry, as we say, will be Linux reseller web hosting and Windows reseller. Each has their signal good and bad points. Therefore, think cautiously before selecting your choice of reseller hosting package.

Your choice of reseller web host might provide you with a choice to upload documents on whether Linux system or perhaps Windows server. This option may be provided to you determined by your individual needs since both platforms are superb in overall performance.

Linux offers a number of advantages to making use of its software to the server system such as:

It can be an open source technological innovation, which is its key advantage throughout its opponents. Consequently you, as a client, do not pay any extra licensing charges to get the software.

Thus, by choosing Linux reseller hosting programs, it is possible to obtain the server system easily and also use it free of charge on any server. Besides, clients keep contributing to the code and also bring about enhancing the computer software over a steady basis.

This is additionally a big benefit the Linux reseller web hosting plans have more than expensive server software program plans.

Should you aren't pleased with Linux reseller hosting computer software and desire to convert to Windows, this platform offers you this capability. It is essential to publish your current documents to your Windows site, effortlessly and seamlessly.

Whatsmore, the site is scalable enough to get altered to match your changing needs. This helps it be the ideal alternative for developing online organizations.

Due to the fact the Linux reseller hosting choice is totally free and an open source technological innovation, it can be extremely cost effective. The only fee a user will need to pay is for distribution that is laid down by the owner or the provider. However, this is a little expense and could be paid for by any consumer.

Customers will discover that Linux system is a lot more appropriate in its different scripting languages when compared with any other platform. It's numerous languages for example Perl, MySQL, and PHP. Linux can supply these languages if a specific site wants them.

Not simply is a compatibility of this reseller hosting program dependable, but it is also very successful.

Being a Linux reseller web hosting client, you'll also have the advantage of utilizing some kinds of databases such as MySQL, mSQL, and PostgreSQL. They may be successfully used to communicate effectively with any site for speedy information access.

This kind of databases is created in a relational manner to ensure that they perform effectively jointly to obtain the finest out of their overall performance when working with every other and the site.

The Linux reseller hosting choice offers far greater stability and also protection to its buyers in comparison with any other competing server programs.

Being open source software, it's stabler when compared with others, and it has, as a result, become a server system of option for professionals throughout the world.

5. HOST LOCATION

Are you searching Linux Cloud Hosting Servers then it is the better appropriate solution if you wish to get your web site or perhaps e-commerce website to get more efficient and also ensure excellent overall performance?

Linux Cloud Hosting Servers affords the clients with additional reconfigurability and also modifications can also de bone fragments according to their particular qualification. This hard drive server provided for you enhances your sites overall performance plus delivers a lot more management on the processing assets offered.

Linux server software makes use of the most recent technological know-how that allows every person to successfully work their very own type involving Linux and also delivering these using superior overall performance, tougher reconfigurability and also superior supply routes.

100 % Uptime is a confirmed this means your blog will be working successfully continuously with virtually no lagging. Regarding making certain your blog is usually about back-up server Auto-failover function is present.

Regarding ensuring utmost stability state-of-the-art, DDOS Safety is provided with Linux server web hosting service. Geographically repetitive DNS and also clientele are forwarded to 8 transit companies.

Linux Shared Web Hosting sustains the most recent and reliable web hosting variations similar to Fedora 7, CentOS 7, Ubuntu age 14. 04 LTS and also Debian 7. 8. The two server and also PC features involving OS are provided towards the clients. These pre-installed hosts are instantaneously deployed which allows clients to work with these in their particular web hosting service offer.

Committed help workers are present that can present specialized alternatives if you're facing any problem together with your web site. Any common and also wide understanding bottom can be provided towards the clientele to guide these using easy requests.

Customers are provided using personal hard drives that have identical creating to order as being a physical server. Linux web hosting service software allows your hosts to plug towards the web by using gigabit uplinks involving Internap's carrier.

Newest section variations are supplied so that clients might have entire management. Internap's

The standard VPS web hosting service is now no more some preferred choice because the carrier's networks slice up the specific hosts for them to easily share these relating to the clientele.

VPS companies employ container technological know-how to segregate this numerous end user on a single discussed Linux type which usually reduces this operation and also productivity.

6. NETWORK CONNECTIONS

uname

uname abbreviates the term "UNIX name". The command displays system information such as the exact name and version of the Linux kernel and the hostname of your computer.

The image below shows the call of the **uname** command with the parameter **-a** (short for --all). The output contains the name of the operating system (Linux), the hostname (debian95), the kernel version and its build date (4.9.8-7-amd64 #1 SMP Debian 4.9.110-1 (2018-07-05)) as well as the architecture of the system (x86_64).

```
user@debian95: ~
File  Edit  View  Search  Terminal  Help
          :~$ uname -a
Linux debian95 4.9.0-7-amd64 #1 SMP Debian 4.9.110-1 (2018-07-05) x86_64 GNU/Linux
          :~$
```

uptime

This command shows how long the system is running. It displays the current time (07:36:47) followed by the uptime in hours (21:56), the number of logged in users (1 user) and the average load (load average: 0.47, 0.43, 0.29) for the last 1, 5 and 15 minutes.

```
user@debian95: ~
File  Edit  View  Search  Terminal  Help
          :~$ uptime
 07:36:47 up 21:56,  1 user,  load average: 0.47, 0.43, 0.29
          :~$
```

In order to see the **uptime** in a nicer way, use the option **-p** (short for --pretty). The image below displays a more human-readable version of the information. The system is up 22 hours and 3 minutes.

```
user@debian95: ~
File  Edit  View  Search  Terminal  Help
          :~$ uptime -p
up 22 hours, 3 minutes
          :~$
```

ip

229

The **ip** command (along with the two keywords **address show**) displays the current network configuration. The image below shows the loopback interface (lo) and the ethernet interface (enp0s3). The ethernet interface is configured with the IP address 10.0.2.15.

```
                        user@debian95: ~
File  Edit  View  Search  Terminal  Help
              :~$ ip address show
1: lo: <LOOPBACK,UP,LOWER_UP> mtu 65536 qdisc noqueue state UNKNOWN group default q
len 1
    link/loopback 00:00:00:00:00:00 brd 00:00:00:00:00:00
    inet 127.0.0.1/8 scope host lo
       valid_lft forever preferred_lft forever
    inet6 ::1/128 scope host
       valid_lft forever preferred_lft forever
2: enp0s3: <BROADCAST,MULTICAST,UP,LOWER_UP> mtu 1500 qdisc pfifo_fast state UP gro
up default qlen 1000
    link/ether 08:00:27:e3:5c:79 brd ff:ff:ff:ff:ff:ff
    inet 10.0.2.15/24 brd 10.0.2.255 scope global enp0s3
       valid_lft forever preferred_lft forever
    inet6 fe80::a00:27ff:fee3:5c79/64 scope link
       valid_lft forever preferred_lft forever
              :~$
```

ping

ping sends ICMP network packets to the given IP address or hostname, and displays the turnaround time. The image below demonstrates this for the host **http://www.google.com**.

```
                        user@debian95: ~
File  Edit  View  Search  Terminal  Help
              :~$ ping google.com
PING google.com (172.217.23.142) 56(84) bytes of data.
64 bytes from fra16s18-in-f14.1e100.net (172.217.23.142): icmp_seq=1 ttl=63 time=36
.9 ms
64 bytes from fra16s18-in-f14.1e100.net (172.217.23.142): icmp_seq=2 ttl=63 time=37
.9 ms
64 bytes from fra16s18-in-f14.1e100.net (172.217.23.142): icmp_seq=3 ttl=63 time=40
.1 ms
^C
--- google.com ping statistics ---
3 packets transmitted, 3 received, 0% packet loss, time 2003ms
rtt min/avg/max/mdev = 36.953/38.353/40.193/1.377 ms
              :~$
```

E. NETWORK AND SYSTEM INFORMATION

If you are going to start using Linux, one of the first things that you will need is a good selection of software. In fact, many people stick with operating systems they hate, simply because they are hesitant to give up their favorite applications. All of the software listed below is completely free, and free to distribute to your friends or family. That should help to convince you that using Linux is a great idea.

You can actually run Windows software in Linux, using a program called Wine. However, you will basically be making your computer pretend to be using Windows. If you would prefer to use dedicated, and often more reliable, methods — you are going to need some great Linux software.

1. NETWORK CONNECTIONS

If you are used to staying in touch with people on your computer, it's important to keep that functionality when you swap over to Linux. Here are some good IM applications that you can try:

- **Skype.** This is an extremely popular instant messenger, and many people would be unwilling to part with using it.

- **Pidgin.** This IM software has been around for a long time, and lets you log onto Facebook, Yahoo, Google, and many other networks.

2. WEB BROWSING

If you are using a computer these days, you probably need to be online, in order to be productive. Luckily, you have plenty of choices for Linux web browsers. You can even use the most popular browsers in Linux, so you won't have to settle for something else.

Here are some great Linux web browsers that you can try:

- **Firefox.** This is one of the most popular web browsers for Linux users. There are faster options out there, as well as newer ones, but Firefox is considered one of the best.

- **Chrome.** You will need to download this from Google, as it won't be in the software repositories. However, you can use Chromium instead, if you insist on using the repositories. This is the number one web browser at the moment, and you will glad to know that Google fully supports Chrome for Linux.

- **In-built browsers.** Whatever version of Linux you choose, it will almost definitely come with a web browser, and that might even be Firefox or Chromium. If you are not fussy about what you use, and just need to check websites every now-and-then, you might be happy to use a default browser.

3. EMAILS

If you need your computer for work, you will probably want a good email client. Windows users will probably be familiar with Outlook, but there are some good alternatives for Linux.

- **Thunderbird.** This is made by Mozilla, the same company that brought you Firefox. It is a lightweight, easy-to-use email client, with lots of different options.

- **KMail.** This is the default for KDE desktop environments. It has loads of features, although you might take a bit of time to get used to its layout.

- **Evolution.** This generally comes with the GNOME desktop environment. It will let you use Google Calendar right away, as well as Microsoft Exchange. It looks good, and is simple to use.

4. COPY AND PASTE

If you want to do something in Linux, and you use your graphical interface to look online for help, you will often find command line text that you can use. You don't need to understand anything about using these commands, and you can still benefit from them. You will need to copy the text, by highlighting it with your mouse in a normal fashion. However, if you try to use the common keyboard shortcut "Ctrl + V" to paste into the command line shell, it will not work. To paste text with command line, press "Ctrl + Shift + V" instead.

5. MATH AND CALCULATIONS

Consequently, you will find many people who use it, and it is largely compatible with MS Office documents. You don't have to install the entire suite, but it contains software for word processing, spreadsheets, graphics, presentations, and databases. If you just want something that will let you get on with your office work, and you only want to try one office suit for Linux — make it OpenOffice.

6. GRAPHICS

One of the most widely used tools in the business world is Microsoft Office. Not long ago, if you were to apply for an office job without any knowledge of MS Office, you just might be laughed out of the room. This might still be the case in many companies. However, the days when MS Office was the one-and-only office suit are in the past.

Here are some great alternatives for Microsoft Office that run on Linux:

- **OpenOffice.** This wonderful, free, opensource office suit runs on Linux, Windows, and Mac OS.

- **LibreOffice.** This one is based off OpenOffice, but the two makers separated in 2010. It is a little less feature-rich than OpenOffice, but will run better on slower machines. That makes it a great choice for businesses using old computers. Because of the small file size of LibreOffice, it can be installed to a USB drive, and used on different computers.

- **Google Docs.** This is a very popular, online office suit, that ties in nicely with the rest of Google's online products. If you already use a Google account, you will not need to do anything but sign in. You can change your settings to be able to work offline, via your Internet browser, so Google Docs is no longer "online only".

7. AUDIO AND VIDEO

If you want to be able to manipulate media files, whether creating a piece of art, recording a song, trimming down the video of your latest vacation, or just watching it — Linux has some create choices on offer.

- **GIMP.** If you want something to replace Photoshop, this is your best choice. However, there are some places where GIMP simply isn't as good.

- **PiTiVi.** If you want to do some basic home movie editing, this is a great choice of software. While it will not give you the more professional functionality of Final Cut Pro, there are plenty of functions to choose from.

- **Audacity.** When it comes to working with sound files, this is the go-to application for Linux users. With it, you can record multi-track audio files, cut them up, rearrange them, and add effects.

- **VLC.** This is a popular media player that is both powerful and reliable. It will let you play more types of files than just about any other media player.

CHAPTER 6: WORKBOOK

Cross Platforms

You could also do cross-platform programming for Linux. For this, you have to keep the following in mind:

1. **windows.h** and **winsock.h** should be used as the header files.

2. Instead of **close()**, **closesocket()** has to be used.

3. **Send ()** and **Receive()** are used, instead of read() or write().

    4. **WSAStartup()** is used to initialize the library.
Protocols of Aliases

Another important protocol of Linux, this one could send requested services and messages to the router, and also has its own protocol number. The difference is that it starts in the IPv4 Header, and is mostly just known as '1'. It also works between octets 0 to 4, where:

1. Code = Control Messages | ICMP Subtype

2. Type = Control Messages | ICMP Subtype

3. Rest of Header = Contents | ICMP Subtype

4. Checksum = Error Checking Data | ICMP Header and Data

Host Resolutions

One thing you have to keep in mind about this is that you should use the syntax **gethostname()** so the standard library could make the right call. This also happens when you're trying to look for the name of a certain part of the program, and when you want to use it for larger applications. It's almost the same as python as you could code it this way

Linux Sockets

What you have to understand about Linux is that it is an Open System Interconnect (OSI) Internet Model which means that it works in **sockets ()**. In order to establish connections, you need to make use of listening sockets so that the host could make calls—or in other words, connections.

Linux Internet Protocols

Internet Protocol is all about providing boundaries in the network, as well as relaying datagrams that allow internet-networking to happen.

The construction involves a **header** and a **payload** where the header is known to be the main IP Address, and with interfaces that are connected with the help of certain parameters. Routing prefixes and network designation are also involved, together with internal or external gateway protocols, too.

Getting Peer Information

In order to get peer information, you have to make sure that you return both TCP and IP information. This way, you could be sure that both server and client are connected to the network. You could also use the **getpeername()** socket so that when information is available, it could easily be captured and saved. This provides the right data to be sent and received by various methods involved in Linux, and also contains proper socket descriptors and grants privileges to others in the program. Some may even be deemed private, to make the experience better for the users.

To accept information, let the socket **TCPAcceptor::accept()** be prevalent in the network. This way, you could differentiate actions coming from the server and the client.

Construct and Destruct

These are connected to the descriptor of the socket that allow peer TCP Ports and peer IP Addresses to show up onscreen. Take note that this does not use other languages, except for C++, unlike its contemporaries in Linux.

Destructors are then able to close any connections that you have made. For example, if you want to log out of one of your social networking accounts, you're able to do it because destructors are around.

Linux and SMTP Clients

As for SMTP Client, you could expect that it involves some of the same characters above—with just a few adjustments. You also should keep in mind that this is all about opening the socket, opening input and output streams, reading and writing the socket, and lastly, cleaning the client portal up. You also have to know that it involves the following:

1. **Datagram Communication.** This means that local sockets would work every time your portal sends datagrams to various clients and servers.

2. **Linux Communications.** This time, stream and datagram communication are involved.

3. **Programming Sockets.** And of course, you can expect you'll program sockets in the right manner!

Echo Client Set-ups

> In Linux, Echo Clients work by means of inserting arguments inside the **socket()** because it means that you will be able to use the IP together with the PF_INET function so that they could both go in the TCP socket. To set up a proper client structure, just remember you have to make a couple of adjustments from earlier codes.

IO Network Models

In order to get peer information, you have to make sure that you return both TCP and IP information. This way, you could be sure that both server and client are connected to the network. You could also use the **getpeername()** socket so that when information is available, it could easily be captured and saved.

To accept information, let the socket **LinuxAcceptor::accept()** be prevalent in the network. This way, you could differentiate actions coming from the server and the client.

Linux and its Sockets

You also have to understand that you can code Linux in C mainly because they both involve the use of sockets. the socket works like a bridge that binds the client to the port, and is also responsible for sending the right kinds of requests to the server while waiting for it to respond. Finally, sending and receiving of data is done.

At the same time, the Linux Socket is also able to create a socket for the server that would then bind itself to the port. During that stage, you can begin listening to client traffic as it builds up. You could also wait for the client at that point, and finally, see the sending and receiving of data to happen. Its other functions are the following:

socket_description. This allows the description of both the client and the server will show up onscreen.

write buffer. This describes the data that needs to be sent.

write buffer length. In order to write the buffer length, you'll have to see the string's output.

client_socket. The socket description will also show on top.

address. This is used for the connect function so that address_len would be on top.

address_len. If the second parameter is null, this would appear onscreen.

return. This helps return description of both the client and the socket. This also lets interaction become easy between the client and the server.

server_socket. This is the description of the socket that's located on top.

backlog. This is the amount of requests that have not yet been dealt with.

You could also put personal comments every once in a while—but definitely not all the time!

CHAPTER 9: QNA FOR BEGINNERS QUESTIONS

QUIZ

1. What is Reading Mode?
2. What is Reading List?
3. What is Increased download protection?
4. What is Cortana Integration?
5. What is Annotations?
6. What is Extensions?
7. What is Other extras?
8. What is Windows 10 Home?
9. What is Windows 10 Professional?
10. What is Windows 10 Enterprise?
11. What is Windows 10 Education?
12 What is Windows 10 Mobile Enterprise?
13. What is Windows 10 IOT?
14. What do you understand by New start menu?
15. What do you understand by Tablet Mode
16. What do you understand by Meet Cortana?
17. What do you understand by Windows Store?
18. What do you understand by Virtual Desktop?
19. What do you understand by Command Prompt Upgrade?

20. What do you understand by Calendar and Mail Application upgrades?

ANSWERS

1. It is another new addition to Microsoft Edge which was taken from more modern browsers like Firefox and Safari. This option, available at the top of the screen at all times will allow you to take any article you are reading and separate it out from the website it is a part of which means you leave all of the ads and other filler out of the equation. You will know the page you are on can be seen in Reading Mode if the book icon animates and starts flipping its pages. The settings menu allows you to modify the way Reading Mode looks with a variety of sizes and settings to suit your current needs.

2. Despite the similar name, the Reading List feature has nothing to do with Reading Mode, instead it functions similarly to a Favorite's list allowing you to pare down your Favorite's into even more specific categories. Adding a site to your Reading List is done from the same star icon as adding an item to your Favorites but will show a thumbnail of the page when saved. To view your Reading List, you click on the button next to the star icon in the top right of the page. Clicking on this icon will display all of your reading list items as thumbnails while choosing one will display the same icon but larger at the top of the page. These pages can also be configured to appear on the New Tab page along with your most frequently visited sites.

3. The downloads page is much the same as those found in other modern browsers, it shows the files you have download and lets you interact with them. What sets Microsoft Edge apart however is that when you begin downloading a file it will tell you if that file is rarely downloaded or potentially harmful to your computer.

4. While you are using Microsoft Edge, at any point you can select a portion of text and right click or hold down on it to

find the option to ask Cortana for more information on the topic. This will open a sidebar with information on the selected topic generally from Wikipedia. While browsing Cortana may also make you aware of Windows Apps that relate to the site you are viewing, provide directions and menus for restaurants whose site you are viewing and provide coupons for products depending on the website.

5. While viewing a website in Microsoft Edge you now have the option to make notes on a webpage and then share the results online. To do this you click on the pen-marking-up-paper icon which will cause the upper part of the browser to turn purple and add additional options including a pen to write notes, an eraser, a highlighter a tool for writing more structured notes in boxes and a cropping tool. These tools all work with either a mouse or a touch input. Once you have finished making notations you can then save your work and share it everywhere from Pinterest to Microsoft OneNote. If you share the results through OneNote you will also have the option to give others the opportunity to edit what you have done adding another level of interactivity to group projects undertaken online.

6. As of January 2016 Microsoft Edge does not yet support extensions which means common browsing tools such as ad blockers or password managers will not yet work. Microsoft has promised that extensions are coming though and a select group of extensions has been confirmed for an upcoming Windows Insider build.

7. Additional common features not yet found in Microsoft Edge as of January 2016 are the abilities to some window or video from certain streaming sites including Vimeo full screen. You will not be able to right-click an image to perform some functions including making an image your desktop. Finally, you cannot open a group of favorited websites all at once with only a single click. The amount you use these

features will no doubt affect your decision when choosing whether or not to switch browsers.

8. This will be the version of Windows 10 that most people will use. It boasts the fewest features and the cheapest cost. This version of Windows will run on personal computers and laptops

9. This version of Windows 10 will be used by technical users and small businesses and will contain more features than the Home version.

10. This version of Windows 10 will be used by large corporations and will have features that reflect this fact.

11. This version of Windows 10 will be prorated for schools and contain additional educational software.

What is Windows 10 Mobile? This version of Windows 10 will function similarly to Windows 10 Home though it will have a mobile specific interface. Windows 10 Mobile will be available on Lumina phones to start with plans for additional options in the works.

12. This version of Windows 10 will be similar to Windows 10 mobile but created with business use in mind.

13. IOT stands for internet of things and this version of Windows 10 is designed to run on industrial equipment such as ATMs or cash registers.

14. When you first boot up the Windows 10 OS after successfully installing it one of the first things you will notice is the new Start menu. Unlike Windows 8, which did away with the commonly known start menu (before public outcry brought the button back at least) for a full screen version. Windows 10 learned from the mistakes of the past and brings back a more familiar start menu which at the same time still takes a few cues from Windows 8.

The new start menu will bring up a modified version of the traditional expanded menu. It will provide a list of commonly used applications (programs are called applications now) which sit above the old standards of settings, file explorer and an option to turn off the device. User's will have the option of storing their ten most used applications on the start menu for easy access. The Start menu also features a search function that works much the same as before except that now it is also connected to Bing so your search will show websites as well as content stored locally.

15. The big push for Windows 10 is to unify all of the disparate Windows platforms and Tablet Mode is a big part of this. Available under settings, this option will switch the standard Start menu into a full screen version reminiscent of Windows 8. This mode will turn on automatically when it is running on a tablet that disconnects from a dock. When this happens the Start Menu becomes full screen and transforms into the main way to interact with your device. The same is true for the Windows Store, the Applications Menu and the Settings Menu. While you will not be able to access the desktop directly in this mode you can still access the desktop folder.

16. The Cortana virtual assistant is one example of the Windows Phone interface bleeding into the primary OS. This feature allows users to ask their OS questions the same way they would when using their smartphones. Cortana is immediately available when you log in to Windows 10, to ask it a question, simply click on the search icon in the lower left corner of the screen and type a question to hear an answer or if you have a microphone connected to your device you can click on the microphone option.

17. The Windows Store survived the transition to Windows 10 and applications downloaded through the service will now feature the ability to be resized along with the standard suite of minimization, maximization and quit options traditional

programs enjoyed. Applications purchased in the Windows Store will be available across all the Windows 10 devices the user connects to.

18. In previous versions of Windows, the programs you had open on multiple monitors showed up on every taskbar making it sometimes difficult to find what you need. The taskbar now includes an option to filter the apps that each taskbar shows.

19. Yes, you read that correctly, after more than two decades the command prompt is getting added functionality. You will now be able to copy and paste data into the command prompt using the keyboard shortcuts.

20. Perhaps one of the most useful features to automatically move between devices running Windows 10, the Calendar Application can pull data from multiple accounts to succinctly sum everything up in one place. The calendar will pull information from your Windows Live account as well as you Windows 10 Mail account as well. Both applications are more responsive and easier to use while at the same time cutting the fat found in earlier versions. Both applications support their Google equivalents if you prefer and resize themselves depending on the version of the platform they are operating on.

CHAPTER 10: TIPS AND TRICKS

Linux is the best Operating System So Far

Even though Linux has been in the market for a long time, offering a better deal than most operating systems, a lot of people are still in the dark as to why they should actually trade the operating system they have been using over time for Linux. The question you should be asking yourself now is this: is the operating system that you have been using all along good enough in all ways? Are there some errors that you wish were improved? Is it working for you just fine? If you were to answer these questions honestly, youwould realize that indeed you have not been getting a good deal from your choice of operating system.

Linux is here to help in ways that other operating systems have failed in order to ensure that computer users are using their computers with minimal or no problems at all.

Some of the problems that you have probably been facing with other operating systems are viruses, malwares, costly computer repairs, slow downs, computer crashes or even licensing fees. You will agree that these are real problems that can stress a computer user so much. If you want nothing to do with such issues in the future, Linux is the operating system to go for!

With Linux, you do not have to live constantly with the fear of losing your data as a result of virus invasion or computer crash. You do not have to worry about taking your computer for a cleanup yearly for it to work well for you. This is a great relief for so many people considering how useful computers have become in our lives lately. We are dependent on computers for practically so many things in our lives and with a problem-free computer, you can achieve a lot all the time.

Why Linux?

a) Zero cost of entry. Linux is absolutelyfree. You can install Linux on as many computers as you have without paying anything for it. There is no server or software licensing as in the case of other operating systems.

b) Easy installation. This is a very easy to install operating system. Newbies will not have a hard time installing it as well. Installing a full server with database server involves a few clicks and only a few commands, which is very easy and straightforward.

c) It is the most reliable operating system. It will never fail you! You will have no problems on your computer, and your data is safe as long as you are using Linux. This is a stress-free operating system for any computer and device user all over the world.

d) As a system administrator, you will have a great time using Linux. You will face zero issues with servers. In fact, once you install the system, you will forget all about it because no problem will ever come up. Even if one of the servers will require restarting or reconfiguring or even upgrading, the rest of the servers will not be affected. This is how easy working with Linux will be for you.

e) Zero troubles for as long as you will use Linux is a guarantee. Many people will attest to using Linux for so many years without experiencing even random computer slowdowns or having to battle with viruses and malware. These will be problems of the past once you start using Linux.

Linux Open Source Licensing

One major advantage of Linux distribution is that of open source licensing. This works under the following philosophies:

1. The freedom for the user to run the program for whatever purpose they may have.
2. The freedom to the user to distribute the program to help out another computer user.
3. The freedom for the user to learn everything about the program and to even change it, if he so wishes, so that it can serve him better.
4. The freedom to distribute the copies of the user's modified program to any user that he wishes to share it with.

This is an operating system that is created by the people and for the people. It is a system that will give you all the privileges and freedom to enjoy working on your computer with no issues at all.

Linux Pros and Cons

On The Desktop

Pros

a) Cost isexclusively free.

b) Far less vulnerable to viruses and malware.

c) Stability.

d) Anti-virus software not required here.

e) Firefox and Chrome are both available.

f) Works very well with old hardware.

Cons

a) An active directory tie-in will work, but it is buggy at times.

b) You will have to look for web solutions for Proprietary Windows/OSX applications because they will not work.

c) Internet Explorer will not work. Therefore, you will not get to enjoy those legacy web applications that need it.

Linux vs Windows

Note: Even if it is said that Linux is safe from virus and malware, it is important for users to take necessary safety precautions just to be safe. If you are a system administrator, do not relax and wait for the invasion to happen. Put safety measures in place to prevent future regrets.

CONCLUSION

Linux operating system is the most dependable, secure, and reliable platforms for the servers as well as desktops. It is an operating system that is gaining so much popularity lately because of the great benefits it has for users. This is a system that is likely to give you a stress-free time as you work on your computer. Computer crashes, for instance, are a thing of the past if you are using Linux.

What you get all the timeis a trouble-free desktop, servers that are always up and minimum support requests, which is what many computer users and system administrators need and deserve.

There is a wide range of Linux versions to choose from. The number of Linux distributions does not stand at what is mentioned here. The number is steadily growing as the developers try to improve on the distributions that have already been released. What you are assured of is that you will get a distribution that will meet all your needs from the distributions that are already in the market.

Linux is easy to customize, ensuring that whenever you are using the system, you are able to create an interface that completely meets your needs.

It is time to switch to Linux if you are still using operating systems that are constantly giving you problems. This is a system for all people; both new users and expert computer users.

JAVA

The Practical Beginner's Guide to Learn Java Programming in One Day Step-by-Step

#2020 Updated Version | Effective Computer Programming

Steve Tudor

Text Copyright ©

All rights reserved. No part of this guide may be reproduced in any form without permission in writing from the publisher except in the case of brief quotations embodied in critical articles or reviews.

Legal & Disclaimer

The information contained in this book and its contents is not designed to replace or take the place of any form of medical or professional advice; and is not meant to replace the need for independent medical, financial, legal or other professional advice or services, as may be required. The content and information in this book has been provided for educational and entertainment purposes only.

The content and information contained in this book has been compiled from sources deemed reliable, and it is accurate to the best of the Author's knowledge, information and belief. However, the Author cannot guarantee its accuracy and validity and cannot be held liable for any errors and/or omissions. Further, changes are periodically made to this book as and when needed. Where appropriate and/or necessary, you must consult a professional (including but not limited to your doctor, attorney, financial advisor or such other professional advisor) before using any of the suggested remedies, techniques, or information in this book.

Upon using the contents and information contained in this book, you agree to hold harmless the Author from and against any damages, costs, and expenses, including any legal fees potentially resulting from the application of any of the information provided by this book. This disclaimer applies to any loss, damages or injury caused by the use and application, whether directly or indirectly, of any advice or information presented, whether for breach of contract, tort, negligence, personal injury, criminal intent, or under any other cause of action.

You agree to accept all risks of using the information presented inside this book.

You agree that by continuing to read this book, where appropriate and/or necessary, you shall consult a professional (including but not limited to your doctor, attorney, or financial advisor or such other advisor as needed) before using any of the suggested remedies, techniques, or information in this book.

INTRODUCTION

Java is a general purpose object oriented programming language. It follows **"write once, run anywhere concept"** which means Java code once compiled on one machine need not be re-compiled anywhere else and can potentially run off the shelf. This is possible because Java is designed to be a platform independent language.

In 1995, the first stable version of Java was released; originally developed by a Canadian computer scientist **James Goslin** while working at **Sun Microsystems**. Sun Microsystems was acquired by **Oracle Corporation** in January 2010. Hence all Java trademarks are owned by **Oracle Corporation** at the time of writing this book.

Why Java?

Java is one of the most popular programming languages today with ever increasing demand in the IT industry. It is extremely popular and sometimes the most obvious choice for developing web applications and web services. There is a good chance that an average computer user comes in touch with technologies offered by or implemented using Java. In fact, some of the most common applications that we use on a day-to-day basis such as **Gmail, ThinkFree Office, Vuze, etc**. are developed using Java either in part or completely.

Using Java, we can develop desktop applications, web applications, video games, mobile applications, etc. In fact, Android application development is primarily done using Java as it is the official android application development language alongside **Kotlin**.

In order to learn Java, no prior programming experience is necessary but is advisable. Having the basic knowledge of C/C++ will help a great deal in learning Java. Having said that, you should be comfortable with using your system and shall have some experience in using Command Prompt on

Windows and Terminal on Linux/MAC. If you are not comfortable with using Command Prompt/Terminal, it is a good idea to learn your way around these tools before beginning Java development.

Java Application Types

Although the Java framework keeps advancing, Java application types can be broadly classified into the following categories:

Desktop applications:

Desktop applications are designed for Windows, Linux and MAC. Can be a console based application that runs from a Command Prompt/Terminal or can have a GUI. These are also known as standalone applications.

Web applications/Web services:

Web applications/services are server side applications. Users normally interact with these applications using a browser.

Mobile/Embedded applications:

These are the applications that are meant for mobile or embedded devices.

Chapter 1 : GETTING READY

While Java is an exciting language, it is easy to get lost in the maze. This is because to create programs using the language, you need to install a few computer peripherals and programs. This is before you can write a single code. The tool (software) also Interface development interface (IDE) we need to write our code is NETBEANS, which is the most popular IDE for writing programs in Java. Here is the kicker; while it is easy to navigate to the NETBEANS URL and download the program, things are never that easy. For NETBEANS to operate (load up) on your system, you need to install some necessary Java files and components. First, you need the Java Virtual Machine.

Java Virtual Machine

We have already stated that Java is independent from any platform and will run on any modern operating system; this component is the reason why Java does not care what OS you are running. Java Virtual Machine is the program that interprets/processes your code correctly. The program is one of the mandatory programs you must install before you can create any Java code or program. You can download the program from the relevant website.

P.s. Across the web, there are many sources of Java related programs. I suggest you only download all your files from the official Sun Microsystems website, Java's parent company.

Once you are on the website, you can proceed to download the Java Virtual machine also known as JRE (Java Runtime Environment). Additionally, while on the website, you can check whether your computer is running a version of JRE by clicking on the relevant **"do I have Java?"** link. The resulting search result will tell you the version of JRE running on your computer, if any.

If you do not have the program installed, install it and restart your computer.

Next is the Java Software development Kit

Java Software Development Kit

After installing the JRE, we are not yet ready to write our first code. At this point, all we have done is installing the support software needed to run Java programs on your computer. You need a tool to write and test code, the Software Development kit, which you can also download from the **Sun Microsystems official** website. I suggest that you download the Java SE (standard edition) and additionally, the JDK 6 that you will find on the Java SE page. When you navigate to the JDK 6 page, you might get confused because there are many options. Depending on the IDE you are using, you can select the relevant option. In our case, we are using NETBEANS so you should locate the following JDK 6 Update X with NetBeans 6.x.

Click on download and head over to the next page to select a download file relevant to your operating system. Download and install the file. It is important to note that the file is a compressed file of over 130 bytes so you should ensure your internet connection is working while you perform the download, otherwise the file might corrupt halfway through the download. So far, we have done everything right. We have downloaded and installed the necessary environments and software needed to write your first code. However, before we launch the applications we have installed, we need to understand the inner working of the world of Java.

Introduction to JDK and NetBeans

In Java, you write your code on a text editor. However, in NetBeans, there is a special area designated for writing your code. The code you write at this point is "the source code" and you save it with the file extension .java. After you create the source code, you have to turn it into Java Byte Code by running it through the JaVac program; we call this process "compiling". The JaVac program then creates a .class extension file if there are no errors in the computing process. This (.class) file is the file you run in the Java Virtual Machine.

Any program you run on NetBeans will run on the output window that you can find at the bottom of your screen directly underneath your code. This design is logical because, with the output window readily available, you do not have to call up the console window or the terminal because in NetBeans, the output window plays the role of the console.

In NetBeans, you can run a program in a number of ways with the easiest being, pressing the F6 key on your keyword. You can also use the menus found at the top of NetBeans to run the program. In the menus, locate the menu Run and execute the run main project option.

Here is the above explanation in steps

1. Create a .java extension source code
2. **Compile a .class extension file by using the JaVac program**
3. Run the complied .class file on the Virtual machine

NetBeans offers you the advantage of creating and compiling for you, behind the scenes. It takes your source code and creates a Java file, then it runs JaVac to compile the .class file. In addition, NetBeans can also run the program within its own software, which saves you the trouble of using a terminal window to type long strings of commands.

This is the inner working of the Java environment/ world. Because you now have a clearer understanding, you can now proceed to launch the NetBeans software and proceed to the next step of our learning process.

Install JDK and NetBeans

Like every other program, if you learn what to expect when NetBeans launches, you will not stare at your screen blankly wondering what to do next. Here is what to expect.

The first time you load NetBeans, the system may be a bit slow as it starts all the resources required to run it. Be patient. When the program does start, you need to navigate to start new project which is on File>New Project part of the NetBeans menu at the top. This should be similar to the Image below.

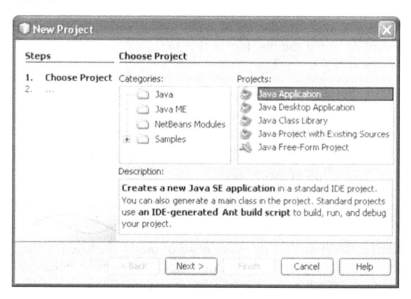

Figure 1

If you look at the above figure, you will notice that the dialog box on the far right hand side has options of the kind of projects you want to create. You can create projects in all the forms available there. In our instance, we are creating a Java application. Therefore, we need to select the Java category and Java application in the project tab and click on next to move on to step two.

When you click on the next button, the program will give you the option of choosing a name for your project. As you type the name of your project, you will notice that the name at the bottom will change to match the name of your project i.e. in "Create Main Class." We shall aptly name our project "First_Project"

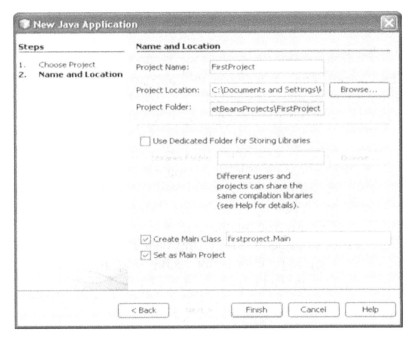

Figure 2

In the above figure, the "Create Main Class" name is first_Project.Main. We cannot leave it like that otherwise; the class will contain the name "Main". We need to change it to First_Project as shown in the figure below.

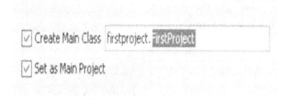

Figure 3

After renaming, the class created will bear the name "First_Project". Notice that the project class name has a capital "F" at the start and a capital "P". Additionally, the package name has the name "first_Project' with a lower case "f" and "p".

The Project Location text box will appear and offer you the option of changing the default save location. If you would prefer to save the file on any other location other than the default area, you can do it here. Additionally, the NetBeans program will also create default folder containing your project name in the same default location you opt for. Clicking on the finish button will prompt NetBeans to work in the background and create the necessary files for use. When it is through, the system will return you to the IDE where you can see and locate all your projects. If by any chance the project area found in the top left corner is not visible, you should navigate to the window>project tab on the menu bar

Figure 4

You can expand your project by pressing the +symbol, after which, your project will look something similar to the figure below.

Figure 5

You should then click the + on the source package to expand it and peek at your project name. We are doing this to see our Java file source code. This is shown in the figure below.

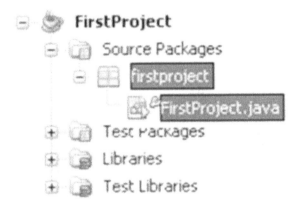

Figure 6

The source code (the same source code) should appear on the right in the text area and will bear the name First_Project.java. Sometimes, the code window will not display. This is not something to be overly concerned about, simply click and press enter on the First_Project.java available in your project window to call up the code window; after this, you can start working on your code. Here is a sample image of the coding window. The @author you part is where your name as an author will appear.

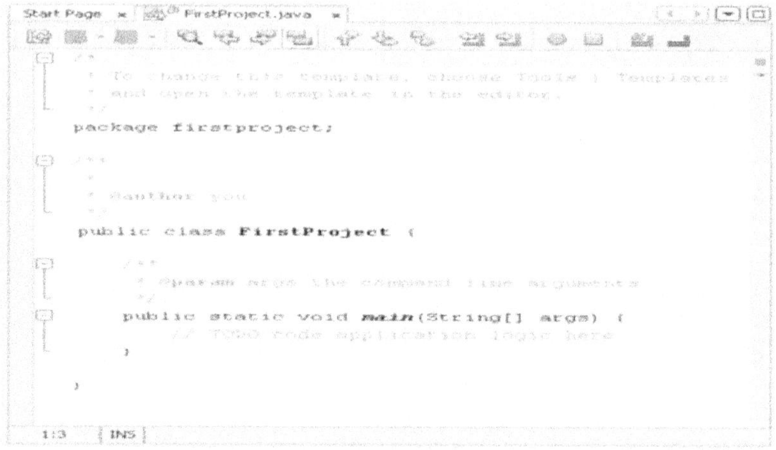

Figure 7

You should note that the class bears the name First_Project.

public class First_Project {

How so you wonder. After all, this is actually the same name as that of your java source file available on your project window, First_Project.java. There is a simple explanation for this. The complier demands of it. Once you run a program, the class name and the source file must match for the compiler to work. What does this mean? It means that if your .java file bears the name first_Project while the class bears the name First_Project, you will receive a compile error simply because the letter class do not match, i.e. the first one is lower class while the second one is upper class.

Remember that our whole project bears the name first project as a working experiment; you can name your package any other name such as **anyprogram** the name package does not necessarily have to bear the same name as the java source file or the class found in the source file. The only two that must match are the name of the class and the java source file.

We have now looked at the basics of creating a java source code within the Java environment. Let us move on swiftly.

Basic structure of a java program

After we have created a new project in the NetBeans program, you may notice that some of the code is grey and contains many asterisks and slashes like in the figure below.

The Structure Of Java Code And How To Run Programs

In the figure, you should notice the package name comes first. Additionally, you should note that a semicolon is what ends the line. The semicolon is important and if you omit it, the program will not compile.

package first_Project;

Next is the class name

public class First_Project {

}

Ideally, you should think of the class as a code segment. However, Java dictates that you tell it where the code segments start and end. You can achieve this by using curly brackets. You can use the left curly bracket at the start of a code, and use the right curly bracket to end the code {this is an example of a curly code segment} you should however note that anything that goes inside the left and right curly is part of the said code segment. Additionally, anything inside both the left and right curly for the class is in fact, a code segment. Here is what I mean:

public static void main(String[ ] args) {

}

More important than anything else is the word "main". Why? Because each time any Java program boots up, it first looks for the method bearing the name 'main'. Simply put, a method is a piece of code. The program then executes codes within the curly as part of the main. There are possibilities that you will get an error message within the Java program if your code does not have a main method. However, since this is the main entry point for your program, there is little chance you will omit it.

The public part of the code (the blue part) simply means that the method is viewable outside that class. On the other hand, static means that the creation of a new object is not necessary while void means that, there is not returnable value and the command gets on with it.

Command line arguments are the parts between the round brackets of the main. Except for the technical bits, you should not concern yourself with this. You should only strive to remember that our class is First_Project, which contains the method main and that both the class and the main use their own set of curly brackets. You should also remember that a huge part of your code is part of the class First_Project.

How to download and install Java on Linux, Windows and Mac.

Check out the figure below.

Figure 10

In the NetBeans tool bar, you will notice a "green play" arrow; you can use this to run a program.

Figure 11

You can also run a program by navigating to your projects window. This is especially effective in ensuring that the correct source code is running. To do this, you need to click on your java source file contained in the project window and then right click for options. Execute the run command. See figure below.

Figure 12

If you use any of the program execution methods above on our code so far, you should get something similar to figure13 below on the output window

Figure 13

In figure 13 above, you can see that the first line is the run command. The second is our code "My First Project." If there is something you are not sure of and would like to run the code again, you can simply press the "two almost fast-forward green arrows" visible on figure 13 above.

Chapter 2: JAVA BASICS

Java tokens

Java tokens are the values that are smaller than other integers. These numbers are going to fall between the value of -32768 and 32767. The code that I have been using is not going to work for shorts, instead I am going to need to use the short function so that I can make sure that the values are going to fall between the set limitations.

Large values are going to be stored inside of a double value along with floating point values. A double does not have to be used if I can use a floating point. As I am storing a floating variable. I am going to need to put a letter at the end of my value amount. This value should be f because it is a floating point number.

Keywords

In Java, the Boolean type refers to false or true values. Java finds out if it is true or false using the reserved keywords. Therefore, an expression Boolean type will assume one of these values. An example to demonstrate include:

There are a few things to note about this program. First, the **println(),** displays a boolean value. Secondly, the boolean values control the flow of an if statement. You don't need to go the long way in writing the boolean type this way: **if (b == true)**

The result shown by the operator such as < is boolean. It is one of the reasons why we have the expression **11 > 8** showing the value **true**. In addition, the other pair of parentheses near the **11 > 8** is important since plus comes before the >.

Identifiers

The top layer of the diagram above is for the identifier or name. This top layer is the name you give to a class. The name should specifically identify and also describe the type of object as seen or experienced by the user. In simple terms, the name or identifier should identify the class.

Operators

Java has an extensive list of operator environment. If you are wondering what an operator is, you can look at it as a symbol which conveys a specific message to the compiler to carry out a logical or mathematical operation. In Java, you will interact with four classes of operators. The four classes include:

- Logical operator
- Bitwise operator
- Relational operator
- Arithmetic operator

Like other computer languages, Java has a defined list of additional operators to take care of certain specific scenarios.

When it comes to learning JAVA programming language, or any programming language for that matter, there are five basic concepts you must understand before you get started. These five basic concepts include:

1. Variables
2. Data Structures
3. Control Structures
4. Syntax
5. Tools

Each of these concepts will be thoroughly explained on a beginner's level to ensure that they are understood.

Separators

They are not suitable for high-level abstraction: note that a lot of these programs make use of low-level constructs which are primarily used for low-level abstraction. The usual approach with these programming languages is that they focus on the machine – how to make a computer do something rather than how these functions can help solve the issues of a user. These languages deal with the minute details, which is already beyond the scope of high-level abstraction, which is the more common approach that we see today. In low-level abstraction, data structures and algorithms are taken separately whereas these are taken as a whole in high-level abstraction.

Literals

When it comes to literals in Java, we mean the fixed values which appear in the form in which human beings can read. We can say the number 200 is a literal. Most of the time, literals can be constants. Literals are important in a program. In fact, most Java programs use literals. Some of the programs we have already discussed in this book use literals.

Literals in Java can fall on various primitive data types. The manner in which every literal is shown is determined by its type. Like it was mentioned some time back, we enclose character constants in single quotes such as **'c'** and **'%'**.

We define literals in integers without involving the fractional part. For instance, 12 and -30 are integer literals. A floating point literal should contain the decimal point plus the fractional part. 12.389 is a floating literal. Java further permits for one to apply the scientific notation for the floating point literals. Integer literals contain int value and anyone can initialize them with a variable of **short**, **byte,** and **char**.

Comments

When this occurs, we call the grey's comments. In the running stages of the program, the grey's (comments) are moot. This is to mean that you can use the comment feature to state or explain what the code you are creating wants to achieve. You can achieve this by typing two slashes and then the comment. Here is a sample.

//Place your single line comment here

You can have more than one comment line by doing either of the following:

//We are going to

//spread the comments into two

Or

/*
This comment spreads over two lines

*/

If you look at the comment above, you will notice that it starts with /* but ends with */

Additionally, if you look at the previous image (figure 8) you will notice that there are comments that begin with a single forward slash and two asterisks (/**) but end with one asterisks and one forwards slash; this is called a Javadoc comment.

Chapter 3 : VARIABLES

what are variables

A variable, on the other hand, is an "object" that contains a specific data type and its assigned or received value. It is called a variable because the value contained can change according to how it is used in the code, how the coder can declare its value, or even how the user of the program chooses to interact with it. A variable, in short, is a storage unit for a data type. Having access to variables allow programmers to conveniently label and call stored values at hand.

Types of variables in Java

Java requires the programmer to use declaration statements, lines of code used to declare variables and define them by specifying the particular data type and name. Java has a specific way of treating variables, by defining variables as containers that contains a certain type and value of information, unlike some languages such as python, which only requires a declaration of a variable, and the variable can dynamically change its type; Java variables are **static**, which retain their type once declared.

Int number = 20;

Boolean completed = true;

String hello = "Hello World!";

The syntax in declaring is seen in the previous examples, with the type of the variable coming first, then the name of the variable, then the value. Note as well that the declaration statement can be composed of multiple declarations in one line, as in the following example:

Int number = 20, Boolean completed = true, string hello = "Hello World!";

Java variables can be declared without any value at the start; in cases such as these, Java chooses to declare these variables with a particular default value, for example:

Byte a;

Short num;

Boolean answer;

Will result in the values 0, 0, and false, respectively. A more complete list of default values is as follows: the byte, short, int, and long data types will all result in a default value of 0, while the float and double data types will have a default 0.0 value, the char data type will result in 'u\0000' value, a string or any other object will have a null default value, and all Booleans will begin with a false default value.

In Java, variables are static when declared, meaning that the programmer must define the data type that the variable will be containing. To illustrate, if we wish to use a variable **num** to store a number, we would first have to declare the variable: "int **num**", before we can assign a value, such as "**num = 10**".

The process above is usually known as and referred to as an "assignment statement", where a value is **assigned** to the variable as declared by the programmer. However, one prominent thing about how Java, and in fact how most programming languages, works is that in the assignment statement, such as in our example of num = 10, the actual value stored is the one on the right side of the equals sign, the value of 10, and num is just the "marker" to call that stored value. This is why there are many Java programmers that tend to prefer the jargon of "getting" a value rather than "assigning", though for the most part, they may be employed interchangeably, and outside of some rare scenario, function mostly the same way.

Note, however, that once values have been assigned to variables, functions need to be carried out in order for the data inside that variable to change its data type.

Naming a variable

Creating variables is an easy task, especially given how Java programmers tend to create and name them after the data type or the purpose of what the variable will store. However, there are a few rules when it comes to naming these variables, else Java will not recognize it and an error message will result. The main restrictions around variable names are that it should not begin with a special character such as an underscore or a number. However, variable names can consist of characters such as letters and numbers, and even an underscore, provided that the underscore is not placed at the start. No other characters may be used, such as the # or even $, as these special characters have different uses in Java, and thus will not be recognized in a variable name.

While those are the major rules, here are some tips when it comes to naming variables. The variable name should be descriptive, as in longer codes it may be difficult to recall just what "x" is for. Having a variable name such as "count" or "output" is much easier to recall as compared to having a generic "x" or "y" and will help in avoiding confusion. In addition to being descriptive, variables will also be easier to use if their names are kept fairly short. While having a variable name such as banking_information_account_records is very descriptive, typing it repeatedly as needed in the program will get exhausting, and having longer variable names increase the chances of typographical errors, which will lead to bugs in the code, resulting in a run - time error or the code not working as intended, or working, but introducing bugs along the way. Note as well that it has always been a practice for Java variables to be written in all lower – case letters, and while there is no restriction on capitalization, keeping things in lowercase simplifies things, as a missed capitalization may result in the variable not being recognized, as Java reads an upper – case letter as an entirely different character versus a lower – case letter.

Java primitive types

Method Naming Conventions

We shall revisit the naming conventions in Java since you will be using member methods. Methods in Java programming perform operations, they also receive any argument provided by a caller, and it can also return a result of an operation to a caller. Here's the syntax for declaring a method:

[Access Control Modifier] Return Type methodName ([set of parameters]) {

   // body of the method

   ......

}

Here are a few rules to remember when you make the names for the methods that you will write. Method names are always verbs or more specifically verb phrases (which means you can use multiple words to name them). The first word of the method name should all be in lower case letters while the rest of the words should follow a camel case format. Here is an example:

writeMethodNamesThisWay( )

Now, you should remember that verbs are used for method names, and they indicate an action while nouns are used for variable names, and they denote a certain attribute.

Following the syntax for declaring a method and following the name conventions for this Java construct, here's a sample code that can be used to compute the area of a circle.

```
public double computeCircleArea() {
return radius * radius * Math.PI;
}
```

Using Constructors in Your Code

We'll just go over some additional details as they relate to object oriented programming. As stated earlier, a constructor will look like a method, and you can certainly think of it and treat it like a special kind of method in Java programming.

However, a constructor will still be different from a method in several ways. The name of a constructor will be the same as the class name. Use the keyword or operator "new" to create a new instance of the constructor and also to initialize it. Here's an example using the class "Employee" and a variety of ways to initialize it in your code:

Employee payrate1 = new Employee( );

Employee payrate2 = new Employee(2.0);

Employee payrate3 = new Employee(3.0, "regular");

A constructor will also implicitly return void – that simply means it doesn't have a return type. You can't put a return statement inside the body of a constructor since it will be flagged by compilers as an error. The only way you can invoke a constructor is via the use of the "new" statement. We have already given you several ways how you can invoke constructors in the samples above.

One final difference is that constructors can't be inherited. Let's go back to the examples provided above – the first line includes "Employee( );" – that is called a default constructor. As you can see, it has no parameters whatsoever. The job of a default constructor is to simply initialize the member variables to a specific default value. In the example above, the member variable payrate1 was initialized to its default pay rate and employee status.

Can constructors be overloaded too? Yes, they can. Constructors behave like methods too so that means you can overload a constructor just the same way you overload a method. Here are a few examples on how you can overload a constructor. We use the Employee class and overload it using different parameters.

Employee( )

Employee(int r)

Employee(int r, String b)

How to initialize a variable

Now that we know how to declare variables, and we know the various types of variables that are available to us, the next thing to do is to learn how to make use of these variables, in something called "expressions". Expressions are the most used building blocks of a Java program, generally meant to produce a new value as a result, though in some cases expressions are used to assign a new value to a variable. Generally, expressions are made up of things such as values, variables, operators, and method calls. There are also some expressions that produce no result, but rather affect another variable. One example would be an expression that changes the value of a variable based on an operation: there is no new value output, and there is no true "assignment" of a new value, but rather there is what is called a **side effect** that results in a changed variable value.

In our previous sample program above, such as the "Hello World" printing program, we introduced raw values into the print function, also known as "hard coding" the output. However, at this point, we should try to incorporate what we have learned about variables. Variables operate much the same way as raw values, as they simply reference a previously stored value by the computer, and as such, the programmer can just use the variable name instead of the value. In order to demonstrate this, let us remember the previous "Hello World" program:

print ("Hello World") ;

input ("\n\nPlease press the return key to close this window.") ;

Now, instead of hard – coding the "Hello World" string, we can simply declare it into a variable and have the program output that variable. This should end up looking as:

String = "Hello World" ;

print(string) ;

input ("\n\nPlease press the return key to close this window.") ;

This should come out with the same result as the previous program, looking something similar to:

Hello World

Please press the return key to close this window.

Variables modified by code

However, the reader may be wondering why we even use a variable in this case, as it makes our code even longer. In very short codes, such as the classic "Hello World", using variables does make it longer, but to demonstrate how they can be used to shorten a code, let's use another code to show the usefulness of variables. For this code, we will attempt to print out a few times table values. In this code we will be using a few iterations and loops, which will be explained further on.

Int num = 9;

byte count = 0 ;

while (counter <10) {

print(num " * ") ;

print(counter "= ") ;

print(num * counter "\n") ;

counter = counter + 1} ;

This basic snippet of code will output the multiplication table of whatever is in the num variable up until times nine. In this program we are to be incorporating a so – called while condition and an iteration function. However, if we break down the components of the code as provided, the "while" condition tells Java to continue iterating the code beneath it until the condition is not true. Since count was initialized at a value of 0, and every time the code runs, the count variable will increase by one, the loop will run for ten times. The code nested within the "while" condition tells the Java program to print an equation of the number multiplied by the "counter" variable, meaning that it will print ten lines, from times zero to times nine. The code should end up looking like the following output:

9 * 0 = 0

9 * 1 = 9

9 * 2 = 18

9 * 3 = 27

9 * 4 = 36

9 * 5 = 45

9 * 6 = 54

9 * 7 = 63

9 * 8 = 72

9 * 9 = 81

Now try and imagine how a more seasoned programmer would think of how to write an algorithm to create a similar table without having a variable that can be changed as the code runs. They would have to "hard – code" all the values and type all the numbers just to get a simple multiplication table. However, due to the power of variables, the coder can simply assign a basic starting value and their code should do the rest.

Variables modified by user input

Variables can have a value declared by the programmer in the code, but the programmer can also have their variables as defined by the user. Remember that user input can be read by the Python code by the use of the input () function. They can do this while declaring the variable, or they may wish to have their user input a new value to an already – declared variable. Let's see how this works using the previous multiplication table code:

Int num = NextInt(input("Please enter a number from 0 – 9 to initialize the multiplication table.")) ;

Int counter = 0 ;

while (counter<10){

print(num " * ") ;

print(counter "= ") ;

print(num * counter "\n") ;

counter = counter + 1 ; }

This code prints an initial line and waits for the user to input a number before the code will run. Note that the user can technically enter a character that is not a number, and this will result in an error. Furthermore, the input function in this case is limited to receiving a single character, so only a number from 0 – 9 can be used, as longer digits will not be read. The variable declaration is a nested function, ensuring that the user input will be converted into an integer, rather than having a character, allowing the code to use mathematical operations.

Chapter 4 : JAVA OPERATORS

Arithmetic operators

Arithmetic operators in Java include:

- \+ represents addition
- \- represents subtraction
- * represents multiplication
- / represents division
- % represents modulus
- ++ represents increment
- -- represents decrement

Operators such as +, -, *, and / all perform the same function just like the rest of other languages.

We have seen that JavaScript has the ability to work with numbers. Hence it also has the ability to work with the operators that can be used with the number data type. Let's look at each of the operators in more detail.

Arithmetic Operators

These are operators that are used to work with numbers. The most common operators are shown below, followed by an example of how it can be applied.

With this program, the output is as follows:

JavaScript Program

The first value is 5

The second value is 10

Addition operator = 15

Subtraction operator = 5

Multiply operator = 50

Division operator = 2

Increment operator = 6

Decrement operator = 5

Modulus operator = 5

Assignment operators

These are operators that are used to determine the value of conditions based on the value of the operands. The relational operators possible in JavaScript are given below.

If a condition evaluates to true, then a value of 1 is returned, otherwise a value of 0 is returned.

With this program, the output is as follows:

JavaScript Program

The first value is 5

The second value is 10

Are the numbers equal = false

Are the numbers not equal = true

Is x less than y = true

Is x greater than y = false

Is x greater than or equal y = false

Is x less than or equal y = true

Logical Operators

These are operators that are used to determine the value of conditions based on the value of the operands, where the operands are Boolean values. The logical operators possible in JavaScript are given below.

With this program, the output is as follows:

JavaScript Program

The first value is true

The second value is true

The third value is false

x AND y = true

y AND z = false

z AND x = false

z AND z = false

The table below shows the logical operators based on the value of the operands for the OR operator.

With this program, the output is as follows:

JavaScript Program

The first value is true

The second value is true

The third value is false

x OR y = true

y OR z = true

z OR x = true

z OR z = false

The following table shows the logical operators based on the value of the operands for the NOT operator.

Assignment Operators

These are operators that are used to make assignment operations easier. The assignment operators possible in JavaScript are given below.

Now let's look at how we can implement these operators in further detail.

With this program, the output is as follows:

JavaScript Program

The first value is 5

The second value is 6

The value of i+j is 11

The value of i+=j is 11

The value of i-=j is 5

The value of i*=j is 30

The value of i/=j is 5

The value of i%=j is 5

Bitwise Operators

These are operators that are used to make bit operations on operands.

With this program, the output is as follows:

JavaScript Program

The first value is 5

The second value is 6

The value of x AND y is 4

The value of x OR y is 7

The value of NOT x is -6

The value of x XOR y is 3

The value Zero fill left shift is 10

The value Signed right shift is 2

The value Zero fill right shift is 2

Chapter 5 : ARRAYS AND STRING

What are strings

A string is a sequence of characters and can also be known as an array of characters

In order declare a string in JAVA, you just use the keyword 'string'

You then name your string whatever you would like

Then you place an equal sign after that

Then in double quotes, place whatever string you want to assign and print it just the same as all the others:

String sample = "Welcome Ron ";

System.out.println(sample)

String Methods

In the above example, there are two variables **message** and **s** of **String** type. The statement *message = s + "Ron";* will append the string **"World"** to the contents of **s** and save it in **message**. Hence, message will now hold **"Welcome Ron"**.

Arrays

An array is similar to a variable but it can store more than one value at a time – the only condition being that even though you can store more than one value in an array, it has to be the same type of values

For example, you would be able to store 10 integers in an array, but if you wanted to store 5 integers and 5 doubles, you would not be able to do it

This is one way of declaring an array: int [] RonArray = {4, 62,1,54,3};

Another way is: int myinarray2[] = {4,62,1,54,3} This way is fine but it is not the preferred way of declaring an array

There are three more ways of declaring arrays

1. int[] RonArray = new int[3];

2. int[] RonArray = {1,2,3};

3. int[] RonArray = new int [ ]{1,2,3};

array methods

The section int [] RonArray indicates that the array is of the primitive variable int declared with the name or reference RonArray. The square brackets [] indicate that it is a reference to an array. The section new int[7] indicates that a new array object is created. The number between the square brackets means that the length of the array is equal to 7. The index of the elements of RonArray consists of the numbers 0, 1, 2, 3, 4, 5 and 6. There are seven elements totally. To find out the element for example at index 2, we use the name of the array, and between square brackets the index of the element: RonArray[2]. In our example, all the seven elements are equal to 0, because they are not initialized. If an int type variable is not initialized its value is by default equal to 0.

The program of example 1 writes seven zeros to the standard output: 0000000

int [] RonArray = new int [7]

The following code changes the value of the fourth element in the array to 11. Remember that the first element index is 0.

intArray [3] = 11

Try to import the package java.util.Arrays of the Java standard API, to learn how to sort the elements of an array.

Primitive types

Primitive data types are data types that Java has already defined for you. This means that you can't use them as names for variables, classes, etc. There are only eight primitive data types defined in Java:

- boolean – boolean data types can only store true or false values and therefore has a very small size of 1 bit.
- byte – byte data types can store integers with a size of only 8 bits.
- short – short data types can also store integers with a larger size of 16 bits
- char – char can store Unicode characters, which would mean one letter/number/symbol, with a size of 16 bits.
- int – int is the most commonly used data type because it can store integers with the standard size of 32 bits – enough to represent most of the integers you'd be using in standard programs.
- long – long is used when a program needs to store a really huge number that int can no longer store. With a size of 64 bits, it has twice the space that int has.
- float – float is used when you need to store numbers with decimal points. Like int it also has 32 bits of allocated space.

- double – double is used when float can no longer accommodate the size of a number with a decimal point. Like long it also has 64 bits of allocated space.

What's special about Java is that there's a special support for strings coming from the java.lang.String class. This means that you can easily create strings by typing a line of code like:

String sentence = "Welcome Ron !";

Remember though that String is not considered a primitive data type, but since its usage is somewhat similar anyway you might as well use it as such.

reference types

To utilize an array as a part of a system, you must declare a variable to reference the array. Besides this, you must determine the sort of array the variable can reference. Here is the syntax for declaring a variable of the type array:

datatype[] RonArray;

Sample Implementation:

The accompanying code bits are illustrations of this concept:

double[] RonArray;

Making Arrays

You can make an exhibit by utilizing the new operator with the accompanying statement:

RonArray = new datatype[sizeofarray];

The above declaration does two things:

- It makes an exhibit with the help of the new operator in the following manner:

new datatype[arraysize];

- It relegates the reference of the recently made array to the variable RonArray.

Proclaiming a array variable, making an exhibit, and doling out the reference of the show to the variable can be consolidated in one declaration, as appeared:

datatype[] RonArray = new datatype[sizeofarray];

On the other hand, you can also make clusters in the following manner:

datatype[] RonArray = {val0, val1, ..., valk};

The components of the array are gotten to through the record. Array lists are 0-based; that is, they begin from 0 to go up to RonArray.length-1.

Sample Implementation:

The declaration shown below declares an array, RonArray, makes a cluster of 10 components of double type and doles out its reference to RonArray:

double[] RonArray = new double[10];

Handling Arrays

Chapter 6 : INTERACTIVE

How to displaying output

The floating type represents fractional numbers. The floating types exist in two types, the double and float. The double represents the double precision numbers while the float represents the single precision numbers.

The double is applied frequently since functions of mathematics use double value. For instance, sqrt() will output a double. You can check its application in the code below. In this example, sqrt() has been applied to calculate the longest side of a triangle when the length of the other sides has been provided.

```
/*
    Use the Pythagorean theorem to
    find the length of the hypotenuse
    given the lengths of the two opposing
    sides.
*/
class Hypot {
  public static void main(String args[]) {
    double x, y, z;

    x = 3;
    y = 4;                    Notice how sqrt() is called. It is preceded by
                              the name of the class of which it is a member.
    z = Math.sqrt(x*x + y*y);

    System.out.println("Hypotenuse is " +z);
  }
}
```

The output from the program is shown here:

```
Hypotenuse is 5.0
```

We need to notice in the example above that **sqrt()** belongs to the **Math** class. But, notice the way the **sqrt()** has been used: first, it has been preceded by the **Math** name. Now, for **sqrt()**, it is similar.

Converters

If you have programmed in another language, you might be thinking that characters in Java are 8. No! Java has Unicode. What a Unicode does is to define a set of characters which represents characters existing in the human languages. The example below demonstrates:

Char th;

th = 'Y';

Still, if you want to display a char value by applying the **println()** statement. This example will show you how to do it:

```
System.out.println("This is th: "+ th);
Given that the char is unsigned 16-bit type, you can do some arithmetic operations
in the char variable. For instance, look at the program below:
Class CharArith {
Public static void main (String args []) {
Char th;
th = 'X';
System.out.println("th has "+ th);
th++; // we increment the th, it is possible to increment a char
System.out.println("th is now "+ th);
th = 90; // we assign th the value Z
System.out.println("th is now "+ th);
}
}
Here is the output of the above program:
"th has X"
"th is now Y"
"th is now Z"
```

This program assigns variable **th** the value **'X'**. Then, it is incremented to **Y**, which is the next character in the Unicode sequence.

formatting outputs

In Java, the Boolean type refers to false or true values. Java finds out if it is true or false using the reserved keywords.

Therefore, an expression Boolean type will assume one of these values. An example to demonstrate include:

```
class BoolPro {
public static void main (String args []) {
 boolean q;
 q = false;
 System.out.println ("q is "+ q);
 q= true;
 System.out.println("q is "+ q);
 // a boolean value can also control the if statement
 If(q)
 System.out.println("This is executed.");
 q = false;
 if(q)
 System.out.println("This is not executed");
 // Describe the results of the relational operator
 System.out.println("11 > 8 is "+ (10 > 8));
}
}
The output:
 q is false
 q is true
 This is executed
 11 > 8 is true
```

There are a few things to note about this program. First, the **println(),** displays a boolean value. Secondly, the boolean values control the flow of an if statement. You don't need to go the long way in writing the boolean type this way: **if (b == true)**

The result shown by the operator such as < is boolean. It is one of the reasons why we have the expression **11 > 8** showing the value **true**. In addition, the other pair of parentheses near the **11 > 8** is important since plus comes before the >.

escape sequences

Surrounding them with single quotes works for the majority of printing characters. However, there are certain characters which have a problem with the text editor. Furthermore, double and single quotes tend to have a unique meaning to

Java. This means you cannot just use them directly. Now, because of the above reason, Java has specific escape sequences, sometimes it is called a **backslash character constant**. This table illustrates:

Escape Sequence	Description
\'	Single quote
\"	Double quote
\\	Backslash
\r	Carriage return
\n	New line
\f	Form feed
\t	Horizontal tab
\b	Backspace
\ddd	Octal constant (where ddd is an octal constant)
\uxxxx	Hexadecimal constant (where xxxx is a hexadecimal constant)

Chapter 7: CONTROL FLOW STATEMENTS

Right now, your programming is sequential, which means that the code is being executed from the top down. It is what we call linear code, with every code line being read by Java, starting with the first line and working down to the last line that you wrote.

We don't always require our programs to work like this, though. Sometimes, you want your code to execute only when and if specific conditions are met. For example, you might want a specific message to be displayed if a user is under 18, while a different one would display for those over 18. What you want is to control how your code flows yourself, and we do this by using conditional logic.

When we talk about conditional logic, we are mostly talking about the IF word. For example, IF user is younger than 18 then display this message; IF user is older than 18, display this message. Luckily, you will find that using conditional logic in Java is easy so let's begin by looking at IF statements.

IF Statements

One of the most common things in computer programming is to execute code when one thing happens instead of something else.

Run the program and check it – Note that NetBeans tends to run the program in bold text in the window for Projects, not the code that you displayed. If you want the code run in your coding window, right-click on the code, anywhere and then click on **Run File** in the menu that appears. The output will now appear in the Output window.

Next, we change the user variable value from 17 to 18; now run the program again.

You should see that the program runs fine, no errors but nothing will be printed. The reason for this is because the message is in between the curly brackets in the IF statement and that statement is looking for values of lower than 18. If the condition isn't met, Java will ignore the curly brackets and anything in between them, moving on to the rest of the code.

Nested ifs

We have previously looked at nested scopes; now we want to look at nested ifs. You will interact most of the time with a nested if. The greatest lesson to learn is nested ifs point to the block of code with the else.

Read the following example:

```
If( i ==10) {
If ( j < 20) a = b;
If (k > 100) c = d;
else a – c; // this else will point to the if (k > 100)
}
else a = d; //this else will point to the if (i ==10)
```

You should be able to note that the last else has not been associated with if(j<20), but associated with the if(i==10).

IF ... ELSE

If you don't want to use two IF statements, there is another way -and IF ... ELSE statement.

So, we have two choices in this code – the user is either 18 or younger, or older than 18. Change your code so it matches what is above and try it. You should now see that the first message is printed out. Change the user variable value to 20 and then run the code again. You should see the message that is between the curly brackets for ELSE displayed in the Output window.

IF ... ELSE IF

The first IF statement will test for the first condition, then we have the ELSE IF, followed by parentheses, in between which goes condition two. If there is anything that the first two conditions do not catch, it will be caught by the last ELSE. Again, we have sectioned the code using curly brackets and each IF, Else IF or ELSE has its own set. If you miss out any of these curly brackets, you will get an error message.

Before you try out any more code, you must first learn about a few more conditional operators. So far, you have used these ones:

- < - Greater Than
- < - Less Than
- >= - Greater Than or Equal To
  - <= - Less Than or Equal To

Here's four more you can use:

- && - AND
- || - OR
- == - HAS A VALUE OF
  - ! - NOT

The first one, a pair of ampersand symbols, is used for testing two or more conditions at once.

We are checking to see if a user is older than the age of 18 but younger than the age of 40 – remember, we are checking what is in the variable called user. The first condition, "greater than 18"; the second condition, "less than 40". Between those two conditions, we have the AND operator so the entire line is saying else if user is greater than 18 AND user is less than 40.

Now run the program and test it again; before it runs you should already be able to guess what is going to print. The user variable has a value of 21 so the message that is between the else if curly brackets will show in the output window.

Nested IF Statements

Look at where the curly brackets are – get one set in the wrong place or miss one out and the code will not run. Nested IF statements might be a little tricky but, really, all you are doing is narrowing the choices down.

Boolean Values

Instead of using int, double or string, you would simply type in boolean (lower case b) and, after the variable name, you assign a TRUE or FALSE value. Notice that we use a single equal sign as the assignment operator. If you wanted to see if a variable "has a value of", you would need to use a pair of equals signs.

This time, we have used the NOT operator in front of the variable called user. The NOT operator is indicated by the use of an exclamation mark, just one, and it will be placed in front of the variable that you are trying to test. This operator tests for negation, which means that it is testing for the opposite of the actual value.

Switch Statements

Another way of controlling flow is to use a switch statement. This provides you with the option of testing for a range of values for the variables and can be used in place of complicated, long IF … ELSE statements.

Start with the word "switch" and then a set of parentheses. The variable you are checking is placed between the switch parentheses and is followed by a set of curly brackets. The rest of the switch statement goes in between the curly brackets.

Chapter 8 : LOOPS IN JAVA

Looping statements allow your program to do something repeatedly for a fixed number of times. There are two types of looping statements:

1. while and do-while statements

while statements are like if-then statements, but this time if the condition specified holds true, then whatever is inside the block of code will be executed again and again until the condition no longer holds true. Of course, this means that you'll have to do something that eventually makes the conditions false within the block of code; otherwise you're going to experience what people call an endless loop. Here are the basic templates for the while and do-while statement:

```
//template for while

while(condition, e.g., ron < 12)

{

    //code here will be executed again and again if the condition still holds true


    //there should be something that eventually breaks the condition, e.g., ron++;

}

//template for do-while

do

{

    //code here will be executed again and again if the condition still holds true
```

> //there should be something that eventually breaks the condition, e.g., ron++;
>
> } while(condition);

The difference between the while and do-while statements is that the do-while statement is guaranteed to execute the code inside at least once, while the while statement has a chance of not executing the code inside at all.

2. for statements

for statements are more compact than while statements and is best used in codes that have rather short conditions for iteration. Here's the basic template for the for statement:

> for(initialize variable, e.g., ab = 0; condition, e.g., ab < 10; iterate variable, e.g., ab++)
>
> {
>
> //do whatever is inside this block as long as the condition specified still holds
>
> }

Branching statements

There are three commands used for branching:

1. break – this command allows you to break outside a loop or a labeled statement. Here's a template for its usage:

> for(initialize variable, e.g., jack = 0; condition, e.g., jack <

10; iterate variable, e.g., x++)

{

//do whatever is inside this block as long as the condition specified still holds

//this next segment of code breaks you out of the for loop as long as condition1 is met.

if(condition1)

{

   break;

}

}

2. continue – continue allows you to go to the next iteration of a loop. Here's a template for its usage:

for(initialize variable, e.g., xyz = 0; condition, e.g., xyz < 10; iterate variable, e.g., xyz++)

{

//this next segment of code allows you to skip whatever comes after the if-statement and go right into the next iteration of the loop if condition1 is met.

if(condition1)

{

   continue;

}

//do whatever is inside this block as long as the condition

> specified still holds
>
> }

    3. return – this statement simply lets you exit the current method you're in. you can either return a value or not, depending on whether or not the method says it needs a value returned. Here are templates for its usage:

```
//returning with a value
if (condition)
{
   return variable;
}
//returning without a value
if (condition)
{
   return;
}
```

Congratulations! You now know how to store data, do stuff to it, and let your program make decisions. You should now be able to create simple programs, like a program that adds two numbers, and other operations. In the final chapter we shall talk about the essential Java classes every Java programmer should know. That chapter should wrap-up everything you've learned so far and give you the power to learn new Java classes all by yourself.

Chapter 9: CLASSES AND OBJECTS IN JAVA

To become a professional Java programmer, you must understand the concept of classes in Java. The class is the main part of any Java program. In other words, it is the basis on which the whole Java language is created, and one reason for this is that the class holds the features of an object.

Inside a class, you will find data defined as well as the code which executes the data. The code exists in the methods. This chapter will take you through a brief understanding of the classes, methods, and objects in Java. It is crucial that you have a basic foundation of the above features so that you can know how to write complicated Java programs.

The fundamentals of Class

Since the start of this book, we have been using Java class. You should have noticed that every Java program has a class. Although we have been using Java classes, the classes were simple and we did not take advantage of the many features which a class comes with. Soon you will discover that the Java class is even more efficient than what we have used previously in the different programs.

So, let's start by looking at the basics of a class in Java. We can look at a class as a blueprint which determines the object properties. It defines in detail the program data and code. And so, a class is like a template which describes how you can create an object. It is vital to be elaborate about a class; it is a logical abstraction. Methods and variable of a class are referred to as members.

The basic style of a class

Whenever you describe a class, you will be declaring its nature and form. To declare a class involves making a specification of its instance variables as well as the methods of the class. While simple classes may only have methods or some might have instance variables alone, the majority of the real-world classes have both the class and instance variables.

The keyword class is used in declaring a class. Here is an easy class definition:

```
class classname {
    // declare instance variables
    type var1;
    type var2;
    // ...
    type varN;

    // declare methods
    type method1(parameters) {
        // body of method
    }
    type method2(parameters) {
        // body of method
    }
    // ...
    type methodN(parameters) {
        // body of method
    }
}
```

A class defined clearly should have a logical entity. For instance, if we have a class which holds telephone numbers and names of people, it will never hold other unrelated information such as average rainfall. The point to note here is that a class which is well-designed will store information that is logically connected. If you store information which is unrelated to the class, it will destroy the structure of your code.

So far, we have used classes which come with a single **main()** method. Soon you will learn how to build other methods, but I want you to know that the basic style of a class is not the way the **main()** method is defined.

We only need the **main()** method in case our class as it is the beginning point of our program. In addition, certain types of Java applications don't need the **main()** method.

Definition of a class

To reveal the concept of Java classes, we shall create a class which will store information about vehicles. The class is called **Vehicle**. This class will have information such as the number of passengers, the capacity of the fuel, as well as the average fuel consumption. In this class, we have three instance variables defined: fuel cap, passengers, and mpg. You should be keen to realize that the class Vehicle is without a method. At the moment, we consider it a data class.

```
class Vehicle {
   int passengers;  // number of passengers
   int fuelcap;     // fuel capacity in gallons
   int mpg;         // fuel consumption in miles per gallon
}
```

By defining a class, it has to create a new data type.

Don't forget that class declaration involves only specifying the type description. No actual object is created. Therefore, the previous example will not enforce the objects of type vehicle to become active.

This statement helps one create an object which belongs to the Vehicle class.

Vehicle minisalon = new Vehicle(); // we have created a variable object called minisalon

When this statement is executed, **minisalon** becomes an instance of the class **Vehicle**. Now, it will be said to have a physical reality. To access any member of a class, the dot operator helps you achieve that:

Object.Member

Take, for instance, we want our **minisalon** to hold the value 12. This is how it is done:

minisalon.fuelcap = 12;

Overall, the dot operator allows you to access the methods and instance variables. You can take a look at this entire program which uses the Vehicle class:

```
/* A program that uses the Vehicle class.

   Call this file VehicleDemo.java
*/
class Vehicle {
   int passengers;   // number of passengers
   int fuelcap;      // fuel capacity in gallons
   int mpg;          // fuel consumption in miles per gallon
}
// This class declares an object of type Vehicle.
class VehicleDemo {
   public static void main(String args[]) {
      Vehicle minivan = new Vehicle();
      int range;

      // assign values to fields in minivan
      minivan.passengers = 7;
      minivan.fuelcap = 16;     // Notice the use of the dot
      minivan.mpg = 21;         // operator to access a member

      // compute the range assuming a full tank of gas
      range = minivan.fuelcap * minivan.mpg;
      System.out.println("Minivan can carry " + minivan.passengers +
                         " with a range of " + range);
   }
}
```

If you want to run this program, you need to run the file with the name **Vehicle.Demo.java**. The main method is found in that class. This program will display:

```
Minivan can carry 7 with a range of 336
```

Reference variables and assignment

When handling the assignment operation in Java, you should underline that the object reference behaves differently from primitive variables. In this case, if you will assign a primitive type variable to another, it is simple. In simple terms, what the left variable does is to store what is held in the variable at right. However, if you choose that you will allot a single object reference variable to the other, the scenario becomes complicated. Why? You will be modifying the object which the reference variable refers to. Here is an example:

Vehicle car1 = new Vehicle ();
Vehicle car2 = car1;

313

By looking at the above code snippet, you might reason that both objects point to separate objects, however, that is not true. In this code, both car1 and car2 point to the same object. Something I would like you to learn here is that even though we have car1 and car2 pointing to the same object. They aren't related.

Methods

As we had said before, methods are members of the classes. At the moment, our Vehicle class has data, but no methods. While having a class which contains data alone is valid, the majority of the classes will have methods. Methods act upon the data which has been defined in the class, and most of the time it offers access to the data.

A method can carry at least one statement. A fully written Java code will contain a method which acts only on one particular task. Every method must be given a name. The name of the method helps one use the method in the code. You can choose to give your method whichever name you want, but note that the **main()** method is meant for the method which will start your program execution. Another important point is that you should never use Java keywords as part of your method name. The syntax for Java methods includes:

```
Type Your_methodname (parameter-list) {
//the body
}
```

In the above example, the **type** represents the type of data you would want your method to return. A **void** method is one which does not return data. We specify method name by **your_methodname**. The **parameter-list** refers to a series of type and identifier differentiated using commas. Parameters point to variables which are going to acquire the arguments which have been passed to the method after it has been called.

We give a method the Java vehicle class

To add a method to the Vehicle class, we will state it in the Vehicle's declaration. In this example, the Vehicle has a method called **range()** which output several types of vehicle:

```
// Add range to Vehicle.
class Vehicle {
    int passengers; // number of passengers
    int fuelcap;    // fuel capacity in gallons
    int mpg;        // fuel consumption in miles per gallon

    // Display the range.
    void range() {    ←──────── The range() method is contained within the Vehicle class
        System.out.println("Range is " + fuelcap * mpg);
    }                                     ↑          ↑
}                                Notice that fuelcap and mpg are used directly, without the dot operator.

class AddMeth {
    public static void main(String args[]) {
        Vehicle minivan = new Vehicle();
        Vehicle sportscar = new Vehicle();

        int range1, range2;

        // assign values to fields in minivan
        minivan.passengers = 7;
        minivan.fuelcap = 16;
        minivan.mpg = 21;
```

315

```
    // assign values to fields in sportscar
    sportscar.passengers = 2;
    sportscar.fuelcap = 14;
    sportscar.mpg = 12;

    System.out.print("Minivan can carry " + minivan.passengers +
                    ". ");

    minivan.range(); // display range of minivan

    System.out.print("Sportscar can carry " + sportscar.passengers +
                    ". ");

    sportscar.range(); // display range of sportscar.
    }
}
```

This program will show the following output:

```
Minivan can carry 7. Range is 336
Sportscar can carry 2. Range is 168
```

We now want to review this program by starting with the method range(). Here is the first line:

Void range() {

What happens here is that we have declared a method whose name is **range**, and it has no parameter. The body of the method has the **System.out.println("......");** construct which will display the range of the vehicle after performing a few calculations. The method **range()** closes when it encounters the closing curly brace. This leads to the main program control

316

to switch to the original caller. Well, let's review the code starting from the main method:

Minivan.range();

What is happening here is that the **range()** method is called by using the object variable minivan. Calling a program causes the program control to migrate to the method. And so, if the method execution comes to an end, control is relayed to the caller, and the program execution resumes from the following code. If we consider the above example, the method **range** here is going to display all the variation of vehicles defined by the minivan, similar to a call done by **sportscar**. Whenever you call **range()**, it will output the range listed by the object.

There is one particular thing you should discover about the method **range()**. Some of the instance variables have been addressed directly using the . operator.

Returning to a method

Generally, we have only two conditions which result in a method returning a value. First, the closing curly brace interacts with the method—this is clear in the method **range()**. The second condition for a method to return happens when a **return** statement gets executed. Don't forget that there are two types of return: the **void** method and the other one which returns values. We shall look at the first form here:

In a void method, it is possible to enforce an immediate termination by applying the **return** statement.

When the return statement is executed, the program control will get back to the caller by jumping all the rest of the code in a method. Consider the following example:

```
void myMeth() {
    int i;

    for(i=0; i<10; i++) {
        if(i == 5) return;  // stop at 5
        System.out.println();
    }
}
```

In this case, the for loop will execute from 0–5 because when it reaches 5, the method is enforced to return a value. You can still develop many return statements in one Java method, especially when you have two pathways.

Returning a Value

While it is rare for a void method to return a value, there are specific methods which return a value. The potential for the method to have a return is an important property of a method. You have perhaps seen an example in the square root function to find the square root. Return value is important in programming to show a given result of a calculation like in the **sqrt()** function.

Sometimes, the return value proves the success or failure of a given method. The syntax used for a method with a return value is:

    return value;

Chapter 10 : ENCAPSULATIONS IN JAVA

Java encapsulation

The entire code can be thought of a capsule, and you can only communicate through the messages. Hence the name encapsulation.

Few notes on Encapsulation in Java :

- In Java, encapsulation is binding the data with its related functionalities
- Here functionalities mean "methods" and data means "variables"
- So we keep variable and methods in one place. That place is "class."
- "Class" is the base for encapsulation.
- With Java Encapsulation, you can hide (restrict access) to critical data members in your code, which improves security
- As we discussed earlier, if a data member is declared "private", then it can only be accessed within the same class. No outside class can access data member (variable) of other class.
- However if you need to access these variables, you have to use **public "getter" and "setter"** methods.
- Setup public "getter" and "setter" method to update and read the private data field. This will allow data access from private class.

Abstraction

Abstraction simply refers to the process of hiding unnecessary details of an object and only showing the ones that are relevant. **Encapsulation** on the other hand simply means the binding of the states and the methods of an object together.

This binding eventually creates something called a class (we'll cover that in a little bit). Finally, **message passing** refers to the ability of objects to interact with other objects.

High – level programming languages, on the other hand, have a much higher level of abstraction, meaning that code goes through a program called a compiler, which acts as the computer's translator, before the computer is able to use it. This level of abstraction is usually to the point where the programming language already has syntax similar to English, a global language. The compiler assumes the role of the translator between the high – level language and the machine. This allows the programmer to write their program in a more natural manner, as it allows for the coder to use more "natural" language, and the higher – level language allows for some functions to be automated, making life much easier for the coder. The trade – off here however is that the code has to go through a compiler, which will take lengthier for the program to run and execute, and the computer will often use more memory as compared to a lower – level language. Amongst these high – level languages are the more frequently – known ones, such as Python, C++, and our topic for today, Java.

Chapter 11: POLYMORPHISM IN JAVA

Static polymorphism

There are two kinds of members that are possible inside a class. One is the instance member and the other static member.

Instance members bind to the each instance of a class we create and have its own copy in memory. So change of a member in once object doesn't change the value of the same member in another object.

On the other side, static members bind to the class and shared by each instance of a class. So when we modify the value of static members in one object, it will get reflected in all other objects. Moreover static members are available once the class got loaded into memory, whereas instance members are available only after we create an object of the class.

dynamic polymorphism

Resolving or interpreting the behavior at run time is called dynamic polymorphism. We already see static polymorphism when we are discussing about "method overloading". Now, here we discuss about the dynamic or runtime polymorphism.

Inheritance and composition

Inheritance is nothing by deriving the characteristics from one entity to other. So we can derive properties of one class to other by using the technique inheritance. We can inherit both the methods and fields from a class to other (of-course there is a restriction with respect to access specifiers, and will discuss later in this chapter).

The class from which properties are derived is called **base class, super class or parent class**. The class which inherits the properties from other class is called **derived class, sub class or extended class**.

Why do I need Inheritance?

Let us consider a scenario in a bank. A bank operate many kind of accounts, say savings account, current account, salary account and many more. In each case (in case of every account), bank stores the account holder details like, name, address, contact details etcetera. Suppose a person has 3 different types of accounts. Now, do I need to repeat all the data again and again?

A big NO. This is the scenario where we could go for inheritance. Just aggregate all the properties that are common to all type of entities into a single class. Now derive each of the specialized entity out of the aggregate entity so that each derive entity inherits the properties of the base entity.

Chapter 12: EXAMPLES WITH JAVA

Assuming that the reader is not a total newbie to programming, and has been introduced to the world of programming using C or another procedural – heavy language, the next logical question would be: why even use object – oriented programming? Well, one of its main advantages is that in the long run, it saves time.

How to build a small game with Java

Procedural programming is usually much quicker and more straightforward in simpler algorithms and programs; rather than having to construct and define a class, and create an object based on that class, all the programmer really has to do is to simply declare the necessary variables and write the functions, and create the algorithm in order to solve the problem that they need the code to address.

However, when it comes to more complex programs, needing more complex solutions, this is where object – oriented programming begins to shine, and this is where it starts to show its strength. In a lot of programs, there will be times that there will be a number of "objects" or data clusters that have to be grouped together, and that the programmer will be treating in a certain way. This is what "classes" are meant to address. Instead of declaring a new set of variables per data cluster, they can simply draw on a pre – made "class" and create a new "object". Let's see how this would work in practice.

Each piece also has different methods of moving, depending on what piece they are. If a programmer were to code a chess game in procedural fashion, then they would have to manually describe each and every piece, all sixteen pawns, four bishops and four knights, four rooks, two queens, and two kings. In addition, they will have to write the functions that allow each piece to move in its own separate way. However, if the programmer makes use of object - oriented programming, instead of having to code sixteen pawns, four bishops, four knights, four rooks, two queens, two kings, they simply have to code six classes: one class to describe each piece on the board. The programmer can now simply include the movement functions within each class, and have the attributes describe their position: whether they're white king's pawn, or black queen's pawn, these are all things that can be inserted through the "attributes" portion of the "pawn" class. Instead of thirty – two clusters of code, the programmer only has to do six. Now it's much easier, much shorter, and also much more elegant.

Chapter 13: Most searched beginner's questions

Installing Java

Given that Java is free, it can easily be downloaded from the Java website, and it will be quite easy to install, with basic instructions that can easily be followed, depending on what operating system the user is running. Here we will cover the three major operating systems, Windows, Linux, and Mac.

Installing Java on Windows

Before installing Java, check the version of Windows that the computer is running, in order to see whether or not it is compatible with the latest Java version. Generally, Windows platforms as far back as Windows XP are still supported, though the support for these older Windows versions is being slowly phased out.

The next step is to disable the Windows firewall. This step is in order to prevent any issues with installing Java, as there are often times when firewall settings disable any automatic or online installation, so in order to avoid these issues, it would be best to simply disable the firewall. However, this step may leave your computer vulnerable, so remember to turn it on immediately after installation of Java, and make sure not to open any suspicious files or visit any suspicious websites while the firewall is turned off.

Once the user has verified whether Java is compatible with their Windows system, and has disabled or limited the firewall, it is time to proceed to the installation process. Navigate to the manual download page for Windows in the Java website and choose the applicable Windows OS option.

Once this is done, an installer should come up, and the user should press the "**Run**" option, which will automatically allow the installer to begin the installation process. If the user wishes to defer installation to a later date, or simply wants to download it for use on another device, they can simply **"Save"** the installer file rather than **Running** it. The Java installation window should then pop up, and this will allow the user to choose what folder they wish Java to be installed in; for convenience, the default folder in C: should suffice for most users, unless they have a special need. The installer may offer to install additional programs other than Java; know that these are unnecessary in order to use Java, so if the user refuses to install them, this will not hamper their use of Java. After a few minutes, the Java program should then be installed, and in some cases the user will have to restart their device. Once the device has been restarted, the user may wish to go back to the Java website through this link: https://java.com/en/download/installed.jsp in order to verify whether or not the installation was completed properly. Once verified, congratulations! The Java software package has been installed and should be ready to use.

Installing Java on Linux

Before installing Java, check the version of Linux that the computer is running, in order to see whether or not it is compatible with the latest Java version. Generally, most Linux packages are supported, but Java runs a 32 – bit version for a lot of these platforms, such as Oracle Linux or SUSE Linux.

The next step is to ensure that the user is installing as a user with root access. This will allow Java to be fully installed with the necessary permissions. In case the user is not one with root access, then they may have to edit the destination folder of their Java installation in order to be able to properly install it, as they may not have the required permissions to install it in the default folder.

Once the user has verified whether Java is compatible with their Linux system, as well as checked whether or not they have the appropriate permissions in order to install the Java Runtime Environment, or JRE, then they can navigate to the

Java home page and choose the compatible version to their software package.

Once this is done, an installer should come up, and the user should press the "**Run**" option, which will automatically allow the installer to begin the installation process. If the user wishes to defer installation to a later date, or simply wants to download it for use on another device, they can simply "**Save**" the installer file rather than **Running** it.

The installer may offer to install additional programs other than Java; know that these are unnecessary in order to use Java, so if the user refuses to install them, this will not hamper their use of Java. After a few minutes, the Java program should then be installed, and in some cases the user will have to restart their device. Once the device has been restarted, the user may wish to go back to the Java website through this link: https://java.com/en/download/installed.jsp in order to verify whether or not the installation was completed properly. Once verified, congratulations! The Java software package has been installed and should be ready to use.

Installing Java on Mac

Before installing Java, check the version of Mac that the computer is running, in order to see whether or not it is compatible with the latest Java version. Generally, Java runs with most macOS versions, but in order to be safe, ensure that your Mac is running the latest macOS version in order to avoid support or compatibility issues.

Once the user has verified whether Java is compatible with their mac system, it is time to proceed to the installation process. Navigate to the manual download page for Mac in the Java website and choose the applicable Mac OS option.

Once this is done, the file jre-8u65-macosx-x64.pkg file should have been downloaded, and the user should press the "**Run**" option, which will automatically allow the installer to begin the installation process. If the user wishes to defer installation to a later date, or simply wants to download it for use on another device, they can simply **"Save"** the installer file rather than **Running** it. The Java installation wizard should then pop up, and this will allow the user to choose what folder they wish Java to be installed in; for convenience, the default folder in C: should suffice for most users, unless they have a special need. The installer may offer to install additional programs other than Java; know that these are unnecessary in order to use Java, so if the user refuses to install them, this will not hamper their use of Java. After a few minutes, the Java program should then be installed, and in some cases the user will have to restart their device.

Once the device has been restarted, the user may wish to go back to the Java website through this link: https://java.com/en/download/installed.jsp in order to verify whether or not the installation was completed properly. Once verified, congratulations! The Java software package has been installed and should be ready to use.

Chapter 14: Tips and tricks

How has java become so successful? Java is such a widespread language for many reasons, and it owes a lot around the key principles it was designed around. One of the first principles of Java is its ease of use. The fundamentals of the Java programming language were adapted from C ++, another extremely popular higher – level programming language. However, though C ++ and its predecessors, C and C # are powerful languages, it tends to be rather complex in terms of syntax, and is not fully adapted for some of the purposes of Java, notably for internet technology integration. Java thus was able to base itself on C ++, and build on this powerful language's fundamentals in order to provide a language that is also similarly powerful, but easier to use and better – suited for some specialized users. Java is also a very reliable programming language, intentionally build in order to reduce and even eliminate the possibilities of fatal errors that arise from programmer errors. This is why Java heavily relies on object – oriented programming principles, which allows the data and the manipulation of data to be packaged together, making Java more robust and reliable, as well as much more modular, allowing for code packages to be switched out and adapted as needed.

In addition to the previous qualities of ease of use and reliability, given Java's nature of initially being designed for mobile devices, it was designed to be able to provide a higher level of security and safety for its programming, as it was initially meant for mobile devices, which by their nature are meant to exchange data over networks, making data security of the utmost priority. Due to this, Java has become one of the most secure programming languages widely available today, making it a highly attractive option to those who wish to write programs that are less vulnerable to exploits. Also, though Java was initially intended for mobile devices, Java has developed into a relatively platform – independent programming language, something that works to its advantage, as programs written in Java tend to work no matter what machine is running the program. Java was written as a language that would be portable and work cross – platform, meaning that it doesn't matter what operating system the machine has, what hardware the machine is running, or what device it's running on. This has led to its adaptability and its widespread use around the world. Due to these core principles prioritized by the Sun Microsystems team that developed Java: Ease of Use, Reliability, Safety, Cross – platform adaptability, Java became and still remains one of the most popular and most widely used programming languages today.

Why Java?

Of course, one of the key reasons to use Java is its focus on Object – oriented programming. Object – oriented programming, or "OOP" is a type of programming language model which allows the program's code to be organized around data, rather than functions and logic, which is known as procedural programming. These "data clusters" are organized into things called "objects", hence the moniker of "object – oriented programming". These objects are created by something called "classes", understood here in the traditional sense of how classes are: types of objects, allowing the programmer to "classify" them according to two major criteria: attributes and methods. The attributes of a class are the raw data that will create the object: these are its descriptors, such as the values that it possesses, and other relevant data that will make up the object. The second criterion is the "method" of the object. This "method" is the behavior, or the logical sequences contained within the class, describing how it interacts or can be interacted with natively.

In order to make this clearer, say that there is a class "Human". This "class" will have attributes such as height, weight, gender, race. The "human" class can also have methods such as "run", "walk", "talk". These theoretical components make up the "human" class, a blueprint for an object. Now that the class has been defined, the programmer, if they so wish, can create an object using the "human" class as a blueprint. They can invoke the class "Human" and "populate" its attributes, giving it a specific height, weight, gender, and race. In addition, the object already has built – in functions such as "run", "walk", and "talk", so upon the creation of an object, let's say named "Mike" from the "Human" class, it already contains the functions to run, walk, and talk, without need for the programmer to code those specific functions again, as they are already "inherent" in the created object.

In a nutshell, that is what Object - oriented programming is meant to be: a way of programming that allows the programmer to draw on pre – defined classes so that it will be easier to describe them and use their internal, or built – in functions in order to operate them.

Assuming that the reader is not a total newbie to programming, and has been introduced to the world of programming using C or another procedural – heavy language, the next logical question would be: why even use object – oriented programming? Well, one of its main advantages is that in the long run, it saves time.

Procedural programming is usually much quicker and more straightforward in simpler algorithms and programs; rather than having to construct and define a class, and create an object based on that class, all the programmer really has to do is to simply declare the necessary variables and write the functions, and create the algorithm in order to solve the problem that they need the code to address.

However, when it comes to more complex programs, needing more complex solutions, this is where object – oriented programming begins to shine, and this is where it starts to show its strength. In a lot of programs, there will be times that there will be a number of "objects" or data clusters that have to be grouped together, and that the programmer will be treating in a certain way. This is what "classes" are meant to address. Instead of declaring a new set of variables per data cluster, they can simply draw on a pre – made "class" and create a new "object". Let's see how this would work in practice.

If a programmer were to code a chess game in procedural fashion, then they would have to manually describe each and every piece, all sixteen pawns, four bishops and four knights, four rooks, two queens, and two kings. In addition, they will have to write the functions that allow each piece to move in its own separate way. However, if the programmer makes use of object - oriented programming, instead of having to code sixteen pawns, four bishops, four knights, four rooks, two queens, two kings, they simply have to code six classes: one class to describe each piece on the board. The programmer can now simply include the movement functions within each class, and have the attributes describe their position: whether they're white king's pawn, or black queen's pawn, these are all things that can be inserted through the "attributes" portion of the "pawn" class. Instead of thirty – two clusters of code, the programmer only has to do six. Now it's much easier, much shorter, and also much more elegant.

Chapter 15: WORKBOOK

1. What is Local Variables?

2. What is Instance Variables?

3. What is Class Variables?

4. What are Constructors?

5. What are Objects?

Answers

1. local variables only function within a method. Once all the lines in that method have been executed the local variables in it get discarded. They can't be used elsewhere in your source code or even in your entire program.

2. instance variables are the variables that can be found within a class but are found outside of a method. Note that methods that are inside the class can use instance variables in that class.

3. these are variables that are also inside a class and also outside any method within that class. The big difference is that class variables are created using the static keyword.

4. This is another important topic in Java OOP. A constructor in Java is a specialized method that you will use to initialize an object. But what if you forget to write a constructor? If that happens, then the compiler will create a constructor for you.

5. Think of objects as bundles of data—a more powerful variable as it were. Now, other than bundles of data (remember, variables only hold or contain data) objects in Java also contain the actual instructions that create some sort of behavior—in other words they contain methods.

Conclusion

This book has taken you through the core fundamentals of Java to help you develop the right foundation to explore deeper concepts in Java. It is important for you to understand the various data types in Java: the variables, strings, and arrays. In addition, mastering the method, classes, and inheritance is crucial. Remember. Java is an object-oriented language. This means that having a deep understanding of the topic of classes, methods, and inheritance is fundamental.

Java is a very powerful language, it powers the majority of enterprises and organizations. It is one of the best languages for developers when they want to implement internet-based applications. Furthermore, software devices which must cross communicate over a given network are developed with the help of Java. Many devices today use Java. This shows how Java is an important computer programming language. While this book has tried to present you with the basics skills of programming in Java, it is highly important to emphasize that it is just a starting point. Java goes beyond the elements which determine the language. For you to become an excellent Java programmer, you need to take time to read deep and master the concepts in Java. Luckily, this book helps you develop the right knowledge to expand more on other areas of Java. Therefore, the next step for you to take after reading this book is to look for a comprehensive Java textbook to read.

PYTHON PROGRAMMING

The Practical Beginner's Guide to Learn Python Programming in One Day Step-by-Step (#2020 Updated Version | Effective Computer Programming)

Steve Tudor

Text	Copyright	©

All rights reserved. No part of this guide may be reproduced in any form without permission in writing from the publisher except in the case of brief quotations embodied in critical articles or reviews.

Legal & Disclaimer

The information contained in this book and its contents is not designed to replace or take the place of any form of medical or professional advice; and is not meant to replace the need for independent medical, financial, legal or other professional advice or services, as may be required. The content and information in this book has been provided for educational and entertainment purposes only.

The content and information contained in this book has been compiled from sources deemed reliable, and it is accurate to the best of the Author's knowledge, information and belief. However, the Author cannot guarantee its accuracy and validity and cannot be held liable for any errors and/or omissions. Further, changes are periodically made to this book as and when needed. Where appropriate and/or necessary, you must consult a professional (including but not limited to your doctor, attorney, financial advisor or such other professional advisor) before using any of the suggested remedies, techniques, or information in this book.

Upon using the contents and information contained in this book, you agree to hold harmless the Author from and against any damages, costs, and expenses, including any legal fees potentially resulting from the application of any of the information provided by this book. This disclaimer applies to any loss, damages or injury caused by the use and application, whether directly or indirectly, of any advice or information presented, whether for breach of contract, tort, negligence, personal injury, criminal intent, or under any other cause of action.

You agree to accept all risks of using the information presented inside this book.

You agree that by continuing to read this book, where appropriate and/or necessary, you shall consult a professional (including but not limited to your doctor, attorney, or financial advisor or such other advisor as needed) before using any of the suggested remedies, techniques, or information in this book.

CHAPTER 1. WHAT IS PYTHON

Python is basically an incredibly useful and powerful language. It's present essentially everywhere. Everything from the scripting side of video games (or the video games themselves) to intensive server-side web applications to the plethora of deep and responsive desktop applications that have been built with it.

When should you use Python? The answer depends upon exactly what you're going to do. But since you're a beginner, I say you should learn anyway.

As you continue to grow as a programmer after this book, you're going to learn when you should and shouldn't use Python just as a matter of intuition. Python is an absolutely fantastic language, but the place where it fails is when you have to get extremely close to a computer's hardware or write incredibly efficient programs. In these areas, Python doesn't excel.

However, that's not to say it doesn't have its perks. In fact, I'd say that's one of the few places that Python falls flat. And what it lacks there, it makes up for in other areas. For example, development time in Python is generally extremely low in comparison to other languages. This is super easy to illustrate. Compare the following excerpts of code, the first from C++, the second from Java, and the last from Python.

A. WHY TO LEARN PYTHON

Learning the ABCs of anything in this world, is a must. Knowing the essentials is winning half the battle before you get started. It's easier to proceed when you are equipped with the fundamentals of what you are working on.

In the same manner that before you embark on the other aspects of python let us level off the basic elements first. You need to learn and understand the basics of python as a foundation in advancing to the more complicated components.

This fundamental information will greatly help you as you go on and make the learning experience easier and enjoyable.

Familiarize yourself with the Python Official Website https://www.python.org/. Knowing well the website of python would give you the leverage in acquiring more information and scaling up your knowledge about python. Also, you can get the needed links for your work

Learn from Python collections. Locate python collections such as records, books, papers, files, documentations and archives and learn from it. You can pick up a number of lessons from these, and expand your knowledge about Python. There are also tutorials, communities and forums at your disposal.

Possess the SEO Basics. Acquire some education on Search Engine Optimization so you can interact with experts in the field and improve your python level of knowledge. That being said, here are the basic elements of Python.

B. DIFFERENT VERSIONS OF PYTHON

With Guido van Rossum at the helm of affairs, Python has witness three versions over the years since its conception in the '80s. These versions represent the growth, development, and evolution of the scripting language over time, and cannot be done without in telling the history of Python.

The Versions of Python Include The Following;

- **Python 0.9.0:**

The first-ever version of Python released following its implementation and in-house releases at the Centrum Wiskunde and Informatica (CWI) between the years 1989 and 1990, was tagged version 0.9.0. This early version which was released on alt.sources had features such as exception handling, functions, and classes with inheritance, as well as the core data types of list, str, dict, among others in its development. The first release came with a module system obtained from Module-3, which Van Rossum defined as one of the central programming units used in the development of Python.

Another similarity the first release bore with Module-3 is found in the exception model which comes with an added else clause. With the public release of this early version came a flurry of users which culminated in the formation of a primary discussion forum for Python in 1994. The group was named comp.lang.python and served as a milestone for the growing popularity of Python users.

Following the release of the first version in the 29th of February, 1991, there were seven other updates made to the early version 0.9.0. These updates took varying tags under the 0.9.0 version and were spread out over nearly three years (1991 to 1993). The first version update came in the form of Python 0.9.1, which was released in the same month of February 1991 as its predecessor. The next update came in the autumn period of the release year, under the label Python 0.9.2. By Christmas Eve of the same year (1991) python published its third update to the earliest version under the label Python 0.9.4. By January of the succeeding year, the 2nd precisely, a gift update under the label Python 0.9.5 was released. By the 6th of April, 1992, a sixth update followed named, Python 0.9.6. It wasn't until the next year, 1993, that a seventh update was released under the tag Python 0.9.8. The eighth and final update to the earliest version came five months after the seventh, on the 29th of July, 1993, and was dubbed python 0.9.9.

These updates marked the first generation of python development before it transcended into the next version label.

- **Python 1.0**

After the last update to Python 0.9.0, a new version, Python 1.0, was released in January of the following year. 1994 marked the addition of key new features to the Python programming language. Functional programming tools such as map, reduce, filter, and lambda were part of the new features of the version 1 release. Van Rossum mentioned that the obtainment of map, lambda, reduce and filter was made possible by a LISP hacker who missed them and submitted patches that worked. Van Rossum's contract with CWI came to an end with the release of the first update version 1.2 on the 10th of April, 1995. In the same year, Van Rossum went on to join CNRI (Corporation for National Research Initiatives) in Reston, Virginia, United States, where he continued to work on Python and published different version updates.

Nearly six months following the first version update, version 1.3 was released on the 12th of October, 1995. The third update, version 1.4, came almost a year later in October of 1996. By then, Python had developed numerous added features. Some of the typical new features included an inbuilt support system for complex numbers and keyword arguments which, although inspired by Modula-3, shared a bit of a likeness to the keyword arguments of Common Lisp. Another included feature was a simple form hiding data through name mangling, although it could be easily bypassed.

It was during his days at CNRI that Van Rossum began the CP4E (Computer Programming for Everybody) program which was aimed at making more people get easy access to programming by engaging in simple literacy of programming languages. Python was a pivotal element to van Rossum's campaign, and owing to its concentration on clean forms of syntax; Python was an already suitable programming language. Also, since the goals of ABC and CP4E were quite similar, there was no hassle putting Python to use. The program was pitched to and funded by DARPA, although it did become inactive in 2007 after running for eight years. However, Python still tries to be relatively easy to learn by not being too arcane in its semantics and syntax, although no priority is made of reaching out to non-programmers again.

The year 2000 marked another significant step in the development of Python when the python core development team switched to a new platform — BeOpen.com where a new group, BeOpen PythonLabs team was formed. At the request of CNRI, a new version update 1.6 was released on the 5th of September, succeeding the fourth version update (Python 1.5) on the December of 1997. This update marked the complete cycle of development for the programming language at CNRI because the development team left shortly afterward. This change affected the timelines of release for the new version Python 2.0 and the version 1.6 update; causing them to clash. It was only a question of time before Van Rossum, and his crew of PythonLabs developers switched to Digital Creations, with Python 2.0 as the only version ever released by BeOpen.com.

With the version 1.6 release caught between a switch of platforms, it didn't take long for CNRI to include a license in the version release of Python 1.6. The license contained in the release was quite more prolonged than the previously used CWI license, and it featured a clause mentioning that the license was under the protection of the laws applicable to the State of Virginia. This intervention sparked a legal feud which led The Free Software Foundation into a debate regarding the "choice-of-law" clause being incongruous with that if the GNU General Public License. At this point, there was a call to negotiations between FSF, CNRI, and BeOoen regarding changing to Python's free software license which would serve to make it compatible with GPL. The negotiation process resulted in the release of another version update under the name of Python 1.6.1. This new version was no different from its predecessor in any way asides a few new bug fixes and the newly added GPL-compatible license.

- **Python 2.0:**

After the many legal dramas surrounding the release of the second-generation Python 1.0 which corroborated into the release of an unplanned update (version 1.6.1), Python was keen to put all behind and forge ahead. So, in October of 2000, Python 2.0 was released. The new release featured new additions such as list comprehensions which were obtained from other functional programming languages Haskell and SETL. The syntax of this latest version was akin to that found in Haskell, but different in that Haskell used punctuation characters while Python stuck to alphabetic keywords.

Python 2.0 also featured a garbage collection system which was able to collect close reference cycles. A version update (Python 2.1) quickly followed the release of Python 2.0, as did Python 1.6.1. However, due to the legal issue over licensing, Python renamed the license on the new release to Python Software Foundation License. As such, every new specification, code or documentation added from the release of version update 2.1 was owned and protected by the PSF (Python Software Foundation) which was a nonprofit organization created in the year 2001. The organization was designed similarly to the Apache Software Foundation. The release of version 2.1 came with changes made to the language specifications, allowing support of nested scopes such as other statically scoped languages. However, this feature was, by default, not in use and unrequired until the release of the next update, version 2.2 on the 21st of December, 2001.

Python 2.2 came with a significant innovation of its own in the form of a unification of all Python's types and classes. The unification process merged the types coded in C and the classes coded in Python into a single hierarchy. The unification process caused Python's object model to remain totally and continuously object-oriented. Another significant innovation was the addition of generators as inspired by Icon. Two years after the release of version 2.2, version 2.3 was published in July of 2003. It was nearly another two years before version 2.4 was released on the 30th of November in 2004. Version 2.5 came less than a year after Python 2.4, in

September of 2006. This version introduced a "with" statement containing a code block in a context manager; as in obtaining a lock before running the code block and releasing the lock after that or opening and closing a file. The block of code made for behavior similar to RAII (Resource Acquisition Is Initialization) and swapped the typical "try" or "finally" idiom.

The release of version 2.6 on the 1st of October, 2008 was strategically scheduled such that it coincided with the release of Python 3.0. Asides the proximity in release date, version 2.6 also had some new features like the "warnings" mode which outlined the use of elements which had been omitted from Python 3.0. Subsequently, in July of 2010, another update to Python 2.0 was released in the version of python 2.7. The new version updates shared features and coincided in release with version 3.1 — the first version update of python 3. At this time, Python drew an end to the release of Parallel 2.x and 3.x, making python 2.7 the last version update of the 2.x series. Python went public in 2014, November precisely, to announce to its username that the availability of python 2.7 would stretch until 2020. However, users were advised to switch to python 3 in their earliest convenience.

- **Python 3.0:**

The fourth generation of Python, Python 3.0, otherwise known as Py3K and python 3000, was published on the 3rd of December 2008. This version was designed to fix the fundamental flaws in the design system of the scripting language. A new version number had to be made to implement the required changes which could not be run while keeping the stock compatibility of the 2.x series that was by this time redundant. The guiding rule for the creation of python 3 was to limit the duplication of features by taking out old formats of processing stuff. Otherwise, Python three still followed the philosophy with which the previous versions were made. Albeit, as Python had evolved to accumulate new but redundant ways of programming alike tasks, python 3.0 was emphatically targeted at quelling duplicative modules and constructs in keeping with the philosophy of making one "and

preferably only one" apparent way of doing things. Regardless of these changes, though, version 3.0 maintained a multi-paradigm language, even though it didn't share compatibility with its predecessor.

The lack of compatibility meant Python 2.0 codes were unable to be run on python 3.0 without proper modifications. The dynamic typing used in Python as well as the intention to change the semantics of specific methods of dictionaries, for instance, made a perfect mechanical conversion from the 2.x series to version 3.0 very challenging. A tool, name of 2to3, was created to handle the parts of translation which could be automatically done. It carried out its tasks quite successfully, even though an early review stated that the tool was incapable of handling certain aspects of the conversion process. Proceeding the release of version 3.0, projects that required compatible with both the 2.x and 3.x series were advised to be given a singular base for the 2.x series. The 3.x series platform, on the other hand, was to produce releases via the 2to3 tool.

For a long time, editing the Python 3.0 codes were forbidden because they required being run on the 2.x series. However, now, it is no longer necessary. The reason being that in 2012, the recommended method was to create a single code base which could run under the 2.x and 3.x series through compatibility modules. Between the December of 2008 and July 2019, 8 version updates have been published under the python 3.x series. The current version as at the 8th of July 2019 is the Python 3.7.4. Within this timeframe, many updates have been made to the programming language, involving the addition of new features mentioned below:

1. Print which used to be a statement was changed to an inbuilt function, making it relatively easier to swap out a module in utilizing different print

functions as well as regularizing the syntax. In the late versions of the 2.x series, (python 2.6 and 2.7), print is introduced as inbuilt, but is concealed by a syntax of the print statement which is capable of being disabled by entering the following line of code into the top of the file: from__future__import print_function

2. The [input] function in the Python 2.x series was removed, and the [raw_input] function to [input] was renamed. The change was such that the [input] function of Python 3 behaves similarly to the [raw_input] function of the python 2.x series; meaning input is typically outputted in the form of strings instead of being evaluated as a single expression.

3. [reduce] was removed with the exemption of [map] and [filter] from the in-built namespace into [functools]. The reason behind this change is that operations involving [reduce] are better expressed with the use of an accumulation loop.

4. Added support was provided for optional function annotations which could be used in informal type declarations as well as other purposes.

5. The [str]/[unicode] types were unified, texts represented, and immutable bytes type were introduced separately as well as a mutable [bytearray] type which was mostly corresponding; both of which indicate several arrays of bytes.

6. Taking out the backward-compatibility features such as implicit relative imports, old-style classes, and string exceptions.

7. Changing the mode of integer division functionality. For instance, in the Python 2.x series, 5/2 equals 2. Note that in the 3.x series, 5/2 equals 2.5. From the recent versions of the 2.x series beginning from version 2.2 up until python 3: 5//2 equals 2.

In contemporary times, version releases in the version 3.x series have all been equipped with added, substantial new features; and every ongoing development on Python is being done in line with the 3.x series.

C. HOW TO DOWNLOAD AND INSTALL PYTHON

In this time and age, being techy is a demand of the times, and the lack of knowledge, classifies one as an outback. This can result to being left out from the career world, especially in the field of programming.

Numerous big shot companies have employed their own programmers for purposes of branding, and to cut back on IT expenses.

In the world of programming, using Python language is found to be easier and programmer-friendly, thus, the universal use.

Discussed below are information on how to download python for MS Windows. In this particular demo, we have chosen windows because it's the most common worldwide – even in not so progressive countries. We want to cater to the programming needs of everyone all over the globe.

Python 2.7.12 version was selected because this version bridges the gap between the old version 2 and the new version 3.

Some of the updated functions/applications of version 3 are still not compatible with some devices, so 2.7.12 is a smart choice.

Steps in downloading Python 2.7.12, and installing it on Windows

1. Type python on your browser and press the Search button to display the search results.

Scroll down to find the item you are interested in. In this instance, you are looking for python. click "python releases for windows", and a new page opens. See image below:

2. Select the Python version, python 2.7.12, and click, or you can select the version that is compatible to your device or OS.

Python Releases for Windows

- Latest Python 2 Release - Python 2.7.12
- Latest Python 3 Release - Python 3.5.2

- Python 3.6.0b1 - 2016-09-12
    - Download Windows x86 web-based installer
    - Download Windows x86 executable installer
    - Download Windows x86 embeddable zip file
    - Download Windows x86-64 web-based installer
    - Download Windows x86-64 executable installer
    - Download Windows x86-64 embeddable zip file
    - Download Windows help file
- Python 3.6.0a4 - 2016-08-15
    - Download Windows x86 web-based installer
    - Download Windows x86 executable installer
    - Download Windows x86 embeddable zip file
    - Download Windows x86-64 web-based installer
    - Download Windows x86-64 executable installer
    - Download Windows x86-64 embeddable zip file

3. The new page contains the various python types. Scroll down and select an option: in this instance, select Windows x86 MSI installer and click.

Files

Version	Operating System	Description	MD5 Sum	File Size	GPG
	Mac OS X	for Mac OS X 10.5 and later			
	Mac OS X	for Mac OS X 10.5 and later			
	Windows				
	Windows				
	Windows				
	Windows	for AMD64/EM64T/x64, not itanium processors			
	Windows				

4. Press the Python box at the bottom of your screen. **<u>Click the "Run" button, and wait for the new window to appear.</u>**

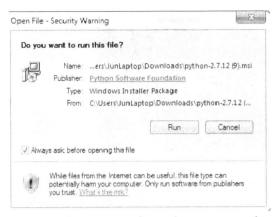

5. Select the user options that you require and press "NEXT".

Your screen will display the hard drive where your python will be located.

6. Press the "NEXT" button.

7. Press yes, and wait for a few minutes. Sometimes it can take longer for the application to download, depending on the speed of your internet.

8. After that, click the FINISHED button to signify that the installation has been completed

Your python has been installed in your computer and is now ready to use. Find it in drive C, or wherever you have saved it.

There can be glitches along the way, but there are options which are presented in this article. If you follow it well, there is no reason that you cannot perform this task.

It's important to note that there's no need to compile programs. Python is an interpretive language and can execute quickly your commands.

You can also download directly from the Python website, by selecting any of these versions – 3.5.2 or 2.7.12. and clicking 'download'. (For this book, 2.7.12 is used, in general, for easy discussions).

See image below:

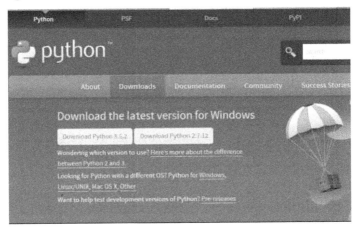

Follow the step by step instructions prompted by the program itself. Save and run the program in your computer.

For Mac

To download Python on Mac, you can follow a similar procedure, but this time, you will have to access the "Python.mpkg" file, to run the installer.

For Linux

For Linux, Python 2 and 3 may have been installed by default. Hence, check first your operating system. You can check if your device has already a Python program, by accessing your command prompt and entering this: python—version, or python3—version.

If Python is not installed in your Linux, the result "command not found" will be displayed. You may want to download both Python 2.7.12 and any of the versions of Python 3 for your

Linux. This is due to the fact that Linux can have more compatibility with Python 3.

For windows users, now that you have downloaded the program, you're ready to start.

And yes, congratulations! You can now begin working and having fun with your Python programming system.

D. WRITING THE FIRST PYTHON PROGRAM

Beginners may find it difficult to start using Python. It's a given and nothing's wrong about that. However, your desire to learn will make it easier for you to gradually become familiar with the language.

Here are the specific steps you can follow to start using Python.

Steps in using Python

Step #1–Read all about Python.

Python has included a README information in your downloaded version. It's advisable to read it first, so you will learn more about the program.

You can start using your Python through the command box (black box), or you can go to your saved file and read first the README file by clicking it.

See image below:

This box will appear.

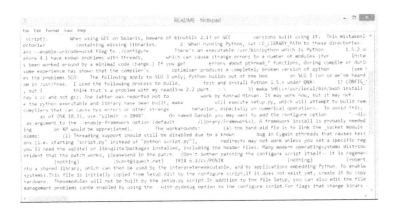

You can read the content completely, if you want to understand more what the program is all about, the file-setup, and similar information.

This is a long data that informs you of how to navigate and use Python. Also, Python welcomes new contributions for its further development.

You can copy paste the content of the box into a Window document for better presentation.

If you don't want to know all the other information about Python and you're raring to go, you can follow these next steps.

Step #2–Start using Python.

First open the Python file you have saved in your computer. Click on Python as show below. In some versions, you just click 'python'for the shell to appear.

See image below:

You can start using Python by utilizing the simplest function, which is 'print'. It's the simplest statement or directive of python. It prints a line or string that you specify.

For Python 2, print command may or may not be enclosed in parenthesis or brackets, while in Python 3 you have to enclose print with brackets.

Example for Python 2:

print "Welcome to My Corner."

Example for Python 3:

print ("Welcome to My Corner")

The image below shows what appears when you press 'enter'.

You may opt to use a Python shell through idle. If you do, this is how it would appear:

In the Python 3.5.2 version, the text colors are: function (purple), string (green) and the result (blue). (The string is composed of the words inside the bracket ("Welcome to My Corner"), while the function is the command word outside the bracket (print).

Take note that the image above is from the Python 2.7.12 version.

You have to use indentation for your Python statements/codes. The standard Python code uses four spaces. The indentations are used in place of braces or blocks.

In some programming languages, you usually use semi-colons at the end of the commands–in python, you don't need to add semi-colons at the end of the whole statement.

In Python, semi-colons are used in separating variables inside the brackets.

For version 3, click on your downloaded Python program and save the file in your computer. Then Click on IDLE (Integrated DeveLopment Environment), your shell will appear. You can now start using your Python.It's preferable to use idle, so that your codes can be interpreted directly by idle.

Alternative method to open a shell (for some versions).

An alternative method to use your Python is to open a shell through the following steps:

Step #1– Open your menu.

After downloading and saving your Python program in your computer, open your menu and find your saved Python file. You may find it in the downloaded files of your computer or in the files where you saved it.

Step #2–Access your Python file.

Open your saved Python file (Python 27) by double clicking it. The contents of Python 27 will appear. Instead of clicking on Python directly (as shown above), click on Lib instead. See image below.

This will appear:

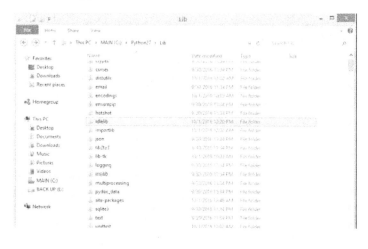

Step #3–Click on 'idlelib'.

Clicking the 'idlelib' will show this content:

Step #4–Click on idle to show the Python shell.

When you click on any of the 'idle' displayed on the menu, the 'white' shell will be displayed, as shown below:

The differences between the three 'idle' menu, is that the first two 'idle' commands have the black box (shell) too, while the last 'idle' has only the 'white' box (shell). I prefer the third 'idle' because it's easy to use.

Step #5–Start using your Python shell.

You can now start typing Python functions, using the shell above.

You may have noticed that there are various entries to the contents of each of the files that you have opened. You can click and open all of them, as you progress in learning more about your Python programming.

Python is a programming language that has been studied by students for several days or months. Thus, what's presented in this book are the basics for beginners.

CHAPTER 2. BASIC OF PYTHON

Python can be used as an active translator or transcriber by interaction through the web. It can also be employed to formulate lessons. In interaction, though, there is one serious concern: that is, it is impossible to keep a copy of what transpired. On the other hand, using lessons allows you to keep a record of the work done. In the interactive translator, you are allowed to open only one display page, while in lessons, you can open as many as you need.

Variables

Python uses information that are not constant, these are used to keep the data. When using these, be sure to put descriptions. These data could be names, age, addresses, gender and other similar material.

Outputs and Inputs

Any computer program requires interfacing between itself and the person using it. The user encodes and that is input, and the output is printing what has been encoded.

Mathematics

Numbers are the common language in computer programs including Python. Mathematical operations are used by Python as you will learn later on. Most of its language are represented by mathematical equations and symbols.

Loop

You need to understand the term loop in python. It is a symbol used to represent repeated word/s or sentence/s in python programming. Anything that is being repeatedly used can employ a loop.

Python categories

It is important to be acquainted with the types of python product categories for easy reference and understanding. Python categories are symbolized by A, B, C that signifies the shifts in language. Examples are 3.3.1 to 3.3.2. This means there are minor changes, but when it employs something like 2.xx to 3.xx it means there are major changes.

Cutting

This is a critical component of python which is used to copy the desired part of a data. It is a method of making programs simple by concentrating on items from a gamut of data. When you do that, you are actually removing components that are not relevant to the program.

Modules

Modules are files of descriptions and declarations of Python. It is a list of all the terminologies used by python with corresponding explanations of each. Python adopts a method of consolidating definitions into one folder called **module**. These modules can be introduced into different modules depending on the needs of the programmer or user.

This is created to allow users to have a better understanding and easy access to the standard library of Python. A programmer or even a beginner can make modules for his use.

Modules can be on: Indexing and searching, Audio and Music, Web development, Console and Database. Python provides an array of modules that you can use. You can also make your own.

Source codes

Generating Python source codes can be tedious,if you don't know how to derive your codes.

Program developers have now an application that converts your Python 2 codes to Python version 3 codes from AST.

You can create your own code as discussed in the chapters, and it's easy to append strings to a list to create a code, but it won't hurt you, if you know how to generate Python source codes. One way of doing this is to use context managers.

These are the most basic elements in python, there are more but with the ones presented, one can already start using python and learn the others, as you go on in your programming.

CHAPTER 3. FULL INSTRUCTIONS ON HOW TO CODE

We have touched on this first topic already, but we will expand and reiterate here. First up is naming conventions.

Comments

Here are some best practices for your comments that will help other readers understand you easier:

- Start with a summary of the sketch and what it will accomplish. Provide any links if it helps the understanding of your design. Try to approach your block comments from a user-friendly stance as much as possible to give a clear idea of what you will be doing.

- Write in the active voice. Use a clear, conversational tone for your writing, as if you were speaking to another person standing next to you.

- For instructions to the user, use the second person, to invoke in the user that they should be the ones to carry out your instructions.

- Use short descriptive phrases rather than complex phrases. It is easier to understand one simple idea at a time.

- Be explicit about what you are doing with your actions. For example: "Next, you'll read the value of the sensor on pin **thisPin**."

- Avoid phrases or words that are 'fluff' or do not contribute to the explanation, e.g. you see, you'd want to, etc. Instead, skip those words and give a statement that's direct to the point, e.g. set the pins.

- Check your assumptions, make sure you have explained all of your ideas and haven't left something that can only be explained 'in your head.'
- Give a description for every variable or constant with a comment of its purpose either before, or in line with the variable or constant.
- Similarly, give an explanation of a block of code that you're about to perform before the instructions are executed, so it's clear what's about to happen.
- Every loop should have comments explaining why this loop exists (e.g. what it is doing), and a verbal explanation of its condition if it's still not clear.

Coding Best Practices
- Follow naming conventions

Do not create one letter variable names! Your naming conventions exist so that you can, at a glance, read your code without having to refer to other places to understand what is going on.

- Write code that is reusable or modular

User-defined functions are a great way to accomplish this. By doing this, you can write a segment of code in just one place and refer to it each time it is necessary. This makes better sense and is much cleaner and simpler to read.

- Write a flow-chart of your sketch **before you start coding**

Seriously, this cannot be overstated how valuable this step is to write clean code. By knowing all the pieces you will need to accomplish your sketch's task ahead of time conceptually, you can successfully plan ahead and use things like functions in a smart way.

- Keep things organize and together

If you make a function to smooth an analog sensor, make sure that's all it does. Don't start doing other parts of your code within that function. If your function needs to, you can have it call yet another function to help it accomplish its task. Again think modular (small pieces make a big part).

- Make yourself a toolbox

Make functions that do specific things. Then use your tools as needed in your code.

- Keep your sketches

Even if you think you won't need a sketch you made anymore, keep them. If you need a piece of code that you've already written for another project and you have followed these practices, you can simply snag that piece of code and drop it into the new project you're working on. Brilliant!

- Write your functions in a generalized way whenever possible for these exact reasons

To put this simply, it means that if you were making a function to draw a square, make a function to draw a rectangle instead since a square is a special case of a rectangle, where the edges are equal.

- Make sure your functions do what they **say** they will do

E.g., if it is a function named 'flickerLeds' (**pinValue**), it better be flickering some LEDs!

- Avoid pointers

We didn't even touch on them in this document, and we are only going to tell you they exist to tell you not to use them unless you're an advanced user. They are the most likely 'tool' to cause the crazy, bad kinds of problems from happening in your coding, and are notoriously tough for a beginner to use properly. So avoid them until you are sure you know what you are doing.

- Embrace self-improvement

Understand from day 1 that as a fledgling coder that you will grow and improve over time. Use each challenge you come across to try writing new sketches as an opportunity to grow and hone your skills.

- Reach out to the community for help and advice!

There are some really fantastic people in our big community of hobbyists that are willing to help you learn and grow as an enthusiast. This is a great way to meet friends and learn so many new ways to do things you may not have thought about previously.

- Try to make things foolproof when you code

Try to make sure your for loops terminate, try to account for unexpected inputs when checking values, try to constrain your data within expected values. These 'tedious' steps are what keeps your program running smooth and bug-free!

- Know how to use debugging tools and techniques

It's a more advanced topic but learning about debugging tools and techniques for large-scale projects such as robotics, or as a controller for something like a pump mechanism will help expand your knowledge further.

- Write both brackets or both braces at the start then fill in the date in-between

When writing functions, loops or anything with brackets and braces, this trick helps to ensure that you will be closing all of your brackets and braces, preventing unexpected results.

- Try new ways to use your Arduino!

This is how you can really develop new skills. When you have more skills, you can think of even more things you can do with the chip! The possibilities with this microcontroller are nearly limitless and are bound only by the limits of your imagination.

More Naming Best Practices

- Functions follow the same rules as variables

The name should start with a lower-case letter, all one word, and additional words are distinguished with capital letters.

- Functions should use verb names to describe their function

E.g. **stepMotor()**, **getValue()**, **smoothReadings()**, etc. All these names explain with an action word what this function should be doing.

- Make the name describe the purpose of the function

- Make sure the for loop variables are clear on what they represent

Having a variable of **x** can work, but it really offers nothing to the person reading your code for them to understand exactly what that variable is for.

CHAPTER 4. HOW TO MAKE PREDICTIONS WITH ALGORITHM

How are you feeling at this stage? Have you encountered any errors? Are you feeling as if you have gained some new knowledge?

Hopefully, things are going smoothly and you are grasping the concepts well at this point. Let's take a look at how to make predictions with algorithms in Python and what it means.

WHAT IS PREDICTIVE ANALYSTICS?

"Predictive Analysis" is regularly talked about with regards to building information, for instance, originating from instruments, specific sensors and associated frameworks in the real world. Business data, at an organization, for example, may incorporate exchange information, deals results, client dissensions, and promote data. Progressively, organizations settle on information-driven choices in light of this important aggregation of data.

With a significant growth in competition, organizations look for a competitive advantage in bringing items and administrations to open markets. Information-focused models typically enable organizations to take care of long-standing issues in creative and unique ways.

Manufacturers, for instance, often think that it is difficult to enhance just its equipment. Item designers can add prescient abilities to existing answers for increased incentives to the client. Utilizing prescient examination for hardware upkeep, or prescient support, can predict future product development disappointments, figure vitality accurately, and decrease working expenses. For instance, sensors that measure certain wave patterns and vibrations in car parts, and in turn, flag the requirements for upkeep before the car/automobile flops during use by an actual consumer.

Additionally, organizations utilize a prescient investigation to make more exact predictions, for example, estimating the increased demand for power on the electrical grids. These figures enable companies to do asset planning, like looking for other power plants, in order to be more efficient and effective.

To extricate an increase in value from all of the information, organizations apply calculations to vast information sets, utilizing new and upcoming technology tools, for example, Hadoop. The information sources may comprise value-based databases, hardware log files, pictures, audio/video, sensory details, or a number of other kinds of information. True innovation is often the result of using and combining data from a variety of different sources.

With this information, these technologies are of critical importance in the discovery of trends and patterns. Machine learning methods are utilized to discover commonalities and patterns in information and to estimate what the outcomes are going to be.

What does Predictive analysis do? What does it mean?

Predictable analytics allows groups in different job roles, ranging from financial, healthcare workers in pharmacy industries, and automobile. This particular analytical process is how we utilize the data that we have analyzed in order to make viable guesses which are largely based on the analyzed information.

Whew! Don't panic.

The great thing is that this process is a predictive model which allows for a systematic approach of delivering outcomes based on a certain set of common criteria.

To define what "predictive analytics" means, this process involves applying a certain statistical approach based on Python machine learning strategies and models which creates realistic and measurable estimations and predictions about future outcomes. Regularly, Python machine learning techniques are used in real-world problem-solving. For example, it is commonly used to estimate the value of something in the near future such as "**How long can my word processor run before needing it to be replaced or require routine maintenance?**"

Constructed on a set of criteria, it can also be used to guess certain customer behaviors. A great deal of banks and financial institutions use this to determine the creditworthiness of their customers, how likely they are to default on their mortgage or car loan, or the probability of excessive overdrafts each month. It's pretty amazing.

Predictive analytics is primarily used in helping companies and organizations make future predictions and meet certain goals. Think about the most common goals of any business: stay in business, make money, and reduce excess waste through the analyzing of data, methods decrease expenses and ability to offer employee bonuses if goals are met. To do something of this scale does require an extensive amount of various data types and inputting them into pre-built models that will ultimately generate concise, measurable, and most importantly—achievable outcomes to maintain a positive bottom line and support growth.

In order to make this click, let's look back at what we said: "predictive analysis" is and what it's for, as it relates to some real-world examples. These are not all inclusive by any means, and more can be found using a simple Google search and research.

Real World Examples of Predictive Analytics:

The Car Industry–Breakthrough technology in cars, designed to gather specific details and information regarding how fast the car is going, how far the car has traveled, its emission levels and the behaviors of drivers are now used with an extremely sophisticated predictive analysis model. This allows the analysts to release extremely beneficial data for car manufacturers, insurance companies, and the racing circles.

Aviation–Determining the viability and health of an aircraft is an application developed by an aviation engineer, it helped improve the performance of aircraft speed and reduce costs to maintain and repair them. This particular application is used to test performance in every critical function of the plan from the take-off, to the control systems, all the way to the efficiency of the fuel and maximum take-off conditions.

The Production of Energy–Electricity companies use predictive analytics in order to determine the cost and demand for electrical supplies. There are a ton of extremely sophisticated models that forecast access, patterns (future and past), the different changes in weather and many other factors.

Accounting and Financial Services–The Development of credit risk models is a prime example of predictive analytics in the real world. Nowadays, banks, credit unions, and many other financial institutions use these models and applications in order to determine a customer or potential client's credit risk.

Equipment and Machine Manufacturing—Testing and determining future machine weaknesses and failures. This particular application is used in helping to improve the efficiency of assembly lines and production of large equipment and machines and at the same time optimizing its operations and workforce.

Modern Medicine–This is last on the list, but certainly not least. Predictive analysis has been used in modern medicine to detect infections and common diseases and even pre-existing conditions. It's also a great way to bridge the communication gaps between those in the medical profession.

Pretty cool, huh? Can you find more ways that predictive analysis is used in real-world situations to improve our life, our economy, and our businesses?

WORKFLOW IN PREDICTIVE ANALYSTICS:

You may or may not be familiar with predictive models at this stage of your learning, but you can think of a real-world example as to what meteorologists use in day to day weather forecasting.

A basic industry utilization of prescient models identifies with any circuit that consumes power and allows a prediction to be made about the demand for power, as it relates here—energy. For this model, network administrators and brokers require precise conjectures of each circuit load to make important choices for integrating them into the electrical grid framework. Huge amounts of information are easily accessible and utilizing these prescient analytics, allowing matrix administrators to transform this data into noteworthy bits of knowledge that can be used to make important decisions and predictions.

Typically, a simple workflow for a predictive analytics model will follow these basic steps outlined here:

- Import information from changed sources, for example, web chronicles, databases, and spreadsheets.

- Information sources incorporate energy load data and information in a CSV record and national climate information demonstrating temperatures and varying dew points.

- Clean the information by evacuating anomalies and joining information sources.

- Distinguish information spikes; especially pinpoint missing information, or even bizarre outputs to expel from the information.

- Make a solitary table including energy load, temperature and dew point.

- Build a precise data model in light of the accumulated information.

- Predicting any type of energy source is a perplexing procedure with numerous factors. You may utilize neural systems to assemble and prepare a prescient model.

- Practice training through your data index to achieve diverse strategies. At the point when the preparation is finished, you can attempt the model against new information to perceive how well it performs.

- Coordinate the model into a front gauging framework in a production type of environment.

- When you locate a model that precisely gauges the outcomes, you can move it into your creation framework, making the examination accessible to programming projects or gadgets, including web applications, servers, or smartphones.

Your aggregated data tells a tale that is certainly complex. To withdraw the insights, you are going to need an extremely accurate design which is predictive. This might not be the best step as a beginner; nonetheless, it is here for reference to the entire picture of Python capabilities.

Predictive analysis is being modeled after major mathematical models to predict a conference or result. These designs forecast the desired outcome at some future time based on modifications placed into data inputs. Using a repetitive procedure, you create the models by choosing a training information set where you will proceed to test and further validate the information. After you examine it to ascertain its reliability and accuracy in predicting forecasts, play around with different methods until you find one that is comfortable for you. The important thing is that you choose one that you can understand, learn and apply without much effort.

To give you an idea of some good examples of such a method, you can try a time-series reversal model for predicting low and even high levels of flight traffic or fuel. Of course, this is certainly predicting based on a linear approach to speed compared to upload and continuing to be extremely beneficial in real-world estimation models for conjecture.

WHAT IS DIFFERENCE BETWEEN PREDICTIVE ANALYSTICS & PRESCRIPTIVE ANALYSTICS?

Businesses that have been able to successfully implement predictive analytics have a competitive advantage to problems, situations and good things in the future. Predictive analytics is a process that creates an estimation of what will happen next—literally. It also gives you tips simple about how to be able to make high-level decisions in a way that maximizes the information you wouldn't have access to.

Prescriptive analytics is just a branch of data analytics that makes use of designs that are predictive guesses to make for the most ideal outcomes. Prescriptive examination depends on advancement and tenets-based procedures for decision-making on a most basic of levels. Anticipating any issues or strains on the framework is absolutely essential in the decision-making process. It means what is to be done is based on the prediction.

CHAPTER 5. INTRODUCTION TO BASIC DATA TYPES

In this Chapter, we will discuss data types, Python implementations, and standard data. I am sure that after reading this Chapter and the book, you will be able to create a program that will allow users to use Python methods and logic to manipulate numbers. All programming languages execute a program differently, and this is the reason for learning different ways of organizing words and separate statements according to the program to avoid experiencing some errors in your code. This chapter will discuss how Python execute commands and how the whole program operates. Working with Python is like dealing with interpreted programming language because of the text interpreter, which enables you to read the content faster. Text interpreter also helps you to quickly understand how to code correctly for the program to run effectively.

In addition to interpreting words, Python is a scripting language that allows programmers to write out the scripts and use extension .py to save them, or even write them and execute all the statements into different Python shell. In fact, Python will compile your program into a byte code just like Java byte code. An excellent example of what Python can compile is the source code, thus makes it easy for Python to execute the code in a short time.

Additionally, you can save byte code files into __pycache__, a subdirectory found in the directory which keeps the file sources. If you write out john.py, for example, it will rename it as john.pyc once it is converted into the byte codes. A programmer can manually compile the code if he/she experiences some problem in running the program. Since Python will carry out this process by itself it is not an issue to the beginners. Usually, Python confirms if there is a compiled version of the .pyc suffix or not when loading in the byte code. Ensure that the file is newer to enable the program to run effectively. Also, Python will create your byte code if it does not exist to execute the program.

IMPLEMENTATION OF PYTHON

Although this might be seen as a new thing, implementation of Python refers to the environment and the program that facilitates the execution of your program within the Python language, and it is represented with CPython. Depending on the type of the CPython you are using, such environment enables you to execute different kinds of the codes and statements you are handling within the program.

In programming, implementation includes everything to enable you to work on your program and complete it successfully on time. Unlike in other programming languages, implementation helps the programmers to get more things done in Python. The Python enables you to work on your program with many different programming languages like Java and C++, and this makes it appealing and straightforward.

Apart from CPython, you can use implementations such as Brython, CLPython, HotPy, IronPython, Jython, PyMite, and PyPy in Python to carry out the specific thing with the Python language. For the beginners, Python is the most suitable for them because it is not confusing like the other programming languages.

STANDARD DATA

Python programming language is suitable for those who are looking for the programming language that will enable them to work on their project using many different data successfully. These data are used to define various operations which the programmers can use to do multiple things when coding. There are five types of data in Python, and these include Numbers, Dictionary, Tuple, List, and String. These data types are essential in programming. You can use any of them to increase the function and the speed of the Python.

Additionally, number data types stores the numerical values and are created as objects after assigning a value to them. Numerical values exist in four types, namely; assigned integers, complex numbers, float point, and long integers shown as octal or hexadecimal. As a programmer, you should use these types of numerical values correctly to ensure that there is no error when running the program. Although Python allows a programmer to use the lowercase mainly when dealing with the long type of number, it is good to use uppercase when working with the letter as it eliminates any confusion the programmer can experience in reading the program.

Because Python is a programming tool that helps individuals to use and read it with ease, it is the best method one should start with when he/she enters programming professional. It is easy to use and read as it has syntax, which allows programmers to express their concepts without necessarily creating a coding page. Generally, Python is the best language for you due to its usability and readability. We are sure that after reading this book, you can now create a program with Python programming language.

CHAPTER 6. INTERMEDIATE AND ADVANCED DATA TYPES

In Python, every value is assigned a specified datatype. Since every aspect of Python consists of an object, data types are in fact classes, and variables are instances or objects of these classes. Python has several data types used in its operations. Listed below are some of the basic, important ones.

PYTHON NUMBERS:

Python numbers is a category constituted by floating-point numbers and integers as well as complex numbers. They are usually defined as int (integer), float (floating number), and complex (complex numbers) class in Python. To determine the class a value or variable belongs in the type() function is used, and to find out if an object belongs in a specific class, the isinstance() function is used.

In python numbers, the length of integers is boundless and can only be limited by the amount of available memory. Also, a floating-point number can maintain accuracy up to 15 decimal places. The presence of a decimal point shows the distinction between an integer and floating points. For example, 1 and 1.0 are the same in basic maths, but in Python, the former (1) is an integer, and the latter (1.0) is a floating number. Complex numbers are usually written in the following format, x + y; where x constitutes the real part of the equation, and the imaginary part is denoted by y.

PYTHON LIST:

A list refers to an ordered sequence of items. In python programming, list is one of the widely used datatypes owing to its relative flexibility. The items contained in a list do not have to share similarities in type to be on the list. Also, the process of declaring a list is quite easy. Items which are separated using commas and are contained within brackets []. The slicing operator [] is used in extracting a specific range of items or a single item from a list. In Python, index begins from the number 0. Lists can be mutable, meaning the value of the elements in a list is capable of being changed.

PYTHON TUPLE:

In Python, a tuple refers to an ordered sequence of items similar to list. The distinction, however, is that unlike lists, tuples are immutable. That is, once they have been created, the elements of a tuple cannot be changed or modified. Tuples are mainly used in place of lists to write-protect data as they are much faster and are incapable of changing dynamically. Tuples are defined with parentheses () where the items within are separated using commas. Moreover, even though a slicing operator [] can also be used to extract items, the values cannot be changed.

PYTHON SET

A set is a collection of special items which are not in any particular order. It is defined by values contained within braces {} and separated using commas. Like sets in basic mathematics, operations can be carried out on python sets such as the intersection and union of two sets.

Every set has a unique value, and since they are unordered, they do not require indexing. In this vein, the slicing operator [] cannot be used on sets.

PYTHON DICTIONARY

Like sets, python dictionary is a collection of key-value pairs in an unordered state. Dictionaries are used when there are vast volumes of data. Dictionaries are optimized to retrieve data. To do this, the key to retrieve a specific value must be known. In python programming, dictionaries exist as items being paired in the format key:value and contained within braces {}.

Moreover, the pair must not necessarily be of the same type. That is, key and value can be different types. In the pair, the key is used to retrieve a respective value, but it doesn't work vice versa.

CONVERSION BETWEEN DATA TYPES:

Conversion can be done from one data type to another using a several type conversion functions such as str(), float(), int() among others.

In converting from float to int, the value would be truncated to make it nearer to zero.

Only compatible values can be used in converting from and to string.

Conversion can also be done from one sequence to another sequence.

In converting to dictionary, every element must exist as a pair.

CHAPTER 7. FUNCTIONS AND MODULES IN PYTHON

In Python programming, functions refer to any group of related statements which perform a given activity. Functions are used in breaking down programs into smaller and modular bits. In that sense, functions are the key factors which make programs easier to manage and organize as they grow bigger over time. Functions are also helpful in avoiding repetition during coding and makes codes reusable.

- **The Syntax of Functions:**

The syntax of functions refers to the rules which govern the combination of characters that make up a function. These syntaxes include the following:

1. The keyword "def" highlights the beginning of every function header.
2. A function named is to identify it distinctly. The rules of making functions are the same as the rules which apply for writing identifiers in Python.
3. Parameters or arguments via which values are passed onto a function are optional in Python.
4. A colon sign (:) is used to highlight the end of every function header.
5. The optional documentation string known as do string is used to define the purpose of the function.
6. The body of a function is comprised of one or more valid statements in Python. The statements must all have a similar indentation level, (typically four spaces).
7. An optional return statement is included for returning a value from a function.

Below is a representation of the essential components of a function as described in the syntax.

def function_name(parameters):

"""docstring"""

statement(s)

- **How functions are called in Python:**

Once a function has been defined in Python, it is capable of being called from another function, a program, or the python prompt even. Calling a function is done by entering a function name with a proper parameter.

1. Docstring:

The docstring is the first string which comes after the function header. The docstring is short for documentation string and is used in explaining what a function does briefly. Although it is an optional part of a function, the documentation process is a good practice in programming. So, unless you have got an excellent memory which can recall what you had for breakfast on your first birthday, you should document your code at all times. In the example shown below, the docstring is used directly beneath the function header.

\>>> greet("Amos")

Hello, Amos. Good morning!

Triple quotation marks are typically used when writing docstrings so they can extend to several lines. Such a string is inputted as the __doc__ attribute of the function. Take the example below.

You can run the following lines of code in a Python shell and see what it outputs:

1. \>>> print(greet.__doc__)

2. This function greets to

3. the person passed into the

4. name parameter

2. The return statement:

The purpose of the return statement is to go back to the location from which it was called after exiting a function.

- **Syntax of return:**

This statement is able to hold expressions which have been evaluated and have their values returned. A function will return the Noneobject if the statement is without an expression, or its return statement is itself absent in the function. For instance:

1. >>> print(greet('Amos'))

2. Hello, Amos. Good morning!

3. None

In this case, the returned value is None.

CHAPTER 8. PYTHON FILE MANAGEMENT

File is a named memory location that is used to store and access data. Python manages file through a file object.

There are 4 basic file operations in Python:

1) opening a file
2) reading from a file
3) writing to a file
4) closing a file

Opening a File

The open() function creates a file object or handle that can be used to call other methods. You will use this function to open the file for reading, writing, or both.

syntax:

file object=open(filename [, access_mode][, buffering])

The filename refers to the file that you want to access.

The access mode is an optional parameter that will allow you to specify the access mode. There are two types of files that can be opened: a text file and binary file. There are several access modes for both files.

Modes for Accessing Text Files

r   read mode (default); opens a file for reading

w   write mode; creates a new file or overwrites existing one

r+   read and write mode

w+   read and write mode; creates a new file or overwrites an existing one

a   append mode; adds data at end of file or creates new file if the file is non-existent

a+   read and append mode: appends data at end of file or creates new file if file is non-existent

x   opens file for exclusive creation and fails if the file is already in existence

Modes for Accessing Binary Files

rb+   read and write

wb+   read and write mode; creates a new file or overwrite an existing file

ab+   read and append mode; adds data at end of file or create a new file if the file is non-existent

The buffering option lets users specify their preferred buffering style. When the value given is one, buffering is implemented as you access files. When the value exceeds one, buffering is carried out according to the specified buffer size. When a negative value is given, Python uses the system default.

To open a file in the default mode, the read mode:

f = open("diary.txt")

To open a file in write mode:

f = open("diary.txt",'w')

To read and write to a file in binary format:

f = open("reflection.bmp",'rb+')

Writing to a File

Before you can start writing to a file, you have to open the file with a file object:

>>> notes = open("myfile.txt", "w")

To start writing to a file, you will use the write method on the file object:

>>> notes.write("A file can be used to store important data.")

43

>>> notes.write("Files are objects that you can use in your program.")

51

Python returns the number of characters written on each line.

When you're done writing to a file, you have to close the file for proper processing and to avoid accidental erasure or alteration:

notes.close()

Reading a File

There are several ways to read a file:

- the readlines() method
- 'while' statement
- through an iterator

The readlines() Method

The readlines() method is a simple way to read and parse lines in a text file.

Using the file you created above, here are the steps:

Use a file object to open the file:

>>> notes = open("myfile.txt", "r")

Use the readlines() method on the file object to read each text line from the file. Create a variable that will store the text lines read:

```
>>> lines = notes.readlines()
```

Type the variable name on the Python prompt to access the contents of the file:

```
>>> lines
['A file can be used to store important data. Files are objects that you can use in your program.']
```

Close the file:

```
>>>notes.close()
```

Reading Files with a 'while loop'

Reading files with a 'while loop' is a more efficient way to read larger files. To illustrate, build a new file with the open() function:

```
>>> message = open("newfile.txt", "w")
```

Write the following lines with a new line character (\n) at the end of each line:

```
>>> message.write("This file stores important messages.\n")
```

\>\>\> message.write("Attendance is a must.\n")

22

Close the file:

\>\>\>message.close()

To read the file using the readline method and the while loop:

\# Open the linefile.txt on read only mode:

message = open('newfile.txt')

\# Read the first line

textline = message.readline()

\# keep reading line one at a time until file is empty

while textline:

   print(textline)

   textline = message.readline()

message.close()

When you run the above program, you will see the following line-by-line output on the Python shell:

This file stores important messages.

Attendance is a must.

Reading files with an iterator:

To read the newfile.txt with an iterator:

```
message = open('newfile.txt')

for x in iter(message):
    print(x)

message.close()
```

Appending Data to a File

To append data to an existing file, you need to open the file on append mode.

For example, to append data to newfile.txt, open the file and assign it to a new file handle:

>>> messages = open('newfile.txt', 'a')

Write a new line using the write method:

messages.write("Appending a line is as easy as writing a new line.")

50

Close the file:

>>> messages.close()

Use readlines() to view the updated newfile.txt:

>>>messages = open('newfile.txt')

>>> lines = messages.readlines()

>>> lines

['This file stores important messages.\n', 'Attendance is a must.\n', 'Appending a line is as easy as writing a new line.']

CHAPTER 9. INTRODUCTION TO OBJECT ORIENTED PROGRAMMING

Classes and objects are really important to how C# and other object-oriented programming languages will work. This is a pretty simple topic that you won't have trouble understanding, but this doesn't mean it's something you should ignore, it is actually very important that you should learn about it because it will help you learn how all of these work. This chapter will take the time to carefully look at how you can work with objects so that they will function the way they should in your code.

Classes and Objects

The first thing that we will spend our time talking about are the objects which are used in this programming language. Programming has changed a lot over the past few years, and this has changed how programmers create their new computer applications. The newest form of programming, known as 'OOP' or object-oriented programming, is the newest idea that most modern coding languages rely on to get the coding done. There are a lot of components that go with this, but it basically makes it easier to sort out and use the coding language.

Automation is the need of the current era, and with Python, you can automate tasks by writing test scripts, and Python surprises you here as well. You need a very little number of lines required to automate. This is because it supports lots of modules and tools, making stuff easy and instant.

Multipurpose

It is like the Swiss Army Knife, which would be used for many purposes. Python is not just a thing that deals with discipline but supports all sources of data like data from SQL or MongoDB. API of Python, which is called PySpark, is used to distribute computing. It has an inbuilt feature of service provision for natural language processing NLTK.

• Python also has many applications in the provision of services for internet protocol like XML, LSON, and HTML.

• Python enables you to draft a user interface for applications already made. To do this, there are tool kits available which are wxWidgets, Kivy which is for writing multi-touch applications and finally QT via PySide.

• It provides great applications for the scientific community like SciPy, which is a package for mathematics, engineering, and science. Pandas is a modeling and data analysis library.

• Python is extremely powerful when it comes to editing and works session recordings.

• Examples of What is OOP?

As a beginner, you may be curious as to what OOP means and how it's relevant to your coding. OOP is a style of coding that relies solely on objects to get the program to work. OOP will provide you with a model type that is based on how things would work in the real world and then you would use this idea and implement it in the codes that you are writing.

In some of the older coding languages, you had to concentrate on abstract ideas to help you to get the coding done. This may sound like a great idea, but it does make things more difficult in the long run. With OOP, you have to work with real objects, rather than these abstract ideas, which makes the coding so much easier. This is the approach that most modern programming languages take and it does make it much easier for the beginner to write their own codes, create their own program, and even solve some of their own problems they might encounter as they go about their programming.

Objects

In this section, we will spend some time working with objects to learn more about them. Programmers use digital objects to help represent the physical objects that they want to place inside of their code. While you are working with an OOP language, it is important to remember that these objects have more than a few characteristics that you should remember. These include:

State

These are the characteristics that will define the object. These can be general or specific.

Behavior

These are the characteristics that will declare all the actions that an object is capable of.

For us to understand exactly how all of this will work, we need to take a look at an example. Let's say that we are looking at a ball. The state of this object or the traits that define its characteristics are things like its color, what the ball is made out of, and the size. The behavior of that ball would refer to what that ball is capable of, such as bouncing, rolling, and so on and so forth.

When you are working on an OOP language, you can easily combine the technique and the information to process them as the same thing. The programming object will then match up to how it would behave or look when it is in the real world and then it will also hold onto the actions and the information until later.

Classes

Within this language, the 'classes' refer to what defines all the characteristics of the objects from above. These classes are in charge of giving you a model or a structure so that you can effectively define the nature of the object. These classes are often considered the foundation of OOP languages, and they will be linked closely to the object. Another thing to note is that each of the objects that you are using can also represent one specific class.

Let's take a look at how this works so that it makes a lot more sense to you. For example, we have a class that we named 'Toys' and while the object will be 'Ball.' In this sample, the ball is one instance of that 'Toy' class that you worked on. However, that the class will also define the state and the behavior of all the 'toys' that you add to the 'class' including the 'ball.'

Classes may sound complicated, and they will make the organization of your code a lot easier to handle, many people often see them as the basis of just about any program. The information they hold onto is meaningful for those who will take a look inside of the class so they can understand exactly what it is. For example, if you have a class that you named 'Toys,' the other users can access or look into the class and see that all the items or objects that were placed inside the code actually belong there. They do not have to be exactly the same, but putting them together in the same class should make sense.

The classes function to define the behavior of an object, such as the kinds of actions you want that object to be capable of performing. The object will also have its own characteristics or attributes. You will see that the attributes appear as different variables in the body of the class while the behavior, on the other hand, is defined by the different methods that fall inside the class.

Let's take a look at how this works by examining the Toy class that we talked about before. When these are applied, you will get the size and the color as the attributes. To make this work, you will need to bring out and use the **move()** and the **stop()** methods.

How to use these classes in your code

We have already spent a little bit of time talking about classes and how you can get them to work inside of your code, but now we need to spend some more time looking at how they work within the program as a whole and how they are useful at changing what you can write out inside of the code. When you are working with the C# programming language, you need to define all of the classes with the help of the 'class' keyword to not only make sure that everything works but to also help make things clear and simple.

After you have started with the code and you typed in the word 'class,' this is when you should indicate the identifier that you would like to see with the variable and the methods that would help make it certain that all of this works. As for making sure that all of this would stay simple, there are specific parts that you need to use since you are working with this kind of code. The different parts that you need to add to the class when working in C# include:

Fields

These are any of the variables that belong to a particular data type.

Methods

You can use these methods to manipulate the data.

Properties

In this programming language, the properties are what will enhance how well the fields work. The property will provide some extra management abilities for the information and give it to the fields.

At this point, it will probably be easier if you take a look at how you can work with making classes and how to make sure that they do exactly what you would like. We will now have a look at an example of how this code will work and the different theories that have been going on with it. In this example, we will use 'book' as the name of the class and then it will have the properties of 'size' and 'type.'

CHAPTER 10. REAL WORLD EXAMPLES OF PYTHON

One might argue that the era of Python was just 2017 when it witnessed some great rise in the popularity and growth across the world. The recent However, according to statistics and data, the recent rise in the growth of Python could not be ignored.

However, why do you think it will keep on attaining the rise in the expansion and in size? To answer the question, we dive into the market data and the scale of Python adoption and acquisition by corporations and companies around the world.

SO the reason behind the popularity of Python is one and simple. It will be as popular and widely used five years from now as it was five years ago. This is a big statement and to prove this, we need to see in detail what makes Python so special for these developers and programmers.

Years ago, when Python came into the market, people believed it would be dead within months of inception. In face when Larry Wall who is also the founder and brain behind programing language Perl was delivering his third annual state of Pearl Opinion said that there are some programming languages out there in the market that are C++, Java, Perl, Visual Basics, Javascript and in the last Python. Back then, the leading language for programming was C++ and Perl was on the third number in the market. Python had very low demand and was not included among the PLs that could grow.

However, in the years to follow, Python grew with tremendous speed and outshined Perl as well. According to Stack Overflow, the visitor volume to question and enquire about Python increased more rapidly than Perl.

Following are the reasons behind the rise and super demand for Python among developers.

Data Science

This is one of the most adored languages among data scientists, unlike R and C++. SO the current era is the era of big data, and since Python supports large sets of libraries, internet, and prototypes, Python is the best and fully suited language for the operations. PyMySQL, PyBrain, and NumPy are the reason why is Python so extensively demanded. In addition, integrations and programming are the things a programmer has to deal in everyday life, and this is the reason behind the huge demand for Python as well because it provides easy integration even of existing apps or sites to other programming languages. This makes it future-oriented and scalable.

Machine Learning

In the industry these days, artificial intelligence and machine learning have created a huge buzz with every industry investing in the areas to maximize their revenue and cut costs. This is not really possible without the induction of Python. It is actually an interpreted language, and its use makes it elucidated enough to be interpreted by machines and to be understood by the hardware. The growth of ML has been on the rise in the last few years, and I think this is also one of the reasons why Python has witnessed a surge in its demand.

Applications in Web Development

According to data, Python is chosen by two out of three developers who in the start worked with OHO, and this is an achievement. The rising trend of Python in the last couple of years shows that it seems like the best alternative. It offers Flask and Django, which makes the process of web development easy and quick. It is due to these reasons and features that leading tech giants like Google, Facebook, Instagram, etc. have been using it for long. Uber and Google use it for its algorithms. In addition, it is super simple, and this is the reason why it is easy to work with and adaptable.

Automation

software development applications are SCons, which is for build control, Roundup, and Trace, which are for bug tracking and project management. For IDE integrated development environments, Roster is used.

• The most important stuff related to Python is that it provides special applications for education.

• Its applications in business include Tryton, which is a 3-tier and advanced level application platform. Another management software called Odoocomes with a huge deal of business applications. This actually makes Python an all-rounder.

• For network programming, we have Twisted Python which provides a platform and framework for the network programming that is asynchronous. It has a simple socket interface.

• We all know that the gaming industry is evolving with great potential and ability to create replicated amount of revenue. The applications of Python for gaming is very safe to use and have been pretty much and widely used. PyGame and PyKyra are bi-development frameworks for games. There is also a variety of 3D rendering options in the libraries.

• Moreover, we have applications which interest the developers to a huge extent and are used widely. We have applications that are console-based, applications for robotics, machine learning and web scraping and scripting and whatnot.

These are the main reason why Python is the best fit in the industry from the point of view of a developer.

According to a report of myTectra, the jobs which were posted in Naukri from 2014 to 2017 have been monitored. The trend of Python jobs is compared to the world's number one language showing different results.

THINGS WE CAN DO IN PYTHON

In this Chapter, we will discuss many things that you can do in Python. Some of the things we can do in Python include the comments, reading and writing, files and integers, strings, and variables. We are sure that after reading this the book, you will be able to create the program that will run effectively. Due to the interactive and descriptive nature of the Python, a beginner can handle many things using it. Therefore, this chapter will discuss some aspects and comments in Python to help you get started. You can make amazing codes in a short time using the Python programming language.

Comment

A comment, in the Python programming, starts with the # sign. This continues until the programmer gets to the end of the line. A good example is;

This is a comment

Print (hello, thanks for contacting us)

It instructs your computer to print "hello, thanks for contacting us". In fact, the Python interpreter ignores all the comments. As a programmer, however, you should not leave a comment after every line. You can put in a comment when you need to explain something. Since long comments are not supported by Python, it is important to use short and descriptive comments to avoid them going across the lines.

READING AND WRITING

You will realize that some program requests specific information or show the text on the screen. Sometimes we start the program code by informing the readers about our programs. To make things look easy for the other coders, it is important to give it the name or title that is simple and descriptive.

As a programmer, you can use a string literal that comprises the print function to get the right data. String literal is a line of the text surrounded by the quotes. They can be either double or single quotes. Although the type of quotes a programmer use matters less, the programmer must end with the quotes that he/she has used at the beginning of the phrase. You can command your computer to display a phrase or a word on the screen by just doing as discussed above.

Files

Apart from using the print function to obtain a string when printing on the screen, it can be used to write something onto the file. First, you will have to open up the myfile.txt and write on it before assigning it the myfile which is a variable. Once you have completed the first step, you will have to assign "w" in the new line to tell the program that you will only write or make changes after the file has opened. It is not mandatory to use print function; just use the right methods like read method.

Read method is used to open specific files to help you read the available data. You can use this option to open a specific file. Generally, the read method helps the programmers to read the contents into variable data, making it easy for them to open the program they would like to read.

Integers

Always make sure that the integers are kept as whole numbers if you are using them. They can be negative or positive only if there are no decimals. However, if your number has a decimal point, use it as a floating number. Python will automatically display such integers in the screen.

Moreover, you cannot place one number next to others if you are using the integers because Python is a strongly typed language; thus it will not recognize them when you use them together. However, you put both the number and the string together by making sure you turn the number into a string first before going to the next steps.

TRIPLE QUOTES

After reading and understanding both the single and double quotes, it is now a time to look at the triple quotes. The triple quotes are used to define the literal that spans many lines. You can use three singles, double, or single when defining an authentic.

Strings

Although a string is seen as a complicated thing to many beginners, it is a term used by the programmers when referring to a sequence of characters and works just like a list. A string contains more functionality which is specific than a list. You will find it challenging to format the strings when writing out the code because some messages will not be fixed easily due to its functionality. String formatting is the only way to go away within such a situation.

ESCAPE SEQUENCES

They are used to donate special characters which are hard to type on the keyboard or those that can be reserved to avoid confusion that may occur in programming.

OPERATOR PRECEDENCE

It will help you to track what you are doing in Python. In fact, it makes things easy when ordering the operation to receive the right information. So, take enough time to understand how the operator precedence works to avoid confusion.

Variables

Variables refer to the labels donated somewhere in the computer memory to store something like holding values and numbers. In the programming typed statistically, the variables have predetermined values. However, Python enables you to use one variable to store many different types. For example, in the calculator, variables are like memory function to hold values which can be retrieved in case you need them later. The variables can only be erased if you store them in the newer value. You will have to name the variable and ensure it has an integer value.

Moreover, the programmer can define a variable in Python by providing the label value. For instance, a programmer can name a variable count and even make it an integer of one, and this can be written as; count=1. It allows you to assign the same name to the variable, and in fact, the Python interpreter cannot read through the information if you are trying to access values in the undefined variable. It will display a message showing syntax error. Also, Python provides you with the opportunity of defining different variables in one line even though this not a good according to our experience.

THE SCOPE OF A VARIABLE

It is not easy to access everything in Python, and there will be differences in the length of the variables. However, the way we define the variable plays a vital role in determining the location and the duration of accessing the variables. The part of the program that allows you to access the variable is called the Scope while the time taken for accessing the variable is a lifetime.

Global variables refer to the variables defined in the primary file body. These variables are visible throughout the file and also in the file that imports specific data. As such, these variables cause a long-term impact which you may notice when working on your program. This is the reason why it is not good to use global variables in the Python program. We advise programmers to add stuff into the global namespace only if they plan to use them internationally. A local variable is a variable defined within another variable. You can access local variables from the region they are assigned. Also, the variables are available in the specific parts of the program.

MODIFYING VALUES

For many programming languages, it is easy for an individual to define a particular variable whose values have been set. The values which cannot be modified or changed, in the programming language, are called constants. Although this kind of restrictions is not allowed in Python, there are used to ensure some variables are marked indicating that no one should change those values. You must write the name in capital letters, separated with underscores. A good example is shown below.

NUMBER_OF_HOURS_IN_A_DAY=24

It is not mandatory to put the correct number at the end. Since Python programming does not keep tracking and has no rules for inserting the correct value at the end, you are free and allowed to say, for example, that they are 25 hours in a day. However, it is important to put the correct value for other coders to use in case they want.

Modifying values is essential in your string as it allows a programmer to change the maximum number in the future. Therefore, understanding the working of the string in the program contributes a lot to the success of your program. One has to learn and know where to store the values, the rules governing each value, and how to make them perform well in a specific area.

THE ASSIGNMENT OPERATOR

Although discussed in this book earlier, we had not given it the specific name. It refers to an equal sign (=). You will be using the assignment operator to assign values to the variable located at the left side on the right of the statement. However, you must evaluate if the value on the right side is an arithmetic expression. Note that the assignment operator is not a mathematical sign in the programming because, in programming, we are allowed to add all types of things and make them look like they are equivalent to a certain number. This sign is used to show that those items can be changed or turned into the part on the other side.

CHAPTER 11. EXAMPLES OF CODING

LOOPS

Loops are generally utilized whenever one computer system is used when there is a program needed to repeat processes more than once. This particular process is referred to as 'iteration' and there will end up being 1 loop that is 'for' and the other is called a 'while' loop in Python. The first image is a representation of the 'for' loop and the 2nd image is the easiest of the two and is the 'while' loop.

WORKING AND STRINGS

Strings as part of python, frequently tend to be a conterminous collection of recognizable possibility delimited through a line or possibly multiple quotes. Python wouldn't possess any kind of distinct information range for a recognizable possibility; therefore, they frequently tend to be portrayed as the lone recognizable string.

Creating strings

It is essentially the string of recognizable possibility; the string takes place to be as part of the fact. The recognizable takes place to be as part of the character. For example, the English language has 26 recognizable possibilities.

Computer systems do not contend with mere possibility. They contend with actual numbers (with decimal points included). It is quite possibly an option, however, that you may not notice any recognizable options on your display screen inside. It takes place to be as part of the fact actually store and analyzed as a series and combinations of zeros (o) and ones (1).

This conversion process recognizable to the number takes place to be a part of fact called encoding. The reverse process takes place to be as part of the fact called decoding. ASCII and Unicode frequently tend to be more of the favored among users and especially beginners, as it relates to Python strings, which tend to take place in a hidden bit of Unicode that remains recognizable.

Unicode was originally coded to include all things considered and bring consistency as a major aspect of encoding. You can take in additional about Unicode from here.

Strings as a Python Feature:

Strings can be made through encasing unmistakable probability inside singular quotation marks or multiple quotes. It is up to you what your desired outcome will be. For the most part, Python is typically used to be a representation of multiple strings and doc-strings.

When you run the program, your specific output will be: If ran and executed properly.

There are numerous tasks that can be performed with the string that makes it a standout amongst the most utilized types of data in Python.

Link of Two or More Strings - Joining of at least two strings into a solitary one is called "concatenation".

The "+" function allows you to compose 2 string literals together and links them.

The " *" function can be utilized to rehash the string for a set number of repetitions.

CHAPTER 12. QUIZ AND WORKBOOK

To optimize your use of the Python program as a beginner, here are significant pointers that can help your learning activity become fruitful.

1. Be positive. Anything new can be daunting – especially a 'foreign' language. Think about learning Korean, Chinese or Spanish, and you won't even want to start. But optimism can make you change your mind. As Master Yoda from "Star Wars' said: "Do, there is no try." Believe that you can do it, and you can. Think about all the benefits you can derive from what you will learn.

2. Python is an extensive program; continue learning. What we have discussed here is only the tip of the iceberg. There are still thousands of complex information about Python that you can learn.

3. If you want to obtain several values from a list, use the 'slice' function, instead of using the index. This is because the 'index' can provide you a single value only.

4. Assign only integer values to indices. Other number forms are not recognized by Python. Keep in mind that index values start from zero (0).

5. Remember to use the 'help' function whenever necessary. Explore the 'help' function, when in doubt on what to do. A little help from Python can go a long way.

6. Python programming is a dynamic language. Thus, you can experiment and come up with a code of your own to contribute towards its advancement.

7. There are some differences among the Python versions. But don't fret, the program itself has built-in modules and functions that can assist you in solving the problems you can encounter.

8. The interactive shell can promptly return results. That's why it's preferable to open a 'New File' first, before creating your statement. But if you're sure of your code, then, go ahead, and use the interactive shell directly.

9. Separate your multiple statements, in a single line, with semicolons. This is easier and more sensible.

10. *The three 'greater than' signs (>>>) or arrows is a prompt from the interactive shell. You can explore their functionality as you create your statements.*

11. The Python interpreter can act as a calculator. Using your interactive shell, you can compute math problems quickly – and continuously. No sweat!

12. The # symbol indicates that the statement is a comment. The # sign is placed before the comment, and after the Python statement, so Python won't mistake it as part of the statement or code.

13. Use the reverse or back slash (\ ) to escape a single quote, or double quotes. Examples of these are contracted words, such as 'don't, "won't", 'aren't'. When using them in Python, they will appear this way: 'don\'t', "won\'t", 'aren\'t'.

14. *A short cut in joining two literal strings (strings literal) is to put them beside each other and enclose each in quotes. Example:*

'Clinical' 'Chemistry'. This will give: ClinicalChemistry.

```
>>>
>>> 'Clinical' 'Chemistry'
'ClinicalChemistry'
>>>
>>>
>>>
```

15. For modifying immutable data, create a new file. These immutable data include strings, numbers, frozen set, bytes and Tuples. By creating a new file, you can modify, add and remove items from your immutable data.

QUIZ

1. Why do you think multi-line statements are necessary we can simply write a single line, and the program statement will run just fine?

2. List the variable scope types?

3. Start IDLE.

Navigate to the File menu and click New Window.

Type the following:

```
food=['omelet', 'fish','rice']
for j in range(len(food)):
    print("I prefer", food[j])
```

ANSWERS

1. Multi-line statements can help improve formatting/readability of the entire program. Remember, when

writing a program always assume that it is other people who will use and maintain it without your input.

2. The following are the scope types:

i. Scope containing local names, current function.

ii. Scope containing global names, the scope of the module.

iii. Scope containing built-in names of the outermost scope.

3. The output of this program will be:

I prefer omelet

I prefer fish

I prefer jazz

CHAPTER 13. BONUS: WORKBOOK

You have already seen that Python can sometimes be rather difficult to operate. But, with a few tips and tricks, you can make Python that much easier for you to use so that you do not have to worry so much about something not making sense in your code.

Strings

As started earlier, triple quotes are going to be the easiest way that you are going to be able to set the definition of a string.

Str.join ( ) can be used when you are using string concentration.

The only time that you are going to use string concentration is when your string is a thousand characters or more.

Example

Print "peanut butter" + "jelly" + "peanut butter" #this type of coding should not ever be done!

Print " " join(["peanut butter" , "jelly" , "and" , "peanut butter"]) #while it does not seem like it, this is going to be more efficient for your code in Python. You may also notice that this is a Python idiom that is used often.

Print "%s %s %s %s %s ("peanut butter," "jelly," "and," "peanut butter") #this is also a method that is pythonic as well as an example for string concentration.

Modules that are used in C

Some modules will actually be faster when the program is running because of the language that they are written in.

The C language is going to be identical to the other languages that are used in Python. The biggest difference is that it is going to be faster because of the implementations that Python uses. Module behavior will end up being different when C is being used, but the differences are not going to be noticed by the user.

C versions are going to be used in more versions of Python than any other language.

Modules will be optimized but only in the event that they are available with the version of Python that you are using.

cProfile is going to be what is going to be used in Python 3.4.

Importation

In the C version of Python, you are going to notice the name of the modules that you use are going to begin with the letter c so that it can be set aside as being written in a different language.

When you are importing this file, you are not going to use the c for the import process.

The reason that you are going to forget the c is because you are going to be using the original Python version. The code will be converted to C in the program.

Example

Import cName as Name

Except Import error for this file.

Import Name

Examples

Python 2.x is going to carry out commands in C over a thousand times faster than if you were to use a different method.

In Python 2.x you are also going to add a c to the string function.

Python 3 is going to replace that c with an io

A cprofile in Python is going to have overhead added to it and that is why it is going to be the one that is recommended for you to use.

If you are using a version of Python that is 3.3 or higher the celementtree is going to be the same as the element tree. Element tree ends up being about twenty times faster and is going to consume less memory than other methods that you have to choose from. As mentioned, if you have version 3.3 then it is going to be done by the program automatically since it is a faster method of keeping the program going.

Comprehension and generators

Smaller loops should be used with a generated expression or through the use of list comprehension.

Comprehension can be also make for loops go faster so that you do not have to worry about making a mistake.

A dictionary is going to be a section of the program that is going to contain files that are going to help the program run the code that you are wanting to be run.

The files that are in the directory is usually going to be used for making sure that all the rules for the loop that you are making are being followed. If conditions are going to make the search through the directory more narrow so that it goes faster.

Expressions that have been generated can be used with a multitude of lists as long as you use the zip function.

Data type

To figure which data type you should use, you are going to need to look at the application and determine how it is going to run with each data type.

In comparing two lists to see if there is anything similar between the two of them, you are going to have to go through each element individually, but this is going to take up too much of your time and you may end up forgetting what you are trying to do.

Instead of going through the list you are going to use a function that is going to go through the list for you and find what each list has in common.

This method should only be used on smaller lists. There is another method that you can use for lists that have more entries so that it is more efficient and less time consuming.

A set is going to help speed up the process when you are using it as a function.

A dictionary is not going to be recommended when you are using a set since sets are mutable, but a tuple is going to be the perfect choice for you.

Dictionaries that have to be used are going to convert your objects into the tuple or list so that you can do the proper operation so that it can be converted back to the form that it should be in for the program.

Methods such as this are going to be faster than attempting to duplicate the string.

Other

Logging and database access is going to be handled by a decorator.

There is no function that has been placed into Python as of yet that is going to enable you to make a list smaller as you work on it. However, you can use a recursive function which is going to do the same thing, but it is going to do it when you have finished creating your list.

A GUI button has been placed in Python that was originally based off of the TcI's Tk. This is going to give you access to things that are in Python 4 and Python 3 that you do not have access to in other versions of Python.

Swapping two numbers

Thanks to Python, there is a way that you can switch the place of two numbers that are all in one line.

Example

Z, t = 15, 5

Print (z, t)

Z, t – t, z

Print (z, t)

First (15, 5)

Second (5, 15)

This function actually makes a new tuple while the previous one is left unreferenced.

After the new tuple is created, it is going to be flagged by the program because of the variables that have been switched.

Comparison operators

Comparison operators can be aggregated so that you can chain the two operators together.

Example

Z = 5

Result = 2 < z < 25

Print (result)

#this statement is true

Result = 1 > z <= 4

Print (result)

#this statement is false

Ternary operators and conditional assignments

A ternary operator is going to be the short way of writing out an if else statement

Syntax

[on_true] if [expression] else [on_false]

Example

Z = 15 if (t == 5) else 50

Class objects can also use ternary operators

Example

Z = (classB if y == 2 else classD)(param4, param7)

When the number of parameters has been set, ternary operators can be used to evaluate the smaller numbers that are in the expression

Example

Def small(d, r, g) :

Return d if d <= r and d <= g else (r if r <= d and r <= g else g)

Print(small(2, 5, 2))

Print(small(6, 3, 3))

Print(small(3, 3, 4))

Print(small(9, 8, 7))

Output

2,3,4,5,6,7,8,9

List comprehension can use ternary operators as well.

Multi-line strings

Backslashes are going to be used with the C language .

Example

multiStr = "choose * from one of the statements \
depending on placement_id < 6"

print(multiStr)

#you are going to choose one from the statements that are listed where the placement_id is 6

Triple quotes work just as well

multiStr = """choose * from one of the statements \
depending on placement_id < 6"""

print(multiStr)

#you are going to choose one from the statements that are listed where the placement_id is 6

When using triple quotes, the indentation is going to be a problem because the quotes are going to get in the way of the indentation. Trying to place our own indentations is going to result in whitespaces.

So, to correct this, the string is going to be split up and there are going to be parentheses that will enclose the entire code.

Example

multiStr = (" choose * from one of the statements"

"where placement_id < 6"

"select by number")

Print (multiStr)

#you are going to select from the multiple rows available where the placement_id is < 6 and selected by number.

Elements placed in a list with new variables

Lists can be used with a great number of variables.

The number of variables that are in your list should never go past the number of elements that are in your list

Example

Listest = [5, 8 2]

Z, u, I = listest

Print (z, u, I)

#The numbers are going to be 5, 8, 5

Interactive operators

Expressions can be tested with a temporary name.

The underscore is going to take the place of the expression that you are wanting to test so that you are not testing the actual expression and potentially messing up your code.

Example

3 + 5

8

_

8

Print _

8

Set comprehension and dictionaries

Set comprehension and dictionaries are going to work just like list comprehension does.

Example

Dicttest = { z: z* z for z in xrange (5) }

Settest = { z * 8 for z in x range (5) }

Print (settest)

Print(dicttest)

#set ([0, 5, 10, 15, 20])

When you are using < : > there is going to be a difference from just the regular commas.

Code that is run in Python 3 is going to replace the xrange with just the normal word of range.

We are happy that you have made up your mind to start the journey of mastering Python. One of the most common questions that new learners want to know is how to learn a given language.

Well, the first step in becoming a master in Python programming is to ensure that you know how to learn. Knowing how to learn is a vital skill in computer programming.

So why is it important for you to know how to learn? Simply put: language changes, new libraries are created, and new tools are released. Thus, if you know how to learn, it will be important to help you remain at par with these changes and become a successful developer.

This chapter will provide you with tips that will help you kick start your journey of becoming a master in python programming.

HOW TO MAKE NEW CONCEPTS STICK

Practice coding daily

Consistency is a key element when trying to learn anything new. Whether you want to learn how to drive a car, how to cook pizza, or even play basketball, you must be consistent. And learning a new language isn't an exception. You may not believe it but the muscle memory plays a huge role in programming. By coding daily, you will be boosting that muscle memory. Although this can be difficult in the first few weeks, you should try and begin with 25 minutes per day, and slowly increase the length of time each day.

Write something down

Concepts will not stick in your brain just by staring at them; you must have a pen and a notebook to take notes. Research indicates that taking notes by hand increases the level of retention. If you want to become a full-time Python developer, then you must take notes, and write down some lines of code.

Once you begin to work on small programs, writing by hand can assist you to know how to plan your code before you shift to the computer. This will help you save a lot of time, especially if you can write out the type of functions, variables, and classes you will need.

Don't be dull but be active

Whether you are learning how to debug an application or learning about Python lists, the Python shell should be your favorite tool. Use it to test out some Python codes and concept.

Give yourself a break

You know that work without play makes Jack a dull boy, so take breaks and allow the concepts to sink. Take a break of 25 minutes, then come back and resume your learning process. Breaks ensure that you have an efficient study session, especially when you are learning new information.

Breaks will be crucial when you start to debug your program. If you get a bug and you can't tell how to fix it, a break could answer to your problem. Step away from your computer and refresh yourself.

Maybe it could be a missing quotation mark that is preventing your program from running, and that break will make a difference.

Love to fix bugs

When it comes to hitting bugs, this is one thing that you will never miss if you begin to write advanced Python programs. Running into bugs is something that happens to everyone who codes. It doesn't matter which language you are using. Don't let bugs get the better of you. So you need to embrace any moment you encounter a bug and think of yourself as a master of solving bugs.

When you start to debug, ensure that you have a methodological strategy to assist you in identifying where things are going wrong. Scanning through your code by following the steps in which the program is implemented is a great way to debug. Once you identify the problem, then you can think of how to solve it.

Work with others

Surround yourself with people who are learning

While coding can appear as a solitary task, it really works well when you collaborate with others. It is very crucial that when you are learning how to program in Python that you have friends who are in the same boat as you. This will give you room to share amongst yourselves the tricks to help in learning.

Don't be scared if you don't have anyone that you can collaborate with. In fact, there are many ways to meet like-minded developers passionate about Python development. You can go to local events and peer to peer learning community for Python lovers and Meetups.

Teach

The best way to master something is to teach others. This is true when you are learning Python. There are different ways you can do this. For example, you can create blog posts that describe newly learned concepts, record videos where you explain something, or even talk to yourself. Each of these methods will solidify your knowledge and reveal any gaps in your understanding.

Try out pair programming

In this approach, two programmers work in a single workstation to finish a task. The two developers then switch tasks. One writes the code and the other one guides the process and reviews the code as it is being written. Switch tasks often to experience the benefit of both sides.

This technique has many advantages. For instance, you get the chance to have another person review your code and also see how the other person could be thinking about the problem. By getting exposed to numerous ideas and approaches of thinking will help you know how to create solutions to problems using Python.

Ask smart questions

You may have heard someone say that there is no bad question but in programming, it is possible to ask a bad question. When asking questions from someone who has very little knowledge or context of the problem you want to solve, it is advised to follow this format:

G: Give context on the area you want to solve.

O: Outline everything you have attempted to fix

O: Offer the best guess of what the problem could be.

D: Demonstrate what is happening

Asking a good question can save a lot of time. If you skip any of the following steps can lead to conflict because of the back-and-forth conversations. As a newbie, you want to ensure that you only ask good questions so that you can learn how to express your thought process. Also, the people who help you can be happy to assist you again.

Create something

Above all, you only learn by doing. Doing exercises will help you make important steps but building something will take you far.

Build anything

For new beginners, there are always small exercises that will boost your confidence in Python. Once you have a solid foundation on basic data structures, writing classes, and object-oriented programming, then you can begin to build something.

What you build is not as important as the method you use. The path of the building is what will help you learn the most. You can only learn a lot from reading Python books, articles, and courses. Most of your learning will originate from developing something. The problems you will solve will help you learn a lot.

If you find it hard to come up with a python practice project to work on, you can get started with the following:

Dice roll simulator.

Number guessing game.

Simple calculator.

Bitcoin price notification system

Participate in open source programs

In the open source system, you can access the source code of a software, and anyone can take part. Python has a lot of open-source projects that you can decide to contribute. Besides that, many companies post open-source projects. In other words, you can contribute to the code written and generated by engineers working in some of these companies.

CONCLUSION

The next step is to go on to more complicated topics. You've started the long and often arduous journey of programming in this book. And the best thing about it? There's no finite end point. There's never going to be a point in programming where you say enough is enough, or where you reach some kind of "peak" in your knowledge. Well, technically speaking, maybe, but only if you quit trying will you have hit a peak.

Programming is one of the most liberating tasks known to man, because it's the ultimate art form. It's the most interactive art form too. When you program, what you're doing is literally talking to the computer, and thereby making the computer talk to the user. Every single program you make is an extension of the effort that you put into it and the time and the code that you've dedicated to it.

Programming, too, is not easy. In fact, it's rather difficult. And there are topics that are sadly too esoteric to cover in this book. For example, we didn't get to the bulk of file operations, nor did we get to things like object-oriented programming. But I hope what I've given you is a very solid foundational understanding of Python so that you can better service **yourself** to learn about these things.

My goal here wasn't explicitly to teach you **Python** or object-oriented programming or any of that: my goal was to teach you the **computer**. The way it thinks, and the way programs are written. Anybody can learn Python keywords. But to learn to program, and to write solid effective code regardless of which programming language that you're using, that's another skill entirely.

C# PROGRAMMING

The practical beginner's guide to learn c# programming in one day step-by-step

(#2020 Updated Version | Effective Computer Languages)

Steve Tudor

Text   Copyright   ©
All rights reserved. No part of this guide may be reproduced in any form without permission in writing from the publisher except in the case of brief quotations embodied in critical articles or reviews.

Legal & Disclaimer

The information contained in this book and its contents is not designed to replace or take the place of any form of medical or professional advice; and is not meant to replace the need for independent medical, financial, legal or other professional advice or services, as may be required. The content and information in this book has been provided for educational and entertainment purposes only.

The content and information contained in this book has been compiled from sources deemed reliable, and it is accurate to the best of the Author's knowledge, information and belief. However, the Author cannot guarantee its accuracy and validity and cannot be held liable for any errors and/or omissions. Further, changes are periodically made to this book as and when needed. Where appropriate and/or necessary, you must consult a professional (including but not limited to your doctor, attorney, financial advisor or such other professional advisor) before using any of the suggested remedies, techniques, or information in this book.

Upon using the contents and information contained in this book, you agree to hold harmless the Author from and against any damages, costs, and expenses, including any legal fees potentially resulting from the application of any of the information provided by this book. This disclaimer applies to any loss, damages or injury caused by the use and application, whether directly or indirectly, of any advice or information presented, whether for breach of contract, tort, negligence,

personal injury, criminal intent, or under any other cause of action.

You agree to accept all risks of using the information presented inside this book.

You agree that by continuing to read this book, where appropriate and/or necessary, you shall consult a professional (including but not limited to your doctor, attorney, or financial advisor or such other advisor as needed) before using any of the suggested remedies, techniques, or information in this book.

Introduction

Most people are scared of learning a new coding language. They know that it would open a lot of doors for what they would be able to do with their computers, but they worry that coding itself is too hard for them to learn how to work with. If you do not take the proper time to learn a new programming language, the whole process of programming could be difficult. But when it comes to finding a good language that will help you write almost any code that you would like, then it is time to take a look at the C# programming language. This chapter will take you through some of the basics that come with using the C# coding language so that you can start using it yourself.

What is special about C#?

The first thing that you might want to look into when it comes to a coding language is to understand why C# is so special and why you would even want to learn how to use this particular programming language.

There are many different coding languages out there to choose from, and they all work differently.

But you will find that there are a ton of benefits that come with using the C# program, and we will explore some of them inside this guidebook. Even though you are just a beginner, this is a great coding language to work with and will allow you to design so many programs of your own.

While there are many different options available if you want to get started with coding, none are as great to work with like C#. Some of the benefits of going with C# rather than some of the other programming languages include:

- **It can utilize a big library**

As a beginner, there are a lot of parts of the code that won't be easy for you to learn. You will learn them as you go, but the library that you can use with C# is a great resource that will be of great help to you. You can place these functions into the code without a lot of hassle being involved. You can even use them to make some changes to the code, so it works the way that you want.

- **Automatically disposes of the functions**

    When you are working with some of the other programming languages, you will have to go through and remove the items that you own. This will take up your time and can be a hassle if you end up missing some of them. Using C# will do all of this work for you to make things faster and easier.

- **Easy to learn**

C# is widely considered as one of the easiest programming languages you can learn how to work with. While there are a few parts that are more complicated than some other coding languages, this is not a difficult one, and you'll start recognizing different parts of the code pretty quickly as you continue to use it.

- **Compatible with Windows computers as well as others**

This programming language was originally created to work on Windows computers and help you design a program for them. But it also works well with some other operating systems such as Mac, Linux, and more as long as you download .NET on it. Windows has some great products that are easy to use, especially for beginners, so you will surely get great results once you get started.

- **Works with .NET which helps make it easy**

This is a program that already comes with the Windows computers, but you can add it to some of the other systems to make C# accessible on these other computers as well.

- **Similar to C and C++**

This makes it really easy to work with this program and learn the basics before going on to these other programs. Even if you choose to stick with this programming language, you will find that it is powerful enough to do most of the coding that you want and without all the hassle you might experience with some of the other programs.

What do I need to get started?
Now it is time to learn what you will need to get started with using this programming language so you can get to make the codes that you want. The first thing that you should look at is to check whether or not your code has the .NET framework in place. You should also have the development kit for this presentation on your Windows computer. Starting on Windows Vista, this framework was automatically placed on the computer for you so this will save you some time if you are working with the right operating system.

If you are on a computer that does not have the .NET framework, you will have to go with Mono Project rather than working with the .NET framework for your projects. You can visit the Microsoft store at www.microsoft.com to find the right framework for the computer that you want to work with.

Remember that this language works the best for Windows computers, but this doesn't mean you can't use it on other systems. If you are working with a MAC or a Linux computer, you have to make sure that you are working with Mono Project rather than the .NET framework. You can check out their website: www.monoproject.com where you can find the right framework for your system.

Getting started with the C# language

After you have gone through and downloaded the things that you need, it is time to get started with using the C# language. When it comes to working with your Windows computer, C# is a great programming language to work with. It is compatible with the .NET framework that should already be found on your Windows computer. The C# language is also really simple and flexible to use, and at the same time, it provides you with the power that your codes will need. If you are someone who is still new to the idea of programming and you like using Windows products, then the C# language is definitely worth your time to learn and use.

Just like when you work with Java, C# will not support any code pointers, and you won't have any access to working with multiple inheritances. It is important to remember this because some other programming languages are capable of doing those things. Rather, memory collection and type checking are what C# can offer. It also has some powerful and useful features that you may recognize if you're familiar with using C++ so you can add a lot of functionality to your codes. Let's take a look at some of the things that you can do with code writing in C#.

Writing out a program with C#

The best thing that you can do while you're still learning how to work with C# is to actually write out a program and see how the code looks. As an example, we will write out a simple program that will help you understand what is going on with C# and how it can be used to help out with other codes that you might want to write in the future.

The first thing that you have to do is launch the text editor that you prefer using. If you are using a computer on the Windows operating system, going with the popular Notepad is a great option. There are also several other options available depending on the type of computer you are planning on working with.

Once the text editor is open and ready to go, write out the following code inside:

```
class FirstProgram
{
    static void Main()
    {
        Console.WriteLine("UsingC# is fun.");
    }
}
```

Now you can access the command prompt and type:

csc FirstProgram.cs

After you issue this command, the compiler for C# will process this file and then create an .exe file in the same location as your code. For example, if you saved the original file on the desktop, you should see a new program come up called 'FirstProgram.ee.' right in the same place. If there is an error in the code that you wrote, you will see an error message come up.

Now you can run this application by entering 'FirstProgram.exe' into the command prompt. If everything was done correctly, you should see that the command prompt will display the message: 'Using C# is fun'.

Analyzing the program

Now that you have written out the program that you want to use, it is time to take a look at the different parts of the code and what they all mean. The code above is pretty simple to work with, and you will find that it will include a variety of the different components that you need to write out a decent code inside of C#. Some of the parts that you should look for include the following:

- **The first line**

In the first line, we will include the identifier and the keyword. The keyword is the word inside the code that has special functions inside the language. With the keyword that we used in the last example, you were creating a new class for the program. The identifier is then in charge of listing out the class, the variable, and the method and the one that we are using here is called 'FirstProgram'.

- **The third line**

In this line, we will define the method Main(). This is what will act as the starting point for any of the applications that are on your computer. The program will always start if the Main() method is executed, no matter where you place it inside the code. Only two words will fit in there, and one of them will be 'static' while the other one is 'void.' These will help to determine the kind of object that is in the code.

- **The fifth line**

This is the final part of the code we are working on. This line is where you write out the message that you want to come up after the code has been executed. This method is called WriteLine() and it's used to make sure that you can write things out in the code. You can also add any message that you like.

In addition to the things that we talked about above, you may have noticed that there were braces placed into the code. These braces are there to tell our computer that there are some blocks of code throughout the program and it will keep everything separated nicely. Keep in mind that when you write your code in C#, you have to use a semicolon the same way you do when writing a code with C and with Java.

Comments in C#

It can be useful to know how to leave comments when you're writing out a code with the C# coding language. These comments are helpful no matter what kind of programming language you prefer to use and can add a little something to the code that you are trying to create. These are like little notes that will remind you or tell the other programmers something important about your code. When you write out the comments properly, the compiler will know that it should skip over them and will not read through them. You can add in as many of these comments as you would like, but it is best if they are only used when necessary, so they do not make the code look too messy.

There are two main types of comments that you can work with inside of C#. The first one is a 'single line' comment. This is written with two forward slashes. These are used only if you need to write out a small sentence or a few words, and you want all of it to stay on one line. If you end up using these slashes, and then you go over that one line, the compiler will notice this and will bring up an error message.

You can also choose to work with multi-line comments. There are times when you might want or need to write out a comment that is a little bit longer. You would not be able to do this with the slashes that we talked about before. If you would like to write out one of these longer comments, you simply have to write /* at the beginning of the comment and then end it with */.

It really is that simple to learn how to work with the C# programming language. It may look a little bit intimidating at first, but with some practice and a willingness to learn some of the basics that we have already been talking about, you can start writing your own codes in no time.

Chapter 1 Data Types

C# is a strongly typed language; hence it expects you to state the data type any time you are declaring a variable. Let us explore some of the common data types and how they work:

1. ***bool*** - this is a simple data type. It takes 2 values only, True or False. It is highly applicable when using logical operators like if statement.
2. ***int*** - this stands for integer. It is a data type for storing numbers with no decimal values. It marks the most popular data type for numbers. Integers also have several data types within C#, based on the size of the number that is to be stored.
3. ***string*** - this is used for storage of text, which is a sequence of characters. C# strings are immutable, meaning that you cannot change a string once it has been created. If you use a method that changes a string, the string will not be changed but instead, a new string will be returned.
4. ***char*** - this is used for storage of a single character.
5. ***float*** - this is a data type used for storage of numbers that have decimal values in them.

The sizeof() method allows us to know the size of a variable or data type. The size is returned in the form of bytes.

Consider the following example:

```
using System;

namespace TypeApp {

  class IntType {
```

```
static void Main(string[] args) {
    Console.WriteLine("Size of int: {0}", sizeof(int));
    Console.ReadLine();
  }
 }
}
```

The code should return:

Which means that an integer takes a storage size of **4** bytes.

Chapter 2 Data Type Conversion

In general, an operator works on arguments that belong to the same type. However, the C# language offers a wide range of data types that you can use for certain situations. To conduct any process on variables that belong to different types, you should convert one of those variables first. In C#, data type conversion can be implicit or explicit.

Each C# expression has a data type. This data type results from the literals, variables, values, and structures used inside the expression. Basically, you might use an expression whose type is incompatible for the situation. When this happens, you'll get one of these results:

- **The program will give you a compile-time error.**

- **The program will perform an automated conversion. That means the program will get the right expression type.**

Converting an "s" type to "t" type allows you to treat "s" as "t" while running your program. Sometimes, this process requires the programmer to validate the type conversion. Check the examples below:

- **Converting "objects" to "strings" will need verification during the program's runtime. This verification ensures that you really want to use the values as strings.**

- **Converting "string" values to "object" values doesn't need any validation. That's because the "string" type is a branch of the "object" type. You can convert strings to their "parent" class without losing data or getting any error.**

- You won't have to perform verification while converting int values to long values. The "long" data type covers all of the possible values of the "int" type. That means the data can be transformed without any error.
- Converting "double" values to "long" values involves validation. You might experience loss of data, depending on the values you're working on.

Important Note: C# has certain restrictions when it comes to changing data types. Here are the possible type conversions supported by this language:

Explicit Conversion

Use this conversion if there's a chance of information loss. For instance, you'll experience information loss while converting floating-point values to integer values (i.e. the fractional section will disappear). You might also lose some data while converting a wide-range type to a narrow-range type (e.g. long-to-int conversion, double-to-float conversion, etc.).

To complete this process, you need to use the "type" operator. Check the examples below:

class Example

{

    static void Main()

        {

```csharp
double yourDouble = 2.1d;

System.Console.WriteLine(yourDouble);

long yourLong = (long)yourDouble;

System.Console.WriteLine(yourLong);

yourDouble = 2e9d;

System.Console.WriteLine(yourDouble);

int yourInt = (int)yourDouble;

System.Console.WriteLine(yourInt);

    }

}
```

If compiled and executed correctly, that program will give you these results:

Implicit Conversion

You can only perform this conversion if data loss is impossible. This conversion is referred to as implicit because it doesn't require any operator. The C# compiler will perform implicit conversion whenever you assign narrow-range values to variables that have a wide-range.

String Conversion

C# allows you to convert any data type to "string". The compiler will perform this conversion process automatically if you will use "+" and at least one non-string argument. Here, the non-string argument will become a string and the "+" operator will produce a new value.

Chapter 3 Arrays and Loops

I solemnly promise not to bore you straight out the gate in this chapter with a long discussion on abstract logic. However, it's important for me to make the case that all of this is highly important in the pursuit of a stronger grasp on programming. A lot of programming books will try to teach you the essentials, but they'll fail to teach you the underlying concepts that actually explain **why** something works the way that it works. This means that in effect, your learning will be incomplete. You may have absolutely no idea why something works in the way that it does.

This is the last place that you want to be when it comes to logic, though. Logic and programming go so intrinsically hand-in-hand. Back in my time in undergrad, I would constantly see people confused about why something worked in one way or another, or why a program didn't work even though they were so sure their logic was sound.

When I would go to review their logic, though, their program would be wrong in some glaring way, at least from a logical standpoint. Because of this, I've really come around to the opinion that logic and the underlying concepts behind programming are some of the most important things that you can grasp.

Let's start our discussion of arrays with a simple question. What would you do if you needed to connect several variables together in some way? As in, what if you needed to access a bunch of variables from the same location?

The simple answer is that you couldn't, at least not with what you know now. This is an issue, and allow me to show you why.

If you had to start take inventory of a bunch of items in your program, then you may find yourself doing something like this:

```
int item1 = 3;

int item2 = 2;

int item3 = 6;

int item4 = 5;
```

As you can see, this would get unwieldy after a while. This is not even to mention the fact that you're creating so many extraneous variables that you really don't need. What could you do instead of creating all of these variables?

The ideal solution would be if you had one singular variable called **item**, from which you could access all of these values stored with in. Well, fortunate for you, you can do exactly that.

The concept of storing a bunch of variables together is known as an **array**, and they are a central concept to computer programming. Let me explain how they work.

Remember how we talked about how computers store values in what are essentially little boxes in the computer's memory that you can reference through the use of a variable (or by directly referring to the given location in memory, but that's for a more advanced language than this one)? Well, arrays allow you to actually set a bunch of boxes aside and declare them all to contain related data. So what does this mean?

Well, for one, it tells the computer that this specific location in memory is related, meaning that when you want to move through this data, it actually goes faster since the computer doesn't have to randomly pull information from different places in memory. Understand that computers don't store values in a rational way, especially not in RAM, and when you're trying to pull information from RAM there's always a pretty decent chance that the computer will have the values scattered all over the place. When all of the boxes are there together and the computer knows they're related, it's easier for the computer to move from box to box efficiently.

However, on top of this, what this essentially means is that to the computer, these things **are** related. That is, all of these boxes connect in one way or another. You've already told the computer how big of something is going to be in these boxes, how many boxes it needs to set aside, and a variety of other information.

Arrays then offer the optimal way to store related information. For the record, this doesn't have **specifically** to do with control flow but it is an extremely important lesson that we needed to cover in this book and it does fit in well to the overall lesson of control flow, so we're going to cover it here.

Let's go back to the inventory example. Let's say that we wanted to create an array of integer values that could hold as many as 10 items. To do this, we would do the following:

    int[] item = new int[10];

This initializes an array with 10 spaces.

You can then start adding values to the array by referencing **indices**. An index of an array is a specific location within the array, or in other words, a specific one of the boxes which was set aside. When you initialize an array like we did above, which you can refer to as a soft initialization, all of the values are zero from the get-go and essentially waiting to be filled in.

To understand how to refer to an index of an array, you have to understand how **computers** understand them. Computers don't count things starting from 1 like we do. They actually start at 0. This means that if you want to refer to the first index in an array, you would refer to the one at index **0**. If you want to refer to the third index in an array, you would refer to the one at index 2, and so on and so forth.

Let's say we wanted to assign the following values:

3, 5, 7, 1, 2, 8, 3, 5, 4, 1

We could do that in two different ways.

The first is through going through the array and assigning each value:

item[0] = 3;

item[1] = 5;

item[2] = 7;

item[3] = 1;

item[4] = 2;

And so on and so forth. But this clearly is pretty clunky. There has to be some better solution to setting up so many values at once, right?

Well, there is. You can also do a **hard initialize**. This is where you declare the values of the array right from the very start when you initialize it. You could initialize an array like so:

int item[] = {3, 5, 7, 1, 2, 8, 3, 5, 4, 1};

You can also do a combination of the two. Let's say, for example, that you wanted to create an array with 15 spaces but you only had 10 pieces of data right now. You could initialize the array to have 15 spaces, but you could only fill the first 10. The last 5 would be initialized to 0 until you changed them.

int item = new int[15] {3, 5, 7, 1, 2, 8, 3, 5, 4, 1};

With that, we've covered the most basic part of arrays. This doesn't seem terribly useful just yet, but bear with me, because we're going to be going into great detail on why this is super handy momentarily.

Now, with all of that out of the way, it's time that we start to talk about another very important part of control flow: loops. We often don't think about it, but we use loop logic all of the time. Loops find their ways into our daily lives so often and generally we fail to appreciate it.

Let's take something as simple as writing a sentence. This may not seem like a loop, but it actually is!

Think about the abstract process.

>You put your pen to the paper.
>
>Write out a letter of a certain shape.
>
>Pick the pen back up.
>
>Check if you're at the end of the line,
>
>If so:

Check if you're at the end of the page,

>>If so, move to the beginning of the back page.
>>
>>If not, move to beginning of the next line.
>
>If not:
>
>Move the pen to the right.

And this repeats until you are done writing whatever it is that you have to write. When expressed in those terms, loop logic is actually relatively intuitive, but it still doesn't come superbly easy to a lot of people and many people aren't terribly aware of just how pervasive loop logic really is.

For the purposes of this chapter, we're going to go ahead and define three different loops: the while loop, the do while loop, and the for loop.

Note that C# most certainly does have more loop types, but they go beyond the scope of this book into what one could consider object-oriented programming, which we aren't discussing in this book. These loops will suffice perfectly to give you a solid introductory idea on loops and how they work.

Let us start by discussing the first major loop on our agenda. This is the while loop. We are starting with the while loop because it is extremely simple in principle. The way that the while loop works is that you simply give it a condition, and then it will run for as long as that condition is met. If the condition ever isn't met, then the loop will quit running and the code will continue past it.

The while loop has a fair bit of utility, but much of it is context dependent. As you will learn as this chapter presses on, every loop has their own strengths and weaknesses. While it may not be immediately apparent to you as a novice programmer, they will most certainly become more apparent as you gain more experience in the world of programming and start to branch out and work on more projects, both your own and those of others.

The while loop takes the syntax like so:

```
while (condition) {

    // code goes here, executes until condition isn't true

}
```

The while loop, since it is has such a unique and simple construction, finds much of its utility in its usage as a game loop. While this can refer to games, it doesn't specifically and only refer to games.

Rather, the game loop refers to the idea of creating a variable such as running or hasWon which you can set to true or false at the start of a variable. The loop will be then set so that it runs for as long as that condition remains true. As a result, the loop will keep running over and over and won't stop until something happens which changes this variable to be set to false.

This is useful when you have numerous exit conditions for the loop, but it also is useful in a general way when a more sophisticated loop condition may be tricky or too exacting. With this, you're able to set the exit condition under things like if statements and so forth to ensure that the loop runs until you're absolutely certain that you don't want it to run.

Let's test out the functionality of a while loop by creating a loop that will count from 1 all the way up to 10. The way that we'd do this is pretty simple.

```
int i = 1;
while (i < 10) {
Console.WriteLine(i);
i++;
}
Console.WriteLine(i);
```

If you were to run and test this loop, you can see that it would run 9 times. Each time, it would print the current value of the integer i, then it would iterate i up by 1. On the 9th run, it iterates 9 up to 10. At this point, the loop exits since i is no longer less than 10. This leaves our i set to 10, and we verify this when we leave the loop by counting the last number.

As is quite clear, while loops are certainly not the most difficult thing that you've ever encountered. The logic behind them is actually rather intuitive and the chances are low that you're going to be particularly at a loss for understanding here. With all of that said, it's time that we move on to the next loop.

The next loop that we need to cover is the do while loop. Do while loops are on the surface very similar to while loops, but there is one major distinction. Do while loops will always run a certain block of code at least once, even if the condition for the loop isn't true. However, if the condition for the loop is true, then the loop will continue running until the condition isn't met.

In order to better illustrate what I mean by this, here is the syntax for a do while loop with appropriate notes tucked inside:

> do {
>
> // This code runs at least once.
>
> // But it will keep running if...
>
> } while (condition); // ... this condition is met, and will run until it isn't.

Because do while loops aren't terribly difficult, we're going to skip the example here and move straight on to for loops.

For loops serve a diametrically different purpose than while loops do, and this purpose is actually readily apparent in the implementations of for loops in some languages. For example, while Python follows the basic structure and philosophy of the for loop from C and C-style languages, it massively differs in the way that it implements it.

The for loop serves its purpose best as an iterative loop. This means that you should most ideally use the for loop whenever you need to work your way through a given set of data. Hopefully, the reason that we spent so long talking about arrays is becoming more and more clear now.

For loops essentially work by allowing you to define a starting variable. This variable is the one which is going to be iterating through the data, and on every instance of the function, it will iterate by a given step. You also will define the range of the loop. This is the domain for which the loop will execute. It's pretty much synonymous with the conditional statement of while loops, but it functions here as a definition of the range of possible iterator variables i over the course of the given domain. Basically, this tell the for loop for how long the statement will execute and over what particular set of data. Lastly, you define the iterative step, which pretty much just says the size of the steps that the iterator variable needs to increase or decrease by. These aren't just incremental and decremental operators, they are anything that can be performed in a systematic and repetitive way and that will change i each time. However, in these terms, there is no doubt indeed that the incremental and decremental operators are the most common ones that you will see.

Let's go back to our definition of the array item for a moment. Create a new project called Chapter3. In the main function of that project, go ahead and type the following:

> int item[] = {3, 5, 7, 1, 2, 8, 3, 5, 4, 1};

Now, let's say that using a for loop, we wanted to iterate through every item in this list, printing each number out one at a time. We can do this very easily. Firstly, we need to look at the syntax of the for loop:

> for (iterator variable initializer, set to lower bound; condition set to upper bound; iterative step) {

// code goes here

}

So, for this specific program, we recognize that the array starts at 0, so we must set the lower bound to 0. The upper bound is the size of the array, because we can't go bigger than the array obviously. We can access the size of the array using the **.Length** property in relation to the array. Lastly, we want the iterative step to be 1, so we're just going to go ahead and put **i++** here. Putting these into the terms used in the creation of the for loop, we get the following:

> for (int i = 0; i < item.Length; i++)

{

// code goes here

}

Now, we just need to print out the value of every item within the array. We can do this by accessing the current index using the **i** variable:

> for (int i = 0; i < item.Length; i++)

{

```
        Console.WriteLine(item[i]);
}
```

With all of that done, you've now defined a for loop. You can go ahead and try running and testing this program. Everything should go off without any real issues and all of the values should print out.

With that, we've covered the second major beast of control flow. We now are going to move on to one of the last major things that we're going to cover in this book: writing functions in C#.

Chapter 4 Operators

In this chapter, you will understand how you can make your program achieve complex tasks—all with the help of Operators! Conditions and operations are the heart of every programming language. These are the things that make your program capable of computing and evaluating inputs and variables.

Operators

There are several types of operators that you can use in C:

1. Assignment Operators
2. Arithmetic Operator
3. Relational Operators
4. Logical Operators
5. Miscellaneous Operators

Assignment Operators

Assignment Operators are used to assign variables their values. Here are some of the basic assignment operators:

Operator	Description
=	Basic assignment. Use this to assign any value to a variable. A= B + C
+=	Add and assign value. A += B translates to A = A + B
-=	Subtract and assign value. A −= translates to A = A - B

*=	Multiply and assign value	
	A *= B translates to A = A * B	
/=	Divide and assign value	
	A /= B translates to A = A / B	
%=	Get modulus and assign value	
	A %=B translates to A = A % B	

Use the codes below to demonstrate how these operators are used:

```
#include<stdio.h>
int main()
{
    int a = 3;
    int b = 9;
    int c ;
    c = a + b;
    printf ("c is the sum of a and b. The value of c is %d\n", c);
    c+=a;
    printf ("c is the sum of c and a. The new value of c is %d\n", c);
    c-=a;
    printf ("c is the difference of c and a. The new value of c is %d\n", c);
    c*=b;
```

```
    printf ("c is the product of c and b. The new
value of c is %d\n", c);

    c/=a;

    printf ("c is the quotient of c and a. The new
value of c is %d\n", c);

    return 0;

}
```

Here's the output:

Figure 1: Assignment Operators Exercise

Arithmetic Operators

Arithmetic Operators allow you to perform formulas with variables. Here are some of the basic arithmetic operators. Let's use the values: a = 3 and b = 9.

Operator	Description
+	Add the values a + b = 12
-	Perform subtraction b − a = 6
*	Perform multiplication a*b = 27
/	Perform division b/a = 3

%	Modulus – show the remainder after division b/a = 0
++	Add one a++=4
--	Subtract one b--=8

Let's put these into action:

```
#include<stdio.h>
```
int main()

    {

  int a = 3;

  int b = 9;

  int c ;

  c = a + b;

  printf ("c is the sum of a and b. The value of c is %d\n", c);

  c = b - a;

  printf ("c is the difference of b and a. The new value of c is %d\n", c);

  c = a * b;

  printf ("c is the product of a and b. The new value of c is %d\n", c);

  c = b/a;

```
    printf ("c is the quotient of b and a. The new value of c is %d\n", c);

    c = b%a;

    printf ("c is the modules of b and a. The new value of c is %d\n", c);

    a++;

    printf ("a is the value of a + 1. The new value of a is %d\n", a);

    b--;

    printf ("b is the value of b - 1. The new value of b is %d\n", b);

    return 0;
```

Paste the code above on CodeChef and see if you get the same results as below:

Figure 2: Arithmetic Operators Exercise

Relational Operators

Relational Operators are used to compare variables, and return a Boolean result of the evaluation. This means it will signal the program if the value is True or False. Let's use the same values: a = 3 and b = 9.

Operator	Description
==	Check for equality a == b; FALSE
!=	Check for inequality

	a =! b; TRUE
>	Greater than
<	Less than
>=	Greater than or equal to a >= 3; TRUE
<=	Less than or equal to a <= 3; TRUE

To see how this works, we will use the if statement. For now, copy and paste the code below on CodeChef.

```
#include<stdio.h>
int main()
{
    int a = 3;
    int b = 9;
    if (a==b) {
    printf ("Values a and b are equal \n");
    }
    if (a!=b) {
    printf ("Values a and b are not equal \n");
    }
    if (a>b) {
    printf ("a is greater than b \n");
    }
```

```
if (a<b) {
    printf ("b is greater than a \n");
}
if (a>=3) {
    printf ("a is greater than or equal to 3 \n");
}
if (a<=3) {
    printf ("a is less than or equal to 3 \n");
}
return 0;
}
```

Did you get the same output messages?

Figure 3: Relational Operator Exercise

Logical Operators

Next, let's get to logical operators. These operators test and compare the output of a statement or condition. The test will either return a True or False value. Let's use the same values: a = 3 and b = 9 and add these values: c = 2, d = a - 1

Operator	Description
||	OR operator . The condition becomes true when the logical state of any of the operands is true. ((a ==b) || (c ==d)) evaluates to TRUE

&&	AND operator. This returns true when all of the operands evaluate to true. ((a ==b) && (c ==d)) evaluates to FALSE
!	NOT operator. It's used to reverse the result of the condition. If the condition below evaluates it to True, using the NOT operator will reverse it to False. !((a ==b) && (c ==d)) evaluates to TRUE

Logical operators make way for assignment, arithmetic, and relational operators to come together in a condition. The logical operator will be used to evaluate the condition. Here's a short code to showcase how logical operators work.

```
#include<stdio.h>
int main()
{
    int a = 3;
    int b = 9;
    int c = 2;
    int d = a - 1;
    if ((a==b) || (c ==d)) {
        printf ("OR Operator: Print this when one or both of the conditions is true \n");
    }
    if ((a ==b) && (c ==d)) {
```

```
        printf ("AND operator: Print this when both of
the conditions are true\n");

        }

        if (!((a ==b) && (c ==d))) {

            printf ("NOT operator: Print this when the
condition becomes true");

            }

            return 0;

        }
```

Here's the output that you should get once you run this on CodeChef:

Figure 4: Logical Operators Exercise

To validate the output, change the values of the inputs and run the code again. Come up with values that will output the message for the AND operator.

Miscellaneous Operators

The C language also gives us other useful operators:

Operator	Description
sizeof	Checks for the variable size – reflects the size of storage for the variable type
? :	Ternary operator: outputs value a if condition is true, otherwise b will be shown

Here's a short code to show how ternary operators and sizeof work:

```c
#include <stdio.h>
int main() {
    int first = 4;
    char second='x';
    int a;
    int b;
    printf("This is the size of the first variable = %d\n", sizeof(first) );
    printf("This is the size of the second variable = %d\n", sizeof(second) );
    a = 3;
    b = (a == 3) ? 100: 200;
    printf( "Therefore, the value of b is %d\n", b );
    b = (a == 11) ? 200: 300;
    printf( "Therefore, the value of b is %d\n", b );
}
```

Add other variable types to see what is the storage size:

Figure 5: Miscellaneous Operators Output

Values

Values basically pass arguments to the various copies in your function, where you have to make changes in the parameters. For this, the swap() function is necessary. For example:

In this chapter, we covered Logic, Keywords and Operators. In the next chapter, you will learn all that you need to know about loops and loop break statements.

Chapter 5 Classes

A class can be seen as a blueprint for an object. Objects in the real world have characteristics like shape, color and functionalities. For example, X6 is an object of car type. A car has characteristics like color, speed, interior, shape etc. This means that any company that creates an object with the above characteristics will be of type car. This means that the Car is a class while each object, that is, a physical car, will be an object of type Car.

In object oriented programming (not forgetting that C# is an object oriented programming language) a class has fields, properties, methods, events etc. A class should define the types of data and the functionality that the objects should have.

With a class, you can create your own custom types by grouping variables of other types together as well as methods and events.

In C#, we use the class keyword to define a class. Here is a simple example of this:

public class TestClass

{

   public string field1 = **string.**Empty;

   public TestClass()

   {

   }

   public void TestMethod(**int** param1, **string** param2)

   {

      Console.WriteLine(**"The first parameter is {0}, and second parameter is {1}"**,

```
                    param1, param2);
    }
    public int AutoImplementedPropertyTest { get; set; }
    private int propertyVar;
    public int PropertyTest
    {
        get { return propertyVar; }
        set { propertyVar = value; }
    }
}
```

The public keyword before the class is an Access Specifier, specifying how the class will be accessed. By being public, it means that it will be accessible by all other classes within the same project. We have given the class the name TestClass.

We have also defined a field in the class named field1. Below this, we have created a constructor for the class. Note that the constructor takes the same name as the class itself, hence the constructor's name is TestClass(). Inside this class, we have also defined a method named TestMethod(), and this method takes in two parameters, param1 and param2, with the former being an integer and the latter being a string.

Here is another example demonstrating how to declare and use a class:

```
using System;
namespace CubeApplication {
    class Cube {
```

```
    public double length;    // Length of the cube
    public double breadth;   // Breadth of the cube
    public double height;    // Height of the cube
}

class Cubetester {

    static void Main(string[] args) {

        Cube Cube1 = new Cube();   // Declare Cube1 of type Cube

        Cube Cube2 = new Cube();   // Declare Cube2 of type Cube

        double volume = 0.0;   // Store the cube volume here
        // cube 1 specification

        Cube1.height = 4.0;

        Cube1.length = 5.0;

        Cube1.breadth = 8.0;

        // cube 2 specification

        Cube2.height = 8.0;

        Cube2.length = 12.0;

        Cube2.breadth = 14.0;

        // volume of cube 1

        volume = Cube1.height * Cube1.length * Cube1.breadth;
```

Console.WriteLine*("**Volume of Cube1 : {0}**",* volume*);*

// volume of cube 2

volume = Cube2.height * Cube2.length * Cube2.breadth*;*

Console.WriteLine*("**Volume of Cube2 : {0}**",* volume*);*

Console.ReadKey*();*

}

}

}

The code will return the following result:

Encapsulation and Member Functions

A member function for a class is simply a function with a definition or prototype within the definition of the class in the same way as any other function. Such a function can operate on any object of the class in which it is a member, and it can access all the class members for the object.

Member functions are simply the attributes of the object (from a design perspective) and they are defined as private so as to implement the concept of encapsulation. We can only access such variables using pubic member functions. Let us demonstrate how we can set and access the various members of a class in C#:

using System*;*

namespace CubeApplication {

class Cube {

private double **length***;* // Length of a cube
private double **breadth***;* // Breadth of a cube

```
    private double height;   // Height of a cube
    public void setLength( double len ) {
        length = len;
    }
    public void setBreadth( double brea ) {
        breadth = brea;
    }
    public void setHeight( double heig ) {
        height = heig;
    }
    public double getVolume() {
        return length * breadth * height;
    }
}
class Cubetester {
    static void Main(string[] args) {
        Cube Cube1 = new Cube();   // Declare Cube1 of type Cube
        Cube Cube2 = new Cube();
        double volume;
        // Declare Cube2 of type Cube
        // cube 1 specification
```

```
Cube1.setLength(4.0);
Cube1.setBreadth(6.0);
Cube1.setHeight(8.0);
// cube 2 specification
Cube2.setLength(10.0);
Cube2.setBreadth(14.0);
Cube2.setHeight(12.0);
// volume of cube 1
volume = Cube1.getVolume();
    Console.WriteLine("Volume of Cube1 is: {0}", volume);
// volume of cube 2
volume = Cube2.getVolume();
    Console.WriteLine("Volume of Cube2 is: {0}", volume);
Console.ReadKey();
    }
  }
}
```

Here is the output from the code:

We used the setter methods to set the values of the various attributes of our two cubes. The getVolume() function has been called to calculate the volumes of the two cubes.

Constructors

A constructor is simply a special member function of a class that is run anytime that we create new objects of the class. A constructor takes the same name as the class and it should not have a return type. The following example demonstrates how to use a constructor in C#:

```csharp
using System;

namespace ConstructorApplication {

    class Person {

        private double height;   // height of the person
        public Person() {

            Console.WriteLine("We are creating an object");

        }

        public void setHeight( double heig ) {

            height = heig;

        }

        public double getHeight() {

            return height;

        }

        static void Main(string[] args) {

            Person p = new Person();

            // set the person's height

            p.setHeight(7.0);

            Console.WriteLine("The height of the person is: {0}", p.getHeight());

            Console.ReadKey();
```

          }
       }
     }

The code should return the following:

A default constructor has no parameters, but it is possible for us to add parameters to a constructor. Such a constructor is known as a parameterized constructor. With such a technique, it is possible for one to assign an initial value to an object during the time of its creation. Here is an example:

using System;

namespace ConstructorApplication {

  class Person {

    private double **height**; // Height of the person
    public **Person**(double **heig**) { // A parameterized constructor

      Console.WriteLine(**"We are creating an object, height = {0}"**, heig);

      height = heig;

    }

    public void setHeight(double heig) {

      height = heig;

    }

    public double getHeight() {

      return height;

    }

```
static void Main(string[] args) {
    Person p = new Person(8.0);
    Console.WriteLine("The height of the person is : {0}", p.getHeight());
    // set the height
    p.setHeight(7.0);
    Console.WriteLine("The height of the person is : {0}", p.getHeight());
    Console.ReadKey();
  }
 }
}
```

Here is the output from the code:

Destructors

A destructor refers to a special member function of a class that is run anytime an object of the class goes out of scope. A destructor takes the same name as a class but it should be preceded by a tilde (~). A destructor cannot take parameters neither can it return a value.

A destructor is a useful tool for releasing the memory resources before leaving a program. You can overload or inherit a destructor. The following example demonstrates how to use a destructor:

using System;

namespace ConstructorApplication {

```csharp
class Person {
    private double height;   // Height of a person
    public Person() {  // A constructor
        Console.WriteLine("We are creating an object");
    }
    ~Person() {  //A destructor
        Console.WriteLine("We are deleting an object");
    }
    public void setHeight( double heig ) {
        height = heig;
    }
    public double getHeight() {
        return height;
    }
    static void Main(string[] args) {
        Person p = new Person();
        // set the height of the person
        p.setHeight(7.0);
        Console.WriteLine("The height of the person is : {0}", p.getHeight());
    }
  }
}
```

Here is the output from the function:

Static Members

To define a class member as static, we use the static keyword. When a class member is declared as static, it means that regardless of the number of objects of the class that are created, there exists only one cope of the static member.

The use of the static keyword means that there is only one instance of a member existing in the class. We use this keyword when we need to declare constants since their values can be retrieved by invocation of the class without the creation of an instance of the same. We can initialize static variables outside a class definition or a member function. Static variables can also be initialized inside a class definition.

Let us demonstrate the use of static variables using an example:

using System;

namespace StaticApp {

  class StaticVariables {

    public static int x;

    public void count() {

      x++;

    }

    public int getX() {

      return x;

    }

  }

```
class StaticTester {
    static void Main(string[] args) {
        StaticVariables var1 = new StaticVariables();
        StaticVariables var2 = new StaticVariables();
        var1.count();
        var1.count();
        var1.count();
        var2.count();
        var2.count();
        var2.count();
        Console.WriteLine("Variable x for var1 is: {0}", var1.getX());
        Console.WriteLine("Variable x for vars is: {0}", var2.getX());
        Console.ReadKey();
    }
}
```

The code returns the following result:

A member function can also declared as static. Such a function will only be able to access static variables. Static functions exist even before the creation of the object. Static functions can be used as demonstrated in the following example:

using System;

```
namespace StaticAppli {
  class StaticVariable {
    public static int x;
    public void count() {
      x++;
    }
    public static int getX() {
      return x;
    }
  }
  class StaticTester {
    static void Main(string[] args) {
      StaticVariable var = new StaticVariable();
      var.count();
      var.count();
      var.count();
          Console.WriteLine("Variable   x   is:   {0}", StaticVariable.getX());
      Console.ReadKey();
    }
  }
}
```

The code will return the following:

Chapter 6 The C Language Variables

In C, the variable type matches the variable's content—the type of value being stored. Integer variables can hold only integer values or whole numbers. Float variables hold floating-point values, which are very large numbers, very small numbers, or numbers with a fractional part.

Character variables hold single values such as the letter 'x.' The C language lacks a string variable type. Instead, a character array is used. We'll discuss how that works in a later chapter.

The int, float, and char are all C language keywords. Additional keywords are also used to declare variables. These include double, long, short, signed, and unsigned. These are all C language keywords that are used to declare different types of variables. Take a look at the code below:

```
1       #include <stdio.h>
2
3       int main()
4       {
5               int age;
6
7               age = 30;
8               printf("The C language is over %d years old!\n", age);
9
10              return(0);
```

| 11 | } |
| 12 | |

This code declares an integer variable at line five. First comes the keyword int, which is used to declare an integer variable. Next come the variable name: age. As this is a statement, it ends with a semi-colon. Variable names can include numbers, letters, and some symbols. They must begin with a letter, or an underline. The name must be unique, with no two variables having the same name, nor should variables have the same name as functions or C language keywords.

At line seven, the variable age is assigned the value 30. In C, values or equations go on the right side of the assignment operator, the equal sign. The value or results of the equation is then assigned to the variable on the left. Because 30 is an integer value, it fits nicely into the integer variable age.

The statement at line nine displays the variable's value by using the printf function. The %d placeholder is used, and the variable age is specified as the second argument. Now go ahead and build and run the code. The whole idea behind the variable is that its value can change. Edit the source code so that the value of the age variable is changed to 34. Make this modification at line seven.

1	#include <stdio.h>
2	
3	int main()
4	{
5	int age;
6	
7	age = 34;

| 8 | printf("The C language is over %d years old!\n", age); |

9

| 10 | return(0); |

| 11 | } |

12

Save the modified code, then build and run it. As you will see, the program's output reflects the new value.

Now, assign a new value to the variable in the code by adding two lines after line eight. First, assign the value 50 to the age variable:

| 1 | #include <stdio.h> |

2

3	int main()
4	{
5	int age;

6

7	age = 34;
8	printf("The C language is over %d years old!\n", age);
9	age = 50;

10

11

12

13   return(0);

14   }

15

Second, type another printf function:

1   #include <stdio.h>

2

3   int main()

4   {

5   int age;

6

7   age = 34;

8   printf("The C language is over %d years old!\n", age);

9   age = 50;

10   printf("The programmer is over %d years old\n", age);

11

12   return(0);

13   }

14

Save the above changes, then build and run the code. See how the age variable is used twice, but hold two different integer values. On your own, you can change this code once more.

This time you can assign your own age to the age variable and simply add a printf statement to say how old you are.

Math can also be performed using variables. Take a look at the code below:

```
1     #include <stdio.h>
2
3     int main()
4     {
5             int age;
6
7             age = 32;
8             printf("%s is %d years old!\n", "James", age);
9             printf("That's %d months!\n", age*12);
10
11            return(0);
12    }
13
```

In line seven, the value 32 is assigned to the variable integer age. Edit the value to reflect your own age in years. The printf function in line eight uses two statements: a string and an integer variable. The string is an immediate value. Change the name "James" to your own name, unless your name is also James.

You don't need to guess how many months you have because that value is calculated as the argument in the printf function at line nine. Save the code, build and run. Of course, the month's value displayed is an approximation, unless today is your birthday. In that case, Happy Birthday!

The int is really one variable type. Another common type is the char or character variable. Take a look at the code below:

```
1     #include <stdio.h>
2
3     int main()
4     {
5             char x, y, z;
6
7             x = 'A';
8             y = 'B';
9             z = 'C';
10
11            printf("It's as easy as %c%c%c\n", x,y,z);
12
13            return(0);
14    }
15
```

Here, three character variables are declared: x, y, and z. You can declare multiple variables of the same type on a single line, as long as each variable name is separated by a comma. Lines 7-9 assign the variables characters—single quotes are used. Then the values are displayed by the printf function at line 11. Save, build, and run the code.

Just as you can change integer variables, you can also change character variables. You can even do math. Edit line eight to read:

```
1          #include <stdio.h>
2
3          int main()
4          {
5                  char x, y, z;
6
7                  x = 'A';
8                  y = x+1;
9                  z = 'C';
10
11                 printf("It's as easy as %c%c%c\n", x,y,z);
12
13                 return(0);
14         }
15
```

Then, edit line nine to read:

```
1          #include <stdio.h>
2
```

```
3       int main()
4       {
5               char x, y, z;
6
7               x = 'A';
8               y = x+1;
9               z = y+1;
10
11              printf("It's as easy as %c%c%c\n", x,y,z);
12
13              return(0);
14      }
15
```

Save, build and run the code. The output is the same. Instead of assigning immediate values to variables y and z, you did a little character math. Adding 1 to the value of character A gives you a B, and adding 1 to the value of B gives you a C.

The final variable type that we would like to introduce is the float. It holds very large values, very small values, or any values with a fractional part. Take a look at the code below:

```
1       #include <stdio.h>
2
3       int main()
4       {
```

5		float pi;
6		
7		pi = 22.00 / 7.0;
8		printf("The ancients calculated PI as %f.\n", pi);
9		
10		return(0);
11	}	
12		
13		

The float variable pi is declared at line five. At line seven, a calculation is made and the result is assigned to the variable pi. The calculation uses floating point values. By adding a .00 to 22 and 7, the compiler assumes that you need floating point values and treats them as such. Otherwise, integers would be used, and the result would be wrong.

When you use a floating point whole number, remember to add the .00. Line eight sends the result to standard output. The %f placeholder is used to represent floating point values in a printf statement. Build and run the code.

The value generated for pi is accurate down to the hundreds place, which is okay for quite a few things in antiquity, but not acceptable for modern calculations.

Chapter 7 Loops in C

Looping is a common programming situation that you can expect to encounter rather regularly. Loop can simply be described as a situation in which you may need to execute the same block of code over and over. C supports three looping constructs, which are as follows:

- *for Loop*
- *do...while Loop*
- *while Loop*

In addition to this, the foreach looping construct also exists. However, this construct will be explained in the chapter on arrays.

The while Loop:

A while loop is a control structure that permits you to rehash an errand a specific number of times. The syntax for this construct is as follows:

while(boolean_expression) {

/Statements

}

At the point when executing, if the boolean_expression result is genuine, then the activities inside the circle will be executed. This will proceed till the time the result for the condition is genuine. Here, key purpose of the while loop is that the circle may not ever run. At the point when the interpretation is tried and the result is false, the body of the loop will be skipped and the first proclamation after the whole circle will be executed.

Sample:

#include<stdio.h>

int main(){

```
int i=5;
while(i<10) {
printf(" i = " + i );
i++;
printf("\n");
}
}
```

This would deliver the accompanying result:

i = 5

i = 6

i = 7

i = 8

i = 9

i = 5

The do...while Loop

A do...while loop is similar to the while looping construct aside from that a do...while circle is ensured to execute no less than one time. The syntax for this looping construct is as follows:

```
do {
/Statements
}while(<booleanexpression>);
```

Perceive that the Boolean declaration shows up toward the end of the circle, so the code execute once before the Boolean is tried. In the event that the Boolean declaration is genuine, the stream of control bounced go down to do, and the code execute once more. This methodology rehashes until the Boolean articulation is false.

Sample implementation:

```
#include<stdio.h>
int main(){
int i = 1;
do{
printf("i = " + i );
i++;
printf("\n");
}while( i<1 );
}
```

This would create the accompanying result:

i = 1

The for Loop

A for circle is a reiteration control structure that permits you to effectively compose a loop that needs to execute a particular number of times. A for looping construct is helpful when you know how often an errand is to be rehashed. The syntax for the looping construct is as follows:

The punctuation of a for circle is:

for(initialization; Boolean_expression; redesign)

{

/Statements

}

Here is the stream of control in a four circle:

- The introduction step is executed in the first place, and just once. This step permits you to pronounce and introduce any loop control variables. You are not needed to put an announcement here, the length of a semicolon shows up.

- Next, the Boolean outflow is assessed. In the event that it is genuine, the assemblage of the loop is executed. In the event that it is false, the assortment of the loop does not execute and stream of control hops to the following articulation past the for circle.

- After the group of the for circle executes, the stream of control bounced down to the overhaul explanation. This announcement permits you to overhaul any circle control variables. This announcement can be left clear, the length of a semicolon shows up after the Boolean declaration.

- The Boolean outflow is currently assessed once more. On the off chance that it is genuine, the loop executes and the scope rehashes itself. After the Boolean declaration is false, the for loop ends.

Sample Implementation

#include<stdio.h>

int main(){

for(int i = 0; i < 5; i = i+1) {

printf("i = " + i);

printf("\n");

}

}

This would deliver the accompanying result:

i = 0

i = 1

i = 2

i = 3

i = 4

The break Keyword

The break keyword is utilized to stop the whole loop execution. The break word must be utilized inside any loop or a switch construct. The break keyword will stop the execution of the deepest circle and begin executing the following line of code after the ending curly bracket. The syntax for using this keyword is as follows:

break;

The syntax of using this keyword is as follows:

continue;

The Infinite Loop

If the condition is the loop is always true, the loop shall continue infinitely. Typically, the 'for' loop construct is used for this purpose. In order to implement the for loop, you don't need to mention any of the three expressions that are written inside the for loop. Sample implementation of the infinite loop is given by:

#include<stdio.h>

int main(){

```
for(;;)
{
//statements inside infinite loop
}
```

Since no conditional statement is present in for loop, the condition is assumed to be always true by the compiler. As a result, the loop becomes infinite. This loop can be terminated using an external interrupt (Ctrl + C).

Chapter 8 Application of Graphical User Interface

In this chapter, we are going to transform our programs from just texts to a graphical interface which will look more appealing and interesting as compared to a line full of codes. In this section, the programmer is free to create images of various shapes as much as they can desire. The creation of interface requires well planning and use of intelligence to be able to express and output appealing products to the end line of the user.

The importance of graphics is that it is able to compress tasks and visualize a massive amount of written codes into an appealing work of art. In other words, the graphical interface makes work easier for the end user to interact with a program and understand the working concept of the whole program in a very short period of time. The picture below is a snippet of the early works of a graphic interface;

Some of the programs that enable the programmer to achieve such high graphical properties include; CAD- Computer Aided Design and CAM- Computer Aided Manufacturing. In this topic we are going to discuss how to incorporate the hardware and software part of graphics in C# programming language to achieve complex programs

The Graphical Hardware and Software

The Graphic Hardware

In modern technology, computers utilize the concept of a **bitmapped display** to output the products of most programs. In other words, the bit-mapped display consists of a screen which is made up of millions of pixels and picture elements. These pixels are usually laid out in a 2-Dimensional grid that can hold up to a range of (800-1560) x (600-1280). These are the numbers of the pixels in the 2-Dimensional grid. The quality of the display can be determined by the number of pixel in the output of the screen. Large numbers of pixels refer to high resolution whereas low numbers of pixels in a screen refer to low resolution. High-resolution images provide very clear and sharp pictures and low-resolution images provide less quality pictures which are sometimes blurry and less visible to the eyes. In terms of storage components, the frame that stores the images in the actual screen is referred to as **buffer frames.** In connection to high-resolution pictures, the buffer frames required are directly related to the number of pixels that are found in the screen. However, a major drawback to the graphics technology is that the higher the resolution the more the memory required in the buffer frames of the screen. This main disadvantage here is that it requires almost four times the number of memory space that could have been used to store the program in text form.

The hardware which provides the display represents every value of the number of pixel in the buffer frame. It works by balancing the three colors which are Red, Blue and Green. The most interesting thing is that the balancing occurs for each and every pixel on the screen regardless of the range of numbers between half a million to two million pixels. It is also important to know that the color intensity of each and every pixel is not permanent but fades away within a fraction of a second.

For stability of a picture, repainting of the pixel is done quickly after the fading of the color intensity in order to avoid flickering of pictures. For these to be accurately achieved, the screen must be well updated and in good condition. The screen should also be refreshed at least thirty to fifty times a second. The user is also at the liberty of editing the balancing of the colors in order to achieve various shed of colors from the pixels. The shapes of images can also be altered by the modification of color intensity of the pixels

In summary, this is the fundamental concept of how the hardware part of the graphical usage operates in order to produce graphical images. In the next subtopic we are now going to discuss the software part of graphical programming.

Graphical software

In this study, we are going to focus on the software part of setting of pixels until a clear image is achieved. We are going to have a deeper understanding of functions from the graphic library that helps in controlling the settings and clearance of the graphical pixels.

In C# programming language, the graphic library that is involved in graphical software is very powerful. The extensive graphic library can be used to create complex figures, shapes, images and very clear pictures. Some of the complex operations that can be achieved in C# programming language include the drawing of geometric figures and shapes, creation of scrolling interfaces, creation of buttons and also menus that pull down.

We are going to get into further studies on how to create C# graphics using Visual Studio program.

Begin with a Windows Form App project. A window called **"Form 1"** will appear on the screen. This is done by the IDE of the C# programming language. It is done automatically but the learner must know that there were a lot of codes that were generated before the automatic creation of the form. The form appears as shown below;

If the student is interested to see the lines of codes that were used to generate the form he or she can click on the ◇ buttons in the windows form. The following lines of code should appear;

```
using                                           System;
using                          System.Collections.Generic;
using                            System.ComponentModel;
```

```csharp
using System.Data;
using System.Drawing;
using System.Linq;
using System.Text;
using System.Threading.Tasks;
using System.Windows.Forms;
namespace GraphicsProgram
{
    public partial class Form1 : Form
    {
        public Form1()
        {
            InitializeComponent();
        }
    }
}
```

Secondly, we want to draw a basic line in the form created above and see the lines of codes that are used to generate the lines in graphical form. We will draw the simple line from point A (21, 21) to point B (101,101). The diagram below shows the illustration;

The line of code that is used to generate the graphic is as shown below;

```csharp
public Form1()
{ //This is the form on which drawing will appear
InitializeComponent(); // initialization of the form
this.Text = "C# Graphics";
Graphics drawingCanvas = CreateGraphics();
Show();
Pen BlackPen = new Pen(Color.Black, 2);
drawingCanvas.DrawLine
(BlackPen, 21, 21, 101, 101);
}
```

Understanding our code

The first line of the statement of the code calls the initialization of the element function. The function is used to automatically generate the form. The second line of statement displays the texts that will appear on the title bar of the window. The third line of statement produces the platform where the line is drawn or the background surface of the form. The line of the statement containing **"Show ();"** enables the form to be shown on the screen.

"Pen BlackPen = new Pen(Color.Black, 2);" is the piece of code that creates the pen that will paint the line on the form.

Practical Exercise

1. Run the following code and note the changes that will occur and the new things that you can observe:

i) public Form1()
   { // This is the form on which drawing will appear
   InitializeComponent(); // initialization of the form
   this.Text = "C# Graphics";
   Graphics drawingCanvas = CreateGraphics();
   Show();
   Pen BlackPen = new Pen(Color.Black, 2);
   drawingCanvas.DrawARectangle
   (BlackPen, 26, 61, 51, 41);
   }

   ii) public Form1()
   { //This the form on which drawing will appear
   InitializeComponent(); // initialization of the form
   this.Text = "C# Graphics";
   Graphics drawingCanvas = CreateGraphics();
   Show();
   Pen BlackPen = new Pen(Color.Black, 2);
   drawingCanvas.DrawEllipse

(BlackPen,-24, 26, 126, 126);
}

iii) public Form1()
{ // This is the form on which drawing will appear
InitializeComponent(); // initialization of the form
this.Text = "C# Graphics";
Graphics drawingCanvas = CreateGraphics();
Show();
Pen BlackPen = new Pen(Color.Black, 2);
drawingCanvas.DrawEllipse
(BlackPen,-20, 20, 120, 120);
}

iv) public Form1()
{ // This isform on which drawing will occur
InitializeComponent(); // initialize form
this.Text = "C# Graphics";
Graphics drawingCanvas = CreateGraphics();
Show();
Pen BlackPen = new Pen(Color.Black, 2);
drawingCanvas.DrawRectangle
(BlackPen, 90, 90, 40, 90);
Brush redBrush = Brushes.Red;
Font f = new Font("Consolas", 12);
drawingCanvas.DrawString
("Stop", f, redBrush,100, 130);
}

Enabling a Mouse and other operations

In order for the mouse to be enabled to click in the C# programming language, an event handler must be initiated in the windows form. This is a piece of code that is able to sense an activity and hence react to the activity.

The program below illustrates the use of Mouse Clicks in a newly created form;

```
private void Form1_MouseClick
(object sender, MouseEventArgs e)
{
int x;
int y;
x = e.X;
y = e.Y;
if((x >= 90) && (x <= 140) &&
(y >= 90) && (y <= 190))
{
MessageBox.Show("User clicked inside" +
" the button");
}
else
{
MessageBox.Show("User clicked outside" +
" the button");
}
}
```

Understanding our code

After the mouse has been enabled, the cursor that is displayed in the form is used to click on to the imaginary created rectangle and hence respond by outputting some feedback message as shown below;

In summary, the knowledge shown above is a simple illustration of a real graphical interface both in hardware and software part. I hope you have understood a simple concept of GUI in C# programming language. Graphical programming enables us to create interesting pictures, objects and images that make programming to be very interesting and fun to engage in.

The following are some of the visual components

- A Form which is used to output the window.
- A Button which is used to output a clickable surface or button.

- A Textbox which is used to output a surface that can be edited.
- A Label which is used to output labels to other objects.
- A radiobutton which is used to output a selectable surface or button.

Chapter 9 Decision Making in C

There are two sorts of decision making constructs in C. They are:

- if constructs
- switch constructs

The if Statement:

An if constructs comprises of a Boolean outflow emulated by one or more proclamations. The syntax for using this construct is as follows:

if(<condition>) {

//Statements if the condition is true

}

In the event that the Boolean construct assesses to true, then the scope of code inside the if proclamation will be executed. If not the first set of code after the end of the if construct (after the end wavy prop) will be executed.

Sample Implementation:

#include<stdio.h>

int main(){

int i = 0;

if(i < 1){

printf("The if construct is executing!");

}

}

This would create the accompanying result:

The if construct is executing!

The if...else Statement

An if proclamation can be trailed by a non-compulsory else explanation, which executes when the Boolean outflow is false. The syntax for this construct is as follows:

if(<condition>){

//Executes if condition is true

}

else{

//Executes if condition is false

}

Sample Implementation:

```
#include<stdio.h>
int main(){
int i = 0;
if( i > 1 ){
printf("The if construct is executing!");
}
else{
printf("The else construct is executing!");
}
}
```

This would create the accompanying result:

The else construct is executing!

The if...else if Statement

An if proclamation can be trailed by a non-compulsory else if...else explanation, which is exceptionally helpful to test different conditions utilizing single if...else if articulation.

The syntax for using this decision making construct Is as follows:

if(condition_1){

//Execute if condition_1 is true

}

else if(condition_2){

//Execute if condition_2 is true

}

else if(condition_3){

//Execute if condition_3 is true

}

else

{

//Execute if all conditions are false

}

Sample Implementation:

#include<stdio.h>

int main(){

```
int i = 0;
if( i > 1 ){
printf("The first if construct is executing!");
}
else if(i == 0){
printf("The second if construct is executing!");
}
else{
printf("The else construct is executing!");
}
}
```

This would create the accompanying result:

The second if construct is executing!

Nested if...else Statement

It is legitimate to home if-else constructs, which implies you can utilize one if or else if proclamation inside an alternate if or else if explanation. The syntax for using this construct Is as follows:

```
if(condition_1){
//Execute if condition_1 is true
        if(condition_2){
        //Execute if condition_2 is true
        }
}
```

```
else if(condition_3){
//Execute if condition_3 is true
}
else
{
//Execute if all conditions are false
}
```

Sample Implementation:

```c
#include<stdio.h>
int main(){
int i = 1;
if( i >= 1 ){
printf("The if construct is executing!");
    if(i == 1){
    printf("The nested if construct is executing!");
    }
}
else{
printf("The else construct is executing!");
}
}
```

This would create the accompanying result:

The if construct is executing!

The nested if construct is executing!

The switch Statement

A switch construct permits a variable to be tried for equity against a rundown of values. Each one value is known as a case, and the variable being exchanged on is checked for each one case. The syntax for using this decision making construct is as follows:

switch(<condition>){

case value1:

//Statements

break;

case value2 :

//Statements

break;

default:

//Optional

}

The accompanying runs apply to a switch construct:

- The variable utilized as a part of a switch explanation must be a short, byte, char or int.

- You can have any number of case explanations inside a switch. Each one case is trailed by the value to be contrasted with and a colon.

- The value for a case must be the same type as the variable in the switch and it must be a steady or an exacting value.

- When the variable being exchanged on is equivalent to a case, the announcements after that case will execute until a break is arrived at.

- When a break is arrived at, the switch ends, and the stream of control bounces to the following line after the switch.

- Not each case needs to contain a break. In the event that no break shows up, the stream of control will fall through to consequent cases until a break is arrived at.

- A switch articulation can have a discretionary default case, which must show up toward the end of the switch. The default case can be utilized for performing an undertaking when none of the cases is true. No break is required in the default case. However, as per the convention, the use of the same is recommended.

Sample Implementation:

#include<stdio.h>

int main(){

char mygrade = 'A';

switch(mygrade)

{

case "A" :

printf("Excellent Performance!");

break;

case "B" :

printf("Good Performance!");

break;

default :

printf("Failed");

}

Aggregate and run above code utilizing different inputs to grade. This would create the accompanying result for the present value of mygrade:

Excellent Performance!

Nesting of switch case constructs are also allowed in C programming language. Therefore, you can have a switch construct inside a case construct.

Chapter 10 Constants and Literals

Constants are variables for which the value cannot be changed during the program's execution. In other words, their values are fixed. These fixed values are called literals. Several types of constants exist. In fact, constants can be of integer, floating point, character, string and enum type in C#. In simple words, constants are exactly like variables. It is just that the values of variables can be changed during the course of the program while the same for constants is not true.

Integer Literals

A hexadecimal or integer literal is associated with Integer Literals. The radix of the literal is determined by the prefix attached to the number. For instance, if the prefix is 0X or 0x, then the number is hexadecimal else the number is decimal. In addition to this, numbers may have a suffix of U or L. While U stands for unsigned, L stands for Long. The prefix and suffix may have any case and appear in any order. Some examples of integer literals include oxFeeL, 85, 212, 30ul, 0X4b and 48u.

Floating Point Literals

Floating Point literals are literals that possess a fractional or exponential part in addition to the integer part. Therefore, they may be represented in decimal form where the integer part is followed by a decimal point and fractional component or in the exponential form.

Some examples of floating point literals are 510E, 3.14159 and 210E-5F. However, literals like .e55 are not allowed because they do not have an integer component. Likewise, constants like 210f are also invalid as they lack a decimal or exponent component. Therefore, the decimal form must have exponent or/and decimal and the exponential form must have fractional part and/or integer part.

Character Literals

It is a practice to enclose character literals within single inverted commas. A character literal can store characters, special characters and universal characters. Characters that are preceded by a backslash have special functionality. For instance, \n is the newline character. Similar to this character combination, several other character combinations also exist in C#. The codes for these special characters are given below.

\'	**' character**
****	**\ character**
\?	**? character**
\"	**" character**
\b	**Backspace**
\a	**Alert or bell**
\n	**Newline**
\f	**Form feed**

\t   Horizontal tab

\r   Carriage return

\xhh .   Hexadecimal number of one or
. .   more digits

\v   Vertical tab

Sample implementation of how escape characters function is provided below for your reference.

using System;

namespace DemoEscapeChar {

class DemoProg {

static void Main(string[] args) {

Console.WriteLine("Hello\t\t\tWorld\n\n\n!");

Console.ReadLine();

}

}

}

Upon execution, this code shall generate the result given below.

String Literals

When you have to declare string literals or character sequences, you must do so within double inverted commas. The string can be a sequence of characters and special characters. Moreover, it can also be multiple lines that are separated using the newline special character or a character with many white spaces. Some examples of string literals include –

1. *"Hello"*

2. **"HelloWorld"**
3. **"Hello**
4. World".

Chapter 11 Command Line Arguments

In C programming, it is perfectly possible to accept and to have command line arguments. These arguments are typically provided after the program name in the operating systems of the command line. Some of these operating systems include Linux and DOS. Command line arguments are then passed on to the created program from your operating system.

To utilize these command line arguments in the created program, you need to completely understand the entire declaration for the main function first. This main function should previously have no arguments to begin with.

Interestingly, the main function can simultaneously accept two types of arguments. The first one would be the number of the command line arguments. The second one would be the entire list of every command line argument included in the program.

The main argument's full declaration somehow appears like this:

    int main (int argc, char *argv[])

For this code, argc is considered as the argument count. The argument count is the given number of command line arguments passed on to the created program. The command line is the origin for this argument. The line argument includes the program's name as well.

The array of the pointers for the character is regarded as the listing of every argument. On the other hand, argv[0] will be the program's name. For the declaration above, it is an empty string in case the name is not yet available. After this, every number of the element in the declaration that is less than the argc string will be considered as one of the command line arguments.

You may handle the command line arguments using main() as your function argument. If you combine it with other commands, argc will be considered as the number of passed arguments. On the other hand, argv[] will be the pointed array. This means that argv[] will point the each of the passed argument to the created program.

You may use each of the argv elements in the same way that you will use a string. Also, you may utilize argv and treat it as a type of two- dimensional kind of array. In any case, the argv[argc] will be considered a null pointer.

The following is an example that can help you check if there are any supplied arguments from the program's command line. Based on what you observed, you can take the necessary action.

#include <stdio.h>[B5]

int main(int argc, char *argv[]) {

if(argc == 2){
   printf("The supplied argument is %s\n", argv[1]);
}
else if(argc>2){
   printf("Too many supplied arguments.\n");
}
else{
   printf("Only one expected argument.\n");
}

}

Compiling and executing the code above without passing any type of argument will eventually yield this result:

$./a.out
One expected argument

If you compile the codes above, and execute them using just one argument, it can produce this result:

$./a/out testing
The supplied argument is testing.

On the other hand, if you compile the codes above and execute them using two arguments, it can produce this result:

   $./a/out testing1 testing2
   Too many supplied arguments.

Take note that the argv[0] is considered the bearer of the program name itself. On the other hand, argv[1] serves as the pointer to your first supplied command line. Given these facts, *argv[n] will be regarded as the last argument. If you do not supply any argument, argc will be considered as one of those. Otherwise, passing one argument will then set argc to 2.

You have to pass all of the command line arguments, and separate them using spaces. However, if the argument itself contains a space, you need to pass this argument by placing them inside quotation marks. You may also use single quotes, or '' for this. To illustrate this, here is an example:

```
#include <stdio.h>

int main(int argc, char *argv[]) {
  printf("Program's name %s\n", argv[0]);
  if(argc == 2){
      printf("The supplied argument is %s\n", argv[1]);
  }
  else if(argc>2){
    printf("Too many supplied arguments.\n");
  }
  else{
     printf("Only one expected argument.\n");
  }
}
```

If you try compiling and executing the code above using a single argument with spaces enclosed within single quotation marks or double quotation marks, it can produce this result:

$./a.out "testing1 testing2"
Program's name ./a.out
The supplied argument is testing1 testing2

It is actually easy to use this argument for your program. Almost any type of program that prefers the parameters set as soon as the program is executed, will definitely use this one. One of the most common uses for this is to create a function that can take the name of a specific given file. The output would be the entire text of the file. This will be displayed on the screen.

```
#include <stdic.h>
int main ( int argc, char *argv[] )
{
if ( argc != 1) /* argc should be 1 for right execution */
{
/* I print argv[0] assuming this is the program's name */
Printf( "usage: %s filename", argv[0] );
}
else
}
// I assume argv[1] will be the filename to be opened
FILE *file = fopen( argv[1], "r" );
/* fopen returns 0, the NULL pointer, during failure */
if ( file == 0 )
{
printf ( "unable to open file\n" );
}
else
{
int x;
```

/* from the file, read one character only at a time, stop at FOF, which somewhat indicates the file's ending. Take note that the idiom stating that "assign it to one variable, then check the value" used at the bottom part will work because the statement

of the assignment eventually evaluates to the assigned value.
*/

```
while ( ( x = fgetc ( file ) ) != EOF )
{
printf ( "%c", x );
}
```

fclose (file);

}

}

}

The program above is relatively short. However, it has effectively incorporated the full version of the main declaration. It even performed one useful function. First, it checks to fully ensure that the program user successfully included the second argument. Theoretically, this will be the file name. The program will then perform another check to verify if the file is valid. This is done by opening the file in question. This is considered a standard operation type. If the operation eventually leads to the opening of the file, then fopen's return value will have a valid FILE*; as the output. In case the opposite is true, that will be 0. In this case, 0 is considered as the NULL pointer.

After this, you just have to execute a loop. The loop will be used to help you print out one character, for instance. The code is somewhat self-explanatory. However, it has some comments included in it. You will have little trouble deciphering how the operation works if you look at it carefully.

Typecasting

Typecasting is considered a way to change one variable from one type of date to another, different kind of data. It is a method of making one variable into one type, like the int variable, to another different type of variable, like the char. This is done for a single operation. For instance, if you are thinking of storing one 'long' value to a kind of simple integer, all you have to do is to type cast the string 'long' into 'int'.

You may even convert your values from one kind to another by explicitly utilizing the cast operator.

(type_name) expression

This example will show you that the cast operator can cause division of an integer variable by another one. It will be performed as a kind of floating point operation.

```
#include <stdio.h>[B7]

int main() {
    int sum = 20, count = 4;
double mean;
    mean = (double)sum/count;
    printf("Value of mean: %f\n", mean);
    return 0;
}
```

If you compile and execute the code given above, it will produce this result:

Value of mean : 5.00000

Take note that your cast operator should have precedence over the division. Therefore, the value of sum command should first be converted to type double. Finally, it should be divided by count. This will eventually yield a double value.

Some type conversions may be implicit. You may automatically perform this function yourself if you prefer. An alternative would be to explicitly specify this by using the cast operator. Using your cast operator when type conversions are needed is actually considered a good practice, as far as programming is concerned.

If you want to typecast a program or an operation, you have to place the variable type, that you prefer the actual variable to, act within the inside parentheses. These should be placed directly in front of your actual preferred variable. For instance, (char)a will create the 'a' function as char.

Here is an example of typecasting "in action":

#include <stdio.h>
int main()
{

/* The (char) is considered a typecast. This instructs the computer to interpret the number 65 as a type of character and not merely as a number. This will provide the character with an output for the equivalent for the number 65 (In the case of ASCII, this will be the letter A). Take note that the %c found below will be considered as the format code of printing just one character.
*/
printf("%c\n". (char) 65);
getchar ();
}

One of the main uses of typecasting is highlighted if you prefer to use some ASCII characters. For instance, in case you want to come up with your own chart of all the 128 ASCII characters, you need to use the typecast function. This will permit you to print out all the integers as the character equivalent.

#include <stdio.h>
int main()
{

```
            for ( int x = 0; x < 128; x++ ) {
    /* Note the function of int type for x to provide output
                        and use
     * of (char) tohelp typecast x to a character that outputs
     * ASCII characters that correspond to current number
                          */
            printf( "%d = %c\n", x, (char)x );
                           }
                      getchar();
   }
```

If you look closely, you will notice something really strange. If you pass the x value to printf to pass off as a char, in theory, it is expected that the intended value will be treated as a type of character when you write the format string as %c. Because the char variety is considered a relatively small integer, adding the typecast will not actually add any form of value to it!

Therefore, the typecast will come in handy if you want to force the right kind of mathematical operation, and have it take place in the program successfully. It will eventually turn out that in C and other types of programming languages, the final output of the integer divisions is also itself treated as another integer. For example, a value of ¼ turns to 0 because this is considered less than a whole number. The process of dividing integers eventually ignores the remaining value.

On the other hand, the division between the floating- point numbers and even between the floating- point number and the integer is enough to make the result show up as a type of floating point number. Therefore, if you are planning to execute a type of fancy division that you do not want to have truncated values, you will need to cast one of your variables into a floating- point kind. For example, (float)¼ will come out as a .25, as per normal expectation.

It is usually reasonable for you to store two different values in the integers. If you are tracking patients with heart problems, you can have a specific function that will help you compute for the age of each patient in years. You may also include the specific number of instances that they came in for complaints, like heart pain. One type of operation that you may want to execute is the frequency of visits that a patient had with their physician, because of angina or heart pain. For this particular situation, the program will look something like this:

```
/* function will return age in years */
int age = getAge();
/* function will return number of visits */
int angina_visits = getVisits();
float visits_per_year = angina_visits / age;
```

The only problem is when you run the created program, the visits_per_year string will give an output of zero. This will take place unless the patient with the heart problem had a really large number of clinic visits for the duration of the entire year. One way to help you resolve this problem is by casting one of the given values that will be divided. This will then be treated as a kind of floating point number. In turn, it will cause you to treat this expression like it were really bound to be a floating- point number:

```
float visits_per_year = angina_visits / (float)age;
/* or */
float visits_per_year = (float)angina_visits / age;
```

Using this sequence will eventually bring in the right values. These values will be stored in the visits_per_year string. Aside from the example shown above, you may even come up with other similar programs to resolve the problem.

Integer Promotion

Integer promotion is the method of converting values with integer types that are smaller than unsigned int or int to unsigned int or int. See the example below:

```
#include <stdio.h>
main() {
int i = 1;
```

```
        char c = 'c'; /* ascii value is 9 */
            int sum;
            sum = i + c;
   printf("Value of sum : %d\n", sum );
            }
```

If you compile and execute the code above, it will produce this result:

      Value of sum: 10

For this particular example, the value of the sum is 10 because you resorted to integer promotion. You also converted the 'c' value to ASCII before you performed the actually operation of addition.

In this chapter, we discussed command line arguments. In the next chapter, get ready to create your first program!

Great progress so far!

Chapter 12 Extension Methods

Extension Methods (introduced in C# 3.0) provides programmers with a simple framework to "extend" the functionalities of existing types in their programs. "Static" in nature, Extension Methods gives you the freedom to add already present methods into your types without a need to create new derived types or modifying old ones. They use a "this" keyword in their parameters / parameters lists. Since they are "static" methods, it's essential for you to use them in static classes. However, they are used as if they were instance methods of the extended type.

In this chapter, we will discuss Extension Methods in depth, and will learn:

Contents

- **What Extension Methods are**
- **How to create them**
- **How to applying Extension Methods to existing types**

i. Extension Methods

The OCP, Open close principle, directs programmers to write code and functions in a way that they are open for extension all the time, but dead end on modification. In C#, Extension Methods are a practical case of OCP, which we can use in both custom defined and system defined user types to cater to our requirements.

It's also important for us to know a few basic facts about Extension Methods and how they work. One, they have only access (and hence can only use) the "public" properties of the data type they are extending. Two, their type signature should never be the same as any existing method of that type. Three, to use Extension Methods, their parent type must be in the namespace of the calling application. Four, in the case of a method overloading (methods with same signature), an instance method will be executed (called) instead of the Extended Method (as per the overload resolution mechanism), and lastly, we cannot apply Extension Methods on events, properties, and fields.

The generic, or old way, of doing that is:

Example 1:

```
    struct MyExample
{
   int num;
   public MyExample(int val)
   {
      this.num = val;
   }
   public int Negative()
   {
      return -num;
   }
}
static void Main(string[] args)
{
   MyExample i = new MyInt(34);
   Console.WriteLine(i.Negative());
                     }
```

While the code is quite basic, where we have created a strict "MyExample()" that has a simple function that returns negative of our passed value.

ii. Creating Extension Methods

The code above works fine, but technically speaking we are not actually extending the type of our existing type. Instead we have created a new type altogether. Hence, if we are really looking to "extend" the functionality of our existing type, we should be doing something better and more generic than that.

Example 2:

```
    static class MySampleExtension
{
    public static int Negative(this int val)
    {
        return -val;
    }
}
static void Main(string[] args)
{
    int i = 53;
    Console.WriteLine(i.Negative());
                                    }
```

While the basic functionality and output of this is similar in that it will output the negative of the passed "int", how it works is different. See the method declaration here: "public static int Negative()". We are adding our method "negative" with type "int" and are bounding it to be called only with the int type. We are not creating a new type as in the previous example, and we are only extending functionality of the type "int". Hence, to create our Extension Methods, we should:

- Have a "Static" class.
- Use a "public static" method with the same name as the class and have an explicit return type.
- Use the parameters type with the "this" keyword.

The "this" keyword is very important since it tells our compiler that we are "extending" this type and are not using it as an expected argument type.

iii. **Extension Methods on existing types**

Using the above created Extension Method, let's now see how we can call an Extension Method on our existing types. Also note that we used the "this" keyword above, but what about the cases where we want to use additional parameters? We can easily do this too by defining all such parameters with their expected data type after specifying our "extending" type with the "this" keyword. The code below will help us to better understand:

Example 3:

```
    static class MySampleExtMethods
{
   public static int Negative(this int val)
   {
      return -val;
   }
   public static int Multiply(this int val, int multi)
   {
      return val * multi;
```

```
    }
}
static void Main(string[] args)
{
    int i = 8;
    Console.WriteLine(' Using Extension method the input yields: {0}', i.Multiply(2));
                    }
```

Note that here we have defined another extension function called "Multiply". While we are extending it on type "int" as specified by "this in val", the second argument "int multi" lacks the "this" keyword. This is because we are using the second argument as an "argument," and extending it with the first type. However, note that we can also pass "strings," "char," or "float" values in "arguments" as our needs warrant.

The rest of the code is quite straightforward. We have created two extension methods and are calling the "multiply" method with such an argument of "2," and are extending it on the value of "I" which is 8. The output of above code will be:

Output 3:

16

Exercise 4

Task:

Create an Extension Method that checks if a string is an int or not, and if it is, convert the string's numeric value into a corresponding int value. For example, string str="2345" should be converted into int or return false otherwise.
Solution

```csharp
using System;
using System.Text;

namespace SampleExtensionMethod
{
    public static class SampleClass
    {
        public static bool IsInt(this string x)
            {
                float outcome;
                return float.TryParse(x, out outcome);
            }

    public static int IntExt(this string str)
        {
            return Int32.Parse(str);
        }
    }
    class Caller
    {
        static void Main       (string      []      args)
        {
         string str= '2345';
         if (str.IsInt())
            { Console.WriteLine('Yes It's an integer');
           int nmb=str.IntExt();
        Console.WriteLine('The output using our custom Integer extension method: {0}', nmb); }
            else
                Console.WriteLine('No, it's not an integer.');

                Console.ReadLine();
                                                                }
                                                                }
                                                                }
        }
```

Chapter 13 Nullable Types

C# provides some special types that consist of an additional null value along with the usual possible range of values of that data type. For example, an int32 data type can store a value ranging from -2147483648 to 2147483647 while the nullableint32 is able to store a null value along with its original possible range. Similarly, in the case of a Boolean variable, the Nullable of a Boolean variable is able to store a true, false, or a null value in it.

In this chapter we will study:

Contents

- Structures of Nullable types in C#
- Syntax of Nullable types
- The HasValue and Has Property
- The Null Coalescing operator

i. Structures of Nullable types in C#

The following table demonstrates the Nullable structure of a primitive data type along with the range of data that each data type can store. Nullable types have an additional value of Null.

Type	Range
Nullable Boolean	True or False or Null
Nullable byte	0 to 255 or Null
Nullable decimal	(-7.9 x 1028 to 7.9 x 1028) / 100

	to 28 or Null
Nullable double	(+/-)5.0 x 10-324 to (+/-)1.7 x 10308 or Null
Nullable DateTime	Represents an instant in Time or Null
Nullable Int16	-32,768 to +32,767 or Null
Nullable Int32	-2,147,483,648 to 2,147,483,647 or Null
Nullable Int64	-9,223,372,036,854,775,808 to +9,223,372,036,854,775,807 0r Null
Nullable Single	Single value or Null
Nullable char	U+0000 to U+FFFF or Null

ii. Syntax for Nullable types in C#

Nullable types can be declared in two ways. The Syntax for the first way to declare a Nullable type is as follows:

System.Nullable<data_type> <variable_name> ;

It starts with the System.Nullable keyword, followed by data_type (i.e., int, double) followed by the variable name.

The Syntax for declaring a Nullable type the other way is:

< data_type> ? <variable_name> = null;

Starting with the data_type (i.e., int, double), it is followed by a question mark and then the name of variable.

Let's now see Nullable types at work.

Example 1:

Namespace nullable
{
　Class program
　　{
　　static void Main ()
　　{
　　int? a= null;
　　int? b=10;
　　if(a==null)

　　{System.Console.WriteLine(b.Value)}
　　else {System.Console.WriteLine('Undefined');}
　　Console.readKey();
　　}

　}

}

In the example above, we have declared two nullable integers a and b. int? a has a null value and int? b has a value of 10. The if/else construct is quite basic too; if "a" has a null value, the program will print out the value of int? b. Otherwise, it will print "undefined".

Output 1:

10

The following example illustrates the Nullable type in action for Boolean and DateTime types.

Example 2:

Namespace nullable

```
{
    Class program
    {
        static void Main ()
        {
            int? a= null;
            int? b=5;

            Double? c=null;
            Double? d=6

            bool? Val= new bool?();

            DateTime? Start= DateTime.today;

            DateTime? End= null;
Console.Writeline('Showing values of Nullables: {0}, {1}, {2}, {3}',a,b,c,d);

Console.Writeline('A Nullable Boolean Variable: {0}',Val);

Console.Writeline(Start);

Console.Writeline('We don't know yet:', End);

Console.readKey();
        }
    }
}
```

In this program, we are using the Nullables of int, double, Boolean, and DateTime. Later, we are simply displaying them on the console. As the program compiles, it shows the values of the variables as:

Output 2:

Showing values of Nullables:, 5, , 6

A Nullable Boolean Variable:

6/8/2015 12:00:00 AM

We don't know yet:

      iii.   The HasValue and Value Property

The Nullable type instances have two properties. These are public and read-only properties.

- HasValue Property:

The HasValue always returns a Boolean value. It can be true or false. If the type contains an integer or a non-null value, the Hasvalue property is true. If the type doesn't have a value or it is null, the Hasvalue property is false.

- Has Property:

The value is of the same type as the declared type. The Has property has a value if the Hasvalue property is true. If the Hasvalue property is false, the Has property will throw an Exception. See the code below to better understand this:

Example 3:

```
using System;
Namespace nullable
{
  Class program
  {
    static void Main ()
    {
      int? a= null;
```

```
        Console.WriteLine(a.HasValue); // HasValue property is false
        Console.WriteLine(a.Value);    // will cause an exception
        Console.readKey();
    }
}
```

Because our variable "a" has a null value the "HasValue" property will be false. If we try to display the "Value" on the console, we get an exception.

Output 3:
> **False**

Example 4:

```
            using System;
Namespace nullable
{
    Class program
    {
        static void Main ()
        {
            int? a= null;

        Console.WriteLine(a.HasValue); // HasValue property is false


            a=5; //assigning value to variable

        Console.WriteLine(a.HasValue); // hasvalue Property is true because a has non-null value

        Console.WriteLine(a.Value);    // returns value of a
```

Console.WriteLine(a);

Console.readKey();
}

}
Output 4:
False

True

5

iv. The Null Coalescing Operator

C# provides an operator to check the Null values. If it finds a Null value variable, it assigns a value to that variable. It is denoted by double question mark (??). We can use this operator for both Nullable types and reference types. It converts an operand to the type of another value type operand if the implicit conversion is possible. Let's see how it works:

Example 5:

```
using System;
Namespace nullable
{
  Class program
  {
    static void Main ()
    {
      int? a= null;
      int? b=3;
      int c=a ?? 5;
```

```
            System.Console.WriteLine('Value of c is: {0}',c);
            C=b ?? 5;
            System.Console.WriteLine('Value of c is: {0}',c);
            Console.readKey();
        }
    }
}
```

Output 5:

Value of c is: 5

Value of c is: 3

Exercise

Task:

Write a program using a Nullable integer and double values implementing the HasValue property and the Null coalescing properties.

Solution:

using System;
using System.Collections.Generic;

using System.Linq;

using System.Text;

using System.Threading.Tasks;

namespace nullable

{

　class Program

　　{

```csharp
static void Main(string[] args)
{
    int? a = null;
    Console.WriteLine(a.HasValue);
            int?                    b=3;
    Double? d=null;
    Double? e = 4;
int c=a ?? 6;
System.Console.WriteLine('Value of Int c when assigned to null is: {0}',c);
c=b ?? 6;
System.Console.WriteLine('Value of Int c reassigning is: {0}',c);
Double f = d ?? 8;
System.Console.WriteLine('Value of Double f when assigned is:{0}', f);
f = e ?? 8;
System.Console.WriteLine('Value of Double f reassigning is: {0}', f);
    a = 1;   //assigning value to variable
    d = 2;   // aasigning value to variable
    Console.WriteLine(a.HasValue);
    Console.WriteLine(d.HasValue);
    Console.WriteLine(a.Value);
```

```
            Console.WriteLine(d.Value);
            Console.WriteLine(a);
            Console.WriteLine(d);
            Console.ReadKey();
        }
}
```

Conclusion

Thank you again for downloading this book!

The next step is to start using all of this. The best way to learn programming is really just to challenge yourself. Start putting yourself out there and seeking programming challenges. Think of something that you want to do and then start looking into whether other people have done it. If they have, look into the way that they did it and try to find a way that you could do it yourself. If they haven't, then this gives you a perfect opportunity to be the first to do something. Get your hands dirty and start looking into and learning as much about things having to do with programming as you possibly can.

I sincerely hope that this book was able to provide you with the knowledge base that you needed in order to be an able programmer. The best way to learn, from here, is to look into a bunch of open source projects as well as to keep reading other more advanced books. This book was enough to give you a firm foundation in programming that will extend beyond just this book and well into the realm of many other C-style languages. However, this is with the condition that you actually take the time and effort to try to learn and perform in these languages.

C#
The practical **intermediate's** guide to learn c# programming in one day step-by-step.

(#2020 updated version | effective computer programming languages)

Steve Tudor

Text Copyright ©

All rights reserved. No part of this guide may be reproduced in any form without permission in writing from the publisher except in the case of brief quotations embodied in critical articles or reviews.

Legal & Disclaimer

The information contained in this book and its contents is not designed to replace or take the place of any form of medical or professional advice; and is not meant to replace the need for independent medical, financial, legal or other professional advice or services, as may be required. The content and information in this book has been provided for educational and entertainment purposes only.

The content and information contained in this book has been compiled from sources deemed reliable, and it is accurate to the best of the Author's knowledge, information and belief. However, the Author cannot guarantee its accuracy and validity and cannot be held liable for any errors and/or omissions. Further, changes are periodically made to this book as and when needed. Where appropriate and/or necessary, you must consult a professional (including but not limited to your doctor, attorney, financial advisor or such other professional advisor) before using any of the suggested remedies, techniques, or information in this book.

Upon using the contents and information contained in this book, you agree to hold harmless the Author from and against any damages, costs, and expenses, including any legal fees potentially resulting from the application of any of the information provided by this book. This disclaimer applies to any loss, damages or injury caused by the use and application, whether directly or indirectly, of any advice or information presented, whether for breach of contract, tort, negligence,

personal injury, criminal intent, or under any other cause of action.

You agree to accept all risks of using the information presented inside this book.

You agree that by continuing to read this book, where appropriate and/or necessary, you shall consult a professional (including but not limited to your doctor, attorney, or financial advisor or such other advisor as needed) before using any of the suggested remedies, techniques, or information in this book.

Introduction

C is a general high-level programming language ideal for creating various firmware or portable applications. C is one of the most used programming languages, as well as one of the oldest existing languages there is. It has led to the creation of other languages such as C++. It's one of the preferred languages because of its power and flexibility.

Even with its low-level proficiencies, C was made to promote cross-platform programming and has achieved a huge following, even in academic communities. It has also been standardized and made a part of POSIX, which stands for Portable Operating System Interface.

The first major creation using C was actually the Unix operating system. Because of that, Unix has been always connected to C. Today, however, C has become independent from Unix but is still viewed as an important language for every programmer to use.

It's good to learn C programming; it has been here for a while but because it's such a low-level language, it's still very powerful and useful. It's a great way to get to learn other languages better. You'll find it easy to move om to other programming languages. C is also relatively easy to use for application development.

C Programming Features

What features does the C Programming Language offer? Here are some of them:

- It has this basic form of modularity; files can possibly be separately linked and compiled.

- You have a set number of keywords that includes control primitives i.e. if, for, switch, while and do while.

- Different assignments can be used in one statement.

- It offers different mathematical and logical operators with bit manipulators.

- You can choose to ignore function return values if not needed.

- Typing is static for C, but weakly enforced. All the data has type, yet can possibly be implicitly converted such as using characters as integers.

Chapter 1 Data Types

In the C programming language, data types allude to a framework utilized for pronouncing variables or functions of distinctive data types. The type of a variable decides the amount of space it will take and how the bit pattern saved in it is utilized. The fundamental classification used for data types is given below:

- Basic Types:

They are number-crunching sorts and comprises of the two following types: (a) integer sorts and (b) floating point sorts.
- Enumerated sorts:

They are again number sorts and are utilized to characterize variables that must be allocated discrete number values all through the system.
- Void type:

The keyword void demonstrates that no value can be assigned.
- Derived sorts:

They incorporate (a) Array, (b) Pointer, (c) Union, (d) Structure and (e) Function.

The array and structure data types are also referred to as aggregate types. The type of a function defines the kind of value the function will return upon termination. We will discuss the essential data types in the accompanying segments.

Integer Types

Here is a list of data types that follow under this category. In addition, the storage space occupied by them and their range are also specified for your reference.

- char
  - Allocated Memory: 1 byte
  - Range: -128 to 127 or 0 to 255

- signed char
    - Allocated Memory: 1 byte
    - Range: -128 to 127
- unsigned char
    - Allocated Memory: 1 byte
    - Range: 0 to 255
- int
    - Allocated Memory: 2 or 4 bytes
    - Range: -32,768 to 32,767 or -2,147,483,648 to 2,147,483,647
- short
    - Allocated Memory: 2 bytes
    - Range: -32,768 to 32,767
- unsigned short
    - Allocated Memory: 2 bytes
    - Range: 0 to 65,535
- unsigned int
    - Allocated Memory: 2 or 4 bytes
    - Range: 0 to 65,535 or 0 to 4,294,967,295
- long
    - Allocated Memory: 4 bytes
    - Range: -2,147,483,648 to 2,147,483,647
- unsigned long
    - Allocated Memory: 4 bytes
        - Range: 0 to 4,294,967,295

To get the precise size of a variable or data type, you can utilize the sizeof operator. The declarations sizeof(<data type>) yields the size of the data type or variable in bytes. Given below is an example, which illustrates the concept, discussed below:

```
#include <limits.h>

#include <stdio.h>

int main() {

printf("Data type char (size in bytes): %d \n", sizeof(char));

return 0;

}
```

Upon compilation and execution of this code, you must get the following output:

Data type char (size in bytes): 1

Floating Point Data Types

Here is a list of data types that follow under this category. In addition, the storage space occupied by them, their range and precision value are also specified for your reference.

- float
    - o   Allocated Memory: 4 byte
    - o   Range: 1.2e-38 to 3.4e+38
    - o   Precision: 6 decimal places
- double
    - o   Allocated Memory: 8 byte
    - o   Range: 2.3e-308 to 1.7e+308
    - o   Precision: 15 decimal places
- long double
    - o   Allocated Memory: 10 byte
    - o   Range: 3.4e-4932 to 1.1e+4932
    - o   Precision: 19 decimal places

The header file named float.h characterizes macros that permit you to utilize these data type values. The following code will allow you to find the exact amount of allocated memory in bytes on your system for the concerned data type.

#include <float.h>

#include <stdio.h>

int main(){

printf("Allocated Memory for float : %d \n", sizeof(float));

printf("Precision: %d\n", FLT_DIG);

printf("Max Range Value: %E\n", FLT_MAX);

printf("Min Range Value: %E\n", FLT_MIN);

return 0;

}

Upon compilation and execution of this code, you must get the following output:

Allocated Memory for float : 4

Precision: 6

Max Range Value: 3.402823E+38

Max Range Value: 1.175494E-38

The void Type

The void data type points out that no value is accessible. It is utilized as a part of three sorts of circumstances:

- Void returned by a function

    You must have commonly noticed the use of the data type void as return type of function. If not, you will see an extensive use of the same as you move forward in your experience with C. The void data type signifies that the function will not return anything. Example of such an implementation is:
    void print(int);

- Function Arguments as void

    There are different functions in C, which don't acknowledge any parameter. A function with no parameter can acknowledge as a void. Example of such an implementation is:
    int print(void);

- Pointers to void

A pointer of sort void * signifies the location of a variable. For instance, consider the following declaration:
void *malloc(size_t size);
This function returns a pointer to void. In other words, this function can return a pointer to a location of any type.

You may not be able to comprehend the use and meaning of the void data type in entirety right now. However, as you move forward, you will find it easier to relate to and use this data type in your code.

Chapter 2 Data Structures, Handling and Functions

Introduction and Significance of Data Structures

In this chapter we are going to learn about the definition of data structures and their significance in the C# programming language. We will learn on the importance of the data structures and when and how to use them during the programming sessions. It is equally important to know that a great programmer writes efficient and effective programs using very appropriate data structures.

Programming is made up of two major components. These are algorithms and data structures. This explains the reason why more attention is given to these two components. A good developer or software engineer is that which has vast skills and knowledge of data structures and efficient in programming.

Before we get deeper into the data structure there are few terms that we should know and understand in order to become a good developer. **Algorithm complexity**-this can be defined as a standard which examines the order of the operations count that is performed and evaluated by an algorithm which becomes a function of input data size. This standard is commonly represented by **O (f) notation** which is referred to as **"Big O notation or asymptotic notation"**. There are many types of complexities such as constant, logarithmic, exponential, linear, cubic and, quadratic.

Enumerations, Arrays and structs

Enumerations

This can be defined as a data type that specifies the number of items by equally assigning them to an identifier for example a name. This is made possible by the consideration of the

underlying pattern of the base type of the components of the specification or the enumeration.
The declaration of an enumeration can be done as shown below;

>enum Months { January, February, March, April, May, June, July, August, September, October, November, December };

Understanding our code
The code above portray elements of enumerations which are displayed as constants as shown below;

>Month = Month.January;
>if (month == Month.February)
>{
>Console.WriteLine("Programming with C# through the months of the year is easy!");
>}

The first element is always a zero when there is no explicit value which is assigned to the specified or enumerated items. The subsequent elements will uptake the successive value after zero. On the other end, the specific values that originate from integral types can always be assigned to specified elements of enumeration as shown below;

>enum Age { Baby = 0, Adolescence = 13, Youth = 18 };
>Age age = Age.Adolescence
>Console.WriteLine("You are an adolescence at the age of {0}.", (int)age);

In addition, values that are underlying in the specified elements of enumeration usually go unused when the grouping function is specific to a certain group of data. It is usually advisable to create a specified element list using base type as compared to int.

Arrays

This is a representation of a group of items of a similar type or those that bear similar characteristics. The declaration of arrays may depend on constants and variables. It is important to note that once the array length has been declared it cannot be altered after declaration as shown below;

// **an array whose length is defined with a constant**
int[] integers = new int[10];
int length = 0;
System.Console.Write("what is the length of an array? ");
System.Console.ReadLine(length);
// **this is an array. Its length has been defined with a variable**

// **Arrays do not change their length after declaration**
double[] doubles = new double[length];

Structs

The keyword that is used to declare a struct is "**struct**". They are referred to as light container weight for objects. They are mostly applied when data is needed for collection of types of variables.

Structs can be compared to classes. Structs have methods, constructors and interfaces. The other major differences include;

- Structs are usually the value types whereas the classes are considered to be reference types.
- Structs cannot inherit as compared to classes.
- Structs require a less memory space and is less expensive as compared to classes.
- Structs have a compulsory default constructor even if it is not required whereas a class gives the allowance to hide the constructors.

Declaration of structs is done as follows;

```
struct Girl
{
public string name;
public System.DateTime birthDate;
public int heightInMtrs;
public int weightInGrams;
}
```

The Person Struct is used as follows;

```
Girl dana = new Girl();
dana.name = "Dana Programmer";
dana.birthDate = new DateTime(1975, 8, 19);
dana.heightInMtrs = 1.75;
dana.weightInGrams = 50000;
if (dana.birthDate < DateTime.Now)
{
Console.WriteLine("Dana Programmer is a genuine programmer!");
}
```

The example below shows how constructors can be used in structs for initialization;

```
using System;
struct Girl
{

string name;
DateTime birthDate;
int heightInMtrs;
int weightInGrams;
public Person(string name, DateTime birthDate, int heightInMtrs, int weightInGrams)
{
this.name = name;
this.birthDate = birthDate;
this.heightInMtrs = heightInMtrs;
this.weightInGrams = weightInGrams;
}
}
public class StructWeeklyBookSample
{
public static void Main()
{
Person dana = new Person("Dana Programmer", new DateTime(1975, 8, 19),
1.75, 50000);
}
}
```

In summary, structs are best used for performance reasons. They work best when they are holding data amounting to 16bytes but if the programmer is in doubt he or she can utilize the classes.

Relationship between Data Structures Using Algorithm Complexities

At this point we are going to study and compare the different data structures using algorithm complexities. We are going to encounter with operations such as searching, addition, deletion and accessing of data by use of indexing. This will also help us in choosing which data structure to use when programming or developing our codes. The table below is an illustration of basic operations done by the complexities;

Data structure	Search	Addition	Deletion	Index Access
Array	O(N)	O(N)	O(N)	O(1)
Dynamic array	O(N)	O(1)	O(N)	O(1)
Linked lists	O(N)	O(1)	O(N)	0(N)
Stack	-	O(1)	O(1)	-
Queue	-	O(1)	O(1)	-

Balance search tree (set)	O(log(N))	O(log(N))	O(log(N))	-
Hash table (set)	O(1)	O(1)	O(1)	-
Balance search tree (Dictionary)	O(log(N))	O(log(N))	O(log(N))	-
Hash table (dictionary)	O(1)	O(1)	O(1)	-

When to choose a data structure

In this section of the book we are going to discuss situations in which the data structures listed in the table above is going to be used.

Array

As discussed before, this is a grouping or collection of number of components of a similar type. We can also refer to the arrays as *"a small container of data having a predefined size"*. **Addition** of new elements into an array as shown in the table is a very slow process. For this to occur successfully, allocation of definite space is done and an extra space that can transfer data from one array to another. **Searching** of an array is also a slow process because the comparison is done in accordance to the needed value. **Deletion** of an element from the array is a slow process because it's a reverse of the addition process. In this case a definite memory is allocated and a single space is subtracted. However, accessing an array is very fast and efficient because it utilizes **indexing.**

Arrays are best for situations like processing fixed amount or number of components which should be accessed by the use of an index.

Dynamic Arrays

This is the most commonly used type of data structure in modern programming. This is because it avoids a fixed list of components and enables direct access of data by the use of indices. Dynamic arrays can also be referred to as an "array or resizable list".

Dynamic arrays usually hold elements in a list of array. The advantage of this array is that the list has a bigger size than the number of stored components. **Addition** into the dynamic array takes a specific constant time. This is because there is always an empty cell before the addition of components. **Searching** the dynamic array is a slow operation because there is traversing through all the stored components in order to find what is being looked for. **Deletion** from the dynamic array is a slow process. The execution of this command is done using linear time. The other reason is that once a deletion is made, the stored elements are moved to the left in order to create an empty cell for addition.

The dynamic array is used in situations that require quick addition and access by the use of indexing.

Linked lists

These can either be singly or doubly linked lists. The major function done by both the singly and doubly linked list is the storage of collection of components by maintaining their order. They are represented in the memory as dynamic and pointer-based.

Addition into the linked list is a very fast process. Although it is slower than dynamic arrays, it is an advanced process. This is achieved by a new allocation of memory space. It is a high-speed process that is always unpredictable. **Searching** is a very slow process because it uses the same principle as dynamic arrays to traverse all the elements during the search. **Deletion** of an element is a slow operation. This is because searching is done before deletion hence the indexing process makes it generally slow.

In summary, a linked list has a fast addition process. It is suitable for situations when addition and removal are needed at a faster rate at both sides of the linked lists.

Stack

This is a linear data structure that has three major steps; addition of components to the top of the specific stack(push), removing components from the top of the specific stack(pop) and inspection of the components at the top of the stack without interfering with the order(peek).

The **addition and deletion** of the stack is a very fast process because a constant time is used. The stack does not have the searching and accessing by index features. It generally works with the LIFO technique where the Last In is the First Out.

Stack is used in situations where LIFO (Last In First Out) is applicable.

Queue

This is also another type of linear data structures that is specific to two operations: addition of a component to the tail (enqueue) and extraction of the component from the head (dequeue). The two processes are fast because it utilizes a constant timing. The operations here are similar to the processes in addition and deletion of linked lists.

The Queue uses the FIFO technique where First In usually leads to the First Out. Similar to stacks, the searching and access by index is not supported by the queue. Apart from FIFO, the queue embraces the concept of **Breadth-first search (BFS).** This works by starting from the first component in the list and hence its surrounding components are aligned in a queue.

Queue is appropriate in situations where the BFS and the FIFO are applicable.

Hash table (Dictionary Implementation)

Implementation by dictionary means storage of key value and search by the latter mentioned key. The format of dictionary implementation makes the hash table to have a very fast addition, search and deletion processes. However, the hash table does not support the access by index feature because the components of the hash table have no particular order.

The components are stored in an array and located by the use of a hash function. It is also important to note that if a function is wrong, or it causes a collision of single cells then the whole implementation becomes inefficient. Hash table is the fastest data structure. This is because it provides for quick addition and searching with the use of a key.

Hash table is appropriate for a situation where fast addition is required as well as fast search by use of a key.

Hash table (Set implementation)

This data structure is a collection or grouping of components that have no duplicates. The basic processes that do happen in this data structure are the addition of components to a set, searching for the components in the set and deletion or removal of the components from the set.

This is a special kind of hash table that contains keys. It is also important to note that searching using indices is not supported. The case is similar when a bad hash function is used. When this occurs, the whole program becomes inefficient. This situation rarely occurs.

Hash table is used in situations where faster addition of components to a collection or a set is required. It is also good for checking and identification of components that do not belong to a specific data set.

Balance Tree (Dictionary Implementation)

This is a type of data structure that stores pairs of key-value where the keys used are sorted. It supports a faster operation of the addition, searching and removal processes. The algorithm complexity that is used in this data structure is logarithmic.

Collisions of functions do not affect the data structure widely as seen in hash tables. In balance trees, there is a very minimum probability of an error and usage of bad hash functions. It is very evident that in balance tree of dictionary implementation there are fast basic operations. Because of faster operations, extraction feature is enabled which is also very first with dictionary implementation.

Balance tree by dictionary implementation is used in situations where there is fast addition, searching and extraction of components that have been sorted by a particular key.

Balance tree (Set implementation)

This is a special data structure that has a red-black tree implementation where the keys and values always coincide.

Similar to the dictionary implementation, the set implementation uses the logarithmic algorithm complexity.

In summary, a balance tree by set implementation is required in situations where fast addition and checking of components is required. In addition, the components of the set are sorted in ascending order.

Practical Example of choice of a Data Structure

Example 1

In this small sub-chapter we are going to examine several examples of implemented data structures. I believe it is going to open our eyes in choices of data structures.

Our first step is to generate the subsets of a set for example;

W= {Sea, wine, computer, joy}

Our objective is to create a simple code that is going to output the subsets of W. We start from an empty set of {}. We add the empty set to each and every component of set W and we get the collection below;

{sea}, {wine}, {computer}, {joy}

Then we add to each element to the subsets from set W so that the ones which have not been included can be reflected in the two elemental subsets. There is freedom of addition up to the N-elemental subset

{sea, wine}, {sea, computer}, {sea, joy}, {wine, computer},{wine, joy}, {computer, joy}

At this point, we are going to focus on and choose the right data structure to implement the above algorithm. In order to choose the right data structure, we are going to consider the type of operations that are needed to be done. At the moment, the main operation to be done is traversing through all the components of the set (subset). This operation can be done efficiently by the array, dynamic array, hast tables and almost all the other data structures.

i) We shall first consider the **array** because it is the simplest data structure to work with.
ii) The next step that comes after picking the data structure is to pick criterion for storing one of the 2-elemental subsets for example {beer, money}
iii) Here we check the operations which will efficiently execute this subset. The operations to be done are addition and checking of the components of the subset. From our previous knowledge, we know that arrays and

linked lists perform a quicker search. We choose the data structure that is fast in addition and searching.

iv) We pick on the hash table (set implementation) and hence keep the collection or grouping of the words in the subsets as shown below;
{sea, wine}, {sea, computer}, {sea, joy}, {wine, computer},
{wine, joy}, {computer, joy}

v) Using the chosen structure, addition and traversing through the components of the subset is very efficient. At this point we get to notice that other data structures such as; stacks, Sets, queue and list also qualify for this characteristic. On the other end, if we study further we notice that this set W works with FIFO technique. At this point we choose the queue.

vi) **Lastly, we obtain that queue is the best data structure for this program.**

Using the queue data structure

We can illustrate and describe the algorithm using the following procedure;

i) Begin the queue with an empty set {}
ii) Dequeue the components of the subset. Add each and every element from W in relation to the subset it is located.
iii) **Repeat until the queue is empty.**

It is very evident that once a developer understands the needs of the program and hence selects the correct data structure, implementation becomes very quick and easy. The example below is how the program will look after applying the correct data structure;

```
string[] words = {"sea", "wine", "computer", "joy"};
Queue<HashSet<string>> subsetsQueue =new
Queue<HashSet<string>>();
HashSet<string> emptySet = new HashSet<string>();
```

```
subsetsQueue.Enqueue(emptySet);
while (subsetsQueue.Count > 0)
{
HashSet<String> subset = subsetsQueue.Dequeue();
// Display the current subset
Console.Write("{ ");
foreach (string word in subset)
{
Console.Write("{0} ", word);
}
Console.WriteLine("}");
// Generating and enqueuing all possible child subsets
foreach (string element in words)
{
if (! subset.Contains(element))
{
HashSet<string> newSubset = new HashSet<string>();
newSubset.UnionWith(subset);
newSubset.Add(element);
subsetsQueue.Enqueue(newSubset);
}
}
}
```

When the program is run through the compiler the following will be displayed;

    { }
    { sea }
    { wine }
    { computer }
    { joy }
    { sea wine }
    { sea computer }
    { sea joy }

{ wine sea }
...

Understanding our code

The coding above was successful but had one major problem. Some of the subsets of W were displayed twice. For example; {sea wine} and {wine sea} is the same subset. Our code experiences the problem of duplication.

How do we overcome duplication?

In order to overcome the problem of duplication we use indices as shown below;

sea	0
wine	1
computer	2
joy	3

In addition, we are going to generate subset using their indices in ascending order. At this point we will avoid the use of the Hash table and implement the **List.** This will place the indices in ascending order. After choosing the list, our program will look at the following;

```
using System;
using System.Collections.Generic;
public class Subsets
{
static string[] words = { "ocean", "beer", "money", "happiness" };
static void Main()
{
Queue<List<int>> subsetsQueue = new Queue<List<int>>();
List<int> emptySet = new List<int>();
subsetsQueue.Enqueue(emptySet);
while (subsetsQueue.Count > 0)
{
List<int> subset = subsetsQueue.Dequeue();
```

```
            Print(subset);
            int start = -1;
            if (subset.Count > 0)
            {
            start = subset[subset.Count - 1];

            }
            for (int i = start + 1; i < words.Length; i++)
            {
            List<int> newSubset = new List<int>();
            newSubset.AddRange(subset);
            newSubset.Add(i);
            subsetsQueue.Enqueue(newSubset);
            }
            }
            }
            static void Print(List<int> subset) {
            Console.Write("[ ");
            for (int i=0; i<subset.Count; i++) {
            int index = subset[i];
            Console.Write("{0} ", words[index]);
            }
            Console.WriteLine("]");
            }
            }
```

After running the compiler through the program it will display the following output;

```
            [ ]
            [ ocean ]
            [ beer ]
            [ money ]
            [ happiness ]
            [ ocean beer ]
            [ ocean money ]
            [ ocean happiness ]
            [ beer money ]
            [ beer happiness ]
```

[money happiness]
[ocean beer money]
[ocean beer happiness]
[ocean money happiness]
[beer money happiness]
[ocean beer money happiness]

Example 2- Sorting the numbers in a phonebook

Here we have a file containing texts that have people's credentials such as their names, the cities they live in and their cell phone numbers. The table below shows the information;

Names	Cities	Cell Phone Numbers
Kennedy	Nairobi	1-234-567-8911
Silas	Lusaka	2-345-678-9112
Joseph	Jerusalem	3-456-789-1112
Diana	Kisumu	4-567-891-2345
Winston	Migori	5-678-912-3456

Task: Write a code which displays all the names of the cities in alphabetical order **and for each one of them prints all** the names of the people in alphabetical order **and their corresponding** phone numbers.

There are many solutions for such an example illustrated in the table above. We are going to utilize the knowledge we have learned in the previous topics about data structures to solve this problem. We shall use the examples of data structures in the Dot Net Framework.

From the requirements of the codes, we need to sort the names of the cities. This makes us open our line of thoughts towards the data structures that can make us achieve the sorting criterion. For this case we can consider a balanced tree either set implementation or dictionary implementation. However, the records of the phonebook also contain the names of the city and hence we have to use dictionary implementation. As a result, the list containing the names of people will be kept with their respective cell phone numbers. We will initialize the key to be the names of the people and the value to be their respective phone numbers

The following is an illustration of the program using dictionary implementation;

```
// Read the file and build the phone book
SortedDictionary<string, SortedDictionary<string, string>>
phonesByTown = new SortedDictionary<string, SortedDictionary<string, string>>();
StreamReader reader = new StreamReader("PhoneBook.txt");
using (reader)
{
while (true)
{
string line = reader.ReadLine();
if (line == null)
{
break;

}
string[] entry = line.Split(new char[]{'|'});
string name = entry[0].Trim();
string town = entry[1].Trim();
string phone = entry[2].Trim();
SortedDictionary<string, string> phoneBook;
if (! phonesByTown.TryGetValue(town, out phoneBook))
{
// This town is new. Create a phone book for it
phoneBook = new SortedDictionary<string, string>();
phonesByTown.Add(town, phoneBook);
}
phoneBook.Add(name, phone);
```

```
    }
  }
  // Print the phone book by towns
  foreach (string town in phonesByTown.Keys)
  {
    Console.WriteLine("Town " + town + ":");
    SortedDictionary<string, string> phoneBook =
    phonesByTown[town];
    foreach (var entry in phoneBook)
    {
      string name = entry.Key;
      string phone = entry.Value;
      Console.WriteLine("\t{0} - {1}", name, phone);
    }
  }
```

If the code were run by the compiler, the following would be the appropriate display;

Town Portland:
Mary - 1-234-765-1983
Town San Antonio:
Laura - 1-454-345-2345
Paul - 1-535-675-6745
Town Virginia Beach:
Donna - 1-387-387-2389
Kenneth - 1-541-754-3010

Summary (How to choose an appropriate Data structure)

At this point of learning, it is very evident that the choice of data structure is dependent on the objective of the program to be written. On another occasion, we noted that we could combine data structures in order to achieve specific unique situations and results.

Before choosing a particular data structure, it is important that one asks him or herself several questions. The questions include;

- What operations will I perform in my program?
- The operation to be performed requires which type of structure?
- Am I familiar with all the data structures that exist in C# programming language?
- Does my program require a single data structure or a combination of two or three?

In conclusion, the choice of data structure is an important step. It is advised that before you choose a particular data structure you should design an algorithm. Never start by choosing the data structure back to the algorithm.

Chapter 3 How to Define Your Classes in C#

Classes are one of the most important things that we are able to do when it comes to the C# language, and other languages as well, and it can make sure that our code is going to work the way that we want. Let's take a look at what we are able to do when it is time for us to really work on defining the classes that are found in this language.

How to Work with These Classes

When you are ready to work with the C# programming language, the class is going to be important because it is the part that is able to define the types of the object, and the types of the data, that you will be able to use right in that point in the program. The object can help us contain the information that will define the class or the container that, that the object is going to be found in.

These classes are great because they will hold onto a lot of the information that we need at this time. Not only will they hold onto the objects, but they can hold onto information that describes the features and the behavior of those objects. This is all of the behaviors that we would want the object to handle as we go along. When we are working with the OOP languages, you will want to work with methods that can help us with this.

So, the first thing that we need to take a look at here is some of the components that are going to show up in the class. With these classes, there are going to be a number of different components that will come into play when it is time to take care of these classes. There are a few parts that we can pay attention to when it is time to handle the class including:

- Declaration—this is the line that will declare the identifier of the class.

- Body—just like with methods, the classes are going to have a single body. You will need to define the body right after you make the declaration. The body is the statement, or several statements, that are found between the curly brackets. An example of this is:

class Example

{

//This is the body of the "Example" class.

}

- Constructor—This is the part that will allow you to create a new object. An example of this is:

Public Sample()

{

//Insert what you want to say here.

}

- Fields—these are the variables that you will declare within your class. The fields are going to contain the values that will represent the exact state of the object they are trying to get to.
- Properties—this part will describe the different attributes of the class. Many programmers will write the class properties right inside the field of their chosen object.
- Methods—a method is basically a named block of code that is executable. It is able to complete some tasks and then will allow objects to attain the right behavior. It can also execute the right algorithms that are present inside the codes.

Before we dive much more into these classes and start to create one of our own classes, you should make sure that there is already some object that is able to fit inside. You can do this with the help of a new keyword and then you can add in all of the constructors that you will need to work with.

When we are creating these codes in the C# language, you will not be able to do any manipulation on the objects that you are trying to create directly. Instead, you will need to be able to assign the objects over to the right objects ahead of time so that you can handle all of the manipulations that you want later without problems. Remember that when you would like to access these methods and the properties that go with the object, you will need to indicate to the compiler which identifier will go with the object, and then make sure the dot operator is there.

Organizing the Classes

It is important here for us to learn the proper manner to use in order to organize the classes that we want to work within this kind of language. There is mainly just one rule that we want to follow to make sure that this works and that rule is that we need to make sure that the classes are saved as a .cs file. This makes them easier to find and work on later when we would like to pull them out.

Technically, the C# language is going to allow us to save all of the classes that we will make in a program in just one big file and the compiler is going to be able to read through it all without an error. But there are going to be a lot of programmers who find that saving their classes in their own individual files makes it easier to bring out the classes when you need them later, and can keep things more organized. You can choose through which method you like working with here.

Another thing that we are going to use here to gain some more familiarity with when working in C# is the namespace. This is going to be a set of classes that are going to be related in some manner. The way that these will relate with one another is going to change based on the situation of how we use this, but they should make sense as to why they are related. These could include their classes, structures, interfaces, and even some of the information that is placed inside of it. It is even possible for us to take a few of these classes together and make our own namespace, even if they are sorted out into different parts of the memory of the computer.

If you are looking to create a new namespace on some of the codes that you worked with previously, you need to make sure that the directive of "using" to make things a little bit easier. Most programmers are going to be able to find that it is easier to put into the very first lines of our file. This ensures that you don't accidentally forget about these later on. After you have been able to insert this directive, then you can go through and declare the namespace.

How to Access Our Classes

The final thing that we are going to work with when it comes to our classes is how to access these. C# is going to allow us to have some support from four different modifiers when it comes to who is able to access each of the classes that we have. these are going to include protected, private, internal, and public. These modifiers are going to make it easier to control who is able to see each of the elements that are found in that class you are working with. The best way to make sure that each of these is going to work will include:

- Private: This is the modifier that will place some strict restrictions on one of your classes. If the class is tagged as a private class, it will not be accessible by the other classes in the code. The C# language will use this as the default modifier if you do not place anything else there. This can help to avoid problems if you forget to add on that modifier.

- Public: You can also choose to make the class public. This means that the modifier will tell other classes that they are able to access this class. This modifier is going to take away all the limitations about how visible this class is to all the others.
- Internal: If your code has the internal modifier on it, this means that this class is going to be accessible, but only to the files that fall in the same project.
- Protected: This is the modifier that you will use if you would like to prevent a user from accessing the element. However, it also allows all the descendant classes to have access to the elements of that class if they need it.

As you can see, each of these elements is going to work in a slightly different way based on what you would like to have happened in regards to the privacy of our classes. If you would like to make sure that the class remains private and that nothing else is allowed to get ahold of it or use the information, then you will want to work with the private setting. However, if you need other classes to have the ability to work with this particular class, then it is just fine to change it to the public modifier.

As we go through some of the programs, you should think about which of these modifiers is going to be the best one for some of the coding that you work with. If you do not add in one of these modifiers before the data that is needed for the class, then it is, by default, the private class. This is not necessarily a bad thing for your code, but if you want one of the other options, then you need to go through and make that change or the program will not offer it.

Remember though this process that these classes are really going to be important when it is time to write out some of the codes that you have. They are going to help ensure that these containers are going to be organized, and it will make sure that you are easily able to pull up the things that are needed inside of your code. This is going to ensure that things are easier to work with. Your code will work so much better and writing out codes in C# and other OOP languages will be easier as well.

When you are choosing which of the objects you would like to add to one of the classes that you are writing, you need to remember that these objects can fit into the same class, only if they really make sense to go with one another. You should be able to get anyone to look inside of the class, and agree that it does make sense to get these objects to be together in the same class. Of course, remember that the objects do not need to be identical all of the time. But they need to make sense of being together.

For example, if you are working with that Toys class that we had before, you would not have to just put one toy in there, or one type of toy inside. You could add in all of the toys that you would like inside and this would still follow the rules that you need. You could also have a class for things that are all of the same color, one for the animals, and one for different types of vehicles. As long as the objects go together and match up with one another, then you will be just fine.

The objects and classes are going to be an important part when you are working with some of the coding that you want to accomplish in the C# language. It is important for us to take a look at some of the work that we want to do with this kind of language, but we need to make sure that we are writing them up in the right manner, and that we are adding in the right objects.

Chapter 4 Creating Loops in C#

In many of the OOP languages that you will want to work on, you will find that it is possible to create something that is known as a loop. This is a really nice thing to work with because it allows you to fit a lot of code into just a few lines, saving you time and hassle in the process. And in this chapter, we are going to take a closer look at what these loops are all about, how you can create them, and even some of the different types of loops that are available for you to work with.

When we talk about looping when we are coding, it is going to be a method that we can use to execute a statement, and sometimes a set of statements, many times depending on the results of the condition that we want to have evaluated in order to execute those statements in the first place. Sometimes the loop is only going to happen a few times, and sometimes it will go through the iteration many times, depending on what you are hoping to get out of the code and how many times you really need it to go through all of this. The result condition should be something that is seen as true to help execute the statements inside of the loops.

For the most part, you will find that the loops that you are working with are going to be divided up into two categories. The first kind is going to be the entry-controlled loops. The loops where you will have the condition tested at the beginning of the loop will be known as the entry-controlled loops. These are going to include the for loop and the while loop.

To see this work, you will need to make whatever condition you are testing to show up at the beginning of the code. The compiler is going to check the condition in the syntax first, and if it is true, then it will run the loop. This works well with most of the loops that you are going to work with, but sometimes it does mean that your loop is not going to run at all because the conditions are never met.

Let's take a look at some of the loops that are going to fit into this. The first type is the while loop. The test condition that is there is going to be seen as the beginning of the loop, and then all of the statements we work with will be executed until the given condition, which is Boolean in these loops, is satisfied. When the condition is considered false with this one, then the control will be out from the while loop and the loop is going to stop completely. Instead, it will move on to the next part of the code and move on from there.

Working with this kind of coding and loop is not that hard to work with. We are going to take a look at an example of how we are able to handle this in a moment. Take a look at the syntax and experiment a little bit with it to see how it is going to work. You can also look for the while part of the code, which is going to tell us where the loop we are working with is going to start. An example of how we are able to work with the while loop will be below:

```
// C# program to illustrate while loop

using System;


class whileLoopDemo

{

    public static void Main()

    {

        int x = 1;


        // Exit when x becomes greater than 4
```

```
while (x <= 4)
{
    Console.WriteLine("GeeksforGeeks");

    // Increment the value of x for
    // next iteration
    x++;
}
}
}
```

With this one, we created a loop that wrote out the words GeekforGeeks three times. The while loop told the syntax to not go through and do it more than three times. If we had the loop do it four times, then the condition would be considered false and then we would not have gotten the results that we were hoping for in the process. This one sees that we are true when we write it out once because that is below four times. The same is true when it writes it out two times and three times. But when the program goes through the loop again, it seems that doing another iteration and writing out the term again would get us to four, and this would get us too high for what we need.

You can definitely go through and change up the terms that you want to use with this one, and figure out what kind of statement you would like to see show up in the coding. And go ahead and mess around with the while loop as well and figure out how many iterations of the statement you would like to work in order to get the results that you want.

Then it is time to move on to the for a loop. This one is going to be similar in terms of functions when it comes to the while loop, but it is going to come with a different kind of syntax. The for loops are going to be the preferred method to work with when the number of times that a loop statement should be executed is known before you even get started.

The initialization of the loop variable, or the condition to be tested, and the increment or the decrement of the loop variable is going to be done in just one single line for the loop, which helps to provide us with a structure of the loop that is shorter and easier to write. And when you run into problems or need to fix parts of the code, you may find that it is actually an easier format of loops to debug later on so it might be one that you want to consider going with.

Now, there are going to be a few different parts that need to come into play when it is time to work with the for loop in C# and to make sure that it works the way that we would like. Some of these are going to include:

1. Initialization of the loop variable: The variable or the expression that is going to control the loop is going to be initialized in this step. It is going to be the starting point of the loop. An already declared variable can be used or a variable can be declared, local to the loop that you are currently working on only.
2. The testing condition: The second thing that we need to focus on here is the testing condition. This is what we are going to use in order to execute the statements that are in the loop. It is going to be used in many situations in order to test the exit condition for the loop. It must return to us a value that is Boolean, which means we are going to get a result of either true or false. When the condition comes out as being false, then the control is going

to be out from the loop, and this kind of loop is going to end for us.
3. Increment and decrement: The loop variable is going to be either incremented or decremented based on the requirement that we put into it, and the control, when this happens, is then going to shift over to the testing condition again.

One thing to note before we go through the process of looking at some of the coding that we want to do with this is that the initialization part is only going to be evaluated just one time before the for loop starts. If you set this up in the manner that you would really like to see, then this is going to be plenty. With this in mind, let's take some of the information that we talked about above and add in the coding to see how this kind of loop is going to work:

```csharp
// C# program to illustrate for a loop.

using System;


class forLoopDemo

{

    public static void Main()

    {

        // for loop begins when x=1

        // and runs till x <=4

        for (int x = 1; x <= 4; x++)
```

Console.WriteLine("GeeksforGeeks");

}

}

Now that we just talked about some of the entry-controlled loops in C#, it is time for us to move on to the second type of loops that we are able to use in our codes. And these are going to be known as the exit-controlled loops. The loops in which the testing condition is going to be present at the end of the body of our loop are going to be known as the exit-controlled loops. The best known of these kinds of loops is going to be the exit-controlled loop.

One thing that we need to note when we are working on these is that the exit-controlled loops will have the body of the loop evaluated for at a minimum one time as the testing condition is present at the end of the body of our loop. With that in mind, we can take a look at how to work with the do-while loop that we want to focus on here.

The do-while loop is a great one to work with, but you may notice that it has a lot of similarities to what we are going to see with the while loop. The main difference that we are going to see between the do while and the while loop is that the do while is going to check the condition after it goes through and executes the statements. What this means is that it is going to execute the body of the loop just one time for sure because it will run the loop, and then go through and check the condition and see if it has been met yet or not, rather than doing it in the beginning.

Now we need to take a moment to look at some of the syntaxes of what we are going to see when it comes to working with the do while loop. These are nice to work with and can provide us with a lot of great codes, but take a look at the example below and notice where they do and the while part shows up, and what kind of information is showing up in between them.

```csharp
// C# program to illustrate do-while loop

using System;

class dowhileloopDemo
{
    public static void Main()
    {
        int x = 21;
        do
        {
            // The line will be printed even
            // If the condition is false
            Console.WriteLine("GeeksforGeeks");
            x++;
        }
        while (x < 20);
    }
}
```

}

Another option that we need to spend some time on here is known as the infinite loops. These are going to be the types of loops where we will find that the test condition is not going to evaluate anything as false ever. This means that they are going to get stuck in the loop and will continue to execute the statement that you have put into place forever, or until you get an external force to work on it and make sure that it stops.

This can often happen when you do not go through and actually put in some of the conditions that your codes need in the first place. You need to make sure that you are going through and adding in the right conditions right away and keeping it all in the right place to ensure that you are not going to fall into the trap of one of these loops and then having to fix your program before it gets stuck there forever.

To see what this kind of loop is going to look like in case you do make a mistake and forget the condition that should be there, take a look at the code that is below and see if you are able to find where the issue is inside of it:

```csharp
// C# program to demonstrate infinite loop

using System;

class infiniteLoop
{
    public static void Main()
    {
```

```csharp
        // The statement will be printed
        // infinite times
        for(;;)
        Console.WriteLine("This is printed infinite times");
    }
}
```

There are some times in the codes that you want to work with that you will need to combine two loops together in the same part of the code. You want to make sure that they are able to combine with one another and both run until both of them are complete. This is going to be important to some of the codes that you want to write, such as creating one of your own multiplication tables along the way. A good example of these nested loops, where you have one loop present inside of another loop, includes:

```csharp
// C# program to demonstrate nested loops
using System;


class nestedLoops
{
    public static void Main()
    {
        // loop within loop printing GeeksforGeeks
        for(int i = 2; i < 3; i++)
```

```
            for(int j = 1; j < i; j++)

                Console.WriteLine("GeeksforGeeks");

    }

}
```

And finally, the last type of loop that we are going to take a look at in this chapter is going to be known as the continue statement. This kind of statement is useful because we can work with it to skip over the execution part of the loop on a certain condition and then move the flow so that it is then on the next part for updating when we need it. This one may seem a little bit confusing when we are first getting started, so a good way to take a look at this is to look at some of the coding that we need to put it together below:

```
// C# program to demonstrate continue statement

using System;


class demoContinue

{

    public static void Main()

    {

        // GeeksforGeeks is printed only 2 times

        // because of continue statement

        for(int i = 1; i < 3; i++)

        {
```

```
        if(i == 2)

            continue;


        Console.WriteLine("GeeksforGeeks");

    }

}
```

There are a lot of different types of loops when you are working with the C#, and this is a good thing because there are many situations where you would want to bring up some of these loops in your codes, and each situation will need a different kind of loop. The good news is that when you use these in the proper manner, you will be able to write out some of the best codes that you need, without having to rewrite a bunch of lines of code at the same time. Spend some time looking at these different loops and what they can offer to you, and try a few out to see how they are going to work for your own codes as well.

Chapter 5 Value types and Reference types

Types in C# can be split into either value types or reference types. The differences between the types in each category stem from differences in copying strategies, which in turn result in each type being stored differently in memory.

Value types

Value types encompass most built-in types (In specific terms, all numeric types, char type, and bool type) as well as custom struct and enum type. These types all have a fixed size, variables of value types directly contain their own values.

Reference types

Reference types comprise all classes, array, delegate and interface types and are handled differently by the compiler. For example, take the Circle Class type (previous code listing). Once you declare a Circle variable, the compiler allocates a small portion of memory which can possibly hold the address of (or a reference to) additional block of memory holding a Circle. Only once an actual Circle object is created (via the new keyword) then the memory is allocated.

Copying value & reference types

When you take a copy of a value type there are two memory locations. For example, should you create a integer variable called **i** and give it the value 42 then an additional integer variable named **copyi** and assign **i** to **copyi**, **copyi** will hold the identical value as **i** (42). Although **copyi** and **i** hold the exact same value, there are actually two blocks of memory holding the value 42: one block for **i** and another block for **copyi**. If you adjust the value of **i**, the value of **copyi** doesn't change:

```
        int i = 42;         // declare i as integer & assign it 42

        int copyi = i;      /* decclare copyi equal to i (i.e
        copyi now holds a
```

copyi of i – its value 42) */

i++;/* incrementing i by 1. copyi is unchanged;

I now holds 43, but copyi still has 42 value*/

This is in marked difference to declaring a variable as a class type where you are essentially copying the same address. E.g. if you declare c as a Circle, c can refer to a Circle object; the actual value held by c is the address of a Circle object in memory. Should you declare a further variable called **refc** (a Circle) and assign c to **refc, refc** will have a copy of the identical address as c. To summarize, both **refc** and c now denote the one Circle object.

Circle c = new Circle(42); // declare new c variable of Cirlce object that = 42

Circle refc = c;// assign c to refc. refc has identical address as c

Note that the behaviour of method parameters hinge on on whether they are value types or reference types.

Null values

The null value identified with the null keyword, indicates that the variable does not refer to any valid object, i.e. it stipulates that a variable is set to nothing. You can assign reference types, pointer types and nullable types the value null. Code that sets a variable to null explicitly assigns the reference to refer to no valid value. It is possible to check whether a reference refers to nothing. The subsequent code demonstrates assigning null to a string variable:

static void Main()

{

String phoneNum;

```
// ...

// Clear the value of phoneNum.

        phoneNum = null;
//..

}
```

Assigning the value null to a reference type is not the same as not assigning it at all. In other words, a variable that has been assigned null has still been set, whereas a variable with no assignment has not been set and therefore, will often result in your program not compiling if used prior to assignment.

Assigning a string value the value null is particularly dissimilar from assigning an empty string, "". Use of null indicates that the variable has no value, whereas "" indicates that there is an empty value – an empty string. This difference is quite valuable in programming, you could take a phone number of null to mean that the phone number is unknown, while a **phoneNum** value of "" could stipulate no phone exists.

Nullable types

Value types can't typically be assigned null since by definition they can't hold references, which includes references to nothing. However, C# defines a modifier that you can use to declare that a variable is a nullable value type. A nullable value type acts in a similar way to the original value type, but you can assign the null value to it. You use the (?) to specify that a value type is nullable, like so:

int? i = null; // valid code

You can ascertain whether a nullable variable contains null by testing it in the same way as a reference type:

if (i == null)

The System.Object class

One of the most important reference types in the .NET Framework is the Object class in the System namespace. To completely appreciate the significance of the **System**.Object class you need under-stand inheritance - described later in this Ebook. For the time being, simply accept that all classes are specialized types of System.Object and that you can use System.**Ob-ject** to create a variable that can refer to any reference type. **System**.Object is such an important class that C# provides the object keyword as an alias for **System**.Object.

In the subsequent example, the variables c and o both reference the same Circle object. The fact that the type of c is Circle and the type of o is object (the alias for System.Object) in effect offers two dif-ferent views of the same item in memory.

> **Circle c;**
> **c = new Circle(42);**
> **object o;**

o = c;

Boxing

As discussed, variables of type object can refer to any item of any reference type. However, variables of type object can also refer to a value type. To illustrate, both the two following statements initialize the variable **i** (of type int, a value type) to 42 and then initialize the variable o (of type object, a reference type) to **i**:

> int i = 42;

object o = i;

In the second there is a bit more happening. Re-member that **i** is a value type and that it lives on the stack. Should the reference inside **o** referred directly to **i**, then the reference would refer to the stack. Nevertheless, all references must refer to objects on the heap; creating references to items on the stack could seriously compromise the robustness of the runtime and create a potential security flaw, so it is not allowed. Therefore, the runtime allocates a piece of memory from the heap, copies the value of integer **i** to this piece of memory, and then refers the ob-ject o to this copy. Boxing is term for automatically copying an item from the stack to the heap.

Unboxing

Because a variable of type object can refer to a boxed copy of a value, it's only reasonable to allow you to get at that boxed value through the variable. You may be thinking that could can access the boxed int value that a variable o refers to via a simple assignment statement like:

int i = o;

This however will result in a compile error. You can't use the int i = o code. The variable o could be referencing absolutely almost anything - not just an integer. Take for example the subsequent code if such a statement were allowable:

> Circle c = new Circle();
>
> int i = 42;
>
> object o;
>
> o = c; // o refers to a circle

i = o; // what is stored in i?

To get the value of the boxed copy, you must utilise what is known as a cast. This operation checks if it's safe to convert an item of one type to another before it actually making the copy. You prefix the object variable with the name of the type in parentheses, as follows:

```
int i = 42;

object o = i; // boxing ok
```

`i = (int)o; // this compiles ok`

The effect of this cast is subtle. The compiler sees that you've specified the type int in the cast. It generates code to check what **o** actually refers to at run time. It could be really anything. Even though your cast says **o** refers to an int, it doesn't mean that it actually does. If **o** does actually refer to a boxed int and everything correlates, the cast will succeed and the compiler will extract the value from the boxed int and copy it to **i**. (i.e. the boxed value will be stored in **i**.) This is called unboxing

However, if o does not refer to a boxed int, there has been a type mismatch and the cast will fail. InvalidCastException is invoked. The following illustrates an unboxing cast that fails:

```
Circle c = new Circle(42);

object o = c; // fails to box since Circle is a reference
variable
```

`int i = (int)o; // compiles ok but throws an exception @ run time`

Note that boxing and unboxing are expensive operations because of the quantity of checking that is required and the need to allocate additional heap memory. Boxing is useful but overuse will really negatively impact the performance of your pro-gram.

Casting data safely

By utilising a cast, you can in your opinion specify that the data referenced by an object has a specific type and it is safe to reference the object by using that type. It is important to note that it is of your opinion. The C# compiler will not check that this is the case, but the runtime will. If the type of object in memory doesnt match the cast, the runtime will throw an InvalidCastException. You should expect this exception and and deal with it appropriately should it occur.

In saying that, catching an exception and attempting to recover in the event that the type of an object is rather an unwieldly approach. C# offers two really useful operators that can help you perform casting in a much more elegant manner: is and as operators.

The is operator

You can utilise the is operator to authenticate that the type of an object is what you assume it to be, like so:

> WrappedInteger wi = new WrappedInteger();
>
> . . .
>
> object o = wi;
>
> if (o is WrappedInteger)
>
> {
>
> > WrappedInteger temp = (WrappedInteger)o;
> >
> > // This is safe;
> >
> > o is a WrappedInteger
> >
> > . . .
>
> }

The is operator accepts two operands: the left - a reference to an object, the right – a type. Should the type of the object, referred to on the heap, has the specified type, it evaluates to true; or else, it evaluates to false. The prior code tries to cast the reference to the object variable **o** only if it knows that the cast will be successful.

The as operator

The as operator achieves a similar role to is but in a slightly condensed method. You utilise the as operator like so:

> WrappedInteger wi = new WrappedInteger();
>
> . . .
>
> object o = wi;
>
> WrappedInteger temp = o as WrappedInteger;
>
> if (temp != null)
>
> { . . .
>
> **// Cast was a success !**

}

The as operator is similar to the is operator in that it takes an object and a type as its operands. The runtime at-tempts to cast the object to the specified type. If the cast is a success, the result is returned and is assigned to the WrappedInteger variable. Should the cast fail, then the as operator appraises to the null value and instead assigns that to temp.

Chapter 6 Enumerations

An enum is a value type that the developer can declare. The key characteristic of an enum is that it declares at compile time a set of possible constant values that can be referred to by name. The subsequent is an example of an enum:

enum Season { Spring, Summer, Autumn, Winter }

Once you have declared an enum, you can use it in the exact same way as any other type. That is, if the name of your enum is Season then you can create variables, fields and parameters of type Season as demonstrated here:

enum Season { Spring, Summer, Autumn, Winter }

```
    class Example
    {
        public void Method(Season parameter) // method parameter
        {
            Season localVariable; // local variable
            . . .
        }
        private Season currentSeason; // private field
    }
```

In order to read an enumeration, you must assign a value to it. You can assign a value that is defined by the enumeration only to an enumeration variable, as is illustrated here:

Season colourful = Season. Autumn;

Console.WriteLine(colourful); // writes out 'Autumn'

You can then assign the null value, as well the values defined by the enumeration, to the variable:

Season? colourful = null;

Structures

Classes specify reference types that are solely created on the heap. However, on some occasions the class may have so little data that the overhead of managing the heap turns out to be disproportionate. In such cases, it is best to define the type as a structure which is a value type. Since structs are stored on the stack, as long as the structure is reasonably small, the memory management overhead is often reduced.

A structure is similar to a class in that it can have its own fields, methods, and constructors.

Declaring a structure is similar to that of a class. You utilize the keyword struct then use the name of the type, then followed by the body of the structure, between opening and closing braces.

Here for example is a structure named Time that contains three public int fields named hours, minutes, and seconds:

```
struct Time
{
    public int hours, minutes, seconds;
}
```

As per classes, it is not recommended to make the fields of a structure public in most cases; as there is no way to control the values held in public fields. Anyone could for example, set the value of minutes or seconds to a value greater than 60. A better idea is to make the fields private and provide your structure with constructors and methods to initialize and manipulate these fields, as shown in this example:

```
    struct Time
{
    private int hours, minutes, seconds;
            . . .
            public Time(int hh, int mm, int ss)
    {
       this.hours = hh % 24;
       this.minutes = mm % 60;
       this.seconds = ss % 60;
    }
    public int Hours()
    {
       return this.hours;
       }
```

When you copy a value type variable, you get two copies of the value. With reference types however, once you copy a variable of reference type, you get two references to the said object. In summary, use structures for small data values for which it's just as or nearly as efficient to copy the value as it would be to copy an address. Utilise classes for larger more complex data where copying is too inefficient.

Differences between structures and classes

Syntactically a structure and a class are somewhat alike, although there are a few significant differences. Firstly, its impossible to declare a default constructor (i.e. a constructor with zero parameters) for a structure. In the next example the code would compile if **Time** were a class, but since **Time** is a structure, it doesn't:

struct Time

{

    public Time() { ... } / Results in compile time error

    ...

}

Secondly in a class, you can initialize instance fields at their point of declaration. In a structure, you cannot. In this next example, the code would compile if **Time** were a class, but because **Time** is a structure, it triggers a compile-time error:

struct Time

{

    private int hours = 0; // Results in compile time error

    private int minutes;

    private int seconds;

...

}

The main differences between a structure and a class as summarized here:

QuestionStructureClass

What type is it?Value type.Reference type.
Are instances on the Structure instancesClass instances known as

stack or the heap?known as values & liveobjects & live on the heap.

on the stack.
Can you declareNo.Yes.

a default construc-tor?
If you declare your own constructor, will the compiler still generate the default constructor?Yes.No.
Will the compiler automatically initialize a field for you in the constructor if you don't?No.Yes.
Can you initialize instance fields at their point of declaration?No.Yes.

Chapter 7 Decision-making

There are many situations when you require a block of statements to be executed only if a particular condition is satisfied or conversely, if the condition concerned is not satisfied. The implementation of such programming scenarios require decision-making constructs. C# supports many decision-making constructs; most of which are variations of the classic if...else construct. All these decision-making elements of the C# programming language are described in this chapter.

If Statement

The if statement is the most basic decision-making construct that tests the condition, which appears in the if statement. If the condition is found true, the block of statements that follow the if statement is executed. On the other hand, if the condition is false, the if block is simply ignored by the system and execution begins from the first statement that lies outside the if block. Sample implementation for the if statement is given below.

using System;

namespace ConditionalStatements{

class DemoIf{

public static void Main(string[] args)

{

int num = 5;

if (num < 5)

{

Console.WriteLine("Inside If Block");

}

Console.WriteLine("If Executed.");

}

}

}

The output for this code is shown in the image given below.

If Else Statement

The if else is a modified version of the standard if construct that tests the condition, which appears in the if statement. If the condition is found true, the block of statements that follow the if statement is executed. On the other hand, if the condition is found false, the block of statements that follow the else statement is executed. Sample implementation for the if else statement is given below.

using System;

namespace ConditionalStatements{

class DemoIf{

public static void Main(string[] args)

{

int num = 5;

if (num < 5)

{

Console.WriteLine("Inside If Block");

}

else

{

Console.WriteLine("Inside Else Block");

}

Console.WriteLine("If Else Executed.");

}

}

}

The output for this code is shown in the image given below.

Nested If Statements

There may be situations where you may be required to test many conditions; each of which being a sub-part of the main condition. In other words, if you have a programming scenario that needs to perform a block of statements if the vehicle is an Audi car. So, firstly, you will need to put a condition that tests if the vehicle is a car. If this condition is found true, the system must check for a condition that tests if the car is an Audi. This requires two if statements, one inside another, or a nested if statement.

You can have multiple if statements, one inside another to test multiple conditions. There is no limit of the amount of nesting that can be performed for if. However, the higher the number of ifs inside one another gets, the time complexity of the program increases. Sample code for implementing the nested if is as follows –

using System;

namespace ConditionalStatements{

```
class DemoIf{
public static void Main(string[] args)
{
int num1 = 5;
int num2 = 2
if (num1 == 5)
{
Console.WriteLine("Inside If Block 1");
if (num2 == 2)
{
Console.WriteLine("Inside If Block 2");
}
}
Console.WriteLine("Nested If Executed.");
}
}
}
```

The output generated upon the execution of this code can be seen in the image given below.

Switch Statement

In order to mitigate the complexity issues associated with nested if statements, C# also provides switch statement, which can test one variable for multiple values and execute corresponding statements for the same. This construct internall creates a table, which is used for making execution faster. The syntax for implementing switch statement is as follows.

Switch (variable_to_be_tested) {

    Value_1:
    Statement;
    break;
    Value_2:
    Statement;
    break;
    Value_3:
    Statement;
    break;
      default:
    Statement;
    break;

}

Nested Switch Statements

There may be programming scenarios that may require you to test multiple variables and this shall require multiple nested switch statements. C# allows programmers to use nested switch statements and there is no limit on the amount of nesting that can be performed.

Conditional Operator

To simplify the conditional construct, C# also provides a conditional operator (?:).

Chapter 8 Arrays

If you wish to store many elements of the same type and don't want to create an individual variable for each of them, then the best data format available for you is an array. The standard definition of array is a collection of elements that are of the same data type. Moreover, the size of the elements is fixed and the order of the same is sequential in the way that contiguous memory is allocated for the storage of the array elements.

One of the best ways to understand arrays is to see it as a collection of variables of the same type. The name of the array points to the first element of the array. The index of the first element is 0. Therefore, the first element of the array is name_of_array[0]. Subsequent elements of the array can be accessed by mentioning the index of the element by using the syntax, name_of_array[0].

Declaring Arrays

In order to declare an array, you need to use the syntax given below –

data_type[] name_of_array;

Here, data_type is the data type of the array, name_of_array is the identifier that will be used for accessing the array and its elements and [] is the rank or number of elements in the array. An example of array declaration is given below.

double[] bal;

Initializing Arrays

While the array declaration statement tells the compiler that an array of this name is to be created, memory for array is actually allocated when the array is initialized. It is only after array initialization that values can be assigned to the elements of the array. Array is initialized using the new keyword in the following manner –

double[] bal = new double[5];

This statement initializes the array named bal of the type double to have 5 elements.

Assigning Values

Like we mentioned, individual elements of the array can be accessed by mentioning the index of the concerned element, inside square brackets, next to the array name in the following manner –

bal[0] = 4.5

This statement initizlizes the first element of the array bal to the double value 4.5. The above-mentioned method initializes individual elements of the array to specific values. Initialization and assignment can be combined together in the following manner –

double[] bal = {4.5, 66.7, 111.6, 34.0, 98.7};

Alternatively, you may also perform this operation in the following manner –

double[] bal = new bal[5] {4.5, 66.7, 111.6, 34.0, 98.7};

double[] bal = new bal[] {4.5, 66.7, 111.6, 34.0, 98.7};

If you wish to copy an array into another array, you can directly use the statement similar to the one given below.

double[] cp_bal = bal;

This statement creates an array cp_bal that points to the same location as that of bal. It is important to mention here that C# also performs auto-initialization of elements depending on the data type of the array. For instance, if an int array is created, all its values are initialized to 0.

Accessing Elements

Just like array elements are initialized using their index, array elements can be accessed an re-initialized using the name of the array followed by the index of the element, which is enclosed within square brackets. An example of this is given below.

double val = bal[4];

This statement assigns the value of the last element of the array to the variable val. The sample code given below demonstrates the working of arrays in C#.

using System;

namespace DemoApp {

class DemoArray {

static void Main(string[] args) {

int [] num = new int[5]; /* num is an int array of 5 elements */

int x,y;

for (x = 0; x < 5; x++) {

num[x] = x + 100;

}

/*Print the values of array elements*/

for (y = 0; y < 5; y++) {

Console.WriteLine("Element[{0}] = {1}", y, num[y]);

}

Console.ReadKey();

}

}

}

The output generated upon the execution of this code is shown below.

Foreach Loop

C# provides a special looping construct that uses the contiguous nature of arrays for performing iterations. The loops iterates through the elements of the array and its syntax is as follows –

foreach (int var_name in array_name)

{

...

}

Here, var_name is the looping variable and array_name is the name of the array, which needs to be involved for looping. Sample implementation of this looping construct is given below.

using System;

namespace DemoApp {

class DemoArray {

static void Main(string[] args) {

int [] num = new int[5];

```
for ( int x = 0; x < 5; x++ ) {

num[x] = x + 100;

}

foreach (int y in num ) {

int x = y-100;

Console.WriteLine("Value of Element[{0}] = {1}", x, y);

}

Console.ReadKey();

}

}

}
```

The output generated upon the execution of this code is shown below.

Arrays in C#

C# supports multi-dimensional arrays and the simplest form of the same is 2-dimensional arrays. Two dimensional arrays are defined and accessed using the format, array_name[][]. Every new dimension adds a square bracket combination in front of the array name. C# also supports the concepts of jagged arrays or arrays of arrays. Besides this, arrays can also be passed as parameters to functions. Lastly, C# has a defined class in the System namespace for arrays. This is the base class for all arrays, with inbuilt functions.

Chapter 9 Creating Objects and Making Them Work

Classes and objects are really important to how C# and other object-oriented programming languages will work. This is a pretty simple topic that you won't have trouble understanding, but this doesn't mean it's something you should ignore, it is actually very important that you should learn about it because it will help you learn how all of these works. This chapter will take the time to carefully look at how you can work with objects so that they will function the way they should in your code.

Classes and objects

The first thing that we will spend our time talking about are the objects which are used in this programming language. Programming has changed a lot over the past few years, and this has changed how programmers create their new computer applications. The newest form of programming, known as 'OOP' or object-oriented programming, is the newest idea that most modern coding languages rely on to get the coding done. There are a lot of components that go with this, but it basically makes it easier to sort out and use the coding language.

What is OOP?

As a beginner, you may be curious as to what OOP means and how it's relevant to your coding. OOP is a style of coding that relies solely on objects to get the program to work. OOP will provide you with a model type that is based on how things would work in the real world and then you would use this idea and implement it in the codes that you are writing.

In some of the older coding languages, you had to concentrate on abstract ideas to help you to get the coding done. This may sound like a great idea, but it does make things more difficult in the long run. With OOP, you have to work with real objects, rather than these abstract ideas, which makes the coding so much easier. This is the approach that most modern programming languages take and it does make it much easier for the beginner to write their own codes, create their own program, and even solve some of their own problems they might encounter as they go about their programming.

Objects

In this section, we will spend some time working with objects to learn more about them. Programmers use digital objects to help represent the physical objects that they want to place inside of their code. While you are working with an OOP language, it is important to remember that these objects have more than a few characteristics that you should remember. These include:

- State

These are the characteristics that will define the object. These can be general or specific.

- Behavior

These are the characteristics that will declare all the actions that an object is capable of.

For us to understand exactly how all of this will work, we need to take a look at an example. Let's say that we are looking at a ball. The state of this object or the traits that define its characteristics are things like its color, what the ball is made out of, and the size. The behavior of that ball would refer to what that ball is capable of, such as bouncing, rolling, and so on and so forth.

When you are working on an OOP language, you can easily combine the technique and the information to process them as the same thing. The programming object will then match up to how it would behave or look when it is in the real world and then it will also hold onto the actions and the information until later.

Classes

While we will discuss this a little bit more in a later chapter, it is important to understand a little bit about what these classes are at this point. Within this language, the 'classes' refer to what defines all the characteristics of the objects from above. These classes are in charge of giving you a model or a structure so that you can effectively define the nature of the object. These classes are often considered the foundation of OOP languages, and they will be linked closely to the object. Another thing to note is that each of the objects that you are using can also represent one specific class.

Let's take a look at how this works so that it makes a lot more sense to you. For example, we have a class that we named 'Toys' and while the object will be 'Ball.' In this sample, the ball is one instance of that 'Toy' class that you worked on. However, that the class will also define the state and the behavior of all the 'toys' that you add to the 'class' including the 'ball.'

Classes may sound complicated, and they will make the organization of your code a lot easier to handle, many people often see them as the basis of just about any program. The information they hold onto is meaningful for those who will take a look inside of the class so they can understand exactly what it is. For example, if you have a class that you named 'Toys,' the other users can access or look into the class and see that all the items or objects that were placed inside the code actually belong there. They do not have to be exactly the same, but putting them together in the same class should make sense.

The classes function to define the behavior of an object, such as the kinds of actions you want that object to be capable of performing. The object will also have its own characteristics or attributes. You will see that the attributes appear as different variables in the body of the class while the behavior, on the other hand, is defined by the different methods that fall inside the class.

Let's take a look at how this works by examining the Toy class that we talked about before. When these are applied, you will get the size and the color as the attributes. To make this work, you will need to bring out and use the **move()** and the **stop()** methods.

How to use these classes in your code

We have already spent a little bit of time talking about classes and how you can get them to work inside of your code, but now we need to spend some more time looking at how they work within the program as a whole and how they are useful at changing what you can write out inside of the code. When you are working with the C# programming language, you need to define all of the classes with the help of the 'class' keyword to not only make sure that everything works but to also help make things clear and simple.

After you have started with the code and you typed in the word 'class,' this is when you should indicate the identifier that you would like to see with the variable and the methods that would help make it certain that all of this works. As for making sure that all of this would stay simple, there are specific parts that you need to use since you are working with this kind of code. The different parts that you need to add to the class when working in C# include:

- Fields

These are any of the variables that belong to a particular data type.

- Methods

You can use these methods to manipulate the data.

- Properties

In this programming language, the properties are what will enhance how well the fields work. The property will provide some extra management abilities for the information and give it to the fields.

At this point, it will probably be easier if you take a look at how you can work with making classes and how to make sure that they do exactly what you would like. We will now have a look at an example of how this code will work and the different theories that have been going on with it. In this example, we will use 'book' as the name of the class and then it will have the properties of 'size' and 'type.' The example of this code is as follows:

Public class Book

{

Private string bookType:

Private string size;

Public string BookType

{

Get

{

Return this. bookType;

}

Set

{

This.bookTyupe = value'

}

}

```
Public string Size
{
    Get
    {
        Return this size;
    }
    Set
    {
        this.size = value;
    }
}

public Book()
{
    this.bookType = "Dictionary";
    this.size = "large";
}

public book(string bookType, string size)
{
    this.bookType = bookType;
    this.size = size;
}
```

```
public void Sample()
{
    Console.WriteLine(" Is this a {0}, bookType):
```

Now, at first, this will look like a really complicated code to work with and you may be worried about how you will keep all of this in order or if you can understand how to use it at all. It is really not that complicated at all to work with though and you can use the ideas that are inside.

With this example, the 'Book' class will define two different properties, the book type, and the size. These properties will hide the values inside the fields of the same names while the code snippet will declare two constructors that will be generated on the Book class. This code will also create a method called **Sample()**.

You can use this code for a number of different things, like adding in more characteristics if you would like, and it doesn't have to be limited to books, toys, vehicles, or anything else. You can mess around with your text editor as much as you want to try out this formula and change it around with some other classes to make it easier to get the program to work for you.

How to create your own objects

Once you have a class in place to help you out, it is time to work on creating some of the objects that you would like to use and place inside a class. Creating your own object is not meant to be difficult to work with so in this part of the book, we will take the time to have a look at the basics that you need to know to get started.

Creating the object

The first thing that we have to do here is to create the object that you want to place inside an existing class. To get this to happen, you need to make your own keywords. Usually, a programmer will choose to assign the new object a variable so that it will stay as the same data type as the class that you want to use. Remember that doing this won't copy the object over to the right variable, but it will help give the variable a reference to the object that it is now assigned to. To make sure that this actually works, use the following code to do so:

Book someBook = new Book()

This is a good example that you can use because it will take the instance of the book and assign it over to the variable that we named 'someBook.' This will ensure that the proper object will the right class as is needed.

System classes

If you are new to working with the C# language, you will find that this language already has a library that is built right in. This library includes a lot of classes that are kind of default such as string, math, and console. As you start to use this language more, you must remember that the library is something that you can easily use and access with the '.Net' applications.

You are definitely going to love how the .NET framework will do the job for you. This is because the library that you need for C# was installed ahead of time. These classes are the parts that you can use all of the time, and they are helpful as you start to learn some of the basics that come with this language, such as networking, text procession, and execution. These classes are also helpful to a beginner who has never worked in programming before because they are prewritten and recognized by the program so you will not have to do as much work.

One thing that you should remember when you are working with these classes is that they will hide all the logical implementations. You need to focus more on what your classes can do, rather than worrying so much about the mechanics behind how they exactly do this. Because of this, the built-in classes with C# are not something that the programmer can actually view. You simply need to use these codes for their general purposes rather than worrying so much about how they really work because that's something you don't really have to think about.

How to assign a parameter to the object

This programming language will allow you to assign some parameters to the object that you created. This is something that's pretty easy to work with, and you just need to have the basic syntax in place to make sure that this will work for you. The syntax that you need to use is this:

Book someBook = new Book("Biography", "large")';

This code will create a new object named 'someBook' and will assign the two different parameters to it as well. With this adjustment, the object's 'type' is now Biography while the size is now large.

Whenever you use the new keyword, the framework of .NET can complete two things:

- It will reserve some of the memory for this new object
- It will initialize the object's data members

This is a process that will occur because of the constructor method. For the code that we wrote above, the parameters that we set out right away are the parameters for a 'class constructor.' This is what will make sure that the object will stay inside the class that you chose to create and it will provide that object with the right characteristics so that it works properly.

Releasing your objects

One thing that you need to concentrate on is learning how to release the object that you are working with. Some other languages that you will work with will make you go through and manually release the objects, but this is not something that is required when it comes to working with C#. This means that you can release any of the objects that are consuming up too much memory in your system without having to go through and manually destroy them. You can just use the CLR system that can be found inside the .NET framework to make all of this work.

When you are working with the CLR system, the computer can automatically detect and then release the objects that were not referenced. The memory that was reserved for these objects is now available again, and you can use them for some of the other objects or variables that you will create inside of your code. If you would like to release an object, you should stop and learn how to destroy the corresponding references as well. An example of how you would go through and do this is the following:

    someBook = null

This process doesn't mean it's going to delete the object, but it will make sure that all references to that object are removed so that the CLR can go through after you are done with it and perform the deletion for you. This is a great process to have because it will help to limit the number of issues that occur in your code and can get rid of some of the bugs that might show up in the code.

The constructors

The last topic that we will discuss in this chapter is the 'constructors.' These constructors are basically methods that will run when the program creates a new object. The idea behind using these is so that you can use it to initialize the data of that new object. You won't get anything of value to show up when you go with this method. In addition, this constructor will use the same name as the class that it comes from, this means you don't have to try and match up a few random names along the way. You also get the choice of assigning the right parameters to this when you work with constructors in C#.

The constructors that come with C# can accept parameters just like any method that you are using in this programming language. You can set up several constructors in the class, but you always need to check to see if the constructors are from different types and numbers of parameters. This will help to make sure that each parameter is unique.

As you are working with constructors, it is important to remember that these will run any time that you create a brand new object in your class. If you are working with a class that has a few different constructors inside of it, you may be curious to figure out which of the constructors are running as a new object is created in the code. This programming language can pick out the right constructor based on what you are working on so you won't be responsible for coming up with all that information. The compiler will take over so things will stay organized without you being stressed out so much about it.

Now that we have talked about the constructor a little bit, let's take a look at an example of how this would work in C#:

```
    public class Device
{
        private string type;
        private string size;
        // A constructor without any parameter
```

```
public Device()
{
    this.type ="laptop";
    this.type = "large";
}
    //A constructor with two parameters.
{
    this.type = type;
    this.size = size;
}
}
```

The parameters that we just set up can help tell the program what are the tasks or functions that need to be fulfilled. It is also responsible for helping the C# compiler to figure out the constructor that you would like the program to use.

How to Define Classes with the Help of C#

Classes are so important when it comes to working with any programming language because they perform a variety of helpful functions, and this is true in C# as well. So, let's take some time to look at how to define classes inside the C# language.

The basics of working with classes

When you are working with a programming language, the class is the part that will define the object types and the data types that you can use at that point in the program. The object is what will contain the information that defines the class or the container that it is held in. These classes can hold a ton of information, and they can be used to describe the behavior of the object as well. These are all the behaviors that the object is capable of doing. When working with OOP languages, you want to use methods that will help describe the behavior of the objects.

Components of classes

When you are working with a class, some different components will come into play to help you get these classes taken care of. There are a few different parts that come with each class including:

- Declaration

This is the line that will declare the identifier of the class.

- Body

Just like with methods, the classes to have a single body. You need to define the body right after you make the declaration. The body is the statement, or several statements, that are found between the curly brackets. An example of this is:

class Example

{

//This is the body of the "Example" class.

}

- Constructor

This is the part that will allow you to create a new object. An example of this is:

Public Sample()

{

//Insert what you want to say here.

}

- Fields

These are the variables that you will declare within your class. The fields contain the values that will represent the exact state of the object they are trying to get to.

- Properties

This part will describe the different attributes of the class. Many programmers will write the class properties right inside the field of their chosen object.

- Methods

A method is basically a named block of code that is executable. It is capable of completing some tasks that will then allow objects to attain the right behavior. It can also execute the proper algorithms that are present in the codes.

Custom classes

Before you decide that you want to work with a specific class, you should make sure that you have an object that will go inside of it. You can do this by starting with a new keyword and then all you have to do is add in the constructors that you will need.

While you are working on the C# language, you won't have the access to manipulate the objects that you are creating directly. Instead, you need to assign your objects to a variable beforehand so that you can manipulate the objects if needed later on. Remember that to access the methods as well as the properties of that object you need to indicate the identifier that goes along with the object and then use your dot operator.

How to organize your classes

It is incredibly important that you can organize the classes that you are using the C# language. There is really only one rule that you must follow to make this all work. This one rule is that the classes must be saved as **.cs** files so that they are easier to find when you want to pull them up later to ensure that the codes will work properly.

Technically, you do have the ability to save all of your classes into one big file, and the compiler should not have any issues with getting these to work without errors. But many programmers prefer to save their classes in different files because it helps them to easily find these classes later on and organize them as needed. It is really up to you how you would like to get this done though.

Another thing that you will eventually gain some familiarity with as you continue working in this programming language is the 'namespace.' This is a set of classes that are all related in some manner. The way that they are related will vary depending on the situation, but if examined, the way these classes relate to one another makes sense. These can include things like structures, interfaces, classes, and even the information that is placed inside of them. You even have the freedom to combine several classes together into a new namespace regardless of where they had been placed in the computer's memory.

If you are interested in creating a new namespace on the codes that you have already worked on, you should make sure that you add in the 'using' directive to make things a bit easier for you. Most programmers will find that it is easier for them to write out the directives that they want to use inside the first few lines of the **.cs** file so that they do not forget to put them there later. After you made sure to insert this directive, you will then be able to declare the namespace.

Accessing the classes

The next thing that we will take a look at is how to access these classes. C# allows support from four modifiers when it comes to who can access each class. These modifiers are 'public,' 'internal,' 'private,' and 'protected.' What these modifiers do is that they allow you to control who will be able to see the elements that are in a particular class. Let's look at how each of these work so you can decide which one to use when writing your own code:

- Private

The function of this modifier is that will place some strict restrictions on one of your classes. If the class is tagged as a private class, it will not be accessible by the other classes in the code. The C# language will use this as the default modifier if you do not place anything else there. This can help to avoid problems in the future in case you forget to add on that modifier.

- Public

You can also choose to make the class public. This means that the modifier will tell the other classes that they have access to this class. This modifier can take away all the limitations about how visible this class is to all the other classes.

- Internal

If your code has the 'internal' modifier on it, this means that this class will be accessible, but only to the files that fall in the same project.

- Protected

This is the modifier that you want to use if you would like to prevent a user from accessing the element. However, it also allows all the descendant classes to have access to the elements of that class if they need it.

As you can see, each of these elements all works in a slightly different way compared to one another based on how much you want your classes to be private in terms of permitted access. If you would like to make sure that the class remains private and that nothing or no one else is allowed to get ahold of it or use the information, then you working in the private setting is obviously the best for you. However, if you need other classes to have the ability to work with this particular class, then it is just fine to change it to the public modifier.

As you go through your program, think about which of these modifiers will work out the best for your code. If you do not place any of these modifiers before your class, then it will default as a private class, which is not that bad of a thing. But if you feel that one of the other options is the best for making your code, then you must make sure that it is written in with the class to avoid issues later.

A final word about classes

The importance of these classes cannot be emphasized enough when it comes to writing out your code. They help you to keep things neat and organized and will also make sure that you can easily pull up the things that you need from the code. This can make things so much simpler to work with. Your code will work better, and you will find that writing your own codes isn't even really that difficult.

When it comes to picking out the objects that go with the class that you are writing, you must remember that these objects need to make sense if you put them together. You should have someone else, like a friend or a co-worker who's familiar with programming, look at the class and agree that it makes sense that those objects ended up together. This does not mean that the objects need to be identical, but they need to at least be related in some way.

For example, if you have a class that is called 'Toys,' you don't just place the same toy inside and leave it as it is. You could include all sorts of 'toys' or other objects inside, but some rules have to be followed. This can work with any kind of class that you would like to work with. You could have a class of things that are colored blue, one for animals, and one for types of vehicles. As long as the objects that go inside match up a little bit, that means you're doing everything right.

It is important to spend some time learning about objects because they are so important to ensure that your code works the way that you would like. They provide the tools to organize your code and make sure it works amazingly well. Try out a few of the different codes that are in this guidebook, and you will quickly see how well these work once you try making your own code.

Conclusion

This really is just the beginning of your C# journey. There is so much more to learn and so much further you can go; this is only the tip of the iceberg. You've learned the syntax and the language conventions; you've learned what goes into a program and how to make things more complex. The most important part of any computer programming language is the logical aspect. Yes, you may have learned how to loop through an array like you would look through a list of grocery items. But, if someone asked you to take an image and process it, would you know how to do it? Would you know how to scale it? Rotate it? Flip it? By using an API and your brain, you could figure it out.

Real programming requires you to use the logical part of your brain. It's much like learning a foreign language. Learning the language conventions and the grammar rules is one thing, but the real skill comes from writing the language in a clean and structured way and in a well-thought-out and logical manner. As a programmer, the skill comes from being able to put your knowledge and logic into practice by writing clean code that makes sense, and most importantly, that works.

Learning a program and truly understanding it is great – it really is the nearest we have to having magic power. You can make something from nothing, build it from the ground up, and have it do exactly what you want it to do.

In this series of guides, you learned C# basics, and while I couldn't possibly teach you everything you need to know, I have at least set you off on a journey of discovery. I hope that you now feel you can take the next step, and that you are prepared to dive deeper into C# and learn it until you are proficient at using it.

Thank you for taking the time to read my guide and I want to take this opportunity to wish you luck on your C# programming journey.

Conclusion

This marks the end of this guide. C# is a compiled programming language developed by Microsoft. C# is also an object-oriented programming language, meaning that it supports concepts like the use of classes, objects, inheritance, encapsulation, polymorphism etc. To program in C#, you need the .Net framework. This framework was also developed by Microsoft. You also need an integrated development environment (IDE). Visual studio is the common IDE used for programming in C#. You can get its free edition online. The .Net framework can only run on the Windows operating system. This means that if you are using Linux or Mac OS, you have to look for an alternative so as to be able to program in C#. You can use Mono, an open source framework that acts as an alternative to the .Net framework. It can be used on both Linux and Mac OS.

C# is an easy programming language, making it good even to the beginners in programming. One only needs to setup the environment and start writing and running their C# code. You can use C# alone to develop a complete computer application.

If you enjoyed getting started with C#, there is so much more to learn and do with this wonderful language. Be sure to continue your journey with the second book in the series, which looks at slightly more complex topics while still being beginner friendly.

C# is a valuable programming language with a large array of uses. It is practical, efficient, and extremely easy to use. It will be a great asset and reference point for your future in programming. If you can think it, you can create it. Don't be afraid to try something new.

Good luck and happy programming!

ARDUINO PROGRAMMING

The practical beginner's guide to learn arduino programming in one day step-by-step

(#2020 Updated Version | Effective Computer Languages)

Steve Tudor

Text Copyright ©
All rights reserved. No part of this guide may be reproduced in any form without permission in writing from the publisher except in the case of brief quotations embodied in critical articles or reviews.

Legal & Disclaimer

The information contained in this book and its contents is not designed to replace or take the place of any form of medical or professional advice; and is not meant to replace the need for independent medical, financial, legal or other professional advice or services, as may be required. The content and information in this book has been provided for educational and entertainment purposes only.

The content and information contained in this book has been compiled from sources deemed reliable, and it is accurate to the best of the Author's knowledge, information and belief. However, the Author cannot guarantee its accuracy and validity and cannot be held liable for any errors and/or omissions. Further, changes are periodically made to this book as and when needed. Where appropriate and/or necessary, you must consult a professional (including but not limited to your doctor, attorney, financial advisor or such other professional advisor) before using any of the suggested remedies, techniques, or information in this book.

Upon using the contents and information contained in this book, you agree to hold harmless the Author from and against any damages, costs, and expenses, including any legal fees potentially resulting from the application of any of the information provided by this book. This disclaimer applies to any loss, damages or injury caused by the use and application, whether directly or indirectly, of any advice or information presented, whether for breach of contract, tort, negligence,

personal injury, criminal intent, or under any other cause of action.

You agree to accept all risks of using the information presented inside this book.

You agree that by continuing to read this book, where appropriate and/or necessary, you shall consult a professional (including but not limited to your doctor, attorney, or financial advisor or such other advisor as needed) before using any of the suggested remedies, techniques, or information in this book.

Introduction

When it comes to creating some of your own robotics products, there are many things that you can consider. You will need to decide what kind of project you want to work on as well as the type of code that will help you to get the work done. One of the best options that you can use is the Arduino platform.

When we are talking about Arduino, we are talking about a software and microcontroller that is programmable, open sourced, and will use the ATMega chip. It is designed to be more of a prototyping platform, there is a huge fan base for this software when it comes to building an electronic project. When it comes to working with an electronic project, you will find that the Arduino platform is good for using either as a temporary addition while you work on the project or you can even embed it as a permanent part of the robotic project when it is done.

The Arduino board is also programmable with the Arduino software, which is pretty easy to use, even for those who are just getting started and have no idea how to work with this kind of software. If you have happened to use the C++ or Java programming languages, you will see that the Arduino coding language is going to be fairly similar. The idea behind using this software is meant to be really simple, but there is a lot of power there to, making it perfect for those who have some experience and for those who are just getting started out.

Arduino is also an open sourced platform, which means that anyone is able to use it, for free, as well as make adjustments to the code to fit their needs. This is a really cool addition for those who are just starting to use the Arduino system because they will be able to access thousands of codes from other programmers, or even make some changes to their own codes, in order to make the program work perfectly.

In addition to finding that many of the codes that you would like to use are already available and developed, beginners are going to enjoy that the Arduino community is pretty large. You will be able to go online and look through forums and communities to ask your personal questions related to your own project, to find out new information, and even watch tutorials to make working with Arduino easier than ever.

The Arduino platform may be pretty powerful to use, but it is also pretty basic. You will find that this platform only comes with two main components for you to use including:

- The hardware: this is going to include the microcontroller, which is also known as the circuit board. You are able to physically program this part. You will find that there are a number of Arduino boards for you to choose from and the choice will vary depending on the type of project that you are putting together.

The software: this would be the environment that you use with the board, or the IDE, that is going to run right on your own computer. You will use the IDE to help you to upload and write the programming codes that you would like to be relayed over to the board. Once you write your programs on the board and transfer them over, the Arduino board should act in the manner that you requested.

These parts are able to come together to help you to get the project to work well. You need to make sure that you have some hardware in place, such as one of the Arduino board types, and then it needs to respond to what you are able to send through with the software. We will spend some time talking about the various things that you are able to do with the software in order to get your project to work later on, but both of these will need to be set up to ensure that the messages from the IDE are getting over to the board and working properly.

With Arduino, you need to have the IDE in place before writing out any code. The IDE for this program is free since it is open sourced, which makes it easier to get ahold of a copy. When writing codes, you will use the Arduino programming language, which will be easy to learn and works well with all of the operating systems on your computer.

One thing to note with the IDE and the coding language with Arduino, if you are working on a Windows 7 operating system or earlier, you will have a few steps that you will need to take, in addition to the regular steps, to make sure that the Arduino board will work with the operating system. It does work with the older versions of Windows, you just need to take some extra time to introduce the board to this system to get it to work.

Whether you are just getting started out with programming or want to use some of your skills to make a great electronic or robotic project, the Arduino platform will be able to help you get this done. It has all the power that you need with a simplistic background that helps even the beginner understand and accomplish what they want.

What can I do when using Arduino?

One of the first questions that you may have when you see the Arduino programming language is what you are able to do with it all? There are many programming languages out there and you are able to choose them to accomplish different things, but Arduino is going to work a bit differently compared to some of the others.

There are many great projects that you are able to do with the Arduino platform. Basically, the coding that goes with Arduino is going to travel from the IDE on your computer over to the hardware that you purchase to go with your project.

You can use just the board or attach it to some electronic project to make it do some amazing things.

There are a lot of things that you can do with your robotics with the help of Arduino and if you are just getting started with your own electronic learning process or you want to try something new, this is the best platform to do so with. You are able to work with the board making sounds, blinking lights, sending out signals to control what is on the screen ahead of it, and so many other things. We will spend some time looking at the different projects that you are able to do with Arduino so you get a better idea of what you are able to do with this great language.

What isn't Arduino able to do?

As we mentioned above, there are quite a few things that you are able to do with the Arduino platform, but there are also some things that you won't be able to do. First, the Arduino language doesn't have a ton of processing power, so if you want to do a task that is considered intensive, you won't be able to do it with the Arduino platform. This means that the Arduino language won't be able to do things like output video or audio, or even record or process them, though you are able to use it to put graphics on a TFT or LCD screen. If you would like to do some of these processes, you would need to choose a different programming language.

In addition, you will find that the Arduino boards should work similar to a computer board, but this isn't true. It is not possible to hook up a webcam, keyboard, or other option to the board and try to use it because these boards don't have an operating system that comes with it. The confusion with this often comes from a similar product, the Raspberry Pi, which looks the same but actually has its own operating system and can work similar to a computer. The Arduino boards do not work this way.

When you write out the codes with this option, you are going to be using the operating system that comes with your computer. Once the code is written, it is not going to tell the computer what to do. Rather, your computer is going to send this code over to the Arduino board and the board will react in the manner that you wish. For example, you wouldn't be able to use this code to hack into another computer or to create your own website, but it can be sent over to the Arduino board to help it to become a remote control for a game.

Who should use Arduino?

One thing that you will like about the Arduino system is that anyone is able to use it for their own personal needs. Many experts in programming and robotics like to use Arduino because of all the variety that comes with it and they can create their own projects, make any changes to the code that they want, and it has enough power to get things done in no time. Beginners like this because it is easy to learn and you will be able to try out a few of the codes right away to create your own project.

Pretty much anyone who would like to create some of their own robotics and electronic projects will find that the Arduino system is one of the best for them to use. It has a lot of power that makes man projects possible but it is still easy enough that a beginner will not get too frustrated when trying to get it to work for the first time.

Why should I choose Arduino?

So far we have spent some time talking about what the Arduino platform is all about and why you would consider using it for your needs, such as what it is able to do. But there are some other choices out there that you can make when it comes to picking out a board that will control your electronic, so why should you choose to go with the Arduino platform? Here are some of the benefits that come with using Arduino and why you should choose this platform over one of the other options:

- Works across many platforms: the IDE that works with Arduino has the ability to work with pretty much any operating system that you want. It will work with Mac OS, Windows, and Linux. You do need to take precautions when using Windows 7 or earlier, but we will discuss later how to make this work even if you do have an older version.
- Simple environment: when you are a beginner, you don't want to pick an environment that is hard to get through. The Arduino environment is similar to the C++ environment, but has been made even simpler to use.
- Open source: the board plans that come with Arduino are published to be open sourced. This means that programmers are able to come and use the platform and the software, as well as make changes to them whenever needed. This can be nice for programmers who are looking to use the platform but want to make some changes to get it to work for their needs and it is nice for the beginners because there are already many codes available for you to choose from.
- Free to use: since this is an open sourced software, the code is free to use. You will be able to use the software as well as the IDE for free, but keep in mind that you will need to purchase the boards that you want to use for your project. The boards are pretty inexpensive and there are a variety of options so you can experiment a bit and find the one that is right for you.

A large community: the community for Arduino is pretty large, which makes it a great option for you to choose as a beginner. You will be able to find many forums and other locations where you can ask questions, look at tutorials, and find that answers that you need when working on your project.

There is so much that you are going to fall in love with when you are using this platform for some of your own projects. If you are just getting into the world of coding and you want to create a great project, or just mess around and learn something new, the Arduino platform is one of the best that you can choose. Let's take a look at some of the steps that you need to take to hook up one of the Arduino boards to your computer as well as some of the projects that you are able to do to get some great results with this platform.

Terminology to help out

When you are learning about a new coding language, there are always some new terminology that you will need to learn. Before we start to work on some of the projects that are later on in this book, we will need to discuss some of the terms that are popular in many of the directions so you know what is going on. Some of the terms that you should know include:

- Breadboard: this is a tool that is reusable for building circuits. It makes it easier to connect the circuits without having to get them permanently attached to the board. It is also a stable surface that will connect all your components together.
- Compiler: the compiler is a piece of software that will take your written program and translate it into something that the Arduino microcontroller is able to understand.
- Device driver: this is a piece of software that makes it so that the computer is able to communicate with the devices that are attached to it, such as the Arduino board. If the device driver doesn't work well, the computer and the Arduino board won't work together.
- EEPROM: this will stand for Electrically Erasable Programmable Read-Only Memory. This is a computer chip that will be written and re-written with the code that you want. You should notice

that it is electrically erasable which is when an electric current will erase the information so that you are able to use it. Keep in mind that all of the information on this will be erased when you use this option.

- External interrupt: the external interrupt means that something that is outside of the processor or the computer system and it needs your attention.
- Flash memory: this is one of your memory choices. It is going to retain the data whether there is power to the system or not. A good example would be the flash drive, which is going to store files, even if it isn't plugged into your computer.
- Digital input/output: digital pins are known to have either a high or a low value. You are able to pick from a wide variety of digital pins based on the type of board that you get.
- Analog input/output: this is opposite of working with digital. The analog is going to receive a continuous electrical signal, while the digital option will focus just on whether the value is either zero or one. Both can be available on your board depending on what you are doing with it.
- Processor: this is the part of the system that is going to take the instructions from the computer, figure out what you would like to have done with these instructions, and then runs them.
- Serial communication: when this kind of communication is occurring, it means that the two systems are sending digital pulses between them at a rate that you determine.
- Sketch: this is what the Arduino code is known as. It is going to consist of the instructions that you will send to tell Arduino how to run. You will need to compile the sketch and then upload it to your board.

SPI: this stands for serial peripheral interface. It is in charge of keeping the data communication protocol over small distances.

Getting started on one of your first projects in Arduino can be an exciting experience. This is a great program to learn how to use whether you are brand new to the world of coding or you are ready to take things to a new level. This guidebook will show you how to download some of your own projects and create them for the first time as well as some of the basics that you need to get the boards to work.

Setting Up Your Arduino Platform

The Arduino platform is really popular and is always seeing a lot of changes, which means that as a beginner, there are always new things that you can learn about this platform in order to make it your own. We are going to focus on the basics that come with using the Arduino platform, but there are so many new projects that you can learn how to use with this option that it is a good idea to try new things out, keep up with some of the forums and communities, and see what is available for you to expand your knowledge with.

At this time, we will stick with the basics of how to use the platform as well as some of the projects that you are able to use. To get started, there are a few essentials that you will need to get ahold of in order to make the program work. These essentials include the Arduino board and the software that will talk to the board.

What is the Arduino Board?

The Arduino board is necessary if you would like to get started on your first project. There are a variety of options that you are able to choose from though and each one works with a different kind of project. This is why it is a good idea to understand some of the basics of the boards before you go out and purchase one, or you may end up with one that isn't what you want. Each board is able to do slightly different things and they may even look a bit different, but they should all have some of the same components in common including:

- Barrel Jack and USB: all of the boards that you can purchase will need to have some means in order to connect them to your power source, such as to the wall or to your computer. Many of them will also have a USB connect so that you are able to hook them to the computer and download the codes to it. You can also use the barrel jack which helps the board plug right into the wall.
- Pins: the pins are basically the points where you will create your circuits when you connect them with wires. There are several types of pins that you are able to use with the Arduino boards and each of them have a different function. There are several types of pins that you can find on your board including:
  - **GND: this is the short for Gourd. These are going to be the pins that are used in order to ground out the circuit you are creating.**
  - **5V and 3.3V: these are the pins that will give the right kind of voltage that your project needs, either the 5 volts or the 3.3 volts.**
  - **Analog: these are basically the pins that are seen right under the Analog In label on the board. These can be used for reading any signals that come in from the analog sensors and then they are turned into a digital value for you to read.**
  - **AREF: this is a short form of the Analog Reference. This is going to be the pin that you will use when you want to set a maximum or an upper limit for the external voltage that goes to the analog pins. You will usually want to pick a maximum of 0 to**

5 volts, but most of the time you won't use these at all.
- PWM: these are found in many Arduino boards and this label is found right next to the digital pins. These pins are used for either normal digital pins or for a signal that is called Pulse-Width Modulation.
- Digital: these are the pins that are fund right across from your analog pins and will be found right under the digital label. These pins are used to show the input and the output that is provided by the digital signal.

- Reset button: this is the button that is going to allow the pin to rest right on the ground and then will restart the code that you already loaded onto your board. It is the one that you will use when you want to test out your code a few times. Keep in mind that it is not going to reset everything on the board and it won't be able to fix issues if they are there.
- Power LED indicator: this is going to be a small LED light that should be right next to the label for ON right by it. This should light up whenever you plug this board into a new power source.

Voltage regulator: this is the part of the board that will be able to control how much voltage you would like to get onto your board at a time. If there is voltage that is above this set limit, it will be able to turn it away. It will not be able to handle anything that is above 20 volts so make sure that your power source is lower than this or you can have issues with destroying the board.

Each of these pins can be important based on the project that you are using your board for. You will need to pick out the board that has the right pins for the project that you need. Many of the beginner projects are going to have information on which board you are able to use and as you get more familiar with how things work, you will be able to figure out which boards are needed for your more advanced projects.

Hooking up the Arduino software

By this point, you will have the right hardware, or the right board, in order to get started with your first project. It is now time to install the software, also known as the IDE, to make sure that Arduino is going to work. The IDE is basically the environment that you need to have in order to write your code before sending it over to the board and to attach all of the circuit components. Without having the right IDE in place, you would never get the code over to the microcontroller and the board would just remain lifeless.

To download the IDE that you would like to use, go to the website *www.arduino.cc* in order to find the link for downloaded. Give the IDE some time to download on your computer, and when it is done, you should see a zip folder. Open up this file and then save it to the right location on your computer; pick the one that you like the best to ensure that you are able to find it later if needed.

When this is done, you can open up the Arduino.EXE file and then run it to get the installation started. There will be a few command prompts that will come up during the process so read through them and click in order to get it all set up. Once the IDE is installed and the components are all in place, it is time to start working on some of the projects in this guidebook in order to see what all Arduino is able to do.

Getting Started with Arduino

Since this is a platform that is widely popular and is constantly expanding and changing, it is important to keep in mind that you will have to continue learning about the programming language as changes to it occur. To begin with though, we are going to spend some time learning the basics that you will need to know to get started with Arduino. To begin, there are two essentials that you will need; the software to make this work, and the Arduino board.

Understanding the Arduino board

Before you go out and purchase an Arduino board, you will need to understand some of the basic features of these boards and their uses. There are a few types of boards that are available, and each of them have different capabilities and benefits. While they will differ in terms of what they are able to do and how they look, most of the boards you come across will have the following components in common:

- Barrel Jack and USB - all the boards will have some method for you to connect them to a power source. Most of them will come with a USB connection so that you can upload your codes onto them. You can also choose to connect them with a barrel jack which will essentially let you plug the board into the wall.

- Pins - the pins are where you are going to construct your circuits by connecting in the wires. There are a few types of pins that you can use on the boards and they are each used for a specific function. Some of the most common pins that you will find include:

- GND: this is short for Gourd. They are the pins that you will use in order to ground your circuit.
- 5v and 3.3V: these are the pins that will supply either 5 volts or 3.3 Volts of power.
- Analog: these are the pins that will be seen under the 'Analog In' label. These are the ones that you can use for reading signals from the analog sensors, and then these signals are going to be converted into a digital value.
- Digital: these are going to be across from the analog pins and will be under the 'Digital' label. These are the pins that are used for the input and output of the digital signal.
- PWM: in many of the Arduino boards, there will be a (PWM~) label that is next to the Digital one. This basically means that the pins are able to be used as either normal digital pins, or for a signal that is called Pulse-Width Modulation.
- AREF: this is short form for Analog Reference. This is the pin that you can use to set the upper limit of the external voltage for the analog pins, usually between 0 and 5 volts, though it is often left alone.

- Reset button - this button should be there to allow the pin to rest to the ground, and to restart the code that is already loaded on the board. It is a good way to test out code a few times. It will not reset everything to a clean state, and won't fix any problems that exist in your code.
- Power LED Indicator - this should be a tiny LED light that should have the word "ON" right next to

it. It is going to light up when you plug your board into a power source.

- Transmit and Receive LEDs - these are in place to give an indication that the board is either receiving or transmitting data. This is useful when you are trying to load up a new program to the board and you want to see if it is being received.

- Main Integrated Circuit (IC) - this is a little black piece that has metal legs that will attach to the board. Think of it as the brains of the board. The IC will differ between boards, but most are from the ATMEL company. Make sure to know which kind of IC you are using before loading up a new program though because this sometimes does make a difference.

Voltage regulator - this is the component of the board that is going to control how much voltage is able to get onto the board. It has the ability to turn away any extra voltage that is trying to get into the board. It is not able to handle anything that is more than 20 Volts though, so make sure to not use a power supply higher than this or it will destroy the board.

In addition to picking the right board for your project, you need to consider the other hardware that you may want to add on. The board can do a lot of stuff on its own, but it gets a lot of the power you are looking for when you add on some additional hardware. For the basics that we will be learning, it is not such a big deal, but as you progress you may want to consider adding on additional components to get a bit more power.

Getting the software hooked up

After you have had some time to go through and pick out the hardware that you would like to use, including the board you want for the project, it is time to install the IDE for Arduino.

This is basically the environment, or the software, that you will need in order to write out the code for the microcontroller and to attach all the circuit components. Without the IDE in place, you would not be able to write out the code and the microcontroller and board would have no idea what you want them to do.

To start, you simply need to visit the Arduino website at www.arduino.cc in order to download the IDE. The IDE will download as a receive a zip folder. Open this up and then save it in a location on your computer that is easy for you to remember.

Once that's done, you will need to run the Arduino.EXE file so that the installation can get started. You simply need to follow the command prompts that come up in order to get everything installed. Once the IDE is set up and you have all the right hardware components, you are ready to move onto the next step of using this programming language!

Chapter 1 Choosing and Setting Up the Arduino

The first step in setting up your Arduino microcontroller will be to choose an Arduino board with which you want to work.

Choosing a Board

When looking at the options for Arduino Boards, there are a few factors you will want to consider before making a choice. Before deciding on a board, ask yourself the following questions:

How much power do I need to run the application I have in mind?

You might not know the exact measure of flash memory and processing power that you require for your project, but there is a clear difference between the functioning of a simple nightlight that changes colors and a robotic hand with many moving parts. The latter would require a more robust Arduino microcontroller board, with faster processing, more flash memory, and more SRAM than the more straightforward night light idea.

How many digital and analog pins will I require to have the functionality that I desire?

Again, you don't need to have an extremely specific idea in mind but knowing whether you need more pins or less will have a great effect on which board you choose. If you are going for a simple first project, you could get away with having less digital, PWM, and analog pins, while if you are looking to do something more complex, you will want to consider the boards with a great number of pins in general.

Do I want this to be a wearable device?

There are a few options for wearable devices so, of course, this question will not entirely make the decision for you. It will, however, help narrow down the choices and steer you in a direction, with Lilypads and the Gemma or other comparable technologies being your best options.

Do I want to connect to the Internet of Things? If so, how?

If you want connectivity to the Internet of Things, your work will be made much easier by the YÚN, the Tian, the Ethernet, the Leonardo ETH, or the Industrial 101. These have the capabilities of Ethernet connection as well as Wi-Fi capability so you will be able to connect to a network like the Internet and share data or interact with and control other devices on the Internet of Things.

Getting Started on Arduino IDE

The Arduino Software runs in an environment called IDE. This means that you will either need to download the desktop IDE to code in or code online on the online IDE.

The first way that you might access IDE, downloading the desktop application, has a few options to suit the various devices that you might be using. First, there is the Windows desktop application. You can also access it from a Windows tablet or Windows phone with the Windows application. Next, there is the Macintosh OSX version, which allows IDE to run on Apple laptops and desktops, but not on Apple mobile devices like iPhones and iPads. Finally, there are three options for running Arduino IDE on Linux: the 32-bit, the 64-bit, and the Linux ARM version. If you prefer this option to the web browser option, you will simply need to visit the Arduino IDE site by heading to https://www.arduino.cc/en/Main/**Software**

There, you can download the appropriate version of desktop IDE. Next, you will run the installation application, click through the options presented, and you should have a running Arduino IDE environment in just a few minutes.

This allows you to access the IDE software from Android devices and Apple mobile devices as well since it is based in a web browser that runs on its own platform rather than on the Android or iOS platforms. You can also run the web browser on various computer types, including Linux, Microsoft Windows, and Apple Macintosh. This will allow you to upload your sketches to the Cloud, that is, to store the information you have coded in a secure location that you can then re-access from another device by connection to the Internet.

Coding a Program for Your Arduino

Next you will write code for a program that you want the Arduino board to run. This allows you to see the entire code at once, allowing for easier debugging, or removing of errors.

Once you write the code, you will want to run it and troubleshoot or debug any errors that you find. You will best be able to do this by applying the coded program to the Arduino board and seeing if it runs. To do this, you will need to proceed to the next step of uploading your sketch.

Connecting to the Arduino Board

Some of the boards come with built-in USB, mini-USB, or micro-USB ports. Examples would be the Uno and the Leonardo, for the more beginning stages of your Arduino career. Simply insert the appropriate end of the USB cord into your computer and the other end into the particular USB port that is present on the board you possess, and the Arduino IDE software should recognize the type of board it is. If it does not, you can always choose the correct board from a dropdown menu.

Sometimes you will need to use a TKDI cable or a breakout board in order to make the Arduino compatible with your computer. This means you will insert the TKDI into the TKDI port on the Arduino microcontroller board and then connect it either to your computer or to another board. If you connect the TKDI cable to a breakout board, you will do as you did with the USB-compatible boards: insert the appropriate end of the cord to the breakout board and the other end to the computer. Again, the computer's Arduino IDE software program should recognize your Arduino board, but you can always choose from a dropdown menu should it fail to recognize it.

Uploading to the Arduino Board

To upload your sketch, the program you just created in code, you will need to select the correct board and port to which you would like to upload. It should be easy enough to select the correct board, as you simply look for the board title that matches the name of the type of board you are using.

To select the correct serial port, the options you might choose are as follows:

Mac

Use **/dev/tty.usbmodem241** for the Uno, Mega256O or Leonardo.

Use **/dev/tty.usbserial-1B1** for Duemilanove or earlier Arduino boards.

Use **/dev/tty.USA19QW1b1P1.1** for anything else connected by a USB-to-serial adapter.

Windows

Use **COM1** or **COM2** for a serial board.

Use **COM4**, **COM5**, or **COM7** or higher for a USB-connected board.

Look in Windows Device Manager to determine which port the device you are using is utilizing.

Linux

Use **/dev/ttyACMx** for a serial port.

Use **/dev/ttyUSBx** or something like it for a USB port.

Once you have selected the correct board and port, click **Upload** and choose which Sketch to upload from the menu that appears. If you have a newer Arduino board, you will be able to upload the new sketch simply, but with the older boards, you must reset the board before uploading a new sketch, else you will have two, possibly conflicting sketches present in the board's memory, causing it to crash.

Running the Arduino with Your Program

There are a few ways to power your Arduino once you have uploaded the program that you have coded to it. First, you can power it by the USB connection to another powered device, such as your computer. Second, you can power by Ethernet on boards with that capability. This means that by connecting to the network, you will be connected to a power source through the Ethernet. Finally, you can power most Arduino's by lithium polymer battery.

Once power is connected, and the specified input is put into the microcontroller, it will perform the function for which it is intended.

Chapter 2 Inputs and Outputs

If you look at the pins on the Arduino panel, you will see that they can be configured as an input or an output. You should remember that a lot of the analog pins have the possibility of needing to be set and used in the same way that a digital pin is going to be used.

Input Pin Configuration

The pins are going to be set to input by default; therefore, they do not need to be declared as an input by using the pinmode ( ) function whenever you want to use them as a contribution. The pins that are configured this way will be in a state of high impedance due to the fact that the input pins are only going to be made to make small demands on the circuit that they sample, which is going to be equal to the series resistor of a hundred megaohm for the front pin.

In other words, it is not going to take much current to switch the input from one state to the next which makes it useful for things like when you need to implement a touch sensor or when you are reading an LED as a photodiode.

The pins that are configured as pinmode will have nothing that is connected to them, if wires are connected to them, then they cannot be attached to another circuit. It has been reported that there are changes in the pins state, environmental commotion picked up through the pins or the capacitive coupling in the situation of a pin that is near the first pin.

Pull Up Resistors

The pull-up resistor is going to be useful when you need to steer the input of a pin to a known state, but you do not have any data present. This is going to be best when there is no input. All you need to do is add a pull-up resistor that goes up to 5 volts, or you can choose a pull-down resistor for the input.

It is best that you use a 10k resistor that is going to be good for pulling up or pulling down the resistor.

Using the Built-In Pull-Up Resistor with the Pins Configured to Input

In the Atmega chip, there are around 20,000 pull-up resistors that are built into it that you are going to have access to in the software. These resistors are going to be accessed through your pinmod () setting by inputting input_pullup. Now you have inverted the behavior of your contribution mode so that high will turn the sensor off and low will turn the sensor on.

The various values for the pull-up are going to depend on what kind of microcontroller you are using. For many AVR panels, the value is going to be between 20 and 50 k ohms. For the Arduino Due, you will find that it is between 50k and 150 k ohms. To figure out what the exact value is, you will need to look at the datasheet for the microcontroller that is installed on your panel.

Whenever you connect sensors to the pins that are configured for input, you need to ensure that the other end is grounded. This is done so that if the pin is reading high, the switch is going to be opened and little means that the switch is pressed. With pull-up resistors, you are going to be able to provide enough current to light up the LED that is connected to the pin.

There are some registers that are going to tell the pin if it is on a high or low while controlling the pull-up resistor. There are also pins that can be configured to have the pull-up resistor turned on whenever the pin is in input mode, which will mean that the pin is turned on to high. Should the pin be switched over to output by use of the pinmode () function, then it is going to work the opposite direction. So, if the pin is on output mode, the high state is going to have the resistor set up to where if switched it will go into input mode.

Example

pinmode (4, input) ; // the pin is set to input

pinmode (6, input_pullup) ;

Pins Configured To Output

Any pin capable of configuration will do so to output with pinmode ( ) and will be the lower state of impedance. With that being said, they are going to be able to provide a large amount of current to other circuits that are hooked up to it. The Atmega pins are going to give you the positive current or the negative current depending on how many milliamps of current the other pieces of equipment are going to need. As long as it is 40 mA or under, you will be able to have enough current to light up an LED brightly, but it is not going to be enough to run any motors.

Whenever you attempt to run a device that is going to require a lot of currents, the pins can become damaged or even destroyed. This can end up destroying the entire Atmega chip which is going to result in a dead pin in your microcontroller. However, the other pins are going to work still, but they may work at a lesser power than they were before. That is why you should hook your output pins up to another device that is either 470 ohms or is a 1k resistor. The only time that you should not is if the current draw that is coming from the pins is required to run a certain application.

Pinmode () function

Pin mode is going to be used whenever you are configuring a specific pin so that it is going to behave as an input or an output pin. There is the possibility that you can enable the internal pull-up resistor through the input_pullup mode. It also makes it to where the input mode is going to disable any internal pull-ups.

Syntax:

Void setup ( ) {

Pinmode (pin, mode) ;

}

1. Pin is going to be the digital representation of pins that you want to set the mode for.

Mode will be either input, output, or input_pullup.

Digitalwrite ( ) function

This is a super function that you can use when you need to write the code containing higher or lower values for the personal digital pin previously setup. Should the pin be configured for output, then the voltage needs to be set to the value of 5 volts. There cannot be any volts for low because it will need to be grounded.

If the pin is on input, then the high setting is going to be disabled while the low is going to be the pullup internally for the pin. We strongly advise that you setup your personal pinmode ( ) function so that input_pullup. Otherwise, it might not be able to pull up the resistor interior of the panel.

If you do not set the pin mode for output and then proceed to connect an LED tot hat pin as you call on the high setting, then the LED is going to appear dimmer than it should be. If you do not explicitly set the pin mode and digital write functions to enable the internal pullup, it is going to do so automatically which is going to act as a massive current capable of limiting the resistor.

Syntax

Void loop ( ) {

digitalWrite (pin, value) ;

}

1. Pin is going to be the digital representation of pins that you want to set to input or output.

Value is the high or low setting.

Analogread ( ) function

The Arduino program is capable of detection of all levels. Here, it can determine whether or not there is voltage, perhaps inadvertently, finding itself applied to one of the pins before it sends the report back through the digitalread ( ) function. You have to know that there is a difference between the on and off sensor so that the analog sensor is constantly charging. To read this type of sensor, you are going to require a different type of pin.

When you look at the lower right of your panel, there are going to be six pins that are marked as analog in. These pins are not just going to tell if there is any voltage being applied to them, but also how much is flowing through it. When you use the analogread ( ) function, you will be able to read the voltage that is applied to just one of the pins.

For this function, a digital representation is going to be returned between 0 and 1023 to represent the voltage between 0 and 5 volts. An example would be if you have a voltage of 2.5 V that is being applied to the pin digital representation 3, you will get a return of 512.

Syntax

Analogread (pin) ;

Pin: the digital representation of which pin to be read from 0 to 5 on a great majority of panels. 0 to 7 if you are using the mini and Nano panels. And then 0 to 15 on the Mega panels.

Vertical Integration Projects

Project 5: Transmitter and Receiver Arduinos
Description

The term i2c is pronounced "I" squared "C" which is protocol that allows multiple devices to interact on a two-wire bus. In this case one Arduino is described as the transmitter (TX). The second Arduino is designated the receiving Arduino (RX). The TX Arduino is the control panel with a switch and two LEDs. The lighted LED shows which route is selected. The second Arduino receives control inputs regarding route selection, which it uses to control two servos attached to two turnouts. Each servo is mounted to a turnout, which is located at the end of a passing track. The second Arduino has one LED that lights up when Route B is selected.

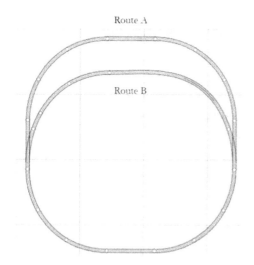

Figure 36: Route A and B on Demonstration

Layout
Material

The material needed for this dual Arduino system includes:
- 2 Arduinos UNO
- Switch
- Multiple LEDs
- 2 servos
- 2 Atlas HO scale "snap" turnouts
- For mounting the servo to the turnout: miscellaneous screws, styrene, wood
- For wiring to the turnout servos: wires, terminal blocks, and cable ties

Challenge

The challenge in this project was getting the two Arduinos communicating, after the authors and others tried several techniques they developed these versions of the TX and RX code in this chapter that work very well.

Diagrams

This project uses Atlas snap turnouts, which have a couple of mounting holes. The figure shows how the servo is mounted to the Atlas turnout. Using a small piece of styrene, a hole is drilled and tapped at one end, and this attaches to the turnout. A second hole is drilled and tapped on the side of the styrene. This is how the servo is mounted to the styrene. Next a small block of wood with a "v" notch filed into it provides the yoke that the servo interfaces with, using a small screw attached to the servo arm. This provides the model railroader with a nicely integrated package. With a few servo rotation tweaks, it will not need to be adjusted. The authors found that setting up turnouts under layout was a challenge. The setup described here allows the minor tweaks to be done above the layout, and then the turnout is installed on the layout with no adjustments needed.

Physical Integration of Servo on Atlas Turnout

The following schematics show how the two Arduinos are connected together. The first schematic shows how the TX Arduino is connected to the LED. The second schematic indicates how to connect the Arduino to the servos on the turnouts.

LED Route A
GND
LED Route B
GND

SDA   **on**
Other
ArduinoSCL on

Other Arduino
Computer Port
Digital
Processor
Chip
OutputAnalogPower
Power

Ground   on
Other Arduino

5 V on Other Arduino

Transmitter Arduino with Two LEDs Indicating which Route is Selected

Servo 1 *5 volt* **+5V**

Ground **GND** *Signal*

GND

+5V *5 volt*

Ground **Servo 2** *Signal*

LED

SDA   on   Other
Arduino   SCL   on   Other
Arduino GND

Computer Port
Digital
4.7 K 4.7 K Processor Chip
Battery Power Sensor Power Analog

Ground   on
Other
Arduino
Ground   on
Servos

5 V on Other Arduino 5 V on

Servos

Receiver Arduino with Servos on Two Turnouts
Note: The authors determined the power should be provided to the RX Arduino otherwise there was not enough power to operate the servos.

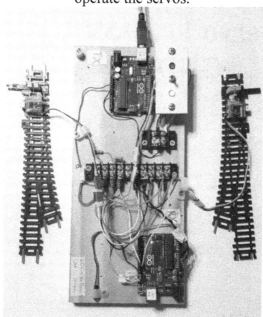

TX and RX Arduinos with Control Panel Transmitter Arduino Code

The goal of this code is for the TX Arduino to transmit the command from a switch to the RX Arduino. It also lights one of two LEDs on the control panel, depending on which route is selected.

// The original code was based:
// I2C Master

```
// By Cornel Amariei for Packt Publishing
//https://www.instructables.com/id/I2C-Between-Arduinos-With-Potentiometer-and-LED/

// i2c_TX_12_23_18 Modified by Fitz Walker, Paul Bradt and David Bradt
//This version works great sends signal to RX and lights LEDs
#include <Wire.h>
const int BUTTON = 4;

int x = 1; //Initialize switch state
int redLED = 7; //connect red LED to pin 7 int greenLED = 6; //connect green LED to pin 6

void setup() {
// Start the I2C Bus as Master
Wire.begin();
pinMode(BUTTON, INPUT_PULLUP); //Setup switch with internal pullup resistor pinMode(redLED, OUTPUT); //setup LED
pinMode(greenLED, OUTPUT); //setup LED
Serial.begin(9600);

}
void loop() {
x = digitalRead(BUTTON); //Read switch input

if (x == LOW) {
Wire.beginTransmission(9); // transmit Swtich state x to device #9 RX Arduino digitalWrite(redLED, HIGH);
digitalWrite(greenLED, LOW);
Wire.write(x);
Wire.endTransmission(); // stop transmitting
Serial.print("Button State: "); // Use for trouble shooting
Serial.println(x); //Send switch state to Serial Port
delay(2000);
```

}

if (x == HIGH) {
Wire.beginTransmission(9); // transmit Swtich state x to device #9 RX Arduino digitalWrite(redLED, LOW);
digitalWrite(greenLED, HIGH);
Wire.write(x);
Wire.endTransmission(); // stop transmitting
Serial.print("Button State: "); // Use for trouble shooting
Serial.println(x); //Send switch state to Serial Port
delay(2000);

}
}

Receiver Arduino Code
After getting a command from the TX Arduino, the RX Arduino controls two turnouts so they operate together for selecting a route on a passing track. It also lights an LED which is located near the turnouts for local indication of route selection.

// The original code was based:
// I2C Slave
// By Cornel Amariei for Packt Publishing
//https://www.instructables.com/id/I2C-Between-Arduinos-With-Potentiometer-and-LED/

// i2c_RX_12_23_2018 Modified extensively by Fitz Walker, Paul Bradt and David Bradt //Compiles LED lights up on RX Arduino(Device # 9) and Servo increments, //returns after switch returned

```
//Data shows up serial bus when Switch thrown on TX Arduino
//Power from RX Arduino

#include <Wire.h> //Start wire library #include <Servo.h> //Start Servo library

int LED = 13; //Setup onboard LED int LED2 = 7; //Attach LED
int x = 0; //Initialize Variable sent from TX

Servo turnOut1; //Setup Servo on turnOut1 Servo turnOut2; //Setup Servo on turnOut2

void setup() {
 // Define the LED pin as Output
 pinMode (LED, OUTPUT);
 pinMode (LED2, OUTPUT);
 turnOut1.attach(9); //Attach turnOut1 servo to pin 9
 turnOut2.attach(11); //Attach turnOut2 servo to pin 11

 // Start the I2C Bus as Slave on address for Device #9 RX Arduino Wire.begin(9);
 // Attach a function to trigger when something is received.
 Wire.onReceive(receiveEvent);
 Serial.begin(9600);

}
 void receiveEvent(int bytes) {
 x = Wire.read(); // read one character from the I2C sent from TX Arduino Serial.print(x);

if (x == 1){
 digitalWrite(LED2, HIGH);
 digitalWrite(LED, HIGH);
 turnOut1.write(60); //Adjust this for turnout throw
 turnOut2.write(60); //Adjust this for turnout throw
 delay(2000);
```

```
}
if(x == 0){
digitalWrite(LED2, LOW);
digitalWrite(LED, LOW);
turnOut1.write(80); //Adjust this for turnout throw
turnOut2.write(80); //Adjust this for turnout throw
delay(2000);

}
}
void loop() {
}
```

Operation

The operation of this two-Arduino system is completed by simply flipping a switch that lights a specific LED along with sending a signal to the second Arduino, which activates two solenoids that position the turnouts to the proper route.

Summary

This project demonstrates the use of one Arduino as a control device and a second Arduino as an effector, operating two servos simultaneously switching the route from one direction to the second direction. The operations in this project could easily be combined on one Arduino. The authors purposely structured this project to demonstrate a vertically integrated system that shows the reader the possibility of separating functions on more than one Arduino.

Project 6: JMRI Interface to Arduino Description

Project 6 uses JAVA Model Railroad Interface (JMRI) to control an Arduino that positions turnouts to the proper route on the layout. JMRI is an incredibly versatile tool that is well suited to controlling many aspects of large layouts. This system uses vertical integration of a computer running JMRI, which sends the signal to the local Arduino, which in turn activates two solenoids that control the turnouts so they move to the proper route configuration.

JMRI is a complex, powerful program, and this book only scratches the surface of its capabilities and highlights one small use for it. If the reader is interested in finding out how to use JMRI, the authors recommend finding an online JMRI group such as **jmriusers@groups.io**, or someone local that is familiar with the program and its features. For this book we are utilizing the Panel Pro section in JMRI and the ability to send commands to a remote effector.

With the proper setup, JMRI could do this on its own without an Arduino, but the authors wanted to develop and implement this solution to demonstrate another way to perform the function.

Material
The material needed for this project:
- Arduino UNO
- 2 servos
- 2 Atlas turnouts
- Miscellaneous screws, styrene, and wood for mounting the servo to the turnout
- Wires, terminal blocks, and cable ties for the wiring to the turnouts
- JMRI loaded on the computer
- Computer Model Railroad Interface (CMRI) and Auto485 libraries download for the code
- Modified Iron Ridge Station kit (Walthers: 931-904)

The only modification to the building is that the opening underneath needs to be expanded.
Diagrams
The following diagrams show the setup of the JMRI Arduino.

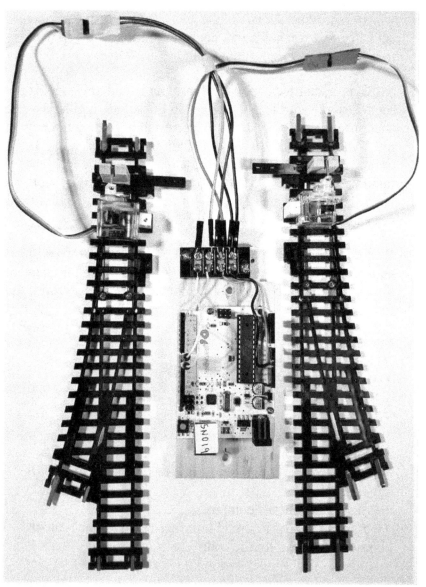

Arduino Set Up to Work with JMRI

Servo 1 Servo 2 *+5V* 5 volt 5 volt *+5V GND*
Ground Ground GND Signal Signal
Computer_{Digital} Port
Processor Chip
_{Sensor Analog}Battery_{Power}
Power
+5V
GND

Schematic for Two Servos on Turnout
Challenges

Connecting the Arduino to the computer and having JMRI operate it to position two turnouts is a significant challenge. JMRI is a little tricky to get working. The following steps, shown here and on the website, should help the user work through these challenges.

Operations and JMRI Setup
The link to the JMRI website is shown below. The website provides a good introductory tutorial for learning the basics of setup and control of both the JMRI and the Arduino.
http://www.motorhomesites.org.uk/jmri-arduino-setup/
The general steps to follow are:
Load JMRI from the following location on to a computer.
http://jmri.sourceforge.net/
Load the CMRI library from the site below.
https://github.com/madleech/ArduinoCMRI
Refer to the library at the site below.

- Start Panel Pro
- Configure the node for Arduino based on the com port it is in
- Open up tables and configure the servos on the turnouts
- Load the Arduino code below
- Restart JMRI and select the turnouts.

Setup and Configuring Nodes

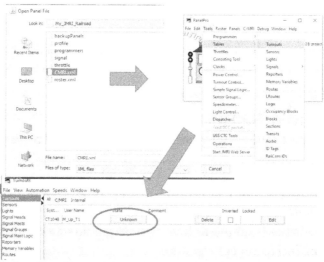

Selecting Control Panel Created and Turnout

If the reader is new to JMRI, the authors recommend walking through all of the tutorials on the site referenced [11]. As noted above, it is a very good introduction to the basics of JMRI and how to recognize and control an Arduino. The website is an excellent reference, but the authors did find one thing that was not needed for our setup. On the website the author indicated the need to rotate the servo back slightly after moving to one position. This part of the code actually caused our servos to hunt and chitter. After removing that part of the code it worked perfectly.

Arduino Code

//SN019 11_15_2018 modified by Paul Bradt and David Bradt code from this site:
//http://www.motorhomesites.org.uk/jmri-arduino-turnout-setup/

#include <CMRI.h> //include CMRI library #include <Auto485.h> //include Auto485b library #include <Servo.h> // include servo library

#define CMRI_ADDR 1 //Define CMRI Address
#define DE_PIN 2 //Define serial connection via Auto485 bus
int turnout1 = 0; int turnout2 = 0;

Auto485 bus(DE_PIN); // Arduino pin 2 -> MAX485 DE and RE pins
CMRI cmri(CMRI_ADDR, 24, 48, bus);
// defaults to a SMINI with address 0. SMINI = 24 inputs, 48 outputs and uses Auto485's bus

Servo turnOut1; Servo turnOut2;

void setup() {
//Setup turnOut and bus turnOut1.attach(9);
turnOut1.write(4);
turnOut2.attach(8);
turnOut2.write(6);
bus.begin(9600);

}
void loop() {
//Starting cmri each time loop runs cmri.process();

```
//Checking out cmri bit 47 and run motor for both turnOut 1
and 2 turnout1 = (cmri.get_bit(47));
if (turnout1 == 1) {

turnOut1.write(36); //Adjust turnout throw if needed }
else {

turnOut1.write(4); //Adjust turnout throw if needed
}
turnout2 = (cmri.get_bit(47));
if (turnout2 == 1) {
turnOut2.write(50); //Adjust turnout throw if needed
}
else {
turnOut2.write(6); //Adjust turnout throw if needed

}
}
```

It should be noted that the JMRI only sees this as one turnout, because the Arduino is controlling both turnouts with one input from JMRI.

Once the setup is configured and working, when it is restarted only four steps are needed, but they must be completed in this order:

Step 1: Connect the Arduino to the exact same USB port on the computer as when it was initially set up.

Step 2: Open Panel Pro

Step 3: Open the Panel that was previously configured.

Step 4: Open the Turnout Table that was previously configured.

It is ready to operate!

Summary

JMRI is a powerful tool and has a number of other capabilities which can seem overwhelming to the novice. The website identified and the information in this chapter provide excellent step-by-step guidance on how to set up and control an Arduino with JMRI. The authors hope the experience shared and the reference website encourage the model railroader to try to use JMRI.

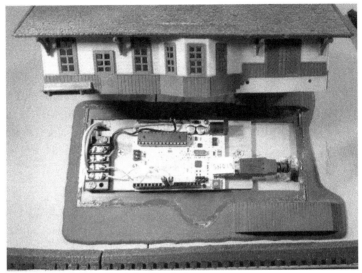

JMRI Arduino Inside Station

Chapter 3 Modulating the On-Board LED and Persistence of Vision

In our blink sketch, we manipulated the on-board LED in the most basic and simple way: we turned it off and on with the same delay.

In our **It's Alive** sketch, we manipulated the on and off times and changed the pattern.

This demonstrated the basic structure of a sketch to control the LED to make any pattern we want.

In this experiment, we will write a sketch which will turn the LED off and on to generate a simple pulse train. This is one of the basic building block signals we will use over and over again.

What you need to know and what you will learn in this experiment

You should be comfortable using the following commands:

void setup()

pinMode(13, OUTPUT);

void loop() {

digitalWrite(13, HIGH);

delay(100);

Serial.begin(9600);

Serial.print("Hello World");

Serial.println(" ");

//comments

In this chapter, we will introduce a valuable feature: variables, their care and feeding. Every sketch we use going forward will use variables. This will introduce you to the abstract thinking of algebra and the essence of programming.

The basic pulse train pattern

A pulse train is a repeating pattern of on and offs. We can describe this pattern with a few **figures of merit**. A figure of merit is a number that characterizes a behavior. It is based on using an ideal pattern as a template with the figures of merit describing specific features. We compare our signal to the template and what value of figure of merit makes the ideal signal match our actual signal.

For example, to describe a pulse train of on's and off's, we could use:

- **On-time**
- **Off-time**
- **Off-voltage (low)**
- **On-voltage (high)**

The generic structure of this ideal pulse train, identifying the figures of merit, is shown in **Figure**

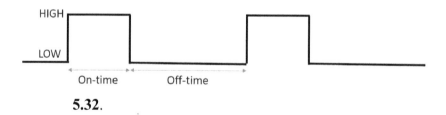

5.32.

Example of a simple pulse train of repeating on-time, off-time, on-time, off-time pulses.

This is exactly the structure of the Blink sketch. We can literally use it and just adjust the on-time and the off-time. Here is how we would use it:

```
void setup() {
    pinMode(13, OUTPUT);
}
void loop() {
    digitalWrite(13, HIGH);
    delay(1000); // on time
    digitalWrite(13, LOW);
    delay(1000); //off time
}
```

This is a great opportunity for you to get your sense of short time intervals calibrated.

Try this experiment: Set the on-time and off-time to be 1000 msec and get familiar with what this time interval feels like. This will give you a calibrated 1 second interval (the on-time) with which to get comfortable.

Then, try this with a 500 msec on-time. Can you train your eye to judge how long ½ a second is?

What is the flicker rate?

As written, the sketch in the last section will modulate the LED with the same on and off time. Using this pattern, we can explore the questions of how fast we can modulate the LED so that it appears to be continuously on.

As we decrease the off and on time, we reach a point where the LED looks like it is no longer blinking, but on continuously. We call this rate the flicker rate.

We already introduced one set of figures of merit that describe this pulse train, the on and off times. We can describe this behavior with another set of parameters or figures of merit.

This is a **periodic** behavior. The same pattern of on and off lights happens over and over again. We call one complete pattern a **cycle**.

One term that describes a property of a cycle is the time it takes to complete. This is called the **period**. If the on-time is 0.5 seconds and the off-time is 0.5 seconds, the period is the total time for one cycle or 1 second per cycle.

An alternative way of describing the properties of a cycle is its **frequency**, how many cycles are completed per second. The frequency of a periodic event is also referred to as a **rate** or **speed**. These terms are a little ambiguous. The **frequency** of the pattern is a better term to always use.

If we know the period per cycle, the frequency is how many cycles occur per second. The frequency is the inverse of the period:

If the period uses units of seconds per cycle, the units of frequency are cycles per second. For historical reasons, we call cycles per second, Hertz, abbreviated Hz.

The flicker rate, or flicker frequency, is the lowest frequency at which the LED appears to be on continuously. At a slightly lower frequency, the LED will appear to noticeably flicker. A higher frequency than the flicker rate and the LED will appear to be on continuously.

To calculate the flicker rate, first decrease the off and on time until the LED appears to not be blinking. The total time, the off-time + the on-time = the **period** of the pulse train. The flicker frequency is

For example, when I adjusted the on and off time, I found that when the on and off time was each 20 msec, the LED appeared to be on continuously. The period was 40 msec = 0.04 sec and the flicker frequency was 1/0.04 sec = 25 Hz.

This is close to the value of 24 frames per second (fps), which is the frame rate used in movies. Why 24 fps? A slower rate and there is perception of individual frames. A faster rate and you use up more film. To reduce the cost of the film, the absolutely lowest rate that is still flicker free was selected. For historical reason, 24 fps was adopted. You can **read about it here**.

Here is my sketch to drive the on-board LED at 25 Hz:

```
void setup() {
    pinMode(13, OUTPUT);
}
void loop() {
    digitalWrite(13, HIGH);
    delay(20); // on time
    digitalWrite(13, LOW);
    delay(20); //off time
}
```

If we pulse the LED at a rate slower than 25 Hz, we can see the LED is flashing. If it is faster than 25 Hz, the flashes blur together in the after image in our eye and it looks continuously on.

Try this experiment: Use the Blink sketch to measure the flicker rate for you and your friends.

In many cars, the red lights used for brake lights or the back lights when the headlights are on, use red LEDs. These are often flashing off and on, but at a rate faster than most peoples' flicker rate.

The way to tell if a car's lights are actually flashing is to move your eyes rapidly around. Your peripheral vision will pick up the lights as streaks. If the light is really being flashed on and off, the streaks will have dashes in them.

When I drive at night, I sometimes move my eyes rapidly side to side when I look at a car's back lights. When I see short dashes in the afterimage, I can tell the car lights are LEDs and they are being modulated.

Changing the apparent brightness

If we use a total period that is shorter than the flicker period, the LED will appear to be on continuously. The persistence of vision in our eyes keeps a little of the image of the on-LED in our vision even when it is off. It's like our vision has some memory to it. The LED has to be off for some period of time for us to forget it was ever on and see it as an off.

To pulse the LED so it looks continuously on, we need to keep the sum of the on and off times shorter than 40 msec.

We can change the apparent brightness of the LED if we make the fraction of time the LED is on shorter or longer.

If we use an on-time of 40 msec, and off-time of 0 msec, the LED will always be on and it will look the brightest.

If the on-time is 20 msec and the off-time 20 msec, the brightness will look mid-range.

If the on-time is 1 msec and the off-time is 39 msec, the LED will look very dim.

Try these experiments:

1. Modulate the LED at the three different brightness levels and compare their relative brightness. Since the fraction of time the LED is on is very precisely controlled, the relative brightness is very linear.

2. This is a chance to calibrate your eye. Does the sensation of brightness match what you set?

3. As you move your eyes around quickly, do you see the length of the LED streak change length with the on-time?

The **apparent** brightness is really related to the **fraction** of the **whole time interval** in which the LED is on. The larger the fraction of time the LED is on in one cycle, the brighter it will look.

We call the fraction of time the LED is on, the **duty cycle**. When the duty cycle is 100%, the LED will be the brightest. When the duty cycle is 50%, it will be dimmer, and when the duty cycle is 2.5%, with the on-time 1 msec out of a total interval of 40 msec, (1/40 = 2.5%), it will be dimmest, before it is finally off.

Try different duty cycles and see if you can calibrate your sensation of brightness with duty cycle.

New Features: Introducing variables and variable types

So far, when we wanted to identify a specific pin, or we wanted a specific delay time, we typed the specific number into the sketch. We call this **hard coding** the number. Every time we wanted to change that number, we had to go in and type a new number. This worked but it was very rigid and awkward. By using **variables**, we dramatically simplify coding.

Variables are names we give to parameters that will hold the value of a number or character. They are a symbolic placeholder for some set of data. We can use the variable name to replace the number or characters in any calculation or operation.

In computer-speak jargon, the **variable** name is the name of the location in memory in which we store the value of the data. Whenever we use the variable name, it points to the data stored in that location.

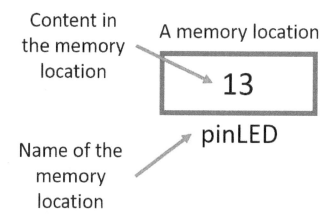

How to think of a variable as a location in memory that stores a number.

In the Blink sketch, pin 13 is the pin to which the on-board LED is connected. We **hard-coded** the number 13 by typing it explicitly in the digitalWrite command. We could have given the on-board pin number a variable name, or memory location label, such as the made-up name, pinLED.

We tell the sketch **pinLED** is a variable and create the variable location by declaring it at the very beginning of the sketch using a special syntax. At the same time we declare the variable, which creates it, we can also place in its memory location the number 13.

At any future time, we could refer to the pin number by this variable name and write the command, for example, as

_{digitalWrite} (pinLED, HIGH);

> In every command in which we need to address pin 13, we could use its variable name, pinLED. Whatever command sees the variable name pinLED will look up in its memory location the value stored there and use this value. If we later decide to use pin 12 instead, we just change the value of the number stored in the pinLED variable name location and pin 12 is used everywhere.

Every variable has three elements:

- **a type**
- **a name**
- **a value**

> The **name** and **value** we described above. There are multiple types of variables based on what sort of data is stored in its location, such as: **int, long, float, Boolean, string, char,** and **arrays.**

In most of the sketches we will write, we will use two types of numbers: **integers** (a whole number with a plus or minus sign) like 448, 12, -94 or -5, and numbers with a decimal point, we call **floating point** numbers, like 4.81 or -2456.12.

The difference between an integer and a floating point number is that a floating point number has a decimal point, but an integer does not.

When we create a **variable** we want to use to represent a number, we have to decide, when we create it, if we want the number to be an **integer** or a **floating-point** number. The **number type** influences the sort of math we do with it and how the variable can be used.

For example, if we want to use the variable as a pin number, it must be an **integer** type. We create integer type numbers using the simple command

    int pinLED;

SOME FUNCTIONS, LIKE DELAY() WILL ONLY USE INTEGERS. HOWEVER, IF YOU TYPE A DELAY OF 145.57 INSIDE THE (), THE DELAY FUNCTION WILL TURN IT INTO AN **INTEGER** BY TRUNCATING EVERYTHING AFTER THE DECIMAL POINT.

If we want to use the variable in a delay function as a delay of some number of milliseconds, it is a good habit to use a number that is an **integer** type. This way, we know exactly what delay value will be used.

The value of a number created from reading an analog pin is an **integer** type.

An **integer** type number has no decimal point. It is only a whole number. If we try to assign a number like 15.3 to a variable we created as an integer variable, only the whole part of the number, 15, will be stored in the variable location.

This means that when we do some algebra like 5/2 and assign the value to a variable that is an integer type, only the integer part of the answer will be stored.

Sometimes, this is a useful feature, such as when we want an answer as a whole number. Sometimes this results in a number we did not want, like when we are taking an average and the average is less than 1. If assigned to an integer variable, its value would be 0.

There are some limitations to the variable type "int". A variable defined as an **int** can only have a value between -32,768 to 32,767.

This is not a very large range. If we use an int variable to count milliseconds, the longest amount of time we can count is only 32.7 seconds.

If the value of our variable is already 32,767 and we add 1 to it, it rolls over to -32768 and counts up from there. This could be very inconvenient if we don't plan for it.

There will be many situations in which we want larger integer values. In this case, there is a different type of integer we can create, called a **long**. Instead of using the **int** command to declare an integer, we use the long command and declare a long integer. The command looks like:

long iCount;

A LONG VARIABLE CAN BE BETWEEN -2,147,483,648 TO 2,147,483,647. IF WE USE A LONG TYPE VARIABLE TO COUNT MILLISECONDS, WE COULD COUNT AS MANY AS 2 MILLION SECONDS, WHICH IS ABOUT 1 ½ MONTHS.

You can never go wrong creating all your integer variable types as long. It will take up a little bit more memory space, but if memory is ever a problem, there are other microcontrollers you can switch over to where memory is not a limitation. They will not be the lowest cost, but they will still be low cost, and higher performance.

We create a variable in the beginning of a sketch before the void setup() function. The syntax is the type of variable and the variable name. We can include an initial value if we want. Here are a few examples:

> int iCounter=0;
>
> long iTime_msec=17;
>
> float V_tempSensor_V;

> Try these experiments:

1. Any number assigned to an integer will always be in the format of an integer. What will int i1= 3.1415 be? Try creating the variable, assigning it this value and printing the variable to the serial monitor.

2. The largest integer you can store is 32,767. if you try to make an integer with a value of 32,768, it will roll over to the very beginning and start up. What value is i1=32768 or higher?

3. If you declare the integer as a long, you can count larger integers. What is long i1=40000, compared to int i2=40000?

4. When we declare a variable at the beginning of a sketch, we can:

    a. just declare the memory space, int i3

    b. declare the memory space and set a value to the variable, int i3 = 12

c. declare the memory space, and perform a simple calculation using other, previously defined variables. long i4 = i2 + i1

5. What is int i2=14+13.6? What is long i9=329000+29?

Remember, you can print a variable's value to the serial monitor using just a few lines of code, like:

int i1=3456;

void setup() {

  Serial.begin(2000000);

}

void loop() {

  Serial.println(*i1*);

}

Floating-point type numbers are numbers with a decimal point. A floating-point **type variable cannot be used as a** counter **in an** if **statement or as a** pin **number or in the delay function.**

However, the **floating-point** type number is incredibly useful when describing a voltage, or a temperature.

Generally, if there is no compelling reason why a number should be an integer, or we think that when we use the variable, it may represent a number with a decimal point, the variable type should be assigned float.

To use a variable, we have to first create it, or in computer jargon, **declare** it, by defining what type of number we want it to be, **integer** or **floating point**. It's a good habit to declare the variable at the beginning of the sketch before the setup() function. The command lines to create an integer or a floating-point variable, labeled as pinLED and sensorVoltage are:

> int pinLED;

> float sensorVoltage;

The command to declare an integer variable is int.

This command allocates a little space in memory, labeled pinLED, that will store an **integer type** number. At some point in the sketch we need to fill this memory location with the value of the number we want. We can both declare the variable and assign it a value all in the same line, such as with

> int pinLED = 13;

In most cases, we place these lines of code which declare the variable and allocate the memory space, at the beginning of the sketch, before the *void* setup()function. We can change the value of the variable anywhere in the code that is appropriate.

A **floating-point type** number can have a value from 3.4028235E+38 to as low as -3.4028235E+38. Each float has 6 or 7 digits and an exponent. Hopefully, you will not encounter a sketch where you need a bigger number.

Try these experiments (think about what you expect to see before you do it and see if it comes out the way you expect):

1. Create an integer and make it equal to 3200, then print it to the serial port, over and over again.

2. Create a floating point variable equal to 25.991 and print it to the serial monitor.

3. Create a new floating-point variable equal to 22.4 and an integer, equal to 10. Then, assign the

integer to equal the floating-point number. Print them both out.

New Features: Variable names

Variables are key elements in every sketch. The hardest part in using variables is thinking of **good names** for them. While we can use almost any name we want, I have certain guidelines that I use based on years of coding in many different languages.

The constraint on variable names is that they can't start with a number and can't have spaces. The only non-letter or number they can use is an underscore, "_".

For example, perfectly good variable names are:

- **a**
- **a5**
- **LED_pin**
- **b4**

    In the olden days, with very limited memory in a computer, variable names were restricted to a single letter and a number. It was always a challenge trying to remember was the temperature sensor value variable name T3 or S2?

But these days, even in an Arduino, variable names can be 64 characters long or longer. So how do we design a good variable name?

As a **Best Design Practice**, the goal in selecting a variable name is to keep it short yet encode valuable information so it is self-documenting. Some of the information we could encode in the variable name are:

- what type of variable: long, float, array, string...

- what element of the Arduino it refers: a pin, an input, out,...
- what the source or use of the number might be- as a specific sensor input, an LED value, a tone value...
- the units of the number stored in the variable

> Good variable names encode the most useful information so that you can remember what they mean a month later, or someone new to the code can decipher what the variable might contain.

If you use a consistent naming approach, your variables will be easy to decipher without having to check in the comment line, easy to remember, and easy to figure out if you don't want to find where it is declared. We want to establish good variable naming habits that are **self-documenting**.

Everyone has a different style when naming **variables**. This makes trying to figure out what is a variable and what type it is, just from the name, can be very confusing when reading someone else's sketch.

Here are two very good descriptions of variable naming conventions:

http://codebuild.blogspot.com/2012/02/15-best-practices-of-variable-method.html

https://dev.to/mohitrajput987/coding-best-practices-part-1-naming-conventions--class-designing-principles

> Generally, I like to use variable names that describe the type of variable, in what general and specific context it is used and include the units of the number contained in the variable location.

To describe an integer, I like to start with the letter "i" or "n", like iCounter, or nptsAve_volts.

The rest of the name describes what the variable is used for and ends with the units. Here are some examples:

nCountCycles

iTimeStart_msec

iTimeStop_usec

sensorTemp1_volts

sensorTemp1_degC

iSensorTemp1_ADU

SensorTemp1_ADU

pinTemp1_hi

pinTemp1_lo

> Any variable that refers to a pin name is unambiguously an integer, so starting with the word "pin" is ok.

The last part of any variable name is the units of the variable. To highlight the units, I set them off with an underscore, _, at the end of the variable name. If it is a time, the units might be _sec, or _msec, or _usec. If it is a voltage, it might be _volts or just _V or _mV.

In the special case of the levels from an **analog pin**, there are no units. The value is dimensionless. However, to help me keep track that the variable is a number from an analog pin, I use the units of **Analog to Digital Units** or _ADU. I always place the characters "ADU" at the end of a variable name that will store the value read from an analog channel.

Even though a number in units of ADU, the number read from an ADC (Analog to Digital Converter), is an integer, sometimes we will make these float type numbers so we can do more accurate math, like when taking averages.

If the variable is used as a simple index number inside of a loop or in an array, which has meaning only as an index number, I would just use the letter i or i1 or i2 or i3.

There are no hard and fast rules. The Best Design Practice is to use variable names that help to describe what the variable refers to so anyone reading your code would have a clear idea. The second-best approach is to be consistent.

It's important to develop good habits early on so that each sketch is an opportunity to practice and so that all of your projects become **self-documenting**.

You can never add too many comments to further clarify each variable.

Let's practice some of these variable principles.

Try these experiments:

1. What would be a good variable name for the pin driving an LED?
2. What is 20/3?
3. What is 20/3.0?
4. What would be a good variable name for the voltage of a sensor, stored as millivolts?
5. What is a good variable name to store the count of the number of times pin 12 has changed from high to low?

On-time, off-time, period and duty cycle

With our new skill at using variables, we can re-write the blink sketch with variables and make it a general pulse train synthesizer.

We will create a repeating pattern of on-times and off-times. We can describe this pattern in one of two ways:

- **in terms of an independent on-time and an off-time**
- **in terms of a repeat period and a fraction of the time it is on, which we call the duty cycle**

I like using the period and duty cycle to control the LED. This is a more intuitive set of figures of merit. To modulate the LED, and use the principles of the BLINK code, we will need to translate the period **and** duty cycle **into the on and off times.**

This is very simple. The on-time and off-time are:

onTime_sec = Period_sec x dutyCycle

offTime_sec = Period_sec x (1-dutyCycle)

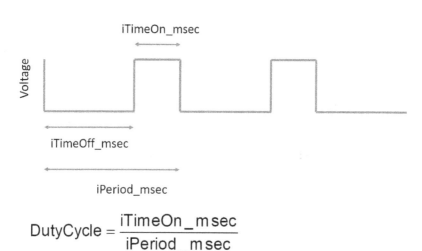

$$DutyCycle = \frac{iTimeOn\_msec}{iPeriod\_msec}$$

The pattern of on and off times of the LED when it is modulated.

The duty cycle controls the apparent brightness of the LED. A duty cycle of 90% means the LED is on for most of the period and it will look bright to us. A duty cycle of only 10% means the LED is on for only a small fraction of the period and it will look dim to our eye.

We will modulate the LED with a period that is short enough so that our eye can't tell the LED is pulsing off and on.

To make the LED flash fast enough so we can't see it flashing, we want the period to be shorter than about 40 msec, or the flash frequency to be faster than 1/40 msec = 25 Hz.

This means we can adjust the on-time from 0 msec to 40 msec. We use delay() commands to adjust the on and off times.

A modified BLINK is all we need to drive the LED with a pulse train. We'll start with a period of 0.040 seconds (40 msec) and adjust the duty cycle from 0% to 100%.

Try this experiment: How would you write the code to set the period and duty cycle for the LED using variables? Use a period of 1 second and adjust the duty cycle. This way you can see the fraction of the time the LED is on.

Make the period shorter and shorter until it is shorter than the flicker rate and watch the LED transition from flashing to appearing on continuously.

If you get stuck, watch this video and I will walk you through setting up this experiment.

My sketch to modulate the LED with a period and duty cycle

```
// introducing variables
long iPeriod_msec = 500;
float dutyCycle_fraction = 0.5;
long iTimeOn_msec = iPeriod_msec * dutyCycle_fraction;
long iTimeOff_msec = iPeriod_msec - iTimeOn_msec;
void setup() {
    pinMode(13, OUTPUT);
}
void loop() {
    digitalWrite(13, HIGH);
    delay(iTimeOn_msec);
    digitalWrite(13, LOW);
    delay(iTimeOff_msec);
}
```

Summary of the commands introduced so far

| Command | Description |

void setup (){
}
}
	This is a function that appears in EVERY sketch. Every command within the brackets will be executed just once

void _loop_ (){
}
}
	This is a function that appears in EVERY sketch. Every command within the brackets will execute over and over again.

pinMode(13, OUTPUT);	This command tells the Arduino that we are going to use a specific digital pin as an OUTPUT, as distinct from an INPUT. We use the pin number to identify the pin we want to setup.
digitalWrite(13, HIGH);	This command controls the output of a digital pin and makes it either a HIGH (logic 1, or 5 V) or a LOW (a logic 0 or a 0 V). Once executed, the pin value will be set to this value.
delay(1000);	This command tells the Arduino to sit there, twiddling its thumbs, doing nothing for a duration of milliseconds as listed inside the (). In this example, the time interval to wait is 1000 msec = 1 sec.
// or /* */	Comments. Everything after these two forward slashes will be ignored by the Arduino sketch. We can use this add comments for our own benefit on any line. For multiple lines add them

	between the /* and the */ lines.
Serial.begin(9600);	This command opens up the serial com link with a baud rated inside the (). In this example the baud rate is 9600 baud. The name Serial is an object, the serial link. The .begin is a verb, telling the object to get set up.
Serial.print("Hello World");	This command will print characters to the serial communications channel. Everything inside the () will be printed. To print a string, enclose the characters within quotes. After printing, the cursor will be left on the same line.
Serial.println(" ");	Does the same thing as the Serial.print command, but moves the cursor to the next line after printing the characters. This starts the next printed content on a new line.
Serial monitor	The terminal emulator that you can print to. This is the primary way of displaying information from the Arduino.
int, long	This will create a new variable that will store an integer. This is a whole number. It is usually placed before the setup() function
float	This will create a new variable that will store a floating point number. This is a number that has a decimal point. It is usually

	placed before the setup() function

Chapter 4 Coding for the Arduino

Coding a program for Arduino means learning a new language, but it is not as hard as you might think. In the same way that mathematics has its own set of symbols to denote various functions like addition, subtraction, and multiplication, there are different symbols and terms used when coding for Arduino. If you have had experience working with coding in the past, learning a new language is easy. For those of you who have never learned to code, translating one form of code to another is like translating one language to another. Though this may seem difficult, the idea of coding is to make coding for other programs easier in the future. Below is a list of the terms and words that are used in Arduino IDE coding and how to use them.

Structure

setup()

This is the function called on when the sketch starts and will run only once after startup or reset. You can use it to start variables, pin modes, or the use of libraries (specific terms you can download for extra functionality).

loop()

The loop function requires the Arduino microcontroller board to repeat a function multiple times, continuously or until a certain variable or condition is met. You will set the condition for it to stop the loop or you will have it loop continuously until you detach the Arduino from the power source or turn it off.

CONTROL STRUCTURES

Control structures show how an input will be received. Just like the name implies, various inputs regarding control determine how your data will be read. Provisional language will also be considered in data analysis. Popular and various control structures are mentioned below.

If

This is what links a condition or input to an output. It means that **if** a certain condition has been met, a specific output or response of the microcontroller will occur. For example, **if** the thermometer to which the microcontroller is attached measures more than 75 degrees Fahrenheit, you might write the code to direct the Arduino to send a signal to your air conditioning unit to turn on to decrease the temperature back to 75 degrees.

If…Else

This is like the **If** conditional, but it specifies another action that the microcontroller will take if the condition for the first action is not met. This gives you an option of performing two different actions in two different circumstances with one piece of code.

While

This is a loop that will continue indefinitely until the expression to which it is connected becomes false. That is, it would perform a certain function until a parameter is met and the statement that is set as the condition is made false.

Do… While

This is like the **while** statement, but it always runs at least once because it tests the variable at the end of the function rather than at the beginning.

Break

This is an emergency exit of sorts from a function of the microcontroller. It is used to exit a **do**, **for,** or **while** loop without meeting the condition that must be met to exit that part of the functionality.

Continue

Return

This is the way to stop a function, and it returns a value with which the function terminated to the calling function or the function that is asking for the information.

Goto

This piece of code tells the microcontroller to move to another place, not consecutive, in the coded program. It transfers the flow to another place in the program. Its use is generally discouraged by C language programmers, but it can definitely simplify a program.

SYNTAX

; (semicolon)

This is used as a period in the English language: it ends a statement. Be sure, however, that the statement closed by the semicolon is complete, or else your code will not function properly.

{} (curly braces)

These have many complex functions, but the thing you must know is that when you insert a beginning curly brace, you **must** follow it with an ending curly brace. This is called keeping the braces balanced and is vital to getting your program working.

// (single-line comment)

If you would like to remind yourself or tell others something about how your code functions, use this code to begin the comment and make sure that it only takes up one line. This will not transfer to the processor of the microcontroller but rather will live in the code and be a reference to you and anyone who is reading the code manually.

/* */ (multi-line comment)

This type of comment is opened by the /*, and it spans more than one line. It can itself contain a single line comment but cannot contain another multi-line comment. Be sure to close the comment with */ or else the rest of your code will be considered a comment and not implemented.

#define

This defines a certain variable as a constant value. It gives a name to that value as a sort of shorthand for that value. These do not take up any memory space on the chip so they can be useful in conserving space. Once the code is compiled or taken together as a program, the compiler will replace any instance of the constant as the value that is used to define it.

NOTE: This statement does NOT use a semicolon at the end.

#include

This is used to include other libraries in your sketch, that is, to include other words and coding language in your sketch that would not otherwise be included. For example, you could include AVR C libraries or many tools, or pieces of code, from the various C libraries.

NOTE: Do NOT add the semicolon at the end of this statement, just as you would exclude it from the **#define** statement. If you do include a semicolon to close the statement, you will receive error messages and the program will not work.

ARITHMETIC OPERATORS

Just as the name implies, arithmetic operators complete codes through use of mathematical symbols. Each symbol connects one line of code to another. When looking for an output resulting in measured values, be sure to check your Arduino setup. Connecting wire with Arduino in the wrong voltage receptors may lead to negative or irrelevant values.

= (assignment operator)

This assigns a value to a variable and replaces the variable with the assigned value throughout the operation in which it appears. This is different than == which evaluates whether two variables or a variable and a set value are equal. The double equal signs function more like the single equal sign in mathematics and algebra than the single equal sign in the Arduino IDE.

+ (addition)

This does what you might expect it would do: it adds two values, or the value to a variable, or two to a fixed constant. One thing that you must take into account is that there is a maximum for variable values in the C programming languages. This means that, if your variable maxes out at 32,767, then adding 1 to the variable will give you a negative result, -32,768. If you expect that the values will be greater than the absolute maximum value allowable, you can still perform the operations, but you will have to instruct the microcontroller what to do in the case of negative results. In addition, as well as in subtraction, multiplication, and division, you place the resulting variable on the left and the operation to the right of the = or ==.

Also, another thing to keep in mind is that whatever type of data you input into the operation will determine the type of data that is output by the operation. We will look at types of data later, but for example, if you input integers, which are whole numbers, you will receive an answer rounded to the nearest whole number.

- (subtraction)

This operation, like the addition sign, does what you would expect: it subtracts two values from each other, whether they both are variables, or one is a constant value. Again, you will have to watch out for values greater than the maximum integer value. Remember to place the resulting variable on the left of the equal sign or signs, and the operation on the right.

* (multiplication)

With multiplication especially, you will need to be careful to define what happens if the value you receive from the operation is greater than the greatest allowable value of a piece of data. This is because multiplication especially grows numbers to large, large values.

/ (division)

Remember to place the resulting variable on the left of the operation, and the values that you are dividing on the right side of the operation.

% (modulo)

This operation gives you the remainder when an integer is divided by another integer. For example, if you did **y = 7 % 5**, the result for y would be 2, since five goes into seven once and leaves a remainder of 2. Remember, you must use integer values for this type of operation.

COMPARISON OPERATORS

Comparison operators compare the values from the left side of the equation to the right. If the left operator does not have the same units as the right, it is still possible to use these operators, but the results may be unpredictable (Arduino.cc).

== (equal to)

This operator checks to see if the data on the left side of the double equal signs match the data on the right side, that is, whether they are equal. For example, you might ask the pin attached to the temperature gauge **t == 75**, and if the temperature is exactly 75 degrees, then the microcontroller will perform a certain task, whether it be turning off the heating or cooling, or turning off a fan.

!= (not equal to)

This is the mirror image of the previous operation. You could just as easily write a program to test **t != 75** and set up the microcontroller to turn on a heating lamp, turn on a fan, or ignite the wood in the fireplace if this statement is true. Between == and !=, you can cover all the possible conditions that input might give your microcontroller.

< (less than)

If this statement is true, then you can program a certain response from your microcontroller, or, in other words, program output for such input.

> (greater than)

INPUT

In the input state, a digital pin will require very little of the processing power and energy from the microcontroller and battery. Instead, it is simply measuring and indicating to the microcontroller its measurements.

OUTPUT

These are very good at powering LED's because they are in a low-impedance state, meaning they let the energy flow freely through them without much resistance. Output pins take their directions from the microcontroller once it has processed the information given by the input pins, and the output pins power whatever mechanism will perform the intended task.

INPUT_PULLUP

This is what mode you will want to use when connected to a button or a switch. There is a lot of resistance involved in the INPUT_PULLUP state. This means that it is best used for Boolean-like situations, such as a switch either being on or off. When there are only two states and not much in between, use INPUT_PULLUP.

LED_BUILTTIN

true

In a Boolean sense, any integer that is not zero is true. One is true, 200 is true, -3 is true, etc. This would be the case when a statement matches reality. One of your pins might be testing a value, and the statement is trying to match **y != 35**, so if the pin receives information that the value of **y** is 25, then the statement **25 != 35** is true.

false

This is part of a Boolean Constant, meaning that a statement is false, or that its logic does not match reality. For example, you could have a statement, **x > 7** and the value the microcontroller receives for x is 3. This would make the statement **false**. It would then be defined as 0 (zero).

integer constants

These are constants that are used by the sketch directly and are in base 10 form, or integer form. You can change the form that the integer constants are written in by preceding the integer with a special notation signifying binary notation (base 2), the octal notation (base 8), or hexadecimal notation (base 16), for example.

floating point constants

These save space in the program by creating a shorthand for a long number in scientific notation. Each time the floating-point constant appears, it is evaluated at the value that you dictate in your code.

DATA TYPES

Data types refer to the type of data received in each of the programming setups you apply. Data received by Arduino are sent to your program of choice to determine various outcomes. Some examples are listed below.

Void

This is used in a function declaration to tell the microcontroller that no information is expected to be returned with this function. For example, you would use it with the **setup()** or **loop()** functions.

Boolean

Boolean data holds one of two values: true or false. This could be true of any of the arithmetic operator functions or of other functions. You will use **&&** if you want two conditions to be true simultaneously for the Boolean to be true, || if you want one of two conditions to be met, either one setting off the output response, and ! for not true, meaning that if the operator is **not** true, then the Boolean is true.

Char

This is a character, such as a letter. It also has a numeric value, such that you can perform arithmetic functions on letters and characters. If you want to use characters literally, you will use a single quote for a single character, **'A'** and a double quote for multiple characters, **"ABC"** such that all characters are enclosed in quotes. This means the microcontroller will output these characters verbatim if the given conditions are met. The numbers -128 to 127 are used to signify various signed characters.

Unsigned Char

This is the same as a character but uses the numbers 0 to 255 to signify characters instead of the "signed" characters which include negatives. This is the same as the byte datatype.

Byte

This type of data stores a number from 0 to 255 in an 8-bit system of binary numbers. For example, B10010 is the number 18, because this uses a base 2 system.

Int

Integers are how you will store numbers for the most part. Because most Arduinos have a 16-bit system, the minimum value is -32,768 and the maximum value of an integer is 32,767. The Arduino Due and a few other boards work on a 32-bit system, and thus can carry integers ranging from -2,147,483,648 to 2,147,483,647. Remember these numbers when you are attempting arithmetic with your program, as any numbers higher or lower than these values will cause errors in your code.

Unsigned Int

This yields the ability to store numbers from 0 to 65,535 on the 8-bit boards with which you will likely be working. If you have higher values than the signed integers will allow, you can switch to unsigned integers and achieve the same amount of range but all in the positive realm, such that you have a higher absolute value of the range.

Word

A word stores a 16-bit unsigned number on the Uno and on other boards with which you will likely be working. In using the Due and the Zero, you will be storing 32-bit numbers using words. Word is essentially the means by which integers and numbers are stored.

Long

If you need to store longer numbers, you can access 4-byte storage, or 32-bit storage in other words, using the long variable. You simply follow an integer in your coded math with the capital letter **L**. This will achieve numbers from -2,147,483,648 to 2,147,483,647.

Unsigned Long

The way to achieve the largest numbers possible and store the largest integers possible is to direct the microcontroller using the unsigned long variables. This also gives you 32 bits or 4 bytes to work with, but being unassigned the 32nd bit is freed from indicating the positive or negative sign in order to give you access to numbers from 0 to 4,294,967,295.

Short

This is simply another way of indicating a 16-bit datatype. On every type of Arduino, you can use short to indicate you are expecting or using integers from -32,768 to 32,767. This helps free up space on your Due or Zero by not wasting space on 0's for a small number and by halving the number of bits used to store that number.

Float

A float number is a single digit followed by 6 to 7 decimal places, multiplied by 10 to a power up to 38. This can be used to store more precise numbers or just larger numbers. Float numbers take a lot more processing power to calculate and work with, and they only have 6 to 7 decimals of precision, so they are not useful in all cases. Many programmers actually try to convert as much float math to integer math as possible to speed up the processing. In addition, these take 32 bits to store versus the normal 16 bits, so if you're running low on storage, try converting your float numbers to integers.

Double

This is only truly relevant to the Due, in which doubling allows for double the precision of a float number. For all other Arduino boards, the floating-point number always takes up 32 bits, so floating does nothing to increase precision or accuracy.

Chapter 5 Ultrasonic Sensor

This sensor is going to be able to determine how far an object is by using a system that is similar to the system that bats use. It is going to give you a great no contact range detection that is highly accurate and going to produce stable readings.

This operation is not going to be affected by things like sunlight or black material, but soft materials such as cloth are going to b somewhat difficult for the sensor to pick up. It is going to be complete with an ultrasonic transmitter and receiver module.

Tech Specifications

1. Measuring angle: thirty degrees
2. **Power supply: five volts**
3. Resolution: point three cm
4. Quiescent current: greater than two milliamps.
5. Ranging distance: two to four hundred cm
6. Working current: fifteen milliamps

Effectual angel: greater than fifteen degrees

Components

1. Arduino Uno R3 (1)
2. **Breadpanel (1)**

Ultrasonic sensor (1)

Code

Const int ping pin = 7 ; // trigger pin with sensor

Const in echo pin = 6 ; /// echo the pin with the sensor

Void setup () {

Serial begin (9600) ; // start serial terminal

}

Void loop () {

```
Long duration, inches, cm ;
Pin mode (ping pin, output) ;
Digital write (ping pin, low) ;
Delay microseconds (3) ;
Digital write (ping pin, high( ;
Delay microseconds (4) ;
Digital write (ping pin, low) ;
Pin mode (echo pin, input) ;
Duration = pulse in (echo pin,high ) ;
Inches = microseconds to inches (duration) ;
Cm = microseconds to centimeters (duration) ;
Serial print (inches) ;
Serial print ( in, ) ;
Serial print (cm) ;
Serial print (cm ) ;
Serial print in () ;
Delay (499) ;
}
Long microseconds to inches (long microseconds) {
Return microseconds / 49 / 2 ;
}
Long microseconds to centimeters (long microseconds) {
```

Return microseconds / 49 / 2 ;

}

Code notes

1. Connect the GND to the GND
2. **The positive five-volt pin to the positive five volt**
3. The echo to pin six

The trigger to pin seven

Result

You are going to see the distance measured by your sensor in inches and centimeters.

Conclusion

Congratulations! Now you have everything you need to go out on your own and start building the projects of your dreams. You learned how to connect any kind of module in order to extend the functionality of the Arduino board, and now you can finally start building more complex projects, such as robots! Start taking over the world and share everything with other Arduino fans and extend your knowledge about electronics, computers, and programming.

Remember, if you feel intimidated by certain topics, or if you think you aren't that great at coding, you shouldn't give up! There's a solution for everything and there are many online communities out there willing to help. Explore the applications step by step, read more module datasheets and reference guides, examine project schematics, and start building! The things you can achieve with the Arduino are incredible, and you should continue practicing because nobody becomes an engineer or a developer overnight without practice.

Congratulations on continuing with the Arduino guide series and advancing to the next level! Keep this guide close, and continue expanding your knowledge with more books, more tutorials, and more practice. Start building your army of Arduino robots today and conquer the world, because why not?

Arduino Programming

The practical intermediate's guide to learn arduino programming in one day step-by-step (#2020 Updated Version | Effective Computer Languages)

Steve Tudor

Text Copyright ©
All rights reserved. No part of this guide may be reproduced in any form without permission in writing from the publisher except in the case of brief quotations embodied in critical articles or reviews.

Legal & Disclaimer

The information contained in this book and its contents is not designed to replace or take the place of any form of medical or professional advice; and is not meant to replace the need for independent medical, financial, legal or other professional advice or services, as may be required. The content and information in this book has been provided for educational and entertainment purposes only.

The content and information contained in this book has been compiled from sources deemed reliable, and it is accurate to the best of the Author's knowledge, information and belief. However, the Author cannot guarantee its accuracy and validity and cannot be held liable for any errors and/or omissions. Further, changes are periodically made to this book as and when needed. Where appropriate and/or necessary, you must consult a professional (including but not limited to your doctor, attorney, financial advisor or such other professional advisor) before using any of the suggested remedies, techniques, or information in this book.

Upon using the contents and information contained in this book, you agree to hold harmless the Author from and against any damages, costs, and expenses, including any legal fees potentially resulting from the application of any of the information provided by this book. This disclaimer applies to any loss, damages or injury caused by the use and application, whether directly or indirectly, of any advice or information presented, whether for breach of contract, tort, negligence,

personal injury, criminal intent, or under any other cause of action.

You agree to accept all risks of using the information presented inside this book.

You agree that by continuing to read this book, where appropriate and/or necessary, you shall consult a professional (including but not limited to your doctor, attorney, or financial advisor or such other advisor as needed) before using any of the suggested remedies, techniques, or information in this book.

Introduction

In case you've never heard of an Arduino before, it is an open-source electronic interface that has two parts: the first is the programable circuit board, and the other is a coding program of your choice to run to your computer. Arduinos come in many forms, including the Arduino Uno, LilyPad Arduino, Redboard, Arduino Mega, Arduino Leonardo, and others which we will explain later on.

If you're unfamiliar with programming, this is a good place to start. The Arduino can be programmed in various types of programming languages, and its wide array of Arduino options can give you more programming experience. Arduinos come with additional attachments, some in the form of sensors, and others can be obtained anywhere and can be attached to the various ports on an Arduino. Arduino is a great stepping stone on the way to understanding programming and sensor interaction.

In programming languages, there is always the well-known program, "Hello World" that is showcased on the screen. In the microcontroller world that we are in, this phase or first program is indicated by a blinking of the light, "on" and "off" to show that everything you have set up works correctly.

We will look at the sketches in their entirety and explain the details after explaining the code. If you go through something that you cannot make something out of, keep on reading, and it will be clear.

Let us look at this program, to show you how we will be breaking down the codes.

Const int PinkL = 13;

Void setup ()

{ pinMode (PinkL, OUTPUT); }

Void loop ()

{digitalWrite(PinkL, HIGH);

delay (600);

digitalWrite(PinkL, LOW);

delay(600); }

On the first part

Const int PinkL = 13;

This line is used to define a constant that is used throughout the program to specify a particular value. All pins are recommended to have this because it makes it easy for software change if the circuit is still the same. In programming in Arduino, the constants are commonly named starting with the letter "k".

The second to part

Void setup ()

{pinMode (PinkL, OUTPUT);}

The OUTPUT is pin 13. This now makes Arduino control the coding to the pins, instead of reading from it.

The third part

Void loop()

{digitalWrite (PinkL, HIGH);

delay(600);

digitalWrite(PinkL, LOW);

Delay(600);}

This is where the core part of the code is. A HIGH is written to the pin that leads to the turning of the LED. When you place HIGH, it means that 5V is the pin's output. The other option we have is LOW, which means that you are putting 0V out.

A delay() is called to delay the number of milliseconds that is sent to it. Since we send 600, there will be a delay of 0.6 of a second. The LED goes off, and this is attributed to the LOW that is written as an output on the pin.

A 600 milliseconds delay will be activated.

This will be the sequence until the Arduino goes off or the power is disconnected from it.

Before you start digesting more content, try this program out and ensure that it works just fine. To test if you have set your LED in reverse order, the following might happen. On the UNO board, you have pin 13 connected to a Light Emitting Diode connected. When it blinks and the breadboard LED does not blink, then you might have connected your LED in reverse. In case you see that it is blinking once in a second, then the program has not been sent to the Arduino successfully.

When you've completed the programming, place comments in the coding lines to instruct the Arduino. These comments can instruct your Arduino to blink the LED intermittently or through various sequences.

The programs we normally write are usually meant for the computers and not for people to understand once they are opened up. There is a good provision that allows us, humans, to read the program easily and the computer will have no clue about it. There are two comments that are possible in this program:

1. The block comment style starts with two characters, /* which progresses until */ is seen. Multiple lines are then crossed and here are a few examples.

/* This is the first line*/

/* the program was successful*/

/* we

*are

*going

*far */

2. Commenting can be done on a line that has the backslash operator //. This is the part that is meant for humans and not machines. It is another way to insert a comment.

When you add comments in a program, you will have a code that looks like the statement above.

You will find in the following pages, that if there is no number next to the line of code, it indicates a comment continuation from the line at the top. We might not showcase this in perfection because we are using a limited space in our book. You will find a hyphen at the line's end that is continued and a hyphen along the continuation line. This is just our way of handling it, but in an IDE, you won't find it and you need not type them.

/*

* Program Name: Blink123

*Author: James Aden

* Date written: 24 July 2017

*Description:

* Turns an LED on for a sixth-hundred of a second, then for another sixth-hundred of a- -second on a continuous repetitive session

*/

/* Pin Definitions */

Const int PinkL = 13;

/*

*Functions Name: setup

*Purpose: Run once after system power up

*/

Void setup(){pinMode(PinkL,OUTPUT);}

/*

Void loop(){digitalWrite(PinkL,HIGH);Delay(600);digitalWrite(PinkL,LOW);Delay(600):}

Gotchas

If you find out that your program does not compile, or it gives you a different result than what you need, here are a few things that people get confused about:

The programming language is normally sensitive to capitalization of letters. For instance, myVar is considered different to MyVar.

Tabs, blank lines, and white spaces are equivalent to a single space, making it easier for one to read.

Code blocks are normally grouped using curly braces, i.e., "{" and "}"

All open parenthesis have a corresponding closing parenthesis, i.e. "(" and ")"

Numbers don't have commas. So instead of writing 1,000, ensure that you write 1000.

All program statements MUST end with a semicolon. This means that each statement except for the following two cases:

-In comments

- after curly braces are placed "}"

Assignment task to test what you have learned:

1. Alter the delay time of your LED before it comes back on to stick to 1.5 seconds. Leave the ON time of the LED limited to 600 milliseconds.

2. From pin 13, change to pin 2, making it the new connection to the LED. Keep in mind that both the circuit & and the program will be different.

This is just a basis for basic Arduino programming. In the rest of the book, we will be looking at how Arduinos can be programmed with respect to different functions. If you're new to programming, don't let the above codes frighten you. Coding takes practice, but it relatively easy to learn, just like a new language.

Chapter 1 Key Terms in Understanding Arduino

hen working with Arduino technologies, it is helpful to understand the terminology of Arduino. You will need to understand the terminology to choose a board, write the coded instructions, set up the microcontroller for use, and finally using the Arduino board. In this chapter, you will find some key terms that will aid you greatly in your endeavor to become an Arduino user.

As mentioned earlier, Arduino is open-source, meaning you can use it and teach it to others without violating any copyright laws. It is based on easy-to-use hardware, which is the actual physical computer board with which you will be working, and straightforward software, the coded instructions with which you will use to direct the hardware to perform a task of your choosing. The software is also known as code, and the individual pieces of instructions are called tools.

Anatomy of the Arduino Board

The board itself contains a good number of parts. The digital pins run along the edges of most Arduino microcontrollers and are used for input, or sensing of a condition, and output, the response that the controller makes to the input. For example, the input might be that the light sensor senses darkness, that is, a lack of light. It will then close a circuit lighting up a bulb as output: a nightlight for your child.

On most boards, there will be a Pin LED, associated with a specific pin, like Pin 13 on the Arduino Uno. This Pin LED is the only output possibility built into the board, and it will help you with your first project of a "blink sketch," which will be explained later. The Pin LED is also used for debugging or fixing the code you have written so that it has no mistakes in it. The Power LED is what its name implies: it lights up when the board is receiving power or is "turned on." This can also be helpful in debugging your code.

There exists on every board the microcontroller itself, called the ATmega microcontroller, which is the brain of the entire board. It receives your instructions and acts accordingly. Without this, the entire board would have no functionality.

Analog in pins exist on the opposite edge of the board from the digital pins on the Arduino Uno. It is an input into the Arduino system. Analog means that the signal which is input is not constant but instead varies with time, such as audio input. In the example of audio input, the auditory input in a room varies with the people in the room talking and with the noises filtering in from outside the room.

GND and 5V pins are used to create additional power of 5V to the circuit and microcontroller. The power connector is most often on the edge of the Arduino board, and it is used to provide power to the microcontroller when it is not plugged into the USB. The USB port can be used as a power source as well, but its main function is to upload, or transfer, your sketch, or set of instructions that you have coded, from your computer to the Arduino.

TX and RX LED's are used to indicate that there is a transfer of information occurring. This indication of communication will happen when you upload your sketches from your computer to the Arduino so that they will blink rapidly during the exchange.

The reset button is as it sounds: it resets the microcontroller to factory settings and erases any information you have uploaded to the Arduino.

Other Terms about Working with Arduino

There are three types of memory in an Arduino system. Memory is the space where information is stored.

Flash memory is where the code for the program that you have written is stored. It is also called the "program space," because it is used for the program automatically when you upload it to the Arduino. This type of memory remains intact when the power is cut off, or when the Arduino is turned off.

SRAM (static random-access memory) is the space used by the sketch or program you have created to create, store, and work with information from the input sources to create an output. This type of storage disappears once the power is turned off.

EEPROM is like a tiny a hard-drive that allows the programmer to store information other than the program itself when the Arduino is turned off. There are separate instructions for the EEPROM, for reading, writing, and erasing, as well as other functions.

Certain digital pins will be designated as PWM pins, meaning that they can create analog using digital means. Analog, as we remember, means that input (or output) is varied and not constant. Normally, digital pins can only create a constant flow of energy. However, PWM pins can vary the "pulse" of energy between 0 and 5 Volts. Certain tasks that you program can only be carried out by PWM pins.

In addition, in comparing microcontroller boards, you will want to look at clock speed, which is the speed at which the microcontroller operates. The faster the speed, the more responsive it the board will be, but the more battery or energy it will consume as well.

UART measures the number of serial communication lines the device can handle. Serial communication lines are lines that transfer data serially, that is, in a line rather than in parallel or simultaneously. It requires much less hardware to process things serially than in parallel.

Some projects will have you connecting devices to the Internet of Things, which essentially describes the interconnectedness of devices, other than desktop and laptop computers, to various networks in order to share information. Everything from smart refrigerators, to smartphones, to smart TV's are connected to the Internet of Things.

Chapter 2 Working with User-Defined Functions

Another thing that we need to take a look at before we end this guidebook is the idea of the user defined function. One of the methods that you are able to keep the code that you are writing, in Arduino and in other languages, clean and organized and modular or reusable, is to make sure that you work with functions inside of that code. In addition, these functions are able to make some of the code smaller because parts of the code, and small sections of it, can be reusable. Functions are going to be like tools that were created in order to serve the particular function that you would like, just like the name is going to suggest.

While we have already gone through and encountered some examples of these particular functions as we go through this guidebook, we now need to go through some of the details that come with them and really understand some of the parts that go with them. This is going to help us to explain some of the features that we may have glossed over in the first place, so that we really know what these functions are like.

The first thing that we are able to do here is to look at the declaration of the function that we want to work with. A good example of how to do this is going to be below:

float employeeEarnings (float hoursWorked, float payrate)
{

float results: // this will be the value that we are going to return when this function has been called up. We want to make sure that it is going to match the type of data that we are using before the name of the function

results = hoursWorked * payrate

Return results // return tells the function that it needs to send a value back once to where it was originally called.

}

Take some time to look over that code and see what it is able to offer in terms of what you are able to do with it, and even what you are able to understand out of the code based on what we have already been able to work with. You can even get some practice in order to get better at this by typing the code out a few times and gaining a feel for it.

This function is going to take on two arguments in order to be successful. It is going to be with the hoursWorked and the payRate in order to handle some of the work that we are doing, and both of these are going to be floats. It does take us some time to work on simple math on these and then it is going to return a float as the value.

The return that we are working on here means that we want to end or terminate the function and then send back the value that was placed with us, after the word return, which is usually going to be a variable, as the results of the calculations that we did. All of this is going to be done to help us understand how these functions work and how we are able to do some stuff with them.

With this in mind, we then need to go through and call up this function. This will allow us to see what the earnings of the employee's are, and can make it easier to see what we are going to get out of this process as well when we work with some of the functions. The code that we are going to need to work with to make this happen will include:

void loop () {

floathoursWorked = 37.5;

float payRate = 18.50;

float result = employeeEarnings (hoursWorked, payRate)

// results will be 693.75

This is a pretty straightforward cod that we are able to work with, but it is definitely going to show us what we are able to do here, and why all of the parts are going to be important along the way. it is also a simple way to get some ideas on how the function is going to work overall.

The first thing that we are going to find here is that the function we want to declare has to be declared independent of and outside of the other functions. This means that we need to be able to write the code for the function that we want to create, doing so either inside of the loop function or the setup function. You can also work with some of the other user defined functions that are there.

We can also go with this and look at another example that will make it easier to see how this is supposed to work. We are going to look at a sample sketch here that is going to be used in many cases to help us smooth out some of our readings of the sensors:

int sensorSmoothin (analogPin) {

in sensorValue = 0;

for (int index = 0; index < 5, index ++)

digitalWrite(LED_BUILTIN, HIGH); //Turn on the LED for smoothing.

sensorValue= sensorValue + analogRead (analogPin)

delay(100) // 100 millisecond delay between the samples

}

digitalWrite(LED_BUILTIN, LOW); //turn off the LED

sensorValue = sensorValue / 5 //average the values over five samples that we are using.

return sensorValue;

}

As you go through some of this, you are going to find that this is going to show up a lot of the functions that we were talking about earlier on. This is going to make it so much easier for us to feel comfortable with some of the work that we are trying to do along the way. The more time that you spend working on some of the coding that we want to do along the way, the easier it is to work with the code because we are comfortable and can recognize things along the way.

This is a good function to work with because it is going to be used to help us to smooth out the input of the data of many sensors, especially if you find that they are prone to inputs that are a bit jittery in the process. This is going to work well because it is able to average out the sample to give us a more consistent flow of data. We are able to see that the code we just did above is going to be similar to some of the sample that we did in the beginning. Let's take along look at it to see what it did there:

With all of this, we are going to be able to work on initializing our sensorValue variable so that it is going to be able to call up the sensorSmoothing() function that we need. This is all going to happen on the analog pin of 0, and can help us out here because it is going to make sure that we are able to average out the results that we have over not just one sample, but over five samples that we are able to use.

Of course, we have to remember that the functions we are working with are not going to always be as smooth and easy to work with as this example. The functions are not always going to need to have parameters or return variables in order to work either. Sometimes the functions can be set up to return no value, and then they can also have no parameters in the process either. All that they are going to do when you bring them up is to execute the few lines of code that you want, and then you can terminate it all, bringing the compiler back to the place in the code where you called them from.

As you can see, these user defined functions are not going to be as difficult as they may seem in the beginning. With a bit of practice, and even trying out a few of the functions that we were able to work with in this chapter, and doing some of your own, you will find that you are able to make these user defined functions work the way that you would like and they will help your Arduino technology complete the project.

Chapter 3 The Serial

While you are not necessarily able to implement the stream class in itself, you are able to go through and implement some of the derivatives of it, and this is where we are going to find a lot of the utility that we need. The serial class that we are going with here is going to be an extension of what we are able to do with the stream class, and it is going to help us to communicate with some of the other devices that we want, such as the computer.

The serial is going to be enacted through both the port on the Arduino for the Serial, as well as on the link for the USB on the computer. We are going to then look at some of the functions that are available with the Serial class, making it easier for you to use this kind of thing and get the most out of this resource along the way as well:

1. Serial.begin(rate): you are already familiar with how this one is going to work. It is a good one to use to help us start out the serial transmission of our data. You are also able to specify the specific rate of the data transmission that you are getting and see it in bits per second.
2. Serial.end): This function is going to allow us to end the communication through this. You can then go through and restart the communication by working with the Serial.begin() function that we did before. While the communication is disabled for whatever purpose, you are able to use the serial pins for generalized entry and exit of the data.
3. Serial.find(string): This is the one that is going to search for the given string within the data that is provided by the Serial. If the string is found, then the method is going to return true. If the string is not found, then the method is going to return the output of false to us.

4. Serial.findUntil(string, OPTIONAL endString): This one is going to take some time to look for a specific string within a serial buffer, until either the string is found or the specified terminating string is found. If the target string is found, then the method is going to return true to us. If the terminating string is found or if the method times out, then you are going to get a return of false.
5. Serial.flush(): This one is going to all you time to halt a process until all of the data that is being sent to the serial has been sent.
6. Serial.parseFloat(): This function is going to work for us by returning the first floating point number to be provided with the serial stream. It is often going to be brought to an end with any character that is not seen as a floating point.
7. Serial.parseInt(): This one is going to be able to work by returning the first integer number to be provided by the serial stream. It is going to be brought to an end by the first character that you are working with that isn't a digit.
8. Serial.peek(): This one is going to return the very next character that should be imported by the serial buffer. However it is not going to remove any of the character from the bugger. This makes it a bit different than he Serial.read() method that we will talk about soon. This means that you are just going to be able to see which of the characters are coming next.
9. Serial.pint(value, OPTIONAL format): You are able to specify the format as well as an option. Otherwise, the integers are going to print as decimals by default. The floats are going to print with two decimal places by default, and so on. You are able to send strings or characters as is to the print statement, and it is going to do the printing that you need without any issues.

10. Serial.pintln(value, OPTIONAL format): This one is going to allow you to prin out some of the values, just like we would expect with some of the other print methods out there.
11. Serial.read(): This one is going to be able to read the data that is showing up through your serial port. This is going to be added to some of the incoming stream of serial data and it is known as the serial buffer. When you read from this buffer, the information will then be destroyed, so we need to make sure that we are saving the data to a variable if we wish to reuse it at one point or another.
12. Serial.readBytes: This one is going to help us read in the characters from the serial port to the buffer. You are able to determine the number of bytes that you would like to see read. Your buffer has to be an array that is a byte or a char.
13. Serial.readBytesUntil: This one is going to work on reading the characters from the serial port, either until the given number of bytes has been read through on there, or until the chosen terminating character is read through as well. In either case, the method will then be able to terminate.
14. Serial.write(): This one is going to write out the data to the serial port. But this method is only going to send over data that is binary to the serial port. If you need to send over other kinds of data, like ASCII, you will need to work with the print method instead.
15. Serial.serialEvent(): The last method that we are going to take some time looking at is this one. Whenever the data you need comes to be available for use with your port of he serial, then this is going to be the function that is called. You can then use this function to help us read the data from the serial port.

As we can see here, we have spent a good deal of time talking about a lot of different topics, especially the functions that we are able to use when we are working with the serial class and how it is going to pertain to some of the programming that happens with the Arduino API. This can help us to get so much done with some of the coding that we need, and can be an important class that will help us to get more done with our API.

Chapter 4 Connecting Switch

The push buttons or switches are going to connect two terminals that are open inside of a circuit.

Pull Down Resistor

The resistor is going to be used when you are working with electronic logic circuits so that it can make sure that the inputs that are on the Arduino panel are settled at the logic levels that are expected. In the event that there are external pieces of equipment that are not connected or are at a high impedance, then nothing is going to be attached to the input pin. This does not mean that it is a logical zero. The pull-down resistor is going to be connected to the ground and the proper pin on the device.

One example would be for the resistor in the circuit to be connected between the supply voltage and the microcontroller pin. In these circuits, the switch is going to be closed while the microcontroller input is high. However, when the switch is open, the resistor is going to pull the input voltage down so that it can prevent an undefined state of the input.

The resistor has to have a massive resistance over the impedance of the logic circuit, or it is going to pull the voltage down lower than it is supposed to be which is going to cause the input voltage to remain at a low value no matter where the switch is.

Components

1. LED (1)
2. **Arduino Uno panel (1)**
3. 4.7 k ohm resistor (1)
    4. 330 ohm resistor (1)

Code

// constants are not going to change they are going to be used to set the pin digital representations

```
Const int buttons pin = 8 // the digital representation of the push button pin
Const int led pin = 2 ; // the LED pin
// variable will change
Int button state = 0 ; // variable for reading the button status
Void setup () {
// initialize the LD pin as an output
Pin mode (led pin, output) ;
// initialize push button as an input ;
Pin mode (button pin, input0 ;
}
Void loop () {
// read the state of the push button value ;
Button state = digital read (button pin) ;
// check if the push button has been pushed
// if yes, then the button state will be high
If (button state == high) {
// turn LED on ;
Digital write (led pin , high) ;
} else {
// turn LED off
Digital write (led pin , low) ;
```

}
}

Chapter 5 Temperature Sensor

The temperature sensor is going to be a precision integrated circuit of temperature pieces of equipment that are going to contain an output voltage linearly proportional to the Centigrade temperature.

The LM35 device is going to have advantages over the linear temperature sensors that are calibrated to Kelvin so that the user is not required to deduct an extensive and continuous voltage from the output to get the Centigrade scaling. This device will not demand any additional calibration from outside sources or trim with a view to obtaining maximum accuracy. Most accuracies are going to be a fourth off either direction.

Technical Specifications

1. Suitable for applications that are remote
2. **Will be calibrated for Celsius**
3. Is going to be rated for temperatures between -55 and 150.
4. Linear to a + 10 -mV/ degree Celsius scale
5. Half a degree ensured accuracy.

Components

1. LM35 sensor (1)
2. **Breadpanel (1)**
3. Arduino Uno R3 (1)

Code

This is the code that you are going to place in the Arduino sketch program after you have created a more up to date file.

Float temp ;

Int temp pin = 1 ;

Void setup () {

Serial begin (8999) ;

Void loop () {

Temp = analog read (temp pin) ;

// read analog volt from sensor and save to variable temp

Temp = temp * 3.939403021 ;

// convert the analog volt to its tempt equivalent

Serial print (temperature =) ;

Serial print (temp) ; // show temperature value

Serial print (F) ;

Serial print in () ;

Delay (300) ; // update sensor reading each one second

}

Notes on the code

1. Connect the GND to the GND that is located on the Arduino
2. **Make sure that you connect the positive Vs. to the positive 5V that you can find on your panel.**
3. Connect the V out to the analog 0 that is on the Arduino board.

The result that you are going to see is the temperature displayed on the serial port monitor which is updated each second.

Water Detector and Sensor

The water sensor brick is going to be designed for detecting water. This is going to be most often used to sense predetermined markers such as any leaks or even water levels.

When you are choosing to connect the water sensor to the Arduino panels, the sensor is going to be able to detect any measurement of water. It can accurately measure the level, presence, volume, or even if there is a complete lack of water. This is a great feature and even has the ability to remind the owner when it is time to water household plants!

You will be able to connect the water sensor to the eighth pin on the Arduino board.this pin is going to enlist an LED that enables us to identify when the sensor has come been exposed to water of any level.

Components
1. 330 ohm resistor (1)
2. **Breadpanel (1)**
3. Led (1)
4. Arduino Uno R3 (1)
5. Water sensor (1)

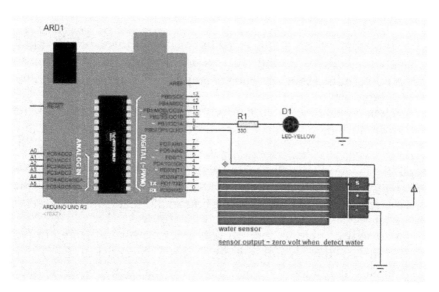

Procedure

Code

define grove water sensor 9 // attach water sensor to Arduino digital pin 8

#define LED 9 // attach an LED to pin 9

Void setup () {

Pin mode (grove water sensor, input) ; // the water sensor will be an input

Pin mode (led, output) ; // the led will be an output

}

Notes on the code

There are going to be three terminals for the water sensor, and it is going to connect as follows.

1. The LED will be connected to the digital pin 9
2. **The positive Vs. willl be tied to the positive side of the five volts.**
3. The GND will be connected to the GND on the panel.
   4. The S will be attached to the eight pin on the Arduino board.

At the point in time that the sensor picks up any water, it is going to cause pin eigh to become weak, and the LED to be turned on.

PIR Sensor

A PIR sensor is going to allow you pick up motions, in other words, it is going to be a motion sensor. The sensor will detect movement inside of the sensors range. You are commonly going to find these sensors outside of homes and businesses. PIR is going to stand for passive infrared, pyroelectric, or IR motion sensor.

Here are some of the advantages of having a PIR sensor.

1. Does not wear out
2. **Small**
3. Easy to use
   4. Has an extensive lens range
5. Low power
6. Easy to interface
7. Low power
   8. *Inexpensive*

A PIR is going to be made of pyroelectric sensors that are going to be located in a round metal can that contains a rectangular crystal in the center. This sensor is going to be able to detect varying levels of infrared radiation. Everything is going to emit some level of radiation. However, the hotter something is, the more radiation it is going to emit. The motion sensor is going to detect the change on the move and not just IR levels. The two halves of the panel are going to snap together which is going to cancel each other out. But, if one half gets more or less IR than the other, the output will end up being high or low.

A PIR is going to be adjustable in the settings while containing a header that is installed on the third pin.

For a lot of the basic projects that you can make to detect a human presence is going to use a PIR sensor. Keep in mind that a PIR is not going to tell you how many people are there or how close to the sensor they are. The lens is going to be fixed in such a way that it can sweep a distance.

Components
1. PIR sensor MQ3 (1)
2. Breadpanel (1)
3. Arduino Uno R3 (1)

Procedure

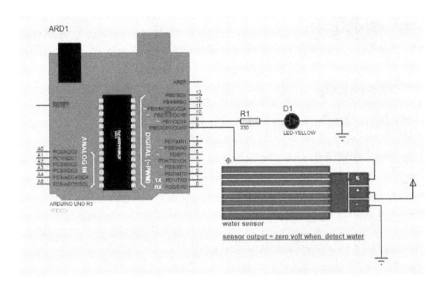

Code

#define pir pin 2

Int calibration time = 30 ;

Long unsigned int low in ;

Long unsigned int pause = 4000 ;

Boolean lock low = true ;

Boolean take low time ;

Int pir value = 0 ;

Void setup () {

Serial begin (9600) ;

Pin mode (pir pin, input) ;

}

Void look () {

```
Pir sensor () ;
}
Void pir sensor () {
if (digital read (pir pin ) == high ) {
if (lock low) {
pir value = 1;
lock low = false ;
serial print in (motion detected) ;
delay (60) ;
}
Take low time = true ;
}
If (digital read (pir pin) == low {
If (take low time ) {
Low in = millis() ; take low time = false ;
}
If (!locklow && millis () – lowin > pause) {
Pirvalue = 0 ;
Locklow = true ;
Serial print in (motion ended) ;
Delay (60)
}
```

}

Notes on code

There are three terminals for the pir.

1. The GND will be connected to the GND
2. **The positive VCC will be connected to the positive side of the five volts**
3. The out will be tied to the second pin on the panel.

You are going to be able to adjust the sensor sensitivity and delay time with two variable resistors that you can find at the bottom of the panel. After the sensor detects motion, the Arduino is going to send you a message to inform you that it has detected motion. The pir sensor is going to be delayed for some time to check if there is any more up to date motion. In the event that there is no more up to date motion detected, the panel will send you a message telling you so.

Chapter 6 Using the Stream Class

This is a topic that is going to be so important to what we are trying to do with some of our work that it really did deserve its own chapter to help us get the work done. While this one is still going to work with the API of Arduino that we talked about before it is going to be pretty broad and will talk about a lot of different parts, so we are going to break off here and work with the stream class, which also allows us to work with strings along the way.

The stream class is going to be a fairly simple concept even though it is really important to work with. The stream class on its own is going to be based on using reading information from a certain source, and then having this as how you make up your own sketch. Because the stream is all about reading the data, it is also important that we talk about working with a mouse and keyboard with the Arduino board in this chapter, even though we may think that these are not going to be related directly to the stream class that we are working with.

When you decide to work with the data, especially when you are readying the data, you will find that there are times when we need to work with sets of characters that are longer, like a sentence. The idea of strings is going to give you the chance to do this on our board. Strings are going to basically just be sets of character values that will be linked together like with an array. This means that they are going to be contiguous in the memory, and the computer is going to see them as one large and interconnected unit. Working with the strings means that we need to learn how to manipulate these units as well as our abilities will allow.

On its own, it is going to be pretty simple. Thought to work with. Strings are just going to be what we know as character arrays. That means that we are still working with some of the C-style strings, which are going to be strings that have abstraction at a very low level. For example, in a lot of the newer programming languages, the strings are not going to be revealed in their character as a character array. Instead of doing this, they are going to be treated as an abstract object instead. Even if they are considered a character array, they will be treated in this manner.

A string is going to be composed of the n + 1 characters, where n is going to be the number of letters that is in the string in general. So, for example, the size of a string for the word "hello" would end up being the six characters. The reason for this is because the string is going to end in a null terminating character, which is going to indicate to us that the end of the array has been reached and that it can be ended.

You are able to go through and define a string in the same manner that you would an array. You are able to also make them bigger than the string that you plan to have them contain. When you go through the process of defining an array you may give it a value right of the bat, but you can also just define the size and expand them out at a later time. this also makes strings, more dynamic and can allow us to change them up later on when we rewrite some of the data that is inside of that string.

This information is going to be useful to a programmer who is just getting started because these strings are going to be fundamental and important to any of the programs that you use that handle information, especially those that are going to handle the input and the output of the file. We have already spent some time looking at this, now, but we also need to go ahead and learn how we are able to define our string. The code that we are able to use for this one will be below:

char myString[6] = "hello";

You can then spend some time referring to this entire string at a later point with the name of the character. Most of the data that is worked with by the board is going to be worked with in terms of how many bytes it is, and most of the actual textual data is going to be worked with in terms of C strings because it is easy to parse these characters when you would like.

It is important that we go over all of these parts so that we learn and develop the right ideas that we need when it is time to treat the strings in this kind of programming and we see what we are able to do with some of these parts as well. Let's dive a bit more into this to see how it will work.

The Serial

While you are not necessarily able to implement the stream class in itself, you are able to go through and implement some of the derivatives of it, and this is where we are going to find a lot of the utility that we need. The serial class that we are going with here is going to be an extension of what we are able to do with the stream class, and it is going to help us to communicate with some of the other devices that we want, such as the computer.

The serial is going to be enacted through both the port on the Arduino for the Serial, as well as on the link for the USB on the computer. We are going to then look at some of the functions that are available with the Serial class, making it easier for you to use this kind of thing and get the most out of this resource along the way as well:

1. Serial.begin(rate): you are already familiar with how this one is going to work. It is a good one to use to help us start out the serial transmission of our data. You are also able to specify the specific rate of the data transmission that you are getting and see it in bits per second.
2. Serial.end): This function is going to allow us to end the communication through this. You can then go through and restart the communication by working with the Serial.begin() function that we

did before. While the communication is disabled for whatever purpose, you are able to use the serial pins for generalized entry and exit of the data.
3. Serial.find(string): This is the one that is going to search for the given string within the data that is provided by the Serial. If the string is found, then the method is going to return true. If the string is not found, then the method is going to return the output of false to us.
4. Serial.findUntil(string, OPTIONAL endString): This one is going to take some time to look for a specific string within a serial buffer, until either the string is found or the specified terminating string is found. If the target string is found, then the method is going to return true to us. If the terminating string is found or if the method times out, then you are going to get a return of false.
5. Serial.flush(): This one is going to all you time to halt a process until all of the data that is being sent to the serial has been sent.
6. Serial.parseFloat(): This function is going to work for us by returning the first floating point number to be provided with the serial stream. It is often going to be brought to an end with any character that is not seen as a floating point.
7. Serial.parseInt(): This one is going to be able to work by returning the first integer number to be provided by the serial stream. It is going to be brought to an end by the first character that you are working with that isn't a digit.
8. Serial.peek(): This one is going to return the very next character that should be imported by the serial buffer. However it is not going to remove any of the character from the bugger. This makes it a bit different than he Serial.read() method that we will talk about soon. This means that you are

just going to be able to see which of the characters are coming next.
9. Serial.pint(value, OPTIONAL format): You are able to specify the format as well as an option. Otherwise, the integers are going to print as decimals by default. The floats are going to print with two decimal places by default, and so on. You are able to send strings or characters as is to the print statement, and it is going to do the printing that you need without any issues.
10. Serial.pintln(value, OPTIONAL format): This one is going to allow you to prin out some of the values, just like we would expect with some of the other print methods out there.
11. Serial.read(): This one is going to be able to read the data that is showing up through your serial port. This is going to be added to some of the incoming stream of serial data and it is known as the serial buffer. When you read from this buffer, the information will then be destroyed, so we need to make sure that we are saving the data to a variable if we wish to reuse it at one point or another.
12. Serial.readBytes: This one is going to help us read in the characters from the serial port to the buffer. You are able to determine the number of bytes that you would like to see read. Your buffer has to be an array that is a byte or a char.
13. Serial.readBytesUntil: This one is going to work on reading the characters from the serial port, either until the given number of bytes has been read through on there, or until the chosen terminating character is read through as well. In either case, the method will then be able to terminate.
14. Serial.write(): This one is going to write out the data to the serial port. But this method is only going to send over data that is binary to the serial port. If you need to send over other kinds of data, like ASCII, you will need to work with the print method instead.

15. Serial.serialEvent(): The last method that we are going to take some time looking at is this one. Whenever the data you need comes to be available for use with your port of he serial, then this is going to be the function that is called. You can then use this function to help us read the data from the serial port.

As we can see here, we have spent a good deal of time talking about a lot of different topics, especially the functions that we are able to use when we are working with the serial class and how it is going to pertain to some of the programming that happens with the Arduino API. This can help us to get so much done with some of the coding that we need, and can be an important class that will help us to get more done with our API.

Chapter 7 Calculated Digital Representations

To generate calculated digital representations, you will use the calculated digital representation functions. You are going to have two functions to choose from.

1. Calculated ()
2. **Calculated seed (seed)**

Calculated Seed (Seed)

This function will reset the pseudocalculated digital representation generator. Even though the dispersion of the digital representations that are returned by the determined function, therefore, making them truly calculated while the sequence becomes predictable. You are going to have to reset the generator to the estimated value. In the event that you have an analog pin that is unconnected, it is going to pick up calculated commotion from the environment that is around the panel. This means that radio waves, electromagnetic interference, and cosmic rays can cause the generator to malfunction.

Example

Calculated seed (analog read (4)) ; //calculatedly pick from the commotion from analog pin 6

Calculated ()

The calculated function is going to create pseudo calculated digital representations.

Syntax

Long calculated (max) // it generates calculated digital representations from zero to max

Long calculated (min, max) // it generates calculated digital representations from min to max

Example

Long rand digital representation ;

Void setup () {

Serial. Begin (4329) ;

// if analog input pin zero is unconnected, calculated analog

// commotion will cause the call to calculated seed () to generate

// different seed digital representations every time that your sketch executes code

// calculated seed () will then shuffle the calculated function

Calculated seed (analog read (1)) ;

}

Void loop () {

// print a calculated digital representation from zero to two hundred and ninety-nine

Serial. Print ("calculated1 =") ;

Rand digital representation = calculated (301) ;

Serial. Println (rand digital representation) ; // print a calculated digital representation from zero to two hundred and ninety-nine.

Serial print ("calculated 2") ;

Rand digital representation = calculated (29, 39) ; // print a calculated digital representation from twenty-nine to thirty-nine

Serial. Print ln (rand digital representation) ;

Delay (29) ;

}

Bits

A bit is going to be a binary digit.

Any binary system that you use is going to use at least two digits, one and zero.

The bit system will work like the decimal digital representation system is going to work, because the digital representations will not hold the same value, the significance of a bit is going to depend on where you locate it in the digital representation line for binary digital representations. Take for example the decimal digital representation three hundred and three is going to be the same digital representations, but they are going to have different values.

Bytes

Bytes are going to consist of eight bits.

In the event that bits are represented by digits, then you can safely assume that a byte will be represented by a digital representation.

All mathematical equations can be completed with a byte.

The digits of a byte are not going to have the same significance.

The leftmost bit is going to have the greatest value, and it is going to be known as the most significant bit or MSB. On the opposite end, it is going to be referred to as the least important bit.

Being that there will be eight ones and zeros that are going to be one byte, at least two hundred and fifty-six of them are going to be used in various ways. The larger decimal digital representation is going to be shown by using a byte which will be two hundred and fifty-five.

Chapter 8 Understanding the Arduino Framework

In this chapter, we're going to actually start looking at the code which fuels Arduino. At this point, we are assuming that you have your Arduino unit and you've got it set up and linked to your computer. This is the first step.

The second step is to get an Arduino compatible IDE. For most beginners and novices, the ones supplied by Arduino themselves will be more than enough. You can navigate to their website and either download the desktop IDE or use the web-based IDE. Either one will work perfectly fine.

So, from here, we need to talk about the structure of sketches.

An Arduino sketch has two basic components that make it up: the 'setup' function and the 'loop' function. Both are essential to the overall functioning of the Arduino sketch, and so you need to make sure that every sketch you run has them. Your sketches, of course, are not limited to just these functions, and you can expand with more functions at ease as we described back in the C chapter.

The Arduino 'language,' so to speak, is just an extension of C and C++, which means that C and C++ coding conventions will work within them, as well as all of the things that we described previously. This makes programming your Arduino unit relatively easy.

The Arduino 'language' is actually a library with various different definitions and functions that are tailored to the Arduino.

This is how the most basic of Arduino programs look, in terms of structure:

```
void setup()
    {
```

// code within

   }

void loop()

   {

// code within

   }

The setup function should be just after the declaration of variables at the start of your sketch. It will always be the first function that your Arduino unit runs, so pay careful attention. You must have your setup function, even if there is nothing within it.

You use the setup function to do things like initializing Arduino relevant variables, like your pin modes. In other words, any necessary setup that you have to do to get everything up and running, those functions should be called from within your setup function.

Do note that not necessarily all of your variables must be declared here. Variables should generally be declared within their primary function or in the global scope. If you fail to define a function at these levels, you won't be able to use it where you want it to. For example, if you defined a variable within the setup function, you wouldn't be able to use it within your loop function since it was defined within another function and isn't global.

The loop function does pretty much exactly what it sounds like: it loops over and over until the program is brought to an end. When the program finally is brought to an end, the loop ends. Programs are generally brought to an end by cutting off power to your Arduino unit, so there isn't much of a way to exit the Arduino loop function. This is the primary function of your program, and everything happens from here.

Consider the fact that when you program something like an Arduino gadget, it really is just looping some function over and over every second, even if that loop is just something like waiting to receive input and then responding respectively when said input is given.

In terms of actual Arduino code from the framework, there are a few that you really need to know at this point.

Constants

Constants are a foundational part of Arduino programming because they allow you to make comparisons or assign certain things easily. Constants are variables which are predefined and do not change. They can be used as references in other functions used within the language.

Two constants are 'TRUE' and 'FALSE.' This harkens back to the language on **Booleans**. TRUE here is defined as anything other than zero, where FALSE is zero.

Two more are 'HIGH' and 'LOW.' These refer to the voltage being given to the pin, and the respective pin levels. HIGH refers to a pin which is 'ON' and which is receiving 5 volts while LOW refers to a pin which is 'OFF' and is receiving zero volts. This is used most often when you are either giving or receiving data from digital pins.

The other two constants that you need to know at this point are 'INPUT' and 'OUTPUT,' which merely allow you to define the mode of something and whether it is for incoming data or outgoing data.

Functions

There are some different functions that are inherent to Arduino programming that we need to cover. While a large amount of Arduino functions will vary depending upon the gadgets you have and the project that you're specifically trying to tackle, there are nonetheless manifold important

The first is **pinMode**, which takes the arguments of **pin** and **mode**. Pin is the respective integer of the given pin, where mode is either OUTPUT or INPUT, as we just said. Therefore, it ties in perfectly to what we were just discussing with the constants. This function will always be called within your setup function.

The next is **digitalRead()**, which takes an argument of a given **pin**, either as a constant or a variable. This will read in a value from a given pin and return either HIGH or LOW, this indicates either true/false, on/off, or 5v/0v.

The next is **digitalWrite**, which takes the arguments of a pin as well as HIGH or LOW, which will essentially turn a given pin on or off.

The next is **analogRead**, which accepts an argument of a given **pin** and will take a value from the analog in pins. It will return an integer value instead of HIGH or LOW.

After that is **analogWrite**, which will take the arguments of **pin** and **value**. **AnalogWrite** allows you to write what is essentially an analog value to a given pin. The value can be from 0 to 255, and the size of the number will indicate how often the signal sent is either 5 or 0 volts; a larger number indicates that the charge will more often be 5 volts than 0 volts. This works in a wave manner and will, therefore, act as a means to regulate how much power is being sent to the given pin.

After the read and write functions is the **delay** function, which pauses the program. It takes an argument of milliseconds, either as a variable or a constant. It will cause a pause in that length.

Beyond that is **millis()** which just returns the number of milliseconds that have passed since the current sketch started as a long. This number resets after several hours.

After that are the min and max functions, which take two arguments both and return either the smaller or larger number respectively. They accept numbers regardless of data type.

After that is **randomSeed** which accepts a given integer as an argument. This creates a seed for a random number generator.

Beyond this are the two random functions. Given one argument, the random function will return any number from zero to the max value. Given two arguments, it will return a number between the two numbers given. You must use **randomSeed** before you use a random function.

The last two functions we need to cover are the 'Serial' functions, which allow you to transmit serial data:

- **Serial.begin()** accepts an argument of the rate of transfer in bits per second. This is called in your setup function. The average rate is 9600 bits per second, so when in doubt, just use this.
- **Serial.println()** accepts an argument of any given data and will then print this to the Serial Monitor.

Chapter 9 Learn the Implementation of Algorithms

In this chapter, we're going to discuss the implementation of algorithms in Arduino programming. Often, algorithms are understated in terms of their importance to Arduino programming, but using them, you're able to do many things that you wouldn't be able to otherwise.

An algorithm is, for lack of a better term, a way of standardizing a sort of procedure. We're going to be discussing two different types of algorithms and how they relate to Arduino programming, as well as discuss in both a theoretical and a practical sense how they can be implemented.

We first will look at the bubble sort algorithm and discuss sorting in relation to Arduino programming. Bubble sorting is the simplest form of sorting, but it will give you a decent look into algorithmic programming and a greater example of how algorithms actually are in practice.

The second thing that we will look at is a Bayesian probability algorithm which is important in statistical programming. Bayesian probability is also used to determine "true probability," which is probability that takes into account false positives and false negatives. We're going to be discussing why probability algorithms may be useful in Arduino programming and how you may find yourself using them in the future depending upon your various different projects.

Let's start by looking at sorting and thinking about when it could be useful to us as Arduino programmers. Sorting is the idea of taking some set of data and then filtering through it and moving things around accordingly. Let's say, for example, that we had an array of ten values. There are times where we may need to sort these. While there do exist certain functions in the Arduino library for getting the minimum or maximum of two values, there is no built-in sorting function for an array, and there's no built-in way to obtain the largest and smallest values within an array.

This is an introduction to algorithmic thinking more than anything else because Arduino is a perfect proxy to building bigger and better technological systems based off of concepts such as artificial intelligence and the internet of things. More than that, algorithms come up in complex programs and having some idea as to how to break down what an algorithm needs to do and then implementing it is a first important step to developing some sort of methodology for programming algorithmically.

The sample language for this example will be C/C++, but the key concepts will remain the same across any language. This is the first time in this book that we're not going to be using pseudocode.

Let's first define an array of 10 random values. You can make them whatever. Here are mine:

int numbers[10] = { 39, 63, 10, 70, 23, 34, 63, 13, 76, 34 };

This is the first important step. Afterward, we need to define the how our algorithm will work. Let's think about this for a second.

What a bubble sort essentially does is look at any given value in an array and compare it to a number either immediately before or after it. If the number before or after is larger or smaller (implementation can vary), then the two numbers will be swapped.

This might seem straightforward: you simply iterate through the array and perform checks to see if a given element is larger than another, right?

Not quite. If you used a single loop to iterate through the array, you're not actually going to be accomplishing much of anything. Instead, you need to use two for loops. The first loop will denote what we can call our **active position**. This will move through every element in the array one by one and perform the necessary checks and swaps until an **n**th element has been checked.

After that, you'll use a second for loop. This creates an **active integer** and compares it against every other element in the array. This is the loop of action. The other is the loop of iteration.

Within the loop of action, we must, therefore, create some kind of check mechanism. We can do this by comparing the active integer against another element in the array. If the other element is smaller, the two elements will swap positions. This means that the smaller element will be pushed towards the front of the array.

By now, we can assume that this means we need two functions: a **sort** function which will contain the logic of our sort mechanism, and a **swap** function which can perform the swap of the two integers given their addresses in memory.

We can implement these two like so:

For the **swap** function, we're going to want it to take the argument of two pointer addresses. Within the function, it will then define a temporary placeholder variable which we can call **i**. The placeholder will be used to store the value of integer 1. Integer 1 will then assume the value of integer 2. Integer 2 then assumes the value of the placeholder, which is the old value of integer 1, meaning integer 1 and 2 have now effectively swapped positions. Here is how I would define this function:

void swap(int *p1, int *p2)

{

int i = *p1;

```
*p1 = *p2;
*p2 = i;
}
```

Easy peasy. The logic behind it is a little rough, but that's all an important part of the learning process!

Now, moving on beyond this, we're going to now work with our **sort** function. The sort function will create two iterative arrays. It will accept the arguments of the array's size and the array itself. It will iterate through these accordingly. Since we're comparing in a forward manner, the active position should only extend to the size of the array minus one element; otherwise, when the last element in the array is reached, there will be an element overflow error, and the program will crash (if it executes at all.)

For the second for loop, we need to iterate according to the size minus the active position minus 1.

Within the second for loop, we need to define an if statement which checks to see whether the active integer is larger than the number immediately ahead of it. If it is, then the two swap positions, meaning we throw the memory addresses of the two to the swap function.

Here is how I would define this function:

void sort(int myArray[], int size)

```
{
for (int i = 0; i < size - 1; i++)
for (int j = 0; j < size - i - 1; j++)
if (myArray[j] > myArray[j+1])
```

```c
        swap(&myArray[j], &myArray[j+1]);
    }
}
```

Again, it's not a terribly difficult algorithm, but it does require a bit of thought and is a decent introduction to algorithmic thinking if you've never done so before. To test this all, we can create a program with our test array that will do all of this, then print it out for us so that we can see if all is in working order:

```c
#include <stdio.h>

void swap(int *p1, int *p2)
{
    int i = *p1;
    *p1 = *p2;
    *p2 = i;
}

void sort(int myArray[], int size)
{
    for (int i = 0; i < size - 1; i++)
        for (int j = 0; j < size - i - 1; j++)
            if (myArray[j] > myArray[j+1])
                swap(&myArray[j], &myArray[j+1]);
}
```

```
int main()
{
    int numbers[10] = { 39, 63, 10, 70, 23, 34, 63, 13, 76, 34 };
    int size = sizeof(numbers)/sizeof(numbers[0]);
    sort(numbers, size);
    for (int i = 0; i < size; i++)
    {
        printf("%d", numbers[i]);
    }
}
```

Your end program should look somewhat like the one above. If so, then you've succeeded.

The next thing that we're going to discuss in an algorithmic sense is probability using a very rudimentary version of Bayes' theorem.

So what exactly is Bayes' theorem, and why is it useful as an Arduino programmer? Well, Bayes' theorem in and of itself is a way of determining true probability of a given situation based upon the likelihood that something has happened in the past. It takes into account various given rates and then returns a certain dimension based on those rates.

For this, we can take two events: event X and event Y. We then have P(X) which is the likelihood of X, and P(Y) which is the likelihood of Y. P(X|Y) is the likelihood of event **X** given that **Y** is true, and P(Y|X) is the likelihood of event Y if event X is true.

Let's say we're trying to find the likelihood of event X given that Y is true, and we have data related to event Y is X is true. Bayes' theorem then allows us to look at it like so:

P(X|Y) = P(Y|X)*P(X) / P(Y)

In other words, the probability of event X given that Y is true is equivalent to the probability of Y given that X is true multiplied by the probability of X, then all of this divided over the probability of Y.

Bayes' theorem is a little difficult to grasp if you aren't looking at it in an intuitive manner. Take, for example, spam filtering, which is a rather common application of Bayes' theorem in the world of computer science.

Let's say that event X is the likelihood that the message is spam, and event Y is the likelihood that it contains certain words flagged as spam. P(X|Y) is the probability that it is spam given that it contains words flagged as spam. P(Y|X) is the probability that a certain word flagged as spam will be in a spam message. P(X) is the probability that any given message is spam, and P(Y) is the probability that the words within are flagged for spam.

Therefore, we can render the equation something like this:

The probability that a message is spam based on flagged words is equivalent to **the probability that the flagged words are in a spam message** multiplied by **the probability that a message is spam**, all divided by **the probability that flagged words are spam**.

This yields:

P(spam|words) = P(words|spam)*P(spam) / P(words)

This could be rendered algorithmically rather simply, and it's a very rudimentary probability equation. However, this does give us a solid starting point. The equation, too, can be mostly given over without much thought given to the conversion process.

For this, we're going to need just one function which returns **x given y** based upon **y given x**, **y**, and **x**. We'll call this function **calc_prob**. We will use this function to return a double value which will be saved to a variable and printed out to the console.

The finished code would look something like this:

#include <stdio.h>

double calc_prob(double ygivenx, double x, double y)

{

return (ygivenx * x) / y;

}

int main()

{

double spam = 3100, words = 6888, wordsgivenspam = 7000;

double spamgivenwords = calc_prob(wordsgivenspam, spam, words);

printf("%.2f", spamgivenwords);

}

With that, you've written your second algorithm. Probability algorithms become massively useful when you need your Arduino programs to be able to act predictively. For example, you could use your Arduino to model certain situations or react accordingly. While it's not powerful enough for hardcore number crunching, it will definitely be powerful enough for basic probability equations. This, for example, is nothing too intensive. So long as it can retrieve information to form a dataset, you can use much of the information in this book to make highly reactive Arduino sketches that could, ideally, change the world.

The purpose of introducing these two algorithms was to give you insight as to how algorithms might impact your programming and how thinking algorithmically can be a major boon to your ability to program in the first place. Consider that the ability to mentally process and break apart certain functions is foundational to being able to think like a programmer, which - in the end - is what this book is trying to help you do.

Chapter 10 Troubleshooting

As you work on your projects, there are specific situations when there will be troubleshooting and debugging.

The more you use Arduino and electronics, the better you become and gain experience. This will end up making the whole process less painful. Don't be frustrated with the problems that you experience. It is much easy than the way it might look at the start.

Since each Arduino project consists of a hardware and software, there are many places to check when things go wrong. Therefore, when debugging, you need to consider these three aspects:

Understanding

You should strive to understand as much as you can in the way the parts you have in your project operate and how they should contribute to the final project. This method will allow you to develop ways in which you can check every component independently.

Simplify and segment

In the ancient Romans, they had what we call divide and rule type of government. You need to break down your project into different components using your intelligence to determine which part of a given function starts and ends.

Exclusion and Certainty

While investigating, you need to check each component individually to ensure that you are sure every component works by itself. You will slowly develop your confidence and note the parts of the project that are doing well and areas that you should fix.

Debugging is the term we refer to the process of fixing errors in software. It was first used by Grace Hopper back in the 1940s. This was the time when computers were majorly electrochemical. It is believed one computer stopped working after an actual insect found its way inside.

However, many of today's bugs are not physical like in this case. Instead, they are virtual and invisible. This means they call for more time and that process can be boring.

Testing the Board

What if the first example of blinking an LED failed to work? That would possibly be frustrating. Let us see what you can do.

Before you throw complains at your project, you need to ascertain that several things are in the right place. This is similar to the way airline pilots follow when they run through a list of things to make sure that there will be no problems when the plane takes off.

The first thing you need to do is to plug your USB into your computer:

- **Verify that the PC is on. This might look obvious, but you could forget to turn on your computer. When the green light labeled PWR lights up, this implies that the computer is powering the board. However, if the LED looks faint, then something is wrong with the power. You can change the USB cable and check the computer USB port as well as the Arduino USB plug port on your computer.**
- **If you are using a new Arduino, the yellow LED labeled L will start to blink.**
- Now, if you had been using an external source of power and you have connected an old Arduino. Just ensure

that the power supply is inserted in and the jumper labeled as SV1 has been connected to the two pins that are close to the external power supply connector.

Another point you need to note is when you are experiencing problems with some sketches, and you want to verify that the board is working. Open and transfer the blink an LED example in the IDE to the board. The onboard LED has to blink in a regular pattern. If you follow all the above steps, then you should be confident that the Arduino is going to work correctly.

Test the Breadboard Circuit

To test your breadboard circuit, join the board to your breadboard by executing a jumper from the GND and 5V connections right between the negative and positive rails of the breadboard. When the green PWR LED goes off, remove the wires. This shows that there exists an error in the circuit and there is a short circuit. A short-circuit leads to an excessive current which cuts off the current as a mechanism to protect your computer.

However, if you are concerned that you might destroy your computer, remember that most machines have safety mechanisms. Besides, the Arduino board has an independently powered USB hub.

If you have a short circuit, it is essential to apply the divide and conquer approach. What you require to do is to look for each sensor in the project and connect each sensor one at a time.

The first thing that you need to begin with is the power source. Review each part of the circuit to ensure that power flows through it. Work procedurally and perform a single change in every step.

Any time you are in the process of debugging and things do not seem to go well, the best thing to do is to handle everything systematically. This is very important because it will help you fix the problem, and that is why it is crucial that you update one at a time.

In addition, do not forget that each debugging process will stick in your head. You will develop an understanding of some of the things to fix up when you encounter a problem. In addition, after some time you will become an expert at doing it.

IDE problems

There are times when you might experience problems with the Arduino IDE, primarily if you are working on Windows. If you receive an error when you double-click the Arduino Icon or nothing happens, you should attempt to execute the run.bat file, which is another option to start Arduino.

Windows users might again run into a problem if the operating system allocates the COM port to a COM10 or higher number to the Arduino. If this takes place, you can let Windows assign a lower port number to the Arduino.

Look for Help Online

If you find yourself stuck entirely such that you are spending a lot of time trying to debug, it might be time to turn to the community of users at the Arduino forum. One of the best things, when you look for help online, is that you will always find someone ready to assist you if you can describe your problem correctly.

Develop a practice of cutting and pasting things into a search engine and wait to check the results if there is a person who has tried to solve it. Look around to discover a solution, nearly every problem you encounter must have an answer.

You, start with checking the main Arduino website before you can move to the playground. Another critical thing to note is before you begin your project, you should search in the playground for a few lines of code or circuit diagram to help you build your project.

Chapter 11 Projects

The Keyboard Instrument

With the help of some buttons, resistors and other devices, you will build a small musical keyboard.

Although you can join a few switches into a digital input and produce different types of tones, in this particular project, you will learn how to build a resistor ladder.

This is a method where you can read some switches by using an analog input. It is an essential technique if you have limited digital data. You will connect some parallel switches into the analog. When you touch each button, there will be a separate voltage level that will flow through the input pin. If you press down two buttons simultaneously, you will find a unique input that depends on the link between the two resistors arranged in parallel. The figure below shows a ladder and five switches.

Let's look at the circuit

1. First, you have to connect the breadboard to the power and ground like the one we did in the previous examples. Hold one side of the piezo and join it to the ground. Connect the remaining side of the pin to your Arduino.
2. Arrange the switches on the breadboard the same way it has been done in the figure above. The pattern of the resistors and switches going into the analog input is the resistor ladder.

Look for something to enclose your keyboard. Take a small cardboard piece that you can cut to fit your buttons. Mark the keys to help you remember the notes that have been triggered by every key.

3. Take a small piece of paper that has holes that belong to the four buttons and the piezo. Decorate it so that it can resemble a piano keyboard.

4. Place the paper on top of the buttons and piezo, and enjoy the creation.

The CODE

This program requires one to have different frequency values which you want to play when you touch the buttons. You can start with the frequencies for the

Parts labeled C, D, E, and F. To achieve this, you must create a variable called array.

An array holds different values of similar type; this can be the frequencies of a musical scale. They are a great tool to help one access information fast. If you want to declare an array, do the same way you declare a variable, but make sure the name follows with a pair of square brackets. The elements of the array remain in the curly brackets.

Anyone who would like to change the elements of the array has to first reference the individual elements by listing the name and index of the element. The index is the order by which things will appear in the array. The first index in an array is 0 and the next is 1. This order follows that trend until the last element is reached.

Creating an array of frequencies

Declare an array to store four notes. Make the array global by making the declaration before the start of the setup() function.

In the loop(), create a local variable to hold the reading of pin A0. Given that each switch has a different resistor value that connects to the source of power, there will be unique values. To see the values, use the line below

Serial.println(keyVal)

We have used an if...else statement to help us allocate every value to its particular tone. This program has used random figures for the size of the resistor. Do not use the exact figures in your program because resistors have some errors, this may fail to work in your case.

```
int buttons[6];
// set up an array with 6 integers

int buttons[0] = 2;
// give the first element of the array the value 2
```

```
1  int notes[] = {262,294,330,349};
```

```
2  void setup() {
3    Serial.begin(9600);
4  }

5  void loop() {
6    int keyVal = analogRead(A0);
7    Serial.println(keyVal);


8    if(keyVal == 1023){
9      tone(8, notes[0]);
10   }
```

Play notes that are similar to the analog value

Call the tone() after every if() statement call. The program tells the array to calculate the frequency to play if the value of AO is similar to the one in the if statements, you can allow the Arduino to play the tone. There is also a possibility that your circuit is noisy and the values can rise when you press the switch. Therefore, it is a good thing to use small values to validate.

If you apply the "&&," look for multiple statements to determine if it is correct. When you press the first button, the notes in the first element will play, touching the second button, the notes in the second element plays and the cycle continues.

To stop the note from playing you use the function noTone(). Just specify as a parameter the pin number you want to stop.

However, in case you have resistors close to one another like in the example program, you should hear sounds originating from the piezo when you press the buttons. If you don't understand, navigate to the serial monitor and make sure that every button is within the range of the notes in the conditional if statement. If you hear a stuttering sound, increase the scale a bit.

Press several buttons simultaneously, and see the type of values that appear in the serial monitor. Use the new values to generate more sounds. Test as many frequencies and expand the musical output.

The tone() function is the best when you want to generate sounds. However, it has some limitations. For instance, the function can only create square waves but not smooth sine waves. Square waves are different from typical waves. While you are about to begin your band, remember that only a single tone can play every time and the function tone interfaces with the analogWrite() on pins 11 and 3.

Note

Finally, remember that arrays are important when you have a similar type of information that you want to classify together. You access arrays using index numbers that point to distinct elements. Resistor ladders provide the right circuit to channel digital signals into a system by inserting into an analog input.

DIGITAL HOURGLASS

In this project, you are going to learn how to build a digital hourglass that switches on an LED after 10 minutes. This will help you know the time you spend working on your projects.

So far you have seen that when you want to make something happen at a specific time interval, you have to apply the delay() function. This is convenient but at the same time limited in what it can achieve. When the delay() is called, it stops the flow of current based on the time of delay. This means that there is no input and output during the delay. Besides, delays are not the best to use to monitor time. If your goal were to do something after every 20 seconds, a delay of 20 seconds would be very long.

The millis() function comes in to provide a much better solution to this problem. The function will record the time the Arduino has been on.

Up to now, we have declared variables as an int. An int consists of a 16-bit number that contains values in the range "-32,768 and 32,767." That is a large number, but not when the Arduino is making a count of 1000 times a second using the millis() function, in just a few minutes you will be out of space. The long data type can store a 32-bit number.

Given that time cannot run back to produce negative numbers, we declare an unsigned long variable to store millis() time. A data type of unsigned type can only be positive. In addition, an unsigned long can extend to 4,294,967,295. This is sufficient space to store time for even 50 days. So, if you compare the function millis() to a given value, you can tell if a certain amount of time has ended.

So when you rotate your hourglass, a tilt switch will update its state, and that begins a different LED cycle.

The tilt switch operates the same way as a normal switch where it has an on and off sensor. In this project, you will use it as a digital signal. Something unique about tilt switches is the way they determine the orientation. Usually, it contains a small cavity with a metal ball. If adjusted correctly, the ball will roll to one particular side of the cavity and join two leads in the breadboard.

1. **The first thing is to connect the power and ground to your breadboard**
2. **The next thing to do is to join the six LEDs to the digital pins 2-7 through the anode. The LEDs have to be connected to the ground through a resistor.**
3. **Connect one lead of the tilt switch to the 5V. The remaining part should be connected to the ground.**

Create a stand using the cardboard and allow power to flow to the Arduino using a battery. You can build a cover that has some numeric displays close to the lights.

Tilt switches are cheap and affordable components to help one tell the orientation of something. Another example of tilt sensors are the accelerometers. In addition, they are quite expensive. If you are only interested to see whether something is up or down, you should go with the tilt sensors.

The Code

Define a constant

In this project, you will need to have several global variables so that you can have everything work. To begin with, define a constant called switchPin.

Declare a variable to store time

Declare an unsigned long variable. This variable will record the last time the LED changed.

Declare variables to hold inputs and outputs

Define variables for both the switch state and previous switch state. The input and output variables will help make a comparison of the switch's position from one state to the next. Declare a variable called **led**. This will make the next LED to switch on. You can start with pin 2.

Variable declaration showing the interval between two events

The last variable to define is the interval between each LED. This is the long datatype.

Determine the time the program started.

Once the loop() begins, you can find the time the Arduino has been on using the function millis() and place it in a variable called currentTime.

Determine the time that has elapsed since the first loop()

With the help of an if() statement, you need to determine whether time has reached to switch on the LED. Perform some mathematical operations by subtracting the currentTime from the original time and test to see if it is more than the interval variable.

Switch on the LED, and prepare for the next

The previousTime displays the last time the LED was on. The moment the previousTime is set, switch on the LED and increase the led variable. If you pass the time interval again, the next LED lights up.

Find out whether all the lights are on

Create another if statement in the program to help you determine whether the LED on pin marked 7 is on. Make sure you do not attempt anything with it.

Towards the end of the loop, save the state of the switch in the prevSwitchState, and compare it with the value you receive for the switchState in next loop().

If you are done with programming the board, look at the time in the clock. Once 10 minutes pass, the first LED has to be turned on. After every 10 minutes, a new light will display. After an hour, all the six light will turn on.

Chapter 12 Spend Time Thinking Outside the Box (and the Arduino)

In this chapter, we're going to talk about how creative thinking and spending time away from Arduino programming both might enable you to be a better Arduino programmer in the end.

This may not make a lot of sense, but the fact is that both of these ideas have a lot of credence. No masterful painter ever got to their mastery by working simply with oils, though they may strongly **prefer** to work with oils. The same applies here: without thinking outside the box and working outside of your comfort zone, you're going to be missing out on a lot of different things that would lead you to become a better programmer and a better Arduino builder in general.

Here's a simple fact for you: all of creativity is based on the way that the brain processes inputs and outputs. Although there is some variety of spontaneous components, you can only ever invent things which are based on those things you've already learned or those things you've already been made aware of. Your ideas will almost always be based on those inputs that you've already dealt with in the past instead of being based on things that are spontaneously generated in terms of new ideas.

Spontaneous generation of ideas can lead to really cool and abstract things, but even the most spontaneous ideas are based on learned stimuli, from a psychological perspective. In other words, no thought that you've ever had has been completely original, because all of your thoughts are formed by the world around you and the unique way in which you happen to process all of that information.

If you want to be a good Arduino programmer, you really need to not stop at Arduino programming. For example, the fundamental languages which power the Arduino language itself, C and C++, have been used for a massive variety of different utilities in the nearly forty years that they've been around. At some point in these languages' long histories, there has been something done that you've never even thought of, surely.

It is by taking in these inputs and getting this practice that you enable yourself to become a better programmer and do more.

I think that a good example would harken back to the phenomenon known as a Magic Mirror. Magic Mirrors are computer monitors which display information fed in by a Raspberry Pi, a microcomputer not too different from an Arduino through a tad bit more powerful and intended for different purposes. The monitor is tucked behind a one-sided mirror such that the information on the monitor displays on the reflective side of the mirror. What results is a mirror that is incredibly science fiction becoming a science reality.

The thing is that while the project itself is simple, the logic behind the program really isn't; for example, to display the data, a modified version of the Chromium browser is used. Within that Chromium browser, a custom page is built using HTML, CSS, and JavaScript (to retrieve information from the web).

It is through the knowledge of how to make these different things happen that a project as ambitious as the Magic Mirror was made possible. If one didn't have the knowledge of how to modify and recompile the Chromium browser, nor if they didn't have the knowledge on how to build web pages using HTML, CSS, and JavaScript, the project simply would have never happened; it would have remained science fiction.

In other words, you may have incredible ideas, but actually being able to take action to make them happen is an entirely different beast altogether. One thing is for certain: building up the knowledge required to, for example, build web pages or modify and recompile a web browser then write a bash script to automatically launch it upon the operating system starting up are things which go well beyond the scope of hobbyist programming for the Arduino.

You can ask for the help of other people, but that will only get you so far and nudge you along a little at a time. So what's the other option, then?

All of this chapter has been building up to this: your ability to program Arduino sketches and to make your dream projects happen is based on you, not programming in Arduino at all.

Programming is a common set of skills that usually transfer across projects, but as an Arduino programmer, you generally are not building these skills in the optimal way. Reading books like this one is a start because they teach you the underlying concepts to all of the computer science mumbo-jumbo that you're being fed, which hopefully acts to help make things click a little bit. But there are a lot of bigger concepts that you aren't going to pick up just within your Arduino IDE. These are things like working with APIs, learning how to read documentation, learning how to create header files or libraries to make your programs more modular, learning in general how to be a better programmer.

These are skills which you gain through continually challenging yourself and trying to come up with new things.

And this has a little perk tacked onto the end of it, too: if you try to work on new things, you will be inspired more often. You'll learn how to do things and start having ideas that you wouldn't have had otherwise, because you'll be enjoying new experiences and getting all sorts of new inputs. When you think about things you've never thought about before, your brain interprets this as a good thing - as a learning experience. This will expand your mind and make you more creative, in turn making you simultaneously a better programmer and a better tinkerer.

So in other words, if you want to be a good Arduino programmer, one of the best things that you can possibly do for yourself is to start working on projects that aren't Arduino-based. You need to be exposing yourself to new things and challenging yourself to become better all of the time.

Chapter 13 Troubleshooting

As you work on your projects, there are specific situations when there will be troubleshooting and debugging.

The more you use Arduino and electronics, the better you become and gain experience. This will end up making the whole process less painful. Don't be frustrated with the problems that you experience. It is much easy than the way it might look at the start.

Since each Arduino project consists of a hardware and software, there are many places to check when things go wrong. Therefore, when debugging, you need to consider these three aspects:

Understanding

You should strive to understand as much as you can in the way the parts you have in your project operate and how they should contribute to the final project. This method will allow you to develop ways in which you can check every component independently.

Simplify and segment

In the ancient Romans, they had what we call divide and rule type of government. You need to break down your project into different components using your intelligence to determine which part of a given function starts and ends.

Testing the Board

What if the first example of blinking an LED failed to work? That would possibly be frustrating. Let us see what you can do.

Before you throw complains at your project, you need to ascertain that several things are in the right place. This is similar to the way airline pilots follow when they run through a list of things to make sure that there will be no problems when the plane takes off.

The first thing you need to do is to plug your USB into your computer:

- Verify that the PC is on. This might look obvious, but you could forget to turn on your computer. When the green light labeled PWR lights up, this implies that the computer is powering the board. However, if the LED looks faint, then something is wrong with the power. You can change the USB cable and check the computer USB port as well as the Arduino USB plug port on your computer.
- If you are using a new Arduino, the yellow LED labeled L will start to blink.
- Now, if you had been using an external source of power and you have connected an old Arduino. Just ensure that the power supply is inserted in and the jumper labeled as SV1 has been connected to the two pins that are close to the external power supply connector.

Another point you need to note is when you are experiencing problems with some sketches, and you want to verify that the board is working. Open and transfer the blink an LED example in the IDE to the board. The onboard LED has to blink in a regular pattern. If you follow all the above steps, then you should be confident that the Arduino is going to work correctly.

Test the Breadboard Circuit

To test your breadboard circuit, join the board to your breadboard by executing a jumper from the GND and 5V connections right between the negative and positive rails of the breadboard. When the green PWR LED goes off, remove the wires. This shows that there exists an error in the circuit and there is a short circuit. A short-circuit leads to an excessive current which cuts off the current as a mechanism to protect your computer.

However, if you are concerned that you might destroy your computer, remember that most machines have safety mechanisms. Besides, the Arduino board has an independently powered USB hub.

If you have a short circuit, it is essential to apply the divide and conquer approach. What you require to do is to look for each sensor in the project and connect each sensor one at a time.

The first thing that you need to begin with is the power source. Review each part of the circuit to ensure that power flows through it. Work procedurally and perform a single change in every step.

Any time you are in the process of debugging and things do not seem to go well, the best thing to do is to handle everything systematically. This is very important because it will help you fix the problem, and that is why it is crucial that you update one at a time.

In addition, do not forget that each debugging process will stick in your head. You will develop an understanding of some of the things to fix up when you encounter a problem. In addition, after some time you will become an expert at doing it.

IDE problems

There are times when you might experience problems with the Arduino IDE, primarily if you are working on Windows. If you receive an error when you double-click the Arduino Icon or nothing happens, you should attempt to execute the run.bat file, which is another option to start Arduino.

Windows users might again run into a problem if the operating system allocates the COM port to a COM10 or higher number to the Arduino. If this takes place, you can let Windows assign a lower port number to the Arduino.

Look for Help Online

If you find yourself stuck entirely such that you are spending a lot of time trying to debug, it might be time to turn to the community of users at the Arduino forum. One of the best things, when you look for help online, is that you will always find someone ready to assist you if you can describe your problem correctly.

Develop a practice of cutting and pasting things into a search engine and wait to check the results if there is a person who has tried to solve it. Look around to discover a solution, nearly every problem you encounter must have an answer.

You, start with checking the main Arduino website before you can move to the playground. Another critical thing to note is before you begin your project, you should search in the playground for a few lines of code or circuit diagram to help you build your project.

Conclusion

Thank you for making it through to the end!

The next step is to purchase the kind of Arduino board that you would like to work with and then go on from there. In the beginning of this guidebook we spent some time looking at what the Arduino board is all about and some of the different options that you are able to use in order to make it do the work that you would like. And picking out the board that is going to help you with some of the projects that you want to complete is going to be an important first step to focus on.

From there, it is time to go through the various steps that we spent our time on in this guidebook so that you can learn a bit about this language and what it is able to do for you. There are many beginners who are worried about learning any kind of coding at all, much less the Arduino language. But you will quickly find that this is a simple language that you are able to work with, one that will help you to see the best results in no time, and is designed for the student, or someone with no engineering or technical experience, to gain some experience on coding in the first place.

There are a lot of different parts that are going to come with this language, and being able to explore it some more, and learn from what is there, is going to make a big difference in the response that we are able to get, and how good we feel about some of our own coding prowess along the way. Don't be worried our scared about the topics that we are going to explore in this guidebook. You will find that they are easy and before long, you will be able to hook up the Arduino machine and get it to work on any project that you want.

In addition to some of those great benefits and the basics of the Arduino, we took it a bit further and looked at some of the things that you are able to do with this system when it comes to coding. We looked at many different parts such as how to turn it into a machine, how to work with the stream class and the Arduino API, and even how to create some of your own user defined functions along the way. all of this came together to help you learn some of the basics of your first coding language, and make it easier for you to get into this world in no time.

There are so many things that you are able to love when it comes to using the Arduino technology to help you out with some of the coding that you would like to accomplish. And getting started on it is easier than you may think. When you are ready to learn how to code, but you want a nice and simple method to use in order to do this, make sure to check out this guidebook to help you get started.

CPSIA information can be obtained
at www.ICGtesting.com
Printed in the USA
LVHW010211141020
668706LV00024B/747